The Women's Liberation Movement

Protest, Culture and Society

General editors:
Kathrin Fahlenbrach, Institute for Media and Communication, University of Hamburg
Martin Klimke, New York University Abu Dhabi
Joachim Scharloth, Technical University Dresden, Germany

Protest movements have been recognized as significant contributors to processes of political participation and transformations of culture and value systems, as well as to the development of both a national and transnational civil society.

This series brings together the various innovative approaches to phenomena of social change, protest and dissent which have emerged in recent years, from an interdisciplinary perspective. It contextualizes social protest and cultures of dissent in larger political processes and socio-cultural transformations by examining the influence of historical trajectories and the response of various segments of society, political and legal institutions on a national and international level. In doing so, the series offers a more comprehensive and multi-dimensional view of historical and cultural change in the twentieth and twenty-first century.

For a full volume listing, please see back matter

The Women's Liberation Movement

Impacts and Outcomes

Edited by

Kristina Schulz

berghahn
NEW YORK • OXFORD
www.berghahnbooks.com

Published in 2017 by
Berghahn Books
www.berghahnbooks.com

Library of Congress Cataloging-in-Publication Data

Names: Schulz, Kristina, editor.
Title: The Women's Liberation Movement : impacts and outcomes / edited by Kristina Schulz.
Description: New York : Berghahn Books, 2017. | Series: Protest, culture and society ; volume 22 | Includes bibliographical references and index.
Identifiers: LCCN 2017015811 (print) | LCCN 2017023366 (ebook) | ISBN 9781785335877 (e-book) | ISBN 9781785335860 (hardback : alk. paper)
Subjects: LCSH: Feminism—History—20th century. | Women's rights—History—20th century. | Women—Social conditions—20th century.
Classification: LCC HQ1154 (ebook) | LCC HQ1154 .W9195 2017 (print) | DDC 305.42—dc23
LC record available at https://lccn.loc.gov/2017015811

British Library Cataloguing in Publication Data

A catalogue record for this book is available from the British Library

ISBN 978-1-78533-586-0 hardback
ISBN 978-1-78533-587-7 ebook

Contents

Introduction

A Success without Impact?

Case Studies from the Women's Liberation Movements in Europe

Kristina Schulz

Historians have underlined feminism's diversity and richness. What feminism was, and is, has been subjected to an ongoing debate, not only for activists but also for scholarship. Twenty-five years ago, Denise Riley suggested that "woman" is an "unstable category" and that "feminism" is the site of the systematic fighting that resulted out of that instability."[1] Others, like Karen Offen, have given a more concrete definition of feminism as a "system of ideas on its own rights"[2] and a movement "for sociopolitical change based on a critical analysis of male privilege and women's subordination within a given society."[3] More recent scholarship has taken to understand feminism as a historical category, trying to work on its historically specific occurrences.[4] There is a large consensus about the assumption that there is not a singular "feminism" but, rather, that it should be thought of in terms of differently "situated feminist experiences."[5] Still, how heterogeneous feminist experiences might be best analyzed with regard to the issue of impact is open to question.

This book is about a very specific moment in the long history of feminism: the women's liberation movements (WLM). In Europe, the organization of women willing to struggle for women's rights first came together in the second half of the nineteenth century. Those who survived the genocide and total war of the twentieth century received a strong, and not always welcome, stimulus from the new and more radical feminist groups that developed within the very different context of the New Left at the end of the 1960s and in the early 1970s. These new groups differed substantially from the older women's movements, which were not, as many "new" feminists used to think, necessarily limited to the struggle for suffrage only but were also focused on access to education, paid work, and, for a minority, sexual/reproductive issues, all sometimes in militant ways not unlike the WLMs in the 1970s. But the newer movements, to a much larger extent, employed unconventional protest forms and organized through informal networks rather than through official membership. Of course, to a certain degree the women's liberation movements were organized. As an internal process that regulates the interrelations of individuals in a collective action pattern, organization is part of every social movement. In addition, social movements can embrace established organizations, often working with progressive elements in socialist parties, or trade unions. But those established groups were not crucial for the specific dynamic of interaction that emerged after 1968. During the early 1970s, in most European countries radical feminists were the driving force in the formation of social movements that – following the example of the United States – were named the women's liberation movement, *Mouvement de libération des femmes, Frauenbefreiungsbewegung,* or used adjectives like "radical," "feminist," or "new" (*movimiento feminista, Neue Frauenbewegung*) in order to distance themselves from older "bourgeois" women's organizations.

Without losing sight of the broader history of feminism in which the WLMs are situated, this book concentrates on the 1970s and 1980s. All the authors are concerned – in very different ways – with the impact that the movements made to the legal, political, and cultural conditions of advanced industrial societies. Of all the social movements that resulted from the political upheavals around 1968, the WLM have been one of the most lasting and visible. The struggle of the movements for women's liberation and autonomy, gender equality policies, reproductive rights, and protection against male violence has been crucial. By increasing its activist base and building alliances with other social groups and organizations, feminism has become an essential part of political culture in many parts of the world. One can therefore say that its strategy of mobilization has been successful. But beyond that, can it also claim to have achieved long-term results? Or was it, to borrow the words of one of the most famous journalists of the Weimar Republic, Kurt Tucholsky (1890–1935), a "success without impact"?[6] Scholars from diverse national and disciplinary backgrounds have pooled their knowledge on post-1968 feminist activism from a European perspective and have attempted a collective assessment in this book. As experts on specific areas of society and on specific national contexts, they evaluate in this volume the impact and outcomes of feminist activism of the 1970s and 1980s.

As Myra Marx Ferree's works on Germany in a global perspective show, the variations of feminism in different countries and contexts can inform us about very general patterns of feminist activism when studied in a systematic way. From here our collective enterprise concentrates on the WLM as a point of departure, understanding them as social movements that, in most of the countries examined here, emerged in the wake of the upheavals of the late 1960s and, after a period of growing public visibility – both in terms of its numbers and prominence in setting national political agendas – transformed over the course of the 1980s, giving way to a multiplicity of networks, associations, institutions, and politicized milieus.

Two distinct – though connected – modes of analysis of the history of feminism and social movements have informed our reflections on impact, all of which ask different questions and draw on different methodological and analytical frameworks.

The first of these approaches is concerned with finding out what precisely feminism is or was in a specific place and moment. It is the attempt to understand who was included under the umbrella of feminism, what at a certain moment of time was considered to be a "feminist" identity (and what was not), and what was understood to be feminist activism, its priorities, and its strategies. When analyzing the impact of the WLM, this perspective investigates what constituted success in the eyes of movement activists at the time. How did they conceptualize the link between collective protest and social change? From this angle, explorations of feminism examine the hopes, the claims, and the action strategies of collective protest in order to further our understanding of the ways that movement activists saw themselves as historical subjects of change, and of their chances to realize their political dreams. What were the expectations of those who engaged with feminism? Within this historicizing approach, reflecting on different notions of "success" can help us to explore the diversity of rival ideas and struggles within a given movement and to investigate how these structured the collective, as well as to identify changes in the goals of a movement and the strategies employed in achieving them. It is to investigate what British feminist activist Sheila Rowbotham called in 1971 the process of "finding a voice."[7] This investigation takes us into the collective imaginary of the movement, to its modes of perception, value systems, and – maybe – collective myths. However, this approach avoids assessing the movement's impact on society. By focusing on expectations, strategies, and self-descriptions, it fails to distinguish between perceptions of success/failure and processes of profound structural change.

The second approach is informed by political and social science and draws on the theories and methodologies of social movement research. With few exceptions, social movement research failed until the late 1990s to elaborate conceptually on the question of effect.[8] But recent reflections on impact and outcome have opened up several new ways of thinking about these important issues.[9] One is to think about the conditions of success. Roland Roth and Dieter Rucht argue that a movement's success depends on "a complex assembly of factors" or even of a "combination of different assemblies of factors."[10] On a general level, the authors distinguish between internal and external conditions. Internal conditions refer to the organizational resources and communication capacities of a movement. They are both a condition and a result of the emergence and stabilization of collective identity formation. The external conditions necessary for success are part of the political opportunity structure, and to access them involves some degree of interaction with the establishment.[11] Though questioning the conditions of success is not well suited to examining any divergences in the collective formulation of the movement's aims, and is also unable to take systematically into account the unintended consequences and effects of social movements, the conceptual differentiation between internal and external conditions needed for success allows us to approach the success or failure of a movement by considering the extent to which movement activists achieved their goals. Still, the question of what is considered to be a legitimate goal is a subject of controversy within social movements and beyond. William Gamson's distinction between "acceptance" and "advances" helps to differentiate the notion of success, distinguishing between the degree to which a challenging group is accepted as legitimate and the degree to which new advantages can be achieved.[12] Yet, this approach, as well as Paul Schumaker's classical distinction between different levels of policy responsiveness to protest group demands,[13] among many other considerations on "how movements matter," concentrate on political demands and thus on the production of legislation.[14] They are helpful for understanding what became of the WLMs' claim for equal rights and for abortion rights, but they are less suited to assessing other dimensions of feminist activism.

More recent approaches offer additional conceptualization to the study of social movement impact. Integrating classifications of movement outcomes, Marco Giugni and Lorenzo Bosi assign social movement impact to three levels: a *political* level, which refers to effects on the movement's political environment; a *cultural* level, which refers to effects on ways of understanding the world, on opinions and values; a *biographical* level, which refers to effects on life-course patterns and to the personal costs and benefits of movement activism.[15] Furthermore, they suggest combining those levels through distinguishing between internal and external impacts. "Internal impacts refer to changes that occur … within the movement …; external impacts refer to the effect that movements have in their external environment." By doing so, they identify six main domains "where effects are possible":[16] first, the power and decision-making structures within a social movement or a movement organization; second, value change within a social movement/movement sector; third, life-course patterns of movement participants; fourth, external policy change or influence on the process of political decision-making; fifth, effects on public opinion and attitudes; and sixth, change of life-course patterns on an aggregate level.

Figure 1

	Internal	External
Political	Power relations within a movement	Substantial (policy) Procedural, institutional change
Cultural	Value change within a movement	Public opinion and attitude
Biographical	Life-course patterns of movement participants	Aggregate-level life-course patterns

It is debatable whether this classification is suited to integrative analysis of all the effects of movement activism. Where would we find the influence that Lucy Delap discusses in her chapter of the effect of feminism on the British men's movement? What about the challenge of categories such as class or race, thoroughly analyzed for the Italian case by Marica Tolomelli and Anna Frisone in this volume? However, such a framework can direct our attention to some crucial areas. To distinguish on an analytical level between possible areas of influence is fundamental to being able to undertake a differentiated analysis. Indeed, without it, the first and the second section of this volume, dealing as they do with different aspects of political and cultural outcomes, would not be possible. But this approach offers no more than a starting point for thinking about the impact of the WLM. It does not take into account that the meaning itself of what was to be considered as "political" or "cultural" was in flux around 1968. In particular, the category of the "political" was the subject of intense debate in the social movements of the 1960s and 1970s and was particularly fought over in and by the WLM that claimed "the personal" to be "political." Furthermore, Giugni and Bosi's classification does not take into consideration the fact that social movements can hardly control the directions taken by the processes they trigger. Depending on contextual factors – such as political opportunities or cultures of protest – they develop their own dynamics. Protest activities may have unintended consequences. Moreover, in order to be heard, social movements need mediators – such as intermediary organizations, parties, unions, or initiative groups – to translate their objectives into politically enforceable demands. In this process of mediation, such objectives may change or even be exploited for other purposes. Such multicausal correlations render the identification of social movement impacts a complex matter. A historical understanding of the impact of social movements, recognized as the result of diverse, uncontrolled, and open processes, therefore might provide a more detailed and source-based account of the struggles, campaigns, institutional responses, and negotiation processes between the actors involved in different social arenas.

Against this backdrop, no decision has been taken in advance on the concepts to employ in this anthology in order to describe social and political change induced by the various groups fighting for women's liberation. To political scientists, this might sound odd, as multiple distinctions have been discussed in social movement research, such as that between "impact" and "outcome" put forward by Charles Tilly and Sidney Tarrow.[17] But this volume is about very diverse movement dynamics, issues, forms, and expressions of collective action in different national settings. If any, the distinction that was binding for all chapters assembled in this volume was that between success in terms of mobilization or immediate satisfaction of concrete demands on the one hand, and multi-dimensional long-term effects on the other hand.

Arguing that the end of the protest cycle that started in many European countries in the aftermath of the social upheavals of the late 1960s was not the "death" of feminism (as neither was the formation period of the WLM in the late 1960s and early 1970s its "birth"), the chapters collected in this volume try to look at the traces that these social movements have left in different European societies – both on the continent and on the British Isles – as well as, for comparative purposes, in the United States.

From here it is useful for us to think about the ways in which social movements end. Social movement research has identified three broad possibilities: transformation into a subsequent social movement, dissolution, or institutionalization.[18] In view of the afterlife of the 1968 protest movement in many Western countries, we might add the possibility of countercultural retreat and terrorist networks. But how do we know in our empirical work that a movement has come to its end? In some cases the answer is clear; for example, when movement activity is reduced to institutional acting. Yet what about when less tangible elements of a movement still exist, such as in subcultures or informal supraregional networks? It seems difficult to determine a definite endpoint of the movement when it comes to women's liberation.

Charles Tilly argues for a more differentiated conceptual approach. He does not discuss the "end" of a social movement but instead suggests the notion of a "future trajectory." According to Tilly, we have to distinguish a number of possible future trajectories for social movements, ranging from extinction through contraction to expansion and institutionalization, and a number of different scales, going from the local through to the regional, national, international, and the global.[19] While undertaking a historical examination of the WLM, it is also worthwhile to utilize a flexible understanding of the concept of "movement" to take into account not only times of obvious formation and mobilization but also what comes after these extraordinarily dynamic periods. How did the mode of organization of women's liberation groups change over time? What became of consciousness-raising groups, and what of the first informal and extracurricular women's studies courses in universities? What of single-issue organizations such as the *Aktion 218* (§ 218 is the paragraph regulating abortion in the criminal code of the Federal Republic of Germany)? Examining the trajectory of expansion and institutionalization, for example, may help us sketch the trajectories of the informal self-help health groups of the 1970s that became institutionalized and accredited health centers by the 1980s and 1990s. Likewise, when analyzing changes of scale, examining the trajectory of young activists from the first days of a WLM group to becoming women's rights advocates in international organizations at the end of the century may be useful.

Based on Tilly's distinction, two contradictory types of trajectories can be seen in the WLM: contraction and expansion. These were first noticeable with regard to institutionalization processes, be it into contraction in the form of counterinstitutions, such as women's or health centers, or into expansion through entering the institutions of the establishment, such as professional women's representatives like equal opportunity offices or parliament. Second, contraction and expansion also mirrored the cultural forms of the movement, be it contraction into a distinct counterculture or successive expansion into the mainstream culture. And, third, we can discuss contraction and expansion in relation to the geographical characteristics of a movement that has become increasingly embedded on a local level, but that at the same time has expanded enormously on an international, even global, level. To examine processes of expansion and contraction adds a historical dimension to the question of external and internal mobilization. Whereas the notion of "internal" and "external" mobilization processes suggests that the borders of social movements are clearly defined – which historically is true in some moments and not in others – "expansion" and "contraction" point more to the fluid character of a social movement.

Expansion and contraction are not mutually exclusive. On the contrary, if we assume the fundamental openness of processes of social change, historical analysis must concentrate on such parallel, overlaying, and sometimes contradictory developments. Several examples in this volume show that the WLM's strategies of outreach did not always make it more accessible for certain social groups and individuals. Producing a journal in order to mobilize women outside the movement, for example, could also unwittingly exclude those who did not have the language skills or the time to participate.

Ironically, attempts at widening the social base of women's liberation could therefore actually exacerbate the exclusion of such groups from feminism.

Whereas "contraction" and "expansion" can provide us with useful ways of thinking about the history of the women's movement, they do not reduce the complexity of the analysis of its effects and outcomes. This is not only because of the prolonged period of investigation but also because, from the 1980s onwards, the WLM became part of a new social, political, and ethical configuration of society that Nancy Fraser has identified as a neoliberal variant of capitalism. In her article "Capitalism and the Cunning of History," Fraser asks the uncomfortable question of whether, by accentuating female autonomy and individuality, the WLM has "unwittingly supplied a key ingredient of what Luc Boltanski and Eve Chiapello called the 'New spirit of capitalism.'"[20] Whether or not we agree with this diagnosis – and with regard to the European scene we might not totally agree[21] – it brings us back to the necessity of making clear distinctions between the intended and unintended consequences of social movements. Even in the national context of one of the countries most committed to the idea of political liberalism – the United States – women's liberation has never been a project reduced to mere economic considerations, nor has "liberation" been reduced to participation in the labor force.

Many of the case studies presented in this volume deal with the tension between processes of contraction and expansion, present in any analysis of the impact of the WLM. The first section explores whether and to what extent the movement successfully changed institutions and how its claims have been echoed in public, political, and academic institutions. Given that such processes of expansion were anything but inevitable, the contributors identify the actors, reconstruct negotiations, and consider strategic compromises. The authors explore such questions in national contexts and shed light on different arenas, such as the WLM's position on the legislation regarding abortion and reproductive technology (Leena Schmitter) and gender equality (Sarah Kiani) in Switzerland, or the influence of feminist theory and practice on academia in West Germany and the United States (Stefanie Ehmsen).

The second section questions the extent of the feminist (counter)culture's advances. It traces the history of women's literature and its producers and investigates its relationship to a feminist – as well as to a broader – public. It analyzes the impact that literary texts, their authors, and the literary practices promoting them have on feminist mobilization. Did feminist (counter)culture contribute to the contraction and/or expansion of the movement? Did the production, translation, and diffusion of texts create new possibilities of inventing a feminist self? Sylvie Chaperon explores Simone de Beauvoir's role in the French Mouvement de libération des femmes, impressively rebutting the assumption that feminists of different status, age, experience, and habitus were not able to collaborate. My own chapter on women and words examines the function that literary practices had within and beyond the WLM in Switzerland, whereas Ana Martins takes a critical look at relations of domination and subordination in what she calls the "second-wave community" by exploring processes of (non)circulation, and (non)canonization, and the selective appropriation of feminist texts from the margins of Europe. Finally Christa Binswanger and Kathy Davis's re-reading of two "feminist" bestsellers, which, at different moments of time, deal with women's sexuality, delineates the essential role of sexuality in women's self-definition and its commitment to feminism.

The third section examines controversies within feminism and the complex ways in which WLMs were entwined with parallel movements such as the workers' or the men's movement. These issues are present elsewhere in the book, but here they are analyzed more systematically. How did activists deal with ethnic and social differences? If we understand the WLM as a social movement, i.e. as a collective actor who acts on the basis of a collective identity,[22] then we must examine how this collective identity was produced and how these processes also resulted in certain social groups being excluded from the movement. Against this background, Christine Bard's chapter explores the relationship between the WLM, lesbianism, and an increasingly distinct lesbian movement in France. Marica Tolomelli and Anna Frisone analyze the theoretical and strategic challenges women's liberation had to face in Italy when confronted with issues of class. Natalie Thomlinson's chapter explores multiracial collectives in Britain, and Lucy Delap reminds us that, again in Britain, women's liberation was, in the very first phase of the movement, closely tied to men's liberation, and that a number of men were engaged in supporting feminist activities.

The fourth section takes a closer look at the transnational dimension of women's liberation by investigating the relationship between French and Russian feminists (Kirsten Harting's chapter) and exploring the possibilities and challenges of feminism in cyberspace (Johanna Niesyto's chapter). These two contributions suggest that the history of women's liberation – as a social movement that acts on a national level but that has always had a strong transnational focus – cannot be written within the confines of "methodological nationalism."

The last section of the book is concerned with methodological questions. That movement impact is difficult to assess has become a commonplace; indeed, this introduction supports rather than refutes this thesis. Yet we need to address these analytical problems in a more concrete way in order to establish which approaches may or may not help us to assess impact more usefully.

Thus, Margaretta Jolly argues that oral history can witness feminist cultural influence that goes beyond the more measurable aspects of campaigns. Elisabeth Elgán's chapter underlines the discrepancies we might find between oral and written history, and it warns us of the pitfalls of both romantic glamorization or subsequent condemnation when either nostalgia or frustration interfere with memory. Karen Offen's contribution on the long-term perspective closes the collection by situating the WLM within the long and fascinating history of feminism.

I am grateful to a number of people and institutions that helped with this book. The Swiss National Scientific Foundation funded a conference on the subject at the University of Bern in 2012. It was the beginning of a collective dialogue that continues. Magda Kaspar was irreplaceable in preparing the different manuscripts for press. I also thank Natalie Thomlinson for her willingness and her invaluable competence in rereading many texts of non-native English speakers. Martin Klimke encouraged me several times to bring the book project to an end, and not to make it a fast book but an interesting and – hopefully – good one. I thank him as well as Joachim Scharloth and Kathrin Fahlenbrach (not to forget Marion Berghahn), for accepting this volume in Berghahn's Protest, Culture and Society series. I owe a lot to them and to the Marie Curie Conference and Training Course "European Protest Movements since the Cold War" that they organized between 2006 and 2010. I also would like to thank the Sozialarchiv in Zurich for providing us the fantastic image now on the cover of this book. It was probably taken in the mid-eighties during a happening called "Die Schaumschlägerinnen" (the egg beaters). Elisabeth Joris was so kind to make some enquiries about the event and the persons involved. Last but not least I am very grateful to Lucy Delap who has been a constant source of knowledge and encouragement in helping this book to appear.

This collection is dedicated to Brigitte Schnegg (1953–2014), pioneer of gender studies in Switzerland. A historian by formation and by conviction, she was also involved in today's feminist campaigns and thinking. She was an irreplaceable source of ideas, confidence, and energy for so many people and projects concerned with gender, its historicity, and its impact. She also cared for this project. In the midst of our discussions about the conclusion for this book, she passed away. We will have to do without her, but not without commemorating her first.

Kristina Schulz, PhD, is Senior Lecturer for Contemporary History and Migration History at the University of Berne. She is a specialist of Western feminist history in comparative perspective and is the author of a book on the French and German WLM: *"Der lange Atem der Provokation": Die*

Frauenbewegung in der Bundesrepublik und in Frankreich (1968–1976). Together with Leena Schmitter and Sarah Kiani she published a source and archive guide about the Swiss Women's Liberation Movement in 2014. With Magda Kaspar she is currently preparing an audio archive and interactive website about the feminist movement in Switzerland from the 1970s to the present (*Frauenbewegun 2.0*).

Notes

1. Denise Riley, *Am I That Name? Feminism and the Category of "Women" in History* (Basingstoke: MacMillan, 1988), 5.
2. Karen Offen, "Defining Feminism. A Comparative Historical Approach," *Signs* 14, no. 1 (1988): 119–57; 150.
3. Ibid., 151.
4. Lucy Delap, "Something in the Air: New Directions on the History of Feminism," unpublished book review on recent scholarship, 2012.
5. Myra Marx Ferree, *Varieties of Feminism: German Gender Politics in Global Perspective* (Stanford, CA: Stanford University Press, 2012), 16.
6. In 1923 Kurt Tucholsky, in a letter to Hans Schönlank, alleged that he had "Erfolg, aber keinerlei Wirkung" ("success but no impact") (*Briefe, Auswahl 1913–1935* [Berlin: Volk und Welt, 1983], 155). In a variant to Franz Hammer in 1931: "Das, worum mir manchmal so bange ist, ist die Wirkung meiner Arbeit. Hat sie eine? (Ich meine nicht den Erfolg; er läßt mich kalt.) Aber mir erscheint es manchmal als so entsetzlich wirkungslos" (ibid., 213). Cf. Uwe Wiemann, "Kurt Tucholsky und die Politisierung des Kabaretts: Paradigmenwechsel oder literarische Mimikry?" in *Studien zur Germanistik 12* (Hamburg: Dr. Kovac, 2004), 30.
7. "[A movement] is the means of finding a voice." Sheila Rowbotham, *Women's Liberation & the New Politics (Spokesman Pamphlets; no. 17)* (Nottingham: Bertrand Russell Peace Foundation, 1971), 12.
8. For early attempts to bring together different perspectives on the topic, see Marco Giugni, "Was It Worth the Effort? The Outcomes and Consequences of Social Movements," *Annual Review of Sociology* 24 (1998): 371–93 and idem; Dough McAdam and Charles Tilly, eds., *How Social Movements Matter* (Minneapolis: University of Minnesota Press, 1999).
9. New literature about that topic is reviewed in Edwin Amenta et al., "The Political Consequences of Social Movements," *Annual Review of Sociology* 36 (2010): 287–307.
10. Roland Roth and Dieter Rucht, "Soziale Bewegungen und Protest—eine theoretische und empirische Bilanz," in *Die sozialen Bewegungen in Deutschland seit 1945: Ein Handbuch*, ed. Roland Roth and Dieter Rucht (Frankfurt: Campus, 2008), 654.
11. For a differentiated account of the notion of "establishment" and it's uses, cf. the introduction to *The "Establishment" Responds: Power, Politics and Protest since 1945*, ed. Kathrin Fahlenbrach, Martin Klimke, and Joachim Scharloth (New York: Berghahn 2012), 3f.

12. William Gamson, *The Strategy of Social Protest,* 2nd ed. (Belmond: Wadsworth Publishing Company, 1990): 28–29.
13. Paul D. Schumaker, "Policy Responsiveness to Protest Group Demands," *Journal of Politics* 37 (1975): 488–521.
14. See: Donatella della Porta and Mario Diani, *Social Movements: An Introduction,* 2nd ed. (Malden: Blackwell Publishing 2006): 231.
15. Marco Giugni and Lorenzo Bosi, "The Impact of Protest Movements on the Establishment: Dimensions, Models, and Approaches," in *The "Establishment" Responds: Power, Politics and Protest since 1945,* ed. Kathrin Fahlenbrach, Martin Klimke, and Joachim Scharloth (New York: Berghahn 2012), 17–28.
16. Giugni and Bosi, "Impact of Protest Movements," 18.
17. Charles Tilly and Sidney Tarrow, *Contentious Politics,* 2nd ed. (Oxford: Oxford University Press, 2015).
18. Joachim Raschke, *Soziale Bewegungen: Ein historisch-systematischer Grundriß* (Frankfurt: Campus-Verlag, 1985).
19. Charles Tilly and Lesley J. Wood, *Social Movements 1768–2008* (Boulder, CO: Paradigm Publishers, 2009). Here, see the last chapter, "Future of Social Movements," 148f.
20. Nancy Fraser, "Feminism, Capitalism and the Cunning of History," *New Left Review* 56 (2009): 98. Nancy Fraser states that "the cultural changes jumpstarted by the second wave, salutary in themselves, have served to legitimate a structural transformation of capitalist society that runs directly counter to feminist visions of a just society" (99).
21. In contrast to the situation in the United States, for instance, feminist criticism of reproductive technology as a path to female self-determination was very prominent in Europe. Many feminists argued that reproductive technology would undermine the woman's autonomy and give control to a growing body of (male) experts. From the mid-1980s on, feminist resistance against reproductive engineering was organized on an international level through the creation of FINRRAGE (Feminist International Network of Resistance to Reproductive and Genetic Engineering).
22. See Joachim Raschke,'s definition: Joachim Raschke, "Zum Begriff der sozialen Bewegung," in *Neue soziale Bewegungen in der Bundesrepublik Deutschland,* ed. Roland Roth and Dieter Rucht, 2nd ed. (Bonn: Bundeszentrale für politische Bildung, 1991), 32f.

Bibliography

Ali, Suki, Kelly Coate, and Wangui wa Goro, eds. *Global Feminist Politics: Identities in a Changing World.* New York: Routledge, 2000.

Allen, Ann Taylor, Anne Cova, and June Purvis, eds. "Special Issue International Feminisms." *Women's History Review* 19, no. 4 (2010).

Amenta, Edwin, et al. "The Political Consequences of Social Movements." *Annual Review of Sociology* 36 (2010): 287–307.

Anderson, Bonnie S., and Judith P. Zinsser. *A History of Their Own; Women in Europe from Prehistory to the Present.* 2 vols. New York: Oxford University Press, 2000.

Bailey, Cathryn. "Making Waves and Drawing Lines: The Politics of Defining the Vicissitudes of Feminism." *Hypatia* 12, no. 3 (1997): 17–28.

Basu, Amrita. *The Challenge of Local Feminisms.* Boulder, CO: Westview Press, 1995.

Davis, Kathy E. *The Making of Our Bodies, Ourselves: How Feminism Travels across Borders.* Durham, NC: Duke University Press, 2007.

Delap, Lucy. *The Feminist Avant-Garde: Transnational Encounters of the Early Twentieth Century.* Cambridge: Cambridge University Press, 2007.

———. "Something in the Air: New Directions on the History of Feminism." Unpublished book review on recent scholarship, 2012.

della Porta, Donatella, and Mario Diani. *Social Movements: An Introduction.* 2nd ed. Malden: Blackwell Publishing, 2006.

———. *The Oxford Handbook of Social Movements.* Oxford: Oxford University Press, 2016.

Dicker, Rory C., and Alison Piepmeier, eds. *Catching a Wave: Reclaiming Feminism for the 21st Century.* Boston: Northeastern University Press, 2003.

Fahlenbrach, Kathrin, Martin Klimke, and Joachim Scharloth, eds. *The "Establishment" Responds: Power, Politics and Protest since 1945.* New York: Berghahn, 2012.

Fell, Alison, and Ingrid Sharp. *The Women's Movement in Wartime: International Perspectives, 1914–1919.* New York: Palgrave Macmillan, 2007.

Ferree, Myra Marx. *Varieties of Feminism: German Gender Politics in Global Perspective.* Stanford, CA: Stanford University Press, 2012.

Fraser, Nancy. "Feminism, Capitalism and the Cunning of History." *New Left Review* 56 (2009): 97–117.

Gamson, William. *The Strategy of Social Protest.* 2nd ed. Belmond: Wadsworth Publishing Company, 1990.

Garrison, Ednie Kaeh. "Are We on a Wavelength Yet? On Feminist Oceanography, Radios, and Third Wave Feminism." In *Different Wavelengths: Studies of the Contemporary Women's Movement,* edited by Jo Reger, 237–56. New York: Routledge, 2005.

Giugni, Marco, Dough McAdam, and Charles Tilly, eds. *How Social Movements Matter.* Minneapolis: University of Minnesota Press, 1999.

Giugni, Marco. "'Was It Worth the Effort?' The Outcomes and Consequences of Social Movements." *Annual Review of Sociology* 24 (1998): 371–93.

———, and Lorenzo Bosi. "The Impact of Protest Movements on the Establishment: Dimensions, Models, and Approaches." In *The "Establishment" Responds: Power, Politics and Protest since 1945,* edited by Kathrin Fahlenbrach, Martin Klimke, and Joachim Scharloth. New York: Berghahn, 2012.

Gubin, Eliane, et al. *Le siècle des feminisms.* Paris: Éditions de l'Atelier, 2004.

Harnois, Catherine. "Re-presenting Feminisms: Past, Present and Future." *Feminist Formations* 20, no. 1 (2008): 120–45.

Lenz, Ilse, Michiko Mae, and Karin Klose, eds. *Frauenbewegung weltweit: Aufbrüche, Kontinuitäten, Veränderungen.* Opladen: Leske + Budrich, 2000.

Morgan, Robin, ed. *Sisterhood Is Global: The International Women's Movement Anthology.* New York: Anchor Press/Doubleday, 1984.

Offen, Karen. "Defining Feminism: A Comparative Historical Approach." *Signs* 14, no. 1 (1988): 119–57.

———. *European Feminism, 1700–1950: A Political History.* Stanford, CA: Stanford University Press, 2000.

———. *Globalizing Feminisms, 1789–1945.* London: Routledge, 2010.

Paletschek, Sylvia, ed. *Women's Emancipation Movements in the Nineteenth Century: A European Perspective.* Stanford, CA: Stanford University Press, 2004.

Raschke, Joachim. *Soziale Bewegungen: Ein historisch-systematischer Grundriß.* Frankfurt: Campus-Verlag, 1985.

———. "Zum Begriff der sozialen Bewegung." In *Neue soziale Bewegungen in der Bundesrepublik Deutschland,* edited by Roland Roth and Dieter Rucht, 31–39. 2nd ed. Bonn: Bundeszentrale für politische Bildung, 1991.

Riley, Denise. *Am I That Name? Feminism and the Category of "Women" in History.* Basingstoke: MacMillan, 1988.

Roth, Roland, and Dieter Rucht. "Soziale Bewegungen und Protest—eine theoretische und empirische Bilanz." In *Die sozialen Bewegungen in Deutschland seit 1945: Ein Handbuch,* edited by Roland Roth and Dieter Rucht, 636–68. Frankfurt: Campus, 2007.

Rowbotham, Sheila. *Women's Liberation & the New Politics (Spokesman Pamphlets; no. 17).* Nottingham: Bertrand Russell Peace Foundation, 1971.

Rupp, Leila. *Worlds of Women: The Making of an International Women's Movement.* Princeton, NJ: Princeton University Press, 1997.

Schumaker, Paul D. "Policy Responsiveness to Protest Group Demands." *Journal of Politics* 37 (1975): 488–521.

Stewart, Abigail J., Jayati Lal, and Kristin McGuire. "Expanding the Archives of Global Feminisms: Narratives of Feminism and Activism." *Signs* 36, no. 4 (2011): 889–914.

Tilly, Charles, and Lesley J. Wood. *Social Movements 1768–2008.* Boulder, CO: Paradigm Publishers, 2009.

Tilly, Charles, and Sidney Tarrow. *Contentious Politics.* 2nd ed. Oxford: Oxford University Press, 2015.

Tucholsky, Kurt. *Briefe, Auswahl 1913–1935.* Berlin: Volk und Welt, 1983.

Wiemann, Uwe. "Kurt Tucholsky und die Politisierung des Kabaretts: Paradigmenwechsel oder literarische Mimikry?" *Studien zur Germanistik 12.* Hamburg: Dr. Kovac, 2004.

Wilmers, Annika. *Pazifismus in der internationalen Frauenbewegung (1914–1920): Handlungsspielräume, politische Konzeptionen und gesellschaftliche Auseinandersetzungen.* Essen: Klartext-Verlag, 2008.

Part I

The Women's Liberation Movement and Institutional Change

Introductory Remarks

Brigitte Studer

There is undoubtedly a consensus that provoking institutional change is one of the most difficult political undertakings. But did the women's liberation movement want to do just this after all? This fundamental question rightly opens the first section of the essays in this collection. Indeed, directly or indirectly the WLM was confronted with many institutions. Institutions like the modern state with its deficits in democracy and restrictive legal order for all "minorities," women in particular; the medical system with its arbitrary authority over contraception and reproduction; or academia with its exclusionary practices against women and critical scholarship were primary targets for provocative confrontation, structural criticism, and satirical denunciation. The sites representing such institutions were objects of demonstrations, occupations, and sit-ins by feminists. Despite their quest for "liberation," which encompassed their claim of each woman's right to self-determination, as well as collective organizational autonomy and their extraparliamentary activity, the feminists of the WLM were campaigning for (and against) state action nearly from the beginning. In this section, two chapters in particular look at this aspect of feminist strategies. Both are concerned with the case of Switzerland, which is distinctive by its political instruments of direct democracy, giving nearly every political force, at nearly all levels, the opportunity to bring their topics on the official political agenda.

Leena Schmitter focuses on the question of abortion rights. Women's control over reproductive functions ("body") was central to the project of women's liberation, autonomy, and self-determination. Charged with a whole complex of meanings, abortion was part of the understanding that "the personal is political" (or that "the private is political" as the slogan went in German). Women's sexual oppression was only one aspect of what feminists wanted to denounce. More generally at issue was the structural subordination of women through the public/private division in modern capitalist societies and the recognition of women as (political) subjects. Schmitter's narrative does not stop at the campaigns for the legalization of abortion in the 1970s in Switzerland. In the second part of her contribution she looks at the challenge to the feminist conceptions of "free choice" and "ownership" of one's own body represented by new reproductive technologies in the 1980s. As she shows, "the fetus" came to be seen or defined as a subject of its own with its own right to life. While the fetus became more and more visible, materially through intrauterine photographs and symbolically in public discourse, women's bodies and claims were made invisible.

At the center of Sarah Kiani's chapter is the interrogation about factors explaining the importance of the issue of workplace equality – or more precisely equal pay legislation – in Swiss feminism after the 1970s, characterized, as Lee Ann Banaszak has shown, by the meeting of the two waves of feminism. Before developing this theme, Kiani devotes part of her chapter to discuss the notions of "wave," "space," and "field." In the end she opts for Pierre Bourdieu's concept of "field" which she terms best adequate for her approach. In her view the personal trajectories explain why the Swiss WLM agreed to collaborate, in the 1980s, with first-wave women's organizations, which were more than single-purpose groups but which had to fight for female suffrage until 1971 and even longer on the local level. As she underlines, the WLM was divided on this issue, with the so-called radical groups refusing to engage on this institutional terrain, contrary to the socialist-feminist tendency of the WLM (influenced by Trotskyism) and to the two leftist-feminist organizations outside of it (of which, unfortunately, only the smaller Maoist group is taken into account). Kiani sustains her thesis on the prominence of Marxist-socialist concepts on gender equality by focusing on two women from the Socialist Party. How far these two can be considered as Marxists remains open to dispute, but what this chapter shows is the influence feminism had through its later appropriation by other protagonists coming from more traditional forces.

In her contribution to this section, Stefanie Ehmsen starts with the statement that, yes, the women's movement did change academia, it influenced the contents of scholarly research, it increased the number of women working there, and it created its own discipline, women's studies. On the basis of a comparison between Germany with its corporatist tradition and the United States with its liberal one, she asks if this institutionalization can also be regarded as a success. Though there were similar controversies, feminist influence in academia took various paths. As the data she provides show, the American educational system fares slightly better, providing more career opportunities for women. But with reference to Nancy Fraser's salient observation that the advancement of women in the academic profession may be connected with the rise of neoliberalism, she considers that the results lead more to ambivalence than unmitigated triumph. For one thing, the glass ceiling has not been broken, she notes. But more importantly, the aim of feminism was not primarily quantitative. Feminism wanted new contents and new curricula. Yet the body of theory provided by women's and gender studies can still be ignored by large parts of students and faculty. Furthermore, with institutionalization, feminism lost its combativeness; its focus is no longer on radical change, but on "mainstreaming" and on individual empowerment.

Indeed, as Mary Douglas has reminded us, institutions are not only constituted by beliefs, they also define the beliefs of their members. Thus, bringing feminist categories of thinking to traditionally patriarchal or at best paternalist institutions is of no minor relevance for feminism. But if we consider also the second part of Douglas's anthropological observation, what happens to feminist beliefs once they are taken over by institutions? As Ehmsen rightly asserts, academia has been resisting radical change. On the other hand, we should not forget that a gender and even a feminist perspective *have* entered most of the disciplines of humanities and social science. Does this mean that they have simply been sort of contaminated? And is it really true that women's and gender studies are simply coherent with a neoliberal agenda? Why, then, are they nowadays under attack in so many places?

As is the case with the topics of the other chapters, there is probably no simple answer to the question of institutional change in academe. Kiani's piece touches upon the circulation of the feminist demand of equal pay. Through intellectual and personal networks, it mobilized well over the frontiers of the WLM. In reality equal pay has a much longer history than shown here, starting with the labor movement, socialism, communism, and the first women's movement. It figures on the agenda of the International Labour Organization, was never realized, but never forgotten either by the early women's organizations. If the principle was finally implemented by Swiss law in 1995, it was probably more thanks to the long historical tradition against this discrimination than to Marxism as Kiani implies. I would argue that the WLM of the 1970s revived the old demand forcing the more traditional political forces like the so-called bourgeois women's organizations and the Social Democratic Party to take it on their agenda again. In this case, indirectly, the feminism of the WLM did have some impact, although not a real success, as equal pay is far from realized. And, more fundamentally, one could add that, as in the case of the steps made into academia, if some women have gained the possibility of an individual career, real equality and collective emancipation remained illusory. Finally, this can also be said for the legislation on abortion examined by Schmitter. If the WLM brought women's sexuality and the right to self-determination to the forefront in the 1970s, the meaning of pregnancy shifted with the social and political use of the new technology of visual reproduction of the fetus. In the end, though only in 2002 and thanks to a Social Democratic female member of parliament, feminism won an institutional success with the legalization of abortion. Up to now this right resisted the attacks by Pro-Life forces. But one has to ask if it is still associated with women's right to sexual self-determination and personal liberation in the comprehensive sense the WLM understood it. History tells us that women's rights can never just be considered as an irreversible gain, they have to be defended again and again. This said, readers will have to judge by themselves if the glass is half full or half empty. The three contributors are quite critical about the achievements of the WLM. The question is still a matter of debate. Other Swiss researchers, lead by Delphine Gardey from the University of Geneva, are more positive, emphasizing the cultural and social changes brought by the WLM. This highlights not only the complexity of feminisms' history, but also the diversity of its interpretations.

Brigitte Studer is full professor of contemporary history at the University of Bern since 1997. She has been teaching at the Universities of Geneva and Zurich and at Washington University in St. Louis (USA). She has been a guest professor at the École des Hautes Études en Sciences Sociales in Paris and at Strathclyde University in Glasgow and a visiting fellow at the University of Vienna and at London University. In her research she focuses on gender history and on social and cultural history of the political (http://www.hist.unibe.ch/ueber_uns/personen/studer_brigitte/index_ger.html). Her most recent publications in English include: *The Transnational World of the Cominternians* (Basingstoke: Palgrave Macmillan, 2015) and "1968 and the Formation of the Feminist Subject," *Twentieth Century Communism: A Journal of International History* 3 (2011): 38–69.

Bibliography

Banaszak, Lee Ann. "When Waves Collide: Cycles of Protest and the Swiss and American Women's Movement." *Political Research Quarterly* 49, no. 4 (1996): 837–60.

Douglas, Mary. *How Institutions Think.* Syracuse, NY: Syracuse University Press, 1986.

Gardey, Delphine (ed.), *Le féminisme change-t-il nos vies?* Paris: Editions textuel, 2011.

Chapter 1

Women's Liberation Movement and Professional Equality

The Swiss Case

Sarah Kiani

Like most other Western countries, Switzerland has experienced a renewal in feminism after 1968. This new feminism encompassed new forms of organization and activism. The women's liberation movement (WLM) favored informal groups and nonhierarchical organization structure, even though most groups tended to become more formalized after 1975. The WLM distinguished itself from the preceding generation of women's rights activists by its themes (first of all body and sexuality) and by its forms of public intervention, such as street demonstrations, provocative and symbolically charged protests, and occupations. Its repertoire of contention, understood as a set of protest-related tools and actions, was largely inspired by the 1968 student movement and challenged the dominant feminist activism of the time, which was mainly organized around women's voting rights. However, to avoid oversimplification, it is worth bearing in mind that parts of the suffragist movement also used street demonstrations and confrontational strategies occasionally, although less extensively.

If the Swiss case seems to perfectly fit the general pattern of Western feminism after 1968, it also has noticeable characteristics that render it unique. The comparatively late achievement of female suffrage at the federal level in 1971 created what Lee Ann Banaszak called a "collision" of two feminist "waves"[1]: women's rights and suffrage associations were still active in the 1970s when women's liberation groups began their activism. What we sometimes call the "old" and the "new" women's movements also met in other national contexts, where some of the feminist associations active since the end of the nineteenth century—mostly the moderate ones—had survived World War II and kept on organizing during the 1950s and 1960s. However, in Switzerland, the women's rights associations of the turn of the century—I will refer to them as "women's rights associations" in this essay to avoid confusion with the WLM—played a role in feminist mobilization processes from the end of the 1960s to the beginning of the 1980s, as did the women's chapters of the left-wing parties and the trade unions. The possibilities offered by the semi-direct democratic system along with the late introduction of women's suffrage created, I would argue, a constellation in which "old" and "new" feminists were more likely to collaborate than in other countries, even though supporters of both strands of Swiss feminism saw each other as antagonists, and are usually seen as such in the historiography of feminism.[2]

The differences between women's rights associations and the WLM created in the aftermath of 1968 were multiple. Aside from age and the generational experiences of their supporters, they involve most importantly, first, the temporal horizon in which feminists situated their activities; second, the relationship toward men and male organizations that led to a claim for autonomy; and, third, the mode of organization. Where women's rights associations mainly believed in the power of slow but steady political lobbying, women's liberation groups thought in terms of "revolution." Women's liberation groups believed in the transformational power of everyday life situations, and their time frame for social change focused on the "here and now." Where women's rights associations sought to collaborate with (male) politicians and trade unionists open to their claims, women's liberation groups pleaded, in the name of autonomy, for women's separatism and gathered in nonmixed groups. Where women's suffrage associations took the classical (male) bourgeois clubs and associations as models for their organizational structure, women's liberation groups sought to meet without the constraints of formal membership, hierarchical organization structures, and division of roles and activities within the movement. But sometimes these distinctions were less rigid than superficial observation might suggest. From time to time, women's rights associations favored "radical" strategies over patient lobbying, as, for example, parts of the socialist and social democratic women's movements or even radical sections of the bourgeois suffragist associations during the first decades of the twentieth century. Also, even though the supporters of the WLM tended to think of the movement as free from organizational hierarchies, an informal hierarchical division of work was frequently reported by former activists. The example of the equality campaign that I will develop in this chapter will also show how, in the Swiss case, the boundaries between "old" and "new" feminism became occasionally fluid. In fact, the 1970s and 1980s witnessed important moments of collaboration between the WLM and the women's rights associations, despite their different understanding of contentious politics.

This chapter explores the ways in which feminists contributed to the campaign for equality legislation between 1975 and 1995. Where earlier accounts of feminist activities during this period have focused on specific associations, groups, and individual political figures, I foreground the practices of collaboration in very specific moments of political mobilization. In those moments, the WLM's principal claim for autonomy was challenged by the strategic need to collaborate. In order to better understand the structure of this coalition and its transformation over time, I will make use of Pierre Bourdieu's concept of the "field." Using this notion will help to highlight the specific evolution of feminist attitudes toward law and institutions: while in the early 1970s the WLM adopted a critical standpoint to campaigning for legislative change, some other groups were willing to work within the framework of the state in the 1980s and the 1990s, mainly concentrating on improving, via legislation, the status of women in the workplace.

The chapter covers the period from the campaign for a constitutional article on gender equality, which was added in 1981, to the application of this constitutional principle through the "law for equality"[3] in 1995. After briefly presenting the concept of the field and advocating its use in research on the women's movement, I will demonstrate its application in the case of Swiss feminism, examining the particular tendencies and situation at that point in time and how personal trajectories played a role in creating this particular field configuration. Finally, I will discuss how this field configuration led to the domination of specific aspects of gender equality in the public arena.

Conceptualizing the History of Feminism(s): "Wave," "Space," and "Field"

The wave metaphor is crucial in the conceptualization of the history of feminism(s). Both activists and scholars have used it in order to better understand a very polymorphous phenomenon.[4] It serves to distinguish between three moments of feminism: the activism of "women's rights" feminism around the turn of the twentieth century, the feminism of the WLM, and a third wave of feminism since the 1990s,[5] presented sometimes as "state feminism" but more often brought together with the concepts of "poststructuralism" and "cyberfeminism," also encompassing an intersectional approach and processes of transnationalization. The wave metaphor has contributed to conceptualizing the history of feminism as a continuum in time with highs and lows as to public visibility and internal cohesion. However, the metaphor also revealed its own limits.[6] This is especially obvious in the Swiss case. If the metaphor of waves entails a temporal notion, meaning that one wave appears after the other, the Swiss history of feminism proves this idea, at least partly, wrong. This has not only to do with the temporal collision of the suffrage movement and the women's liberation movement in this country, but it is also due to the fact that the WLM in Switzerland, although committed theoretically to ad-hoc mobilization dynamics that aim at convincing people through provocation and not through organization, was characterized by a pragmatic approach toward political intervention in the direct democratic political system of Switzerland, even though this position and the will to work with the law and institutions varied, depending on the nature of the groups and periods. Even if there was a deep suspicion from the WLM toward the law system because of its profound patriarchal structures,[7] the abortion debate and the equality legislation show that at least for a part of the women's movement, which may not include all of the autonomous movements, legislative change was considered to be a means of women's emancipation at several specific moments. In this the WLM was closer to the women's rights organizations than it thought. Some women's liberation activists in Switzerland careered in law-oriented areas in order to be able to contribute expert knowledge to the struggle for legislative change according to a feminist agenda. Moreover, if the wave metaphor does not offer the most adequate theoretical tool to conceptualize feminism in Switzerland, this is also because it fails to present contradictions and struggles within the same "wave." It shows neither how nor why these waves appear; or in other words, it does not show why feminism changes and renews itself over time. Applied as a rigid model—opposing patient lobbying to provocation—the "wave" metaphor shows an inability to think about the diversity of feminisms at a particular moment in time.

Laure Bereni, French sociologist, suggests utilizing an "espace de la cause des femmes" (literally: "space of the women's issues") to conceptualize the women's movement. The aim is to take into account forms of mobilization that do not fit easily into the classical definition of a movement. According to Bereni, the concept "restitutes the important plurality of mobilizations, their scattering and their embedding in various and multiple visions. In a few words, we can define it as the *configuration of mobilization sites for the women's issue in a plurality of social spheres.*"[8] This conception insists on the plurality of mobilizations, a plurality that was particularly important in the women's movement of last third of the twentieth century. To give an illustration of this, when examining personal trajectories inside the movement, it is apparent that activists had several career opportunities available to them, ranging from movement activism to being part of a trade union or an official political party (frequently socialist), holding an academic position in the field of gender studies, working at a center for female victims of violence, opening a women's library, or even entering parliament. Conceptualizing these different biographical trajectories while taking into account several forms of militantism or political participation in a broader sense may be the most difficult task for scholars of the women's movement to achieve.

While Bereni's conceptualization helps us to take into account the plurality of feminism, Bourdieu offers us a concept representing social issues as a space crossed by logics of domination and conflicts for the possession of a specific *capital*—a dimension less emphasized in Bereni's work—without minimizing the importance of collaboration, alliance, and friendship. According to Bourdieu, the field constitutes a structured space of positions. The concept of the field is antagonistic as fields are characterized by struggles in which the dominant position holder defends her or his position against agents who want to enter it as newcomers. The structure of a field in a specific moment is the result of struggles for the gain of capital: "The structure of the field is a *state* of the power relations among the agents or institutions engaged in the struggle, or, to put it another way, a state of the distribution of the specific capital which has been accumulated in the course of previous struggles and which orients subsequent strategies."[9] Bourdieu's concept of the field is complex.[10] For the purpose of my analysis here, I focus on Bourdieu's idea that the structure of the field depends in a dynamic way on the positions that the actors of the field take in a specific moment of time. In other words, it is possible to understand important changes in feminism by analyzing the trajectory of actors within the field, and, especially, who is dominant at a particular moment: "these struggles aiming to conserve or to transform the instituted power relation in the field of production obviously have the effect of keeping or transforming the structure of the field."[11] As in this chapter I wish to emphasize the idea of feminism as a "field" rather than as coherent "movement," I will hereafter refer to a "feminist field." This notion enables me to use a broad definition of feminism that does not exclude the institutional arena, neither social movements nor informal groups, but rather puts the emphasis on the *relations* between the different actors of the field active on a particular question. With such an analytical tool I also avoid deciding who is feminist and who is not; rather, I propose a careful observation of all parts involved in favor of specific campaigns, here, the equality campaigns.

Feminism after 1968: New Orientations, New Divisions

The feminist field in Switzerland in the decades after World War II was built around female voting rights. If discrimination against women through matrimonial law and the regulation of labor were also subjects of feminist reflection, it was the ongoing political exclusion of women that became central to women's rights associations in the whole country. The fight was generally won when the (male) electorate accepted female suffrage on the federal level in 1971, although women in some cantons had to wait much longer to obtain vote rights.[12] The strategies of the suffrage movement broadly involved negotiations with the authorities, the launch of petitions, and moderate campaigning. Exceptionally, the women's rights movement attempted to gain greater public attention beyond parliament and its lobby through street demonstrations, a political tool that was highly controversial internally.[13]

At the very same moment when universal suffrage was extended to women in Switzerland, a new generation of feminists—readers of Simone de Beauvoir, Juliet Mitchell, and Kate Millett, who were inspired by new theories and movements from North America, France, Italy, and Germany, and politically formed in the 1968 movement—entered the feminist field. They gained increasing influence at the beginning of the 1970s, thereby modifying the structure of the field.

The entering generation was manifold in itself, embracing different strands and groups that made use of different labels such as "autonomous," "radical," or "revolutionary." Most of them claimed to be part of a wider women's liberation movement. Some named themselves after their American and French counterparts as *Frauenbefreiungsbewegung* (FBB) and *Mouvement de Libération des Femmes* (MLF). Others were closer to leftist standpoints and operated with names such as *Femmes en Lutte/Frauen Kämpfen Mit* (FEL/FKM) (Women in Struggle) or *Organization für die Sache der Frauen* (OFRA) (Organization for Women's Matters). The feminist milieu in Switzerland was tight and open at the same time. People could easily switch from one group to another, support one feminist campaign and turn away from another, join a leftist group or party and confess at the same time to radical feminism, and so on. This makes it difficult to grasp the underlying structure of the feminist field.

I suggest two elements of the cognitive orientation of different groups and strands to be a key to a systematic understanding of controversy and coalition within the feminist field: the conception of the origin of women's oppression and the mode of organization. Both elements were crucial to the choice of action strategies and coalition building. The first element, the conception of the origin of women's oppression, was clearly reflected in the opposition between those groups committed to the analysis of patriarchy as the departure point of women's oppression and those declaring capitalism to be the main enemy of equality between women and men. Most of the FBB and of the MLF stood for a feminist standpoint that put forward solidarity (and some, love) between women ("sisterhood is powerful"), the search for women-only spaces, and the fight for autonomy from political parties and movements, from men in general and from the state as a patriarchal institution per se. The *Radikalfeministinnen Bern-Biel-Fribourg* (Radical feminists) that split from the FBB in 1977 was also part of this tendency. In contrast, the *Progressive Frauen Schweiz* (PFS) (Progessive Women Switzerland) was much closer to class struggle approaches represented by different groups and organizations of the Left. The group developed within the *Progressive Organizationen Schweiz* (POCH) (Progressive Organisations Switzerland)—a far left political party created by supporters of the 1968 protest movement—from 1974 on and opened out into the OFRA in 1977. Like *Femmes en lutte,* the OFRA members intended to link women's oppression with issues of social condition and rights of women; in other words, socialism and feminism. Some of those groups referred to Marxist thinking; others were influenced by Maoism or Trotskyism.

The second element, the mode of organization, was connected to the first. Interestingly enough, it brought feminist groups oriented toward socialism closer to women's rights associations then to women's liberation groups. The latter organized in a decentralized and lose way, hardly defining supporters as "members" and even less obliging them to join a national membership corporation. In some regions, the FBB/MLF was constituted as a registered association, which, according to the code of praxis in Switzerland, allowed for holding a bank account. But this formal foundation had little influence on the structure of autonomous feminism. One of its principles was that groups could be built at any moment from anyone feeling concerned with a certain topic. The topics were not to be defined top down from elected board members but would instead reflect the concerns and interests of women at the grassroots level. It was decided at a plenary meeting in Zurich in 1973 that "in the future, the FBB will be exactly as active as are its working groups, or rather its active members."[14] The organizational structure of the OFRA, in contrast, differed to that of autonomous women's liberation groups. While it stood for an antihierarchical approach and nonconventional political tools, the OFRA criticized what its supporters saw as a lack of structure and organization of the WLM. The OFRA had regional sections in different parts of Switzerland and a national coordination office. From the point of view of organization, the OFRA was closer to women's rights associations active on the suffrage question and to leftist parties, and, unlike the WLM, the organization believed in traditional political tools, in particular making use of the popular initiative.

Against this backdrop it is useful to relativize the importance of the division between a "new" and an "old" feminism, which would run the risk of invisibilizing other conflicts. Indeed, the division between class struggle and what was sometimes—with reference to North American groups—called radical feminism and even conflicts within socialist feminism itself, are the best documented: in Geneva, for example, the group *salaire pour le travail ménager* (Salary for Household Work), which tended to encourage women staying home to get paid for their work in the so-called domestic sphere, split from a group *lutte des classes* (Class Struggle). The WLM indeed was diverse and, as the second part of this chapter shows, so were the relations to the political tools of direct democracy.

Campaigning for Equality

The popular initiative to inscribe gender equality into the Swiss Constitution was launched by a committee of fifteen women mostly in their fifties and sixties, highly educated and politically active in liberal political parties for the majority. Noticeably, the committee was made of a very high presence of former suffragist activists. As a response to the initiative, the government proposed an alternative constitutional amendment, taking into account most of the concerns of the popular initiative. The popular vote took place in 1981. The alternative amendment of the Federal Council was accepted, and thus "equality" between men and women entered the federal constitution. The text that was added to the constitution (article 4 bis) codified: "Men and women are equal. Men and women have the same rights and duties in the family. Men and women can claim the same salary for an equivalent work. Men and women can claim an equal treatment in education, school and professional training, employment and occupation."[15]

During the late 1970s, at the time of the campaign for constitutional equality, the WLM was undergoing an important mobilization process, especially regarding the issue of abortion rights, which was at stake in demonstrations, nonconventional public actions such as street theater, and sit-/go-ins addressed to the representatives in parliament. At that moment, the women's liberation groups cared little for the women's rights associations (and vice versa), and, except for some individuals, very little communication existed between the two. The vast majority of the women's liberation groups, and especially the numerically largest ones such as Zurich's FBB, therefore did not contribute to the equal rights campaign. In Geneva, one member of the MLF was very committed, but the rest of the group appeared reluctant to get involved in any action requiring a close collaboration with either so-called bourgeois groups or the state.[16] A member of the Lausanne MLF explained during an interview that the lack of interest of the group for this campaign was the logical consequence of a strategic decision that corresponded with its political convictions. Refusing to work on legislation in order to transform women's situations was integral to their political strategy. In the opinion of the MLF, it was not an effective method through which to change society and modify existing power relations between men and women. Furthermore, the idea of "equality" was not especially popular among women's liberation activists. It was seen as "reformist," while their aim was to fundamentally change society as a whole—"revolution" rather than "reformism." For many activists, the praxis of women's liberation involved *consciousness-raising* rather than fighting for legislative change: "It is not a law that will make us gain the free control of our body."[17]

The equality campaign reveals that one of the most important conflicts in the feminist field of the 1970s was about legislation in favor of women, or, more broadly, the question of what role the laws, institutions, and the state should and could play in the achievement of equality between women and men.[18] The question was controversial, and reactions to the equality campaign were accordingly charged. The ambivalence was especially obvious in the case of the newcomers to the feminist field of the 1970s. They explicitly declined to use the institutional channels provided by the system of the semi-direct democracy; at the same time, some of them joined the campaign for constitutional equality by organizing street protests and gathering signatures for the initiative.[19] In fact, in spite of its skepticism towards institutional politics, the WLM used political campaigning in the context of popular initiatives more than once, as the pro-choice campaign and the campaign for maternity leave shows. How can we understand this seemingly paradoxical attitude?

A closer look reveals that those groups within the WLM who where likely to support institutional lobbying, were the most compatible with institutional politics. That is the case of groups with a relatively stable organization structure and an ideological affinity to the traditional Left, such as the OFRA. The OFRA mobilized successfully from 1977 on, exactly at the same moment when autonomous groups, such as the FBB and the MLF, where about to split up into various smaller groups and projects. The MLF in Lausanne ceased to meet in 1979, the FBB in Bern in 1980, and the national coordination of the FBB was dissolved in the same year. Only the largest group, the FBB Zurich, survived until 1989.

The OFRA was not the only group to benefit from the demobilization of autonomous feminism. From the mid-1970s, other socialist feminists began to mobilize and to create structures separately from the FBB/MLF. Some activists got involved with the progressive trade unions, with the Social Democratic Party of Switzerland (SP), or with the POCH. By the end of the 1970s socialist feminism had gained influence on the feminist agenda, whereas supporters of the MLF/FBB were less and less able to control the direction of change. As the following suggests, those changes in the field can specifically be observed in the 1980s.

The Transformation of the Feminist Field in the 1980s and 1990s

I use analytically the term "socialist" here to define broadly the portion of the 1970s women's movement favoring a lecture of feminism, in which the struggle for women's liberation was linked to criticism on capitalism. In Switzerland, as well as in other countries that experienced the renewal of feminism in the late 1960s and the beginning of the 1970s, schisms occurred frequently between so-called autonomous groups and socialist and social democratic feminists. An early schism took place in 1973 with the creation of the *Femmes en luttes* (FEL) in the city of Lausanne. Several years later, other regional groups appeared, the FKM/FEL. These groups grew in importance, with further organizations created in Basel, Zurich, and Winterthur before 1980.[20] In the city of Bienne, the class struggle tendency was especially strong: no MLF was created, but a branch of FKM/FEL was.[21] FEL also existed in Geneva.

The importance of feminist groups inclined to socialist ideas within the Swiss WLM has been underestimated in the historiography until now. This may be because of their late emergence, which took place after the period of street mobilization around abortion rights had already ended.[22] Looking at the WLM from a long-term perspective that takes into account the trajectory of the social movement and of its activists, we can see that several supporters of the WLM continued their activism in trade unions. By the late 1970s and early 1980s, women's groups were created in those trade unions under the aegis of members of the WLM or FKM/FEL who became female unionists. It is also worth bringing attention to the fact that the labor movement apparently started to give women in politics better chances, such as in the case of Anne-Catherine Ménétrey, a prominent feminist who became a deputy of the Council of States for the canton of Vaud and who used to be active in the socialist *Parti Ouvrier et Populaire* (Labour and Popular Party) (POP).

The careers of two women, Christiane Brunner and Yvette Jaggi, are paradigmatic for feminist trajectories between women's liberation and labor movement activities, social democracy included. Brunner was first involved with the trade union movement at the time of the equality article campaign, in which she participated (though not as a leading activist) within the Swiss Federation of Trade Unions (*Gewerkschaftbund/ Union syndicale Suisse*).[23] She finally became national counselor—narrowly missing the position of federal counselor—and president of the SP, while Yvette Jaggi was also elected national counselor. Brunner became famous as a leading organizing force of the 1991 women's strike, involved as the president of the women's group of the Swiss Federation of Trade Unions. The strike, an important success for women's organizations in Switzerland, was launched to protest against the ineffectiveness of the constitutional equality article, which was considered unsuited to enforce equality between women and men. The 1991 strike also showed a surprising revival of the strategies adopted by the WLM twenty years earlier, such as the appropriation of the public sphere, spectacular protests, and street demonstrations accompanied by ironic and playful slogans and songs.

If these two women were not primarily women's liberation activists, they clearly could be seen as being influenced by its themes, analysis, and strategies. When examining the main themes that women brought on the agenda of trade unions, influences from the WLM become obvious, especially on the way the trade unions approached the relationship between women's (under- and unpaid) work and women's oppression.[24]

These developments make a strong point for a conceptualization of feminism as a field in constant motion, in which different groups and strands were coexisting in a complex and interdependent interplay. Although Brunner had not been active in the WLM, the starting point of her "politicization" was the reading of women's liberation texts from France, Germany, and the United States, written by Alice Schwarzer, Benoîte Groult, and Betty Friedan. She described herself as being "close to women's liberation (MLF)" in the 1970s.[25] Yvette Jaggi put forward a motion as early as 1983, demanding a law to render effective the equality article on equal pay, which can be seen as the first step toward the law for equality *Gleichstellungsgesetz/ loi pour l'égalité*). She was active in the 1968 student' movement, as were many WLM's activists. Jaggi and Brunner where prominent members of the SP; like many other—and less known—women active in that party from the 1980s on, they had been taking part in debates launched by the WLM in the 1970s. Several supporters of the WLM appear to have careered in the labor movement: Maryelle Budry, member of Geneva's MLF, was, for example, active in the women's group of the Trade Union of the Public Services, SSP (*Syndicat des services publics*).[26]

However, the rise of feminism in the social democratic political left and the unions from the late 1970s on, which Ménétrey or Brunner do represent quite paradigmatically, is not worthy of attention simply because of the sheer number of women who continued their careers—or even started them—in the labor movement and in political organizations or the trade unions; it is also important for understanding the evolution of feminist concerns. When observing the evolution of feminist "mainstream" themes from the implementation of the constitutional article until the law for its application, the law for equality it is striking to see the extent to which the question of gender equality in the workplace has become the main focus for Swiss activists over the years. Indeed, it is even more surprising when one looks at the content of the equality article in 1981, which mandates equal pay but also equality within the family and within education. From a WLM feminist point of view, the workplace was not the most important arena in which to achieve gender equality per se. I argue here that the reason for the success of the concept of "equality in the workplace" in the last decades of the twentieth century was due to the configuration of the field at that time. Feminists that were close to the trade unions and the political left gained more importance from the late 1970s on because they could rely on established institutional resources, and they were also, sometimes, given career opportunities, which allowed them to implement women's concerns in the organizations' program and structure.

After 1981, several actions were established on the federal level to render the equality article effective. First of all, the Federal Council was charged—with its new government body for gender equality, the Federal Commission for Women's Issues (*Eidgenössische Kommission für Frauenfragen/Commission fédérale pour les questions féminines*), instituted in 1976—to investigate discrimination against women in the law, social welfare, education, marriage, and so on. Important work was undertaken over the following years to identify some aspects of this discrimination. As an increasing number of former WLM activists held academic and governmental positions, they tried to forward a feminist agenda, which gradually gained importance over the years. While the small and mostly informal WLM groups disappeared little by little, women's groups in trade unions continued to exist and to be very active. The women's strike organized by the Swiss Federation of Trade Unions, led by Christiane Brunner, constituted a memorable success for feminism in the 1990s, with the campaign for equal pay also attaining a degree of prominence.

Conclusion

In the early 1970s, women's rights associations were no longer seen to constitute the vanguard of women's activism. Female activism had moved to another generation, using other forms of activism and rejecting a reformist strategy. In the mid-1970s however, women's rights activism became—once again—an important current that would grow in the following years: yet surprisingly, it was one of the aims of the campaign launched by this movement—that of workplace equality—that eventually became increasingly dominant within the feminist field more broadly. After the Swiss population voted for the equality article in 1981, feminists frequently put the effectiveness of the article into question: only very few women undertook legal actions to claim an equal pay. Gender inequalities in the workplace after 1981 gradually started to become the most widely discussed feminist issue, within the movement but also in society in general. This brought new attention to those feminist groups who had been campaigning for equal pay for a long time. Indeed, socialist women had been campaigning for such change since the nineteenth century, especially the Swiss Federation of Trade Unions. However, before the middle and late 1980s, equal pay issues had never attained prominence in the public and institutional arenas; in particular, it had never been as widely discussed at the Federal Council or in the press before. This can be seen as a direct outcome of the constitutional article for gender equality, which favored a public discussion in order to render different Swiss laws and amendments compatible to the Constitution. Most strikingly, this issue had never been a prominent object of discussion in feminist circles before this point. The women's strike of 1991 initiated by the Swiss Federation of Trade Union (following the idea of female members of the trade union for workers in the industry, construction and services, *Fédération de l'industrie, de la construction et des services* FTMH)—brought wider attention to the multiple inequalities in the workplace while enforcing the position of female trade unionists such as Christiane Brunner. Other activists who were involved either in the labor movement or the SP also contributed to bringing wider attention to the struggle for equal pay. It was, for example, Yvette Jaggi who submitted a parliamentary motion in 1983 to implement a law to enforce the provisions of the equality article. The need for such a law was clearly communicated during the 1991 strike. Such a law was finally implemented in 1995 under the guise of being a "law for equality,"[27] a generic term suggesting that all the aspects of gender equality were to be addressed, whereas, in fact, it only addressed equality in the workplace.

Sarah Kiani obtained her PhD in contemporary history in 2014 from the University of Bern. She is currently a postdoctoral fellow at the Centre Marc Bloch in Berlin, where she works on the state surveillance of homosexuals in the GDR between 1970 and 1990.

Notes

1. Lee Ann Banaszak, "When Waves Collide: Cycles of Protest and the Swiss and American Women's Movements," *Political Research Quarterly* 49 (1996): 837–60.
2. For Switzerland, for example, May B. Broda, Elisabeth Joris, Regina Müller, "Die alte und die neue Frauenbewegung," in *Dynamisierung und Umbau: Die Schweiz in den 60er und 70er Jahren,* ed. Mario König (Zurich: Chronos, 1998), 202–26; Julie de Dardel, *Révolution sexuelle et mouvement de libération des femmes à Genève (1970–1977)* (Lausanne: Antipodes, 2007); Renate Schär, "Der Schweizerische Frauenkongress und der Antikongress von 1975: Mobilisierungshöhepunkt der Neuen Frauenbewegung," in *1968–1978, une décennie mouvementée en Suisse/Ein bewegtes Jahrzehnt in der Schweiz,* ed. Janick Marina Schaufelbuehl (Zurich: Chronos, 2009), 205–19.
3. *Loi pour l'égalité* (LEg), *Gleichstellungsgesetz* (GIG).
4. See, for example, Martha Weinman Lear, "The Second Feminist Wave," *New York Times* 10 (1966): 24–33; Jo Freeman, "Waves of Feminism," *H Women* (May 1996); Joni Lovenduski, *Women and European Politics: Contemporary Feminism and Public Policy* (Brighton: Wheatsheaf Books, 1986).
5. See, for example, Leslie Heywood and Jennifer Drake, ed., *Third Wave Agenda: Being Feminist, Doing Feminism* (Minneapolis: University of Minnesota Press, 1997); Silke Redolfi, *Frauen bauen Staat: 100 ans de l'Alliance de sociétés féminines suisses* (Zurich: NZZ Verlag, 2000).
6. Astrid Henry, for example, puts into question the supposed internal coherence of each "wave" and stresses the arbitrariness of creating categories of feminism: Astrid Henry, "Feminism's Family Problems: Feminist Generation and the Mother-Daughter Trope," in *Catching a Wave: Reclaiming Feminism for the 21st Century,* ed. Rory Cooke Dicker and Alison Piepmeier (Boston: Northeastern University Press, 2003). Catherine Harnois, in a similar vein, argues that the "wave" metaphor tends to negate diversity: Catherine Harnois, "Re-presenting Feminisms: Past, Present and Future," *Feminist Formations* 20, no. 1 (2008): 120–45. Cathryn Bailey puts into question one of the most solid considerations underlining the metaphor: its temporality. Indeed, she argues that the temporality on which the "waves" are constructed is typically North American and not suitable in other geographical contexts: Cathryn Bailey, "Making Waves and Drawing Lines: The Politics of Defining the Vicissitudes of Feminism," *Hypatia* 12, no. 3 (1997): 17–28.
7. Sarah Kiani, "Equal Rights and Strategies of the Swiss Women's Movement (1975–1996)," *Femina Politika: Die Zeitschrift für feministische Politikwissenschaft* 2 (2012): 85–96. On the question of the relation between law and feminism in latin Europe, see Laure Bereni, Alice Debauche, Emmanuelle Latour, Anne Revillard, *Quand les mouvements féministes font (avec) la loi: les lois du genre (II), Nouvelles Questions Féministes* 29, no. 1, 2010.
8. Laure Bereni, "Penser la transversalité des mobilisations féministes: l'espace de la cause des femmes," in *Les féministes de la deuxième vague,* ed. Christine Bard (Rennes: Presses universitaires de Rennes, 2012), 27. My emphasis and my translation from French to English.

9. Pierre Bourdieu, *Sociology in Question* (London: Sage Publications, 1993), 73. First published in French: Pierre Bourdieu, *Questions de Sociologie* (Paris: Les éditions de Minuit, 1984).
10. For further explanation, see Bourdieu, *Questions de sociologie*; Pierre Bourdieu, *Raisons pratiques: Sur la théorie de l'action* (Paris: Seuil, 1994); Pierre Bourdieu and Loïc J. D. Wacquant, *Réponses: Pour une anthropologie réflexive* (Paris: Seuil, 1992).
11. Bourdieu, *Raisons pratiques,* 71. My own translation from French to English.
12. Suffrage groups were organized both regionally and nationally, with national organizations becoming especially prominent from the beginning of the twentieth century when several groups came together under the name of "Alliance of Swiss Women's Organisation *Bund Schweizerischer Frauenorganisationen/Alliance de sociétés féminines suisses.* A book about to the history of the group was published for its centenary: Redolfi, *Frauen bauen Staat.* See also on this subject: Sybille Hardmeier, *Frühe Frauenstimmrechtsbewegung in der Schweiz (1890–1930): Argumente, Strategien, Netzwerke und Gegenbewegung* (Zurich: Chronos 1997).
13. Examples of controversy include the protest of 1929 organized by the first exhibition on women's work, the SAFFA, *Schweizerische Ausstellung für Frauenarbeit* during which the activists lugged a gigantic snail to symbolize the slowness of the political process regarding suffrage, and in 1969 the "march on Bern," during which women whistled and protested in front of the building of the Federal Council.
14. FBB Frauen Befreiungsbewegung, "Minutes" (without exact date [Summer 1973]), in Kristina Schulz, Leena Schmitter, and Sarah Kiani, *Frauenbewegung: Die Schweiz seit 1968. Analysen. Dokumente. Archive* (Baden: hier + jetzt, 2014), 47.
15. "Mann und Frau sind gleichberechtigt. Das Gesetz sorgt für ihre Gleichstellung, vor allem in Familie, Ausbildung und Arbeit. Mann und Frau haben Anspruch auf gleichen Lohn für gleichwertige Arbeit." (My translation from German to English).
16. The Geneva women's liberation movement (MLF) has kept extensive archives on its activities in the 1970s and the 1980s, when the group dissolved. These archives are situated in Carouge and are in possession of a former activist: http://www.archivesmlf.ch/. In the archives I was not able to find a single sentence regarding the initiative; however, an activist who was part of the MLF and whom I interviewed at the end of 2010 in Geneva has stated that she herself was very active in the campaign, even though her comrades were not. After the MLF dissolved, however, another group that counted among its membership some women from the MLF, the *dispensaire des femmes, Women's Health Center* did support some campaigns regarding equal rights.
17. Femmes du centre femme, *Personne ne décidera pour nous: Nos luttes sur l'avortement. Auto-examen. Attaque contre les gynécos* (Carouge: Centre femmes, 1977), 2. (My translation from French to English).
18. Broda et al., "Die alte und die neue Frauenbewegung," 218.
19. In Switzerland, the system of direct democracy offers two different tools to citizens: the referendum and the initiative. While the former proposes to change an existing law, the latter proposes the inclusion of a new constitutional article. In order to be validated, the initiative has to be signed by 100,000 citizens, although at the time of the initiative for gender equality the number of signatures needed was only 50,000. For this reason, collecting signatures was an important part of campaign work.

20. The information is given in the editorial of the first journal written by the group of Lausanne *Femmes en Luttes,* in 1978. The paper mentions the growth of Marxist groups in the German-speaking part of Switzerland.
21. Interview with a prominent member of the Bienne FEL, December 2011.
22. On the institutionalization of the women's movement, see, among others, Claudie Baudino, "La cause des femmes à l'épreuve de son institutionnalisation," *Politix* 13 (2000): 81–112.
23. The participation of both women can be seen in various internal documents. Christiane Brunner was active in a work group for the initiative, and this is also mentioned in a letter to Jacqueline Berenstein-Wavre, president of the initiative committee in 1979 (USS archives, G.41111 1978–1987).
24. This can be seen very well during the 1991 women's strike, organized by the Swiss Federation of Trade Unions: if the question of paid work was at the center of the event, the question of domestic work was also debated, which was particularly exemplified by the strike of the "housewives." Other themes, such as lesbianism, were also discussed.
25. Christianne Brunner interviewed in *L'Hebdo,* May 30, 2002, http://www.hebdo.ch/laquojamais_je_ne_vous_dirai_si_jai_avorteacuteraquo_13620_.html.
26. Maryelle Budry, "Des unes aux autres," in Maryelle Budry and Edmée Olagnier, eds., *Mais qu'est-ce qu'elles voulaient ? Histoires de vie du MLF à Genève* (Lausanne: Editions d'en bas, 1999), 12.

Bibliography

Banaszak, Lee Ann. "When Waves Collide: Cycles of Protest and the Swiss and American Women's Movements." *Political Research Quarterly* 49/4 (1996): 837–60.

Baudino, Claudie. "La cause des femmes à l'épreuve de son institutionnalisation." *Politix* 13 (2000): 81–112.

Bereni, Laure. "Penser la transversalité des mobilisations féministes: l'espace de la cause des femmes." In *Les féministes de la deuxième vague,* edited by Christine Bard. Rennes: Presses universitaires de Rennes, 2012, 27-43.

Bereni, Laure, Alice Debauche, Emmanuelle Latour, and Anne Revillard. "Quand les mouvements féministes font (avec) la loi: les lois du genre (II)." *Nouvelles Questions Féministes* 29/1 (2010).

Bourdieu, Pierre. *Questions de sociologie.* Paris: Les éditions de minuit, 1984.

———. *Sociology in Question.* London: Sage Publications, 1993.

———. *Raisons pratiques: Sur la théorie de l'action.* Paris: Seuil, 1994.

Bourdieu, Pierre, and Loïc J. D. Wacquant. *Réponses: Pour une anthropologie réflexive.* Paris: Seuil, 1992.

Broda, May B., Elisabeth Joris, and Regina Müller. "Die alte und die neue Frauenbewegung." In *Dynamisierung und Umbau: Die Schweiz in den 60er und 70er Jahren,* edited by Mario König, 202–26. Zurich: Chronos, 1998.

Budry, Maryelle, and Edmée Olagnier, eds. *Mais qu'est-ce qu'elles voulaient? Histoires de vie du MLF à Genève.* Lausanne: Editions d'en bas, 1999.

Dardel, Julie de. *Révolution sexuelle et mouvement de libération des femmes à Genève (1970–1977).* Lausanne: Antipodes, 2007.

Femmes du centre femmes. *Personne ne décidera pour nous: Nos luttes sur l'avortement. Auto-examen. Attaque contre les gynécos.* Carouge: Centre femmes, 1977.

Freeman, Jo. "Waves of Feminism." *H-Women* (May 1996).

Hardmeier, Sybille. *Frühe Frauenstimmrechtsbewegung in der Schweiz (1890–1930): Argumente, Strategien, Netzwerke und Gegenbewegung.* Zürich: Chronos 1997.

Heywood, Leslie, and Jennifer Drake, ed. *Third Wave Agenda: Being Feminist, Doing Feminism.* Minneapolis: University of Minnesota Press, 1997.

Kiani, Sarah. "Equal Rights and Strategies of the Swiss Women's Movement (1975–1996)." *Femina Politika: Die Zeitschrift für feministische Politikwissenschaft* 2 (2012): 85–96.

———. "Une femme obligée à effectuer les travaux ménagers n'est pas forcément une bonne mère: Les vagues féministes et la campagne pour l'égalité en Suisse dans les années 1980." *Thirdspace: A Journal for Feminist Theory and Culture* 11 (2013).

Laughlin, Kathleen A., Julie Gallagher, et al. "Is It Time to Jump Ship? Historians Rethink the Wave Metaphor." *Feminist Formations* 22, no. 1 (2010): 76–135.

Lovenduski, Joni. *Women and European Politics: Contemporary Feminism and Public Policy.* Brighton: Wheatsheaf Books, 1986.

Redolfi, Silke. *Frauen bauen Staat: 100 ans de l'Alliance de sociétés féminines suisses.* Zurich: NZZ Verlag, 2000.

Schär, Renate. "Der Schweizerische Frauenkongress und der Antikongress von 1975: Mobilisierungshöhepunkt der Neuen Frauenbewegung." In *1968-1978, une décennie mouvementée en Suisse/Ein bewegtes Jahrzehnt in der Schweiz,* edited by Janick Marina Schaufelbuehl, 205–19. Zurich: Chronos, 2009.

Schulz, Kristina, Leena Schmitter, and Sarah Kiani. *Frauenbewegung: Die Schweiz seit 1968. Analysen. Dokumente. Archive.* Baden: hier + jetzt, 2014.

Weinman Lear, Martha. "The Second Feminist Wave." *New York Times Magazine* 10 (1966): 24–33.

Chapter 2

How the Women's Movement Changed Academia

A Comparison of Germany and the United States

Stefanie Ehmsen

At first sight, the answer to the question of how the women's movement changed academia seems to be obvious for both Germany and the United States. First, the movement expanded the realm of scientific approaches; second, the women's movement created its own discipline and established presence within academia; third, it increased the number of women working in academia on every level.

While these results are more or less measurable, the question of whether or not this can be considered a "success" of feminism is more difficult to answer. On the one hand, many protagonists of women's studies have interpreted the outcome as a great accomplishment. Marilyn Boxer's dictum, for instance, is quite clear and leaves little room for doubts: "Today we have occasion to celebrate," she states, and draws the simple conclusion: "The more institutionalization, the better."[1] On the other hand, a number of academic feminists tend to express at least ambivalence about the path and the current state of institutionalized feminism. In "Feminism, Institutionalism, and the Idiom of Failure," Robyn Wiegman states, "I want to register how unsure, even insecure, academic feminism has become about the meaning, practices, and goals of its own project of institutional intervention."[2] Similarly, German feminists were looking to express their views about the institutionalization in a dialectical manner as "partially successful" (Sabine Hark), "excluding inclusion," or "marginalizing integration" (Angelika Wetterer).[3]

Ambivalence, it seems, is to be expected in view of a process that has been contested from the outset. When a social movement, in this case the women's movement, enters an institution, in this case academia, many questions about potential pitfalls and shortcomings need to be addressed: How does the institution react? What is the outcome, i.e. to what degree will the institution be reformed, challenged, radically changed? Will the movement be resisted, assimilated, transformed? To be sure, from demanding half the sky to talking about leaking pipelines, the movement has come a long way. How can we come to terms with measuring the "success" of a movement that once started out so radically, with a new definition of the political, new forms of politics, and a strong will for change?

Empirical research indicates that institutions possess strong mechanisms for resisting reform. To complicate things further, institutional resistance to change takes place not only on a structural level but also on a habitual one.[4] So the apparent question is not only how feminism *changed* academia but also how it did *not* change it.

In the 1950s Simone de Beauvoir argued that women as a group are heterogeneous in terms of social preconditions and that their political interests seem to be disparate. She concluded that women therefore tend to be more in solidarity with men of their group than with other women.[5] Forty years later, Ute Gerhard pointed out that, considering the differences among women, it might rather be seen as an astonishing fact that women bond politically and organize collectively at all.[6] Looking at the last several decades of development from this perspective, we do not see a homogenous movement turned heterogenous but rather a turn from political alliance among women to political disalliance.

Generally speaking, we can argue whether the glass is half full or half empty. But if we are going to seriously approach the question of "success," i.e. "how the women's movement changed academia," we need to assess the historic determinants of feminism challenging academia, and how these determinants have changed, in order to understand the state of academic feminism today. For success can only be qualified *in relation to* how the institution was before. This assessment is further complicated by the fact that this is not simply a matter of linear development, as the institution is embedded in—and interacts with—a larger society that constantly changes as well. In this case, the decades of the institutionalization process in question have witnessed the rise of a neoliberal regime (at the expense of the interventionist Fordist welfare state) that has profoundly changed the conditions in which academia (and hence the institutionalization of feminist demands) operates. According to Nancy Fraser, we even need to take into account the possibility that there may be a connection between the rise of neoliberalism and the advances of women in the academic professions.[7]

Fraser's thesis, however, cannot be empirically put to test in this essay. Instead, I will analyze quantitative and qualitative aspects of institutional change, i.e. address the question of how the institution has been affected by the women's movement's feminist demands. In order to include the abovementioned dimension of societal development and its effects on academia in the assessment, I am going to compare two countries—Germany and the United States—that have experienced both the feminist challenge and institutional change. Therefore, I will start by analyzing the historical and political framework in which academic feminism emerged in these two countries. In the next step, I am going to highlight the most important achievements of and obstacles to academic feminism. In conclusion, I will discuss how the political context has impacted the process of institutionalization.

Liberal versus Corporative Tradition: The United States and Germany

Looking at the conditions that shape the nature of political movements in general and of the women's movement in particular, two major differences between the United States and Germany are striking: first, a weak (United States) versus strong (Germany) state leading to a strong (United States) versus weak (Germany) movement tradition; and second, how the coincidence of civil rights and women's rights demands specific to the United States gave birth to analytically and politically different models—one stressing the difference (Germany) and the other one the equality (United States) between men and women.[8] Both aspects are rooted in profoundly diverging constitutional and democratic traditions.

As the "First New Nation"[9] the United States has, in contrast to European societies, no history of feudalism. The first civic constitution was shaped by the fight for independence from British colonial power and is based on a strong protection of individual rights against state arbitrariness. It was groundbreaking in formulating universal rights for all citizens, though at the same time these so-called universal rights were de facto granted only to a small part of society, white male property owners.

For social movements these specific origins mean that the "liberal tradition" (Louis Hartz) has tended to limit a direct state influence in support of individual rights and freedom. This, in turn, has fostered a strong movement tradition in the United States. At the same time, however, the contradiction between supposedly universal rights and de facto discrimination had to be fought from the outset. The antagonism between the "American Creed" and legally protected institutional racism was addressed by the abolitionist and civil rights movements. Both movements have heavily influenced the historical context in which the women's rights movements evolved.

Despite this fundamental contradiction, the democratic tradition dates back significantly longer than in Germany. Here, the implementation of liberal democracy failed after several attempts because of the successful resistance of the traditional ruling classes. The short-lived Weimar Republic was followed by the Nazi regime, and after World War II democracy had to start all over again, and under the auspices of the western allies. In contrast to the United States, one could call the German tradition "corporative."

However, the founding of the Federal Republic of Germany did provide women and men with a constitution (*Grundgesetz*) that explicitly included gender equality. Despite this comparatively modern constitutional framework, gender politics in Germany had a very conservative core—not surprisingly if one takes into account the long tradition of corporativism and the more recent fascist family ideology. When the women's movement rose in the late 1960s it was facing a dominant tradition of conservative gender politics that—even in its modernized form—consolidated gender differences by legally privileging the nuclear family with the husband as provider and the wife as mother and housewife. At the same time, the traditionally important role of the state tended to weaken the influence of social movements.

This tradition also influenced the Fordist welfare state in which the women's movement emerged. "State money" for individuals and organizations was accessible to movement activists and provided many with a comparatively stable economic environment. Many of the early women's projects in Germany, which perceived themselves as politically radical, were able to get access to state funding for so-called "autonomous" projects.[10]

Whereas the German movement started in the context of a weak democratic tradition and a constitutional framework that granted gender equality while simultaneously emphasizing gender differences, the American movement faced different contradictions. The longstanding and modern democratic constitutional foundation was curtailed by the existence of slavery and the subsequent denial of basic civil and human rights on the basis of skin color. The struggle for the abolition of slavery and Jim Crow motivated women to address gender inequality and to phrase their demands analog to the struggles fighting institutionalized racism.

Whereas the German model focused on the biological difference between men and women to bring about equality—e.g., by implementing maternity leave and special protection for pregnant women at their workplace, supporting single mothers—the American model strove for equal opportunity that explicitly refrained from taking into account any form of difference based on race, color, religion, national origin, or sex. In Germany, the institutionalization of women's demands thus resulted in political aid shaped after the needs of women (*Frauenförderung*, i.e. advancement for women). The American path, however, linked differentiating categories in concepts of equal opportunity and affirmative action. The U.S. concepts evolved in the 1960s and 1970s, in the context of the black liberation movement when the social movements were at their peak; in Germany they evolved in the 1980s, when the women's movement was still vibrant but others were already in decline.

The Political Context of the Women's Movement

Given these conditions, how did all this affect the emergence of academic feminism? As Linda Gordon put it in 1975, "Women's Studies did not arise accidentally, as the product of someone's good idea, but was created by a social movement for women's liberation with a sharp political critique of the whole structure of our society."[11] This is true for the United States as well as for Germany, and it explains a lot about the high expectations linked to women's studies as a discipline as well as about the controversies that have been part of this movement from the start.

In both countries the "new feminism" was motivated by left political movements but also by a disappointment with these movements' shortcomings. In the United States women could build on the struggle of the civil rights movement by successfully demanding the inclusion of sex as a category into the Civil Rights Act of 1964. Many of the women activists were part of the New Left, the student movement, or the Black Power movement, each of which demanded more than just legal equality. These movements challenged society on a much deeper level: racism and poverty were analyzed as fundamental parts of capitalist society, and the Vietnam War was conceived of as a symbol of U.S. imperialism. In general, politics was criticized in much more radical terms. The activists were striving "to build a democratic society in which Vietnams are unthinkable, in which human life and initiative are precious."[12] Disappointment arose once women had to find out that changing society did not inherently involve a change of gender role models. As Barbara Epstein put it, "SDS members criticized certain aspects of American culture, but the sexism of American culture was for the most part adopted uncritically."[13]

In Germany, it was exactly this kind of attitude that motivated Sigrid Rüger to throw tomatoes at the German SDS members when they refused to discuss feminist interventions, presented by Helke Sander.[14] In many ways, the German student movement developed in a similar manner as the American one. It, too, mobilized to protest foreign policies of "the West," and it also developed more or less socialist ideologies directed at fundamentally changing the existing society. The more recent German past, however, was a distinct feature—since the protesting students were the children of a generation actively involved in the crimes of the Nazi regime, they tended to criticize authoritarian structures and continuities between the Germany before and the one after 1945. In this context, the university system was scathed for employing professors and using curricula from the Nazi regime and for its authoritarian structure that, among other things, gave tenured professors the power to appoint their faculty and determine their universities' politics in an almost absolutist manner.

Second-wave feminism emerged in the context of the 1968 protest movements, partly in response to the shortcomings of left theories that did not take into account gender differences and imbalances. The new feminism conceptionalized gender oppression as an integral part, and finally as the core of the society the New Left claimed to oppose radically. Feminist theory was supposed to help in understanding the history, nature, and potential change of the category gender. That means that the academic arm of the women's movement emerged as a reaction to the shortcomings of a broad, in fact heterogenous but clearly left movement that challenged the contemporary societies of both countries. While second-wave feminists, as Barbara Epstein states, "especially in the intoxicating early years of the movement, tended to believe that they could speak for all women,"[15] they remained to a large degree shaped by the left movements of the late 1960s and 1970s.

Female Representation and Women's Studies: Quantitative and Qualitative Aspects

When feminism entered academia with a mission to bring about radical change, its task was not only manifold but highly contested from the outset. It faced institutional resistance as well as controversies within the movement. When the women's movement started to confront academia with feminist ideas, it affected the institution on two levels: *quantitatively*, by demanding the employment of more women, and *qualitatively*, by challenging existing curricula and educational methods. In doing so, the activists were hoping that the former goal would eventually also contribute to the latter.

By the time the second wave evolved, women were highly underrepresented in academia—in Germany even more so than in the United States. Whereas the United States had—notwithstanding the general limitations of the time—a tradition of both women in academia and separate women's colleges that goes back well into the nineteenth century, in Germany women were denied access to higher education until 1908. Another difference is that the American educational system provides better career opportunities for women than the German system, which has much stronger hierarchies and requires an additional degree (*Habilitation*) for the tenured university professorship.

In 1975 women held 18 percent of professorships with tenure in the United States, whereas in Germany they held 2.5 percent of the highest-paid and tenured professorships (C4) in 1980.[16] Since then, both countries have seen a significant increase in the percentage of women employed on every level. In Germany, women today hold 19.9 percent of full-time professorships and 10.7 percent of the highest-ranking C4 professorships.[17] In the United States, women in 2009 represented 32.5 percent of assistant professors, 29 percent of associate professors, and 21 percent of full professors (full-time faculty only).[18]

While this data demonstrates that the number of women within academia has significantly increased over the course of the last decades, it also shows that the higher the position ranks in terms of pay and prestige, the smaller the percentage of women still is. At the same time, the overall increase of female faculty took place "in the dramatically changed social context of rising neoliberalism."[19] As a result, this means that many women employed in academia only hold part-time and precarious job positions.[20]

But the movement did not only strive for equal representation; it wanted to expand academic curricula and teaching methods in ways that were supposed to change the institution in its very nature. In this respect, the quantitative aspects, i.e. the rising number of women especially in decisive academic positions, has clearly affected the qualitative one, i.e. the expansion of feminism in the academic setting. Basically, more women simply meant more potential resources for implementing feminism in the curricula. (This is even more the case for Germany than for the United States.)

Academia, however, was shielded against these changes. As Jane Roland Martin puts it, "Had women in the 1970s been aware of the gendered underpinnings of the academy, let alone known how powerful and persistent our educational-gender system is, the women's studies movement might never have been launched."[21] This is particularly important because feminists in both countries claimed to undertake no less than a "Copernican revolution": challenging established science by questioning its traditional methods and by criticizing that what science claimed to be objective or neutral was in fact gender biased. This claim required theoretical work "from the bottom up": by exploring the social dimension of gender (as opposed to the dominant biological understanding of it), by broadening the meaning of "the political" to include the so-called private, and by avoiding a simple "add women and stir" approach. In doing so, early feminists laid the groundwork for future generations of scientists analyzing their subjects from a gender perspective, opening up new areas for research that had been "naturalized" and therefore had not been previously contested.

Another ambitious project was changing the curricula. This required the inclusion of new (feminist) theoretical frameworks as well as the consideration of women's work in the respective academic fields. The controversies about what would be the best way to do so reflect how strong the ties between early academic feminism and the movement were.

Besides fundamental critiques of academic feminism as being elitist and exclusive—providing career options for a few, not taking into account the different (and much harder) living conditions of other women—the main question in both countries was whether one should try to build an independent discipline and independent structures within academia (such as centers, departments, degrees) or rather strive to "infiltrate" the existing disciplines, forcing them to integrate gender as a category into every aspect of theory, teaching, and learning. Though the controversies were similar in both countries, they nevertheless took different paths, reflecting their historical backgrounds as well as the structural preconditions of their respective academic systems.

Following the path of the black studies programs that had started in the mid-1960s as an offspring of the civil rights movement, feminists in academia not only pushed for individual women's studies seminars but also for establishing women's studies programs. In the following decades, the number of such programs grew quickly. The first women's studies program in the United States was founded in 1969 at the University of California at San Diego. In the early 1980s there were already three hundred such programs, and this number doubled by the end of the century.[22] Today there are more than eight hundred women's studies programs nationwide.

This progress was made possible by several different factors, not least the strong pressure from the civil rights movement that led the way for the women's movement in many ways. On an institutional level, outside money and support from individuals within administration and faculty were important factors.[23]

In Germany, where the academic system historically had an even more conservative structure and the exclusion of women was more thorough than in the United States, approaches aiming at the centralization and coordination of feminists' efforts were not seen as feasible. In general, the corporative tradition and the role of the state made social movements—including the women's movement—more suspicious of any kind of institutional approach. Therefore, feminists were first fighting for recognition in their respective disciplines rather than trying to establish centers or programs. The first centralized approaches came into being in the 1980s, when the Free University of Berlin founded the first Center for Women's Studies. Most of today's degree-granting institutions in this field were actually established in the twenty-first century.[24] This context demonstrates that the institutional implementation took off at a time when the organized movement itself was already in decline.

Comparing the numbers of women's studies programs as benchmarks for successful implementation, in terms of institutionalization, the U.S. model—centralizing and concentrating the efforts in order to change the academic system more effectively—was more successful. At the same time, however, women seem to have reached a certain limit—whether we call it the "glass ceiling," "leaking pipeline," or "Bermuda triangle," it indicates that men and women still occupy different spaces in the society as well as in academia. This proves the ambivalence of progress. On one hand, women's and gender studies have reached a certain level of "normality" today, at least in Germany and the United States. It is possible and quite "normal" to do research in this field, to get a degree, and to focus at least a part of your academic education on understanding gender as an integral category of society. On the other hand, skepticism about whether this reflects a sustainable change in both countries is justified because "feminism has simultaneously become institutionalized and marginalized. It has been rhetorically accepted, but the wind has gone out of its sails."[25] The contradictory process of institutionalization means that you can still study a subject, get a degree, and pursue an academic career without ever paying attention to the question of gender, even in the humanities.

The Women's Movement, Academia, and the Rise of Neoliberalism: Concluding Remarks

A comparison of the origins of the second wave's academic feminism in the United States and Germany clearly demonstrates how much has changed in recent decades. There are a lot more women in universities and colleges, more programs and departments dedicated to the analysis of gender relations, more publications by and about women, and there is—to some degree—even some kind of mainstream recognition. At the same time, however, the movement that was the root cause for the institutionalization has changed and declined, if not disappeared.

In essence, the women's movement changed academia to a significant degree. The overall result, however, bears some ambivalence: while the number of women in academia has significantly increased on all levels, the glass ceiling has not been broken. This is particularly evident in the fact that the higher the employment positions in terms of pay and prestige, the lower the proportion of women. In addition, there has been an explosion of feminist theory, a rich and diverse resource for everybody dealing with gender as a social category; but this body of theory can still can be academically ignored or downplayed if students or faculty do not want to deal with this issue. Finally, and accompanying the general demise of the women's movement, the focus is no longer on radical change but rather on "mainstreaming."

The generation of women that shaped the feminism of the 1960s and 1970s is different from the generations that came after it. Growing up in the 1950s in both countries meant facing the politics of postwar gender reconstruction. Marilyn Boxer even goes so far as to state that "thanks to the new historians of women we came to understand the 1950s as the worst decade in American history for women who aspired to personal achievement outside familial roles."[26] The women's movement therefore fought fiercely against these and other gender limitations—private as well as economic ones.

Today, girls grow up very differently from the second wave's founding mothers' generation, and they experience gender realities differently; therefore, "A girl today may learn at two, three, or four to name parts of her body that went unrecognized by some of us until, at twenty, thirty, or forty, we read of them in *Our Bodies, Ourselves.*"[27] That is—at least partly—due to the movement's success, and it needs to be taken seriously. Today, women have access to knowledge and education that they did not enjoy before, and the options of what they want to (and can) do with their lives are much broader.

There has been a change in terminology that, in fact, is the outcome of a change in theory. Today, we talk about women's studies, women's and gender studies, gender studies, queer studies, or diversity studies. This change reflects a postmodern expansion in views, an awareness of diversity that the early movement did not (and could not) have. At the same time, this development is often seen as causing disassociation from a common path and as making it more difficult to come together, to act politically. Academic feminism seems to have emancipated itself from the movement by taking different paths that did not always relate to a specific political goal.

In the United States as well as in Germany, the economic and political context has profoundly changed. Whereas legal equality, one of the major goals of the movements, has been reached and (life) opportunities have been expanded, neoliberalism poses new challenges to emancipatory movements and to academia. Since the late 1960s, the United States and Germany have seen a shift from the Fordist welfare state implementing antidiscrimination policies and nearly full employment to a dramatically growing income gap (especially in the United States), growing unemployment, and an increase in precarious employment. On the ideological level, neoliberalism has supported a strict individualism, thereby shifting responsibilities from society to the individual. Group-oriented approaches have come under attack. Nancy Fraser points us to the fact that the rise of neoliberalism has also deeply affected the development of modern feminism: "I chart not only the movement's extraordinary successes but also the disturbing convergence of some of its ideals with the demands of an emerging new form of capitalism—post-fordist, 'disorganized,' transnational."[28]

Finally, the movement that had been the driving force behind academic feminism has changed. Today, we see the movement's effects on every institutional level, but its strength in terms of visibility, the power to challenge the institutions to their core, and the activists' "inner passion"[29] seem to have disappeared. This can simultaneously be seen as a success being less exclusive and broader as well as wiser in perspective and as weakness, insofar as it can be reduced to a "flea-market feminism" that is no longer cohesive and therefore politically less influential.[30]

Feminism in academia developed in the context of strong movement support, a quick expansion of the educational system, comparatively secure job settings and—even in the United States—antidiscrimination policies supported by the federal government. These days are long gone. Today we are confronted with a situation in which not only movement support has faded away but the educational system itself is facing severe cutbacks. In neoliberalism, academia is—even in the traditionally state-supported German system—increasingly forced to watch out for sources of outside money, to apply for grants, etc. At the same time, employment patterns in educational settings have followed the general neoliberal development in that the proportion of precarious jobs has significantly increased. This has been interpreted as the economic underpinning for the way feminist theory has developed. The "shift away from the public works philosophy" to "free market fundamentalism," as Heywood and Drake describe it, "clearly contextualizes the third wave tendency to focus on individual narratives and to think of feminism as a form of individual empowerment."[31]

The history of feminism in academia can therefore teach a lesson about the opportunities and limitations for emancipatory change within existing institutions. While incorporating some of the demands, like the inclusion of more female employment, the institutions have been successful in resisting radical change. Robyn Wiegman describes the work that is required by the institutionalization process itself as "overwhelming in its time consumption and profoundly constitutive of a subjective focus that threatens to become overdetermined by the foals of institutionalization as ends in themselves."[32]

In Germany, resistance or prejudice against academic feminism is still vivid. This indicates that its very existence threatens the male dominance that seems to be an important underpinning of academia. Because of this, today's feminism should be aware of the danger that its greatest successes might fit neatly into neoliberalist paradigms, as Nancy Fraser has warned.

While society is drifting apart, so are common interests among women, as Simone de Beauvoir emphasized. The centrifugal forces of a neoliberal society represent a grave danger for academic feminism in particular. Obtaining a paid job in a university or college is, after all, quite a privileged position. The academic focus these days seems to be on "glass ceilings" and the underrepresentation of women in high-paying leadership positions. But if we do not take into account that the vast majority of women today are rather threatened by what's happening in the domestic and precarious service work sector, by precarious labor conditions and declining wages (which are still way below the males' wages), we are in danger of being trapped by neoliberalism. An ideology of "Trickle-Down Feminism"[33] won't help.

It might be unlikely or even naive to expect women as a group to act in a common interest. And movement-building is certainly not a task of science as such—it may not be fair to criticize academic feminism for not doing so. It might be more important to ask what we expect critical science to explore and to explain in order to build a just society from an inclusive perspective—with partnerships that fit this purpose.

Stefanie Ehmsen wrote her PhD in political science on the institutionalization of the women's movement in the United States and Germany. From 2009-2011, she was visiting professor for gender and diversity at the Beuth Hochschule für Technik in Berlin. Since 2012, she has been co-director of the Rosa Luxemburg Stiftung's New York office.

Notes

1. Marilyn Boxer, "Women's Studies as Women's History," *Women's Studies Quarterly* 3–4 (2002): 48.
2. Robyn Wiegman, "Feminism, Institutionalism, and the Idiom of Failure," *differences: A Journal of Feminist Cultural Studies* 11, no 3 (1999): 109.
3. Daniela Heitzmann, "Zwei Schritte vor, einer zurück: Zur Institutionalisierung der Frauen- und Geschlechterforschung," *soFid: Sozialwissenschaftlicher Fachinformationsdienst Frauen- und Geschlechterforschung,* no. 1 (2010): 11.
4. Stefanie Ehmsen, *Der Marsch der Frauenbewegung durch die Institutionen* (Münster: Westfälisches Dampfboot, 2008).
5. Simone de Beauvoir, *The Second Sex* (New York: Vintage, 1989).
6. Ute Gerhard, "Westdeutsche Frauenbewegung: Zwischen Autonomie und dem Recht auf Gleichheit," *Feministische Studien,* no. 2 (1992).

7. Nancy Fraser, "Feminism, Capitalism, and the Cunning of History," *New Left Review* (March/April 2009): 71–94.
8. Angelika von Wahl, *Gleichstellungsregime: Berufliche Gleichstellung von Frauen in den USA und Deutschland* (Opladen: Leske und Budrich, 1999).
9. Seymour Martin Lipset, *The First New Nation. The United States in Historical and Coparative Perspective* (New York: Basic Books, 1963).
10. See Sabine Hark, *Dissidente Partizipation: Eine Diskursgeschichte des Feminismus* (Frankfurt am Main: Suhrkamp, 2005), 225.
11. Linda Gordon, "A Socialist View of Women's Studies: A Reply to the Editorial," *Signs* 1 (1975): 559.
12. Speach by SDS president Paul Potter on April 17, 1965, quoted in Judith Albert and Stewart Albert, eds., *The Sixties Papers* (New York: Praeger, 1984), 223.
13. Quoted in Alice Echols, *Daring to Be Bad: Radical Faminism in America 1967–1975* (Minneapolis: University of Minnesota Press, 1989), 26.
14. See Kristina Schulz, *Der lange Atem der Provokation, Die Frauenbewegung in der Bundesrepublik und in Frankreich 1968–1976* (Frankfurt am Main: Campus, 2002), 83.
15. Barbara Epstein, "What Happened to the Women's Movement?" *Monthly Review* 53 (2001): 5.
16. Ehmsen, *Der Marsch der Frauenbewegung durch die Institutionen,* 259.
17. Statistisches Bundesamt, *Frauenanteile der Studierenden, Absolventen und des Personals an Hochschulen,* Wiesbaden 2013.
18. U.S. Department of Education, *Digest of Education Statistics 2011* (Table 264).
19. Fraser, "Feminism, Capitalism, and the Cunning of History," 71.
20. Roland Bloch and Anke Burkhardt, "Arbeitsplatz Hochschule und Forschung für wissenschaftliches Personal und Nachwuchskräfte," Hans Böckler Stiftung, ed., Arbeitspapier, 207; Mary Ann Mason, "Is Tenure a Trap for Women?" *Chronicle for Higher Education* (April 22, 2009).
21. Quoted in Boxer, "Women's Studies as Women's History," 42.
22. Ehmsen, *Der Marsch der Frauenbewegung durch die Institutionen,* 150.
23. See Joan Tronto, interview, in Ehmsen, *Der Marsch der Frauenbewegung durch die Institutionen,* 163f.
24. Zentraleinrichtung zu Förderung von Frauen- und Geschlechterforschung, ed. "Studiengänge und Studien- und Forschungsschwerpunkte Frauen- und Geschlechterforschung/Gender Studies an deutschsprachigen Hochschulen," December 3, 2012.
25. Epstein, "What Happened to the Women's Movement?"
26. Boxer, "Women's Studies as Women's History," 45f.
27. Ibid., 48.
28. Fraser, "Feminism, Capitalism, and the Cunning of History," 12.
29. Barbara Holland-Cunz, *Die alte neue Frauenfrage* (Frankfurt am Main: Suhrkamp, 2003), 173.
30. Heidi Hartmann and Martha Burk, *The Shape of Equality: An Overview of the U.S. Women's Movement* (New York: Rosa Luxemburg Stiftung, 2012), 18ff.
31. Leslie Heywood and Jennifer Drake, "'It's All about the Benjamins': Economic Determinants of Third Wave Feminism in the United States," in *Third Wave Feminism:*

A Critical Exploration, ed. Stacy Gillis, Gillian Howie, and Rebecca Munford (New York: Palgrave Macmillan, 2004): 14.

32. Wiegman, "Feminism, Institutionalism, and the Idiom of Failure," 112.
33. Sarah Jaffe, "Trickle-Down Feminism," *Dissent* (Winter 2013): 25–30.

Bibliography

Albert, Judith, and Stewart Albert, eds. *The Sixties Papers.* New York: Praeger, 1984.

American Association of University Professors. AAUP Faculty Gender Equity Indicators 2006, www.aaup.org.

Bloch, Roland, and Anke Burkhardt. "Arbeitsplatz Hochschule und Forschung für wissenschaftliches Personal und Nachwuchskräfte." Hans Böckler Stiftung, ed., Arbeitspapier.

Boxer, Marilyn. "Women's Studies as Women's History." *Women's Studies Quarterly* 3–4 (2002): 42–49.

Beauvoir, Simone de. *The Second Sex.* New York: Vintage, 1989.

Collins, Patricia Hill. "Learning from the Outsider Within: The Sociological Significance of Black Feminist Thought." *Social Problems* 33, no. 6, Special Theory Issue (October–December, 1986), 14–32.

Echols, Alice. *Daring to Be Bad: Radical Feminism in America 1967–1975.* Minneapolis: University of Minnesota Press, 1989.

Ehmsen, Stefanie. *Der Marsch der Frauenbewegung durch die Institutionen.* Münster: Westfälisches Dampfboot, 2008.

Epstein, Barbara. "What Happened to the Women's Movement?" *Monthly Review* 53 (2001): 1–13.

Faludi, Susan. "Death of a Revolutionary." *New Yorker* (April 15, 2013): 52–61.

Fraser, Nancy. "Feminism, Capitalism, and the Cunning of History." *New Left Review* (March/April 2009): 71–94.

Gerhard, Ute. "Westdeutsche Frauenbewegung. Zwischen Autonomie und dem Recht auf Gleichheit." *Feministische Studien,* no. 2 (1992): 35–55.

Gordon, Linda. "A Socialist View of Women's Studies: A Reply to the Editorial." *Signs* 1 (1975): 559–66.

Hark, Sabine. *Dissidente Partizipation: Eine Diskursgeschichte des Feminismus.* Frankfurt am Main: Suhrkamp, 2005.

Hartmann, Heidi, and Martha Burk. *The Shape of Equality: An Overview of the U.S. Women's Movement.* New York: Rosa Luxemburg Stiftung, 2012.

Heitzmann, Daniela. "Zwei Schritte vor, einer zurück. Zur Institutionalisierung der Frauen- und Geschlechterforschung." *soFid: Sozialwissenschaftlicher Fachinformationsdienst Frauen- und Geschlechterforschung,* no. 1 (2010): 11–22.

Heywood, Leslie, and Jennifer Drake. "'It's All about the Benjamins': Economic Determinants of Third Wave Feminism in the United States." In *Third Wave Feminism: A Critical Exploration,* edited by Stacy Gillis, Gillian Howie, and Rebecca Munford, 13–23. New York: Palgrave Macmillan, 2004.

Holland-Cunz, Barbara. *Die alte neue Frauenfrage.* Frankfurt am Main: Suhrkamp, 2003.

Jaffe, Sarah. "Trickle-Down Feminism." *Dissent* (Winter 2013): 25–30.

Mason, Mary Ann. "Is Tenure a Trap for Women?" *Chronicle for Higher Education* (April 22, 2009).

Mann, Susan Archer. "Third Wave Feminism's Unhappy Marriage of Poststructuralism and Intersectionality Theory." *Journal of Feminist Scholarship* 4 (Spring 2013): 54–73.

Mirza, Heidi Safia. "Decolonizing Higher Education: Black Feminism and the Intersectionality of Race and Gender." *Journal of Feminist Scholarship* 7/8 (Fall 2014/Spring 2015): 1–12.

Rogers, Mary F., and C. D. Garett, eds. *Who's Afraid of Women's Stuides? Feminisms in Everyday Life.* Walnut Creek, CA: AltaMira, 2002.

Sauer, Birgit. "Totem und Tabus: Zur Neubestimmung von Gleichstellungspolitik. Eine Einführung." In *Gleichstellungspolitik—Totem und Tabus: Eine feministische Revision,* edited by Elke Biester et al., 7–35. Frankfurt am Main: Campus, 1994.

———. "Politikwissenschaftliche Frauen- und Geschlechterprofessorinnen im deutschsprachigen Raum: Zwischen Besonderheit und Besonderung oder auf dem Weg zur Normalität?" *Femina Politica* 1 (2015): 126–34.

Schulz, Kristina. *Der lange Atem der Provokation: Die Frauenbewegung in der Bundesrepublik und in Frankreich 1968–1976.* Frankfurt am Main: Campus, 2002.

Statistisches Bundesamt. *Frauenanteile der Studierenden, Absolventen und des Personals an Hochschulen.* Wiesbaden 2013, www.destatis.de.

U.S. Department of Education. *Digest of Education Statistics 2011.*

Wahl, Angelika von. *Gleichstellungsregime:Berufliche Gleichstellung von Frauen in den USA und Deutschland.* Opladen: Leske und Budrich, 1999.

Wiegman, Robyn. "Feminism, Institutionalism, and the Idiom of Failure." *differences: A Journal of Feminist Cultural Studies* 11, no 3 (Fall 1999): 107–36.

———, ed. *Women's Studies on Its Own.* Duke University Press, 2002.

Zentraleinrichtung zu Förderung von Frauen- und Geschlechterforschung, ed. "Studiengänge und Studien- und Forschungsschwerpunkte Frauen- und Geschlechterforschung/Gender Studies an deutschsprachigen Hochschulen." December 3, 2012.

Chapter 3

Female Bodies—Fetal Subjects?

New Reproductive Technologies, Feminist Claims, and Political Change in Switzerland in the 1970/1980s

Leena Schmitter

The fight for abortion rights in Switzerland was long and provoked strong emotions on the both sides of the issue. Only three weeks after women's suffrage on the federal level came into effect,[1] a nonpartisan committee launched a popular initiative asking for the unconditional decriminalization of abortion.[2] Within a few months, the committee and its supporters successfully collected about 59,000 signatures and submitted the initiative to the Federal Chancellery. However, Swiss citizens were never given the opportunity to vote on this legislative change. Realizing that it would neither pass in parliament nor receive the required people's vote, the committee withdrew this first initiative and launched a new one that asked for abortion on demand within the first trimester of a pregnancy.[3] Swiss voters rejected this proposition in 1977, and it was only in June 2002 that—after several political attempts—Swiss abortion legislation was liberalized. From then on, abortion within the first twelve weeks was decriminalized if the pregnant woman could claim hardship and had undergone a consultation with the doctor performing the procedure.[4]

The change of law was the result of a long and intensive campaign of informing, lobbying, and coalition-building among the supporters of the decriminalization of abortion, of which feminist groups were merely one part. Since the early 1970s, the Swiss women's liberation movement (WLM) had publicized the issue of abortion, although the first attempts to legalize abortion in the 1970s were—as in the UK, but unlike in many other countries—not made by feminists but by a nonpartisan committee that included bourgeois milieus and represented moderate liberal ideas. What was the relationship between the WLM, which understood itself as "autonomous" and whose mobilization strategy was based on extraparliamentary activities, and political pressure groups that articulated their claims within the formal channels of the semi-direct democratic system?

This chapter will examine feminist concepts of autonomy and self-determination as formulated since the late 1960s. It focuses on the 1980s, when these concepts were challenged dramatically with the rise of new reproductive technologies. In this context feminists were confronted with the rise of a new political and legal subject: "the fetus."[5] The possibility of creating human life outside the female body, and new imaging techniques, gave "the embryo" and "the fetus" a quasi-iconographic status. They were no longer seen as part of the female body, but were given new and autonomous legal and subject status: embryos were constituted as autonomous human beings while pregnant women were constructed as merely their "uterine environment," absented and disembodied.[6] In this chapter I will analyze how feminists constructed and interpreted abortion as a matter of social struggle in these radically new contexts. In particular, I am interested to explore how the WLM reinterpreted supposedly private matters as political issues and how this reinterpretation shaped feminist interpretations of abortion.[7] The empirical material of this study—which is based on my PhD thesis—consists of a variety of unpublished and published historical sources, which are listed in the bibliography.

The first part of this chapter will give an overview of the development of abortion rights in Switzerland. The second part focuses on the WLM and its campaign for the legalization of abortion, analyzing how the personal came to be seen as political. Parts three and four shed light on the feminist critique of genetic and reproductive technologies in the 1980s and show how feminist discourses were shaped by the construction of "the fetus" as a new political subject. I conclude with some reflections on how the WLM not only identified the political sphere as a male-dominated field but also shifted the boundaries of what popularly was understood to be "political." In a more general way my aim is to enable a broader understanding of politics, feminist claims, legal norms, and social change engendered by these shifts. Ultimately, I will demonstrate how abortion can be understood as a "contested zone of politics"[8] and how feminist body politics broadened the understanding of the political sphere.

Abortion, Self-Determination, and Women's Liberation in the 1970s

Reproductive freedom, contraception, and the safe and legal ability to terminate a pregnancy have been core issues in the Swiss feminist movement since the late 1960s. The WLM fought for free abortion in the name of self-determination and women's right to control their own bodies. The WLM in Switzerland was an important supporter of the campaign for the decriminalization of abortion: feminist activists belonging to the *Frauenbefreiungsbewegung* (FBB)[9] collected one-fifth of the signatures within three months. This was in spite of the fact that feminist claims went much further than the initiative asked for; in fact, feminist groups requested that the cost for abortions be covered by health insurance, and they also asked for sex education in schools, information centers for women and teenagers, free provision of contraception (under medical supervision), and governmental financial support for single mothers. Feminists understood the legal, safe, and affordable termination of a pregnancy as a means of women controlling their own lives and, thus, as a prerequisite for their full participation in society. They argued that motherhood should be freely chosen, and they criticized the existence of a law that prevented women to decide themselves if and when they wanted children or not—in the interests of future children, as well as themselves.[10]

Feminists understood the law concerning abortion as an expression of sexism in society, but also as a result of the intersection of sexism and capitalism: they pointed to the sexist character of the prohibition of abortion, as it treated women as "second class citizens."[11] They also viewed the current laws as an expression of a capitalist order where few could afford to go abroad or pay a qualified doctor. Inspired by a similar campaign in Frankfurt,[12] the FBB in 1979 organized a weekend visit to the Netherlands for the purpose of accessing the safe and legal abortion service offered there. Five pregnant women and four FBB activists (among them a doctor and a hospital nurse) traveled by bus to a clinic in Scheveningen, arguing that the situation in Switzerland was forcing them to go to Holland to have an abortion. With the help of a feminist group in Amsterdam, the FBB organized private accommodation and an exchange program with local activists.[13] The aim of the Holland protest bus was to show that unpunished, safe, and affordable abortions should be provided in Switzerland. This public demonstration took on a profoundly political character by illustrating the unsatisfying legal situation in Switzerland.[14] The FBB criticized the fact that abortion was a taboo subject, with its prohibition denying women's right to self-determination and literally pushing them across the border.[15] By crossing national boundaries, the "Holland bus" revealed the transnational character of feminist opposition against repressive reproduction regulation. Although national policies differed, feminist issues were at stake across the globe. In many Western countries, feminist campaigns for free abortion were accompanied by the same slogan: "The Personal is Political."[16] It is therefore important to understand how this slogan functioned in a feminist discourse that dealt simultaneously with individual rights *and* collective discrimination.

The "Personal" as a Political Matter?

Family, domestic, and intimate life, especially sexuality and the body, have often been viewed as part of the private—and female—sphere, while state and society were traditionally public—and male.[17] Following Joan Scott, gender as an analytical category can be useful in historical research because it is a "constitutive element of social relations" and a "primary way of signifying relationships of power."[18] One such power relation, which is inextricably linked with symbolical representations, normative concepts, and institutions, is the political sphere.[19] Yet women have, for a very long time, been excluded from the institutional political sphere, being considered as "non-actors"[20] assigned to the private, supposedly ahistorical and apolitical field. Because this distinction—and the construction of the distinction—pervades our language, thinking, and perceptions so completely that we might consider the split in these two spheres self-evident, it must be stressed that the public-private distinction is not natural, but it is instead the product of gender and politics, categories that in turn have been shaped by this dichotomy. It has to reflect critically the alleged boundaries between "the political" and "the apolitical" that correspond most of the time—though not always—with the constructed boundaries between "public" and "private." It is in this sense that I use the term "the political" heuristically in this chapter.

In claiming the personal as a political issue, the WLM did not only intend to make relationships or sexuality a matter of public discussion, but they also expected to acknowledge and fight the subordination of women as a structural problem, revealing the gendered dichotomy of the private/public division. With this interpretation, they went further than their male comrades, who claimed that "the personal is political" during the protests of 1968.[21] At that time, the same slogan stood—in theory—for the criticism of authorities in general. In practice, the slogan was also used euphemistically to mean "free love." Free love was equated with having many different sexual partners—which in reality often transpired to mean many female sexual partners for men. This was strongly criticized by feminists. For them, the slogan was not just about the public declaration of individual, sexual, or domestic disturbances but about unveiling the "microstructures of domination"[22] and questioning the boundaries between the private and the public sphere to broaden understandings of what constituted the "political." In

1980 an unknown feminist activist answered a question about the relevance and meaning of politics for her as follows: "To be a woman and stand by it; how I live; how I deal with my body and my relationships; how I am with other women; is political for me."[23]

Talking about one's own experiences had an impact on the collective consciousness-raising that the women's liberation movement aimed at. Discussing abortion in female self-help groups was an important factor for the mobilization of the movement. But the movement also pursued an external mobilization strategy: with its public demonstrations advocating for the safe and legal terminations of pregnancies, it addressed a larger public. Furthermore, the women's liberation movement not only cultivated forms of subcultural retreat but also raised its own voice publicly by making clear that free abortion involved "much more than a paragraph [in the law]."[24]

The feminist interpretation of "abortion" as a political issue differed substantially from a liberal interpretation as it was put forward by the initiative committee and by most of traditional women's rights associations. These groups referred to individual personal rights, and their claims were formulated in the language of political liberalism, stressing the need to protect individual autonomy. From their point of view, abortion regulation needed to be adapted to social reality. A law that was systematically violated was no longer able to guarantee the social order. The punishment of abortion was questioned because it violated privacy, and with that, an important pillar of bourgeois society.[25]

In declaring the private a political matter, the women's liberation movement went further: from a feminist's point of view not just social equality was at stake, but social justice as well. The position of the women's liberation movement was that women had a right to choose for or against the early termination of a pregnancy, independently of husbands, doctors, jurists, and clerics. Consequently, the slogan adopted by feminists was "a woman's right to choose."

Although the FBB helped promote the political campaign for abortion on demand, they considered it conservative. Unlike many in the mainstream political campaign, the FBB called not only for the legalization of abortion under certain circumstances but also for free abortions. They identified the abortion ban as misogynistic—a method of curtailing women's right to self-determination—and as an instrument of patriarchy.

I will now move forward into the 1980s and discuss the feminist critique on genetic and reproductive technologies. I will then clarify how fetuses and embryos were constructed through these discourses as autonomous human beings and the effects that this development had on feminist discussions on abortion.

"Women's Liberation" or "Total Control over Women?" Feminist Critiques of Genetic and Reproductive Technologies

Feminist debates on genetic and reproductive technologies arose in the United States and Switzerland in the early 1980s and in the Federal Republic of Germany in the mid-1980s.[26] They were characterized by two positions: on the one hand, technologies such as in-vitro fertilization (IVF), embryo transfer, and surrogate motherhood were seen to allow women to gain more reproductive freedom. The proliferating discourses about these technologies were interpreted as informative, offering women more knowledge about their reproductive choices. As such, both new reproductive technologies and the discourses around them were, on the one hand, seen to increase women's reproductive self-determination. On the other hand, these technologies were interpreted as the exact opposite, as procedures that would foster paternalist attitudes among the (male) medical profession and disempower women during pregnancy. Hence, in the words of a feminist activist, "Maybe we are about to experience the separation of reproduction from woman's body.... The 'female character' with its ability to give birth, which is imagined in all patriarchal societies as 'original female nature' now seems tamable and thus controllable. The desire of men to have control over the female body is as old as patriarchy itself. Step by step, female control and knowledge about their own bodies were taken away. Today we are, especially in the field of medicine, depending on men, exposed to the technologies developed by them."[27] Reflecting on the technological possibility of separating reproduction from the female body, she worried—as did the majority of Swiss feminists—about women's loss of control and knowledge over their bodies. Especially in the medical field, she argued, women would increasingly come to depend on men and on the technologies developed by them.

In debates about prenatal diagnostics, particularly the possibility of genetic selection and eugenics became subject of discussion, and a critical standpoint—as stated in the second position—prevailed in the Swiss WLM.

In 1988 a group called *Mutterschaft ohne Zwang* (MoZ) (Motherhood without coercion) was founded. One of its members declared in the same year, "Neither in abortion ... nor in prenatal diagnostics ... women's self-determination is ensured. PD [prenatal diagnostics] create new economic and social constraints to abort so-called 'inferior' fetuses while at the same time there is a moral coercion to abort so-called 'healthy' fetuses under no circumstances."[28] She acknowledged that the methods of prenatal diagnostics required choices, which she interpreted to be as important as the decision on abortion. She and her group went on to argue that the required examinations and medical interventions were—from a population policy point of view—very worthwhile, because they could be used to identify (and abort) female fetuses in order to fight "problems of overpopulation."[29] These procedures could therefore be abused to help "an old patriarchal dream [to come] true."[30] They criticized the fact that while women in industrial states were encouraged to have children at all costs, women in the global south were frequently the targets of population-control policies that curtailed their right to have children.[31] The development of prenatal diagnostics accompanied by the selection of "desirable" fetuses was interpreted as a modern form of social Darwinism and the first step toward a neo-eugenics.[32] Through new reproductive technologies, feminists argued, the "expropriation of female corporeality"[33] was heightened: women were to lose autonomy over their bodies, and access to the female body was going to be monopolized by doctors.

The concept of "ownership," as formulated in the slogan "My body belongs to me," and the concepts of "choice" and "autonomy," which have been crucial in feminist rhetoric since the early 1970s, were challenged in the 1980s by the rise of these new reproductive technologies.[34] Through prenatal diagnostics, women were confronted with more options; but from the point of view of critical feminists, this supposedly greater choice was deceptive. For them, new reproductive technologies gave women a choice only from a certain set of options by so-called experts.[35] Hence, in 1995 a feminist lawyer addressed this issue: "If we want to assess the possible impacts of prenatal diagnostics on the self-determination of women[,] ... it is not about a decision against the embryo as an individual, but a decision over the whole issue, the pregnancy itself. Self-determination from a feminist perspective is not about choosing from offers of a patriarchal society. It must be compatible with the demand for a greater freedom of decision of all women."[36]

This quote demonstrates further important development: the distinction between the "embryo as an individual" and "a decision over the whole issue, the pregnancy itself." What was this distinction about?

"The Fetus"

From the late 1970s onward, pro-abortionists were challenged with the rise of a new political and legal subject: "the fetus." On a political level this confrontation reached a first point of culmination in 1985 when Swiss citizens were asked to vote on a people's initiative, which aimed to implement a "right to life" in the federal constitution. "Life," in the view of the initiators, started with the act of conception and lasted until death. The initiative didn't pass, but the Swiss Federal Council still rejected abortion on demand in 1998 because for them it was too much about women's self-determination.[37]

Two developments accompanied the perception of the fetus as a political and legal subject. First, new visual technologies made it possible to "see" the fetus quite clearly and in detail. What formerly was just imagined now became a "scientific truth."[38] Second, talking "on behalf" of the fetus not only gave it a face but also a name, an age, a voice, and other attributes of a living person. Both developments are reflected in a "diary of an embryo," published in 1976 by a member of the Swiss People's Party (*Schweizerische Volkspartei,* SVP) and board member of *Helfen statt Töten,* a "pro-life" committee.[39] Written from the perspective of an unborn, the "diary" starts with the picture of a fertilized egg and the caption: "Today I was brought to life in an act of love by my parents. I am here, although I am smaller than the dot after this sentence." A later "diary entry" states, "My ears are finished now and resemble those of daddy." And a couple of days later, "Today my mother heard that I am with her. But why is she worried—we are both alive and kicking." After that, "Today—at the urging of my father—my mom got me killed." The diary ends with a picture of a half-year-old baby smiling in the camera with the caption, "It could have also ended like this." As this "diary" shows, at the moment of conception, the fertilized egg has become a talking subject, a "living person," and a specific icon of "life."[40]

A further example of the construction of fetuses as persons can be seen in the photographs of Lennart Nilsson, a Swedish medical photographer.[41] In 1965 he produced images of a fetus in a woman's body, until then only visible to experts. Special effects showed translucent fetuses floating in a black surrounding, like astronauts in space.[42] As such, the fetus became disembodied from its actual environment—inside a living woman.

These pictures demonstrate that invoking "the womb" when discussing the termination of pregnancy became very difficult in this new and different light. While women seemed to vanish, fetuses became ubiquitous in their "maternal environment."[43]

Conclusion: Female Bodies—Fetal Subjects?

The WLM located its activism for free abortion within a feminist framework of social criticism. This was the case especially in Switzerland, where feminist activists used their democratic right of the people's initiative as a tool to frame the issue of abortion in the larger context of women's oppression in general (inside and outside feminist groups).[44] In discussing the problem of the abortion ban, they aimed to demonstrate the connection between personal experience and women's position in society[45]: What was formerly associated with the private sphere, namely female bodily experience, was politicized in the course of discussing the legalization and liberalization of abortion. The 1970s, therefore, were characterized by rhetoric and slogans that claimed women's status as political subjects. In talking about abortion, feminists did not just discuss the act of terminating a pregnancy but also the meanings of "self-determination," "autonomy," and "emancipation"—and thus the situation of women in society in general. Decriminalization stood not only for the decriminalization of abortion but for the recognition of women as (political) subjects.

From the 1970s on, the debate on abortion allowed feminists to formulate an understanding of "self-determination" as an emancipatory concept. Women became seen as active agents shaping their own lives, claiming freedom from social constraints. Self-determination was seen as giving women the opportunity to have agency in their own lives, without being placed under duress by gynecologists or religious or moral standards.[46] Framed in the context of abortion, self-determination and autonomy were understood to mean that abortion and pregnancy for women should be matters of personal choice, regardless of social norms and women's supposed "biological destiny."

In the 1980s, female life and body experiences were challenged through the rise of the "public fetus," which was supported by genetic and reproductive technologies on the one hand and by the proliferation of visual images of the fetus and the embryo on the other.[47] These developments in the fields of technology, law, and religion restricted women's efforts at autonomy and their demand for self-determination, and sometimes even overrode them. In Swiss society, abortion was increasingly no longer seen as the termination of a specific condition but as an attack on the medically, religiously, technologically, and legally constructed fetus with its own right to life. This development also was connected to the ideological construction of "life" disseminated by right wing political parties.[48] Pregnancy was not discussed as a symbiotic relationship but as a competition between two antagonistic subjects that had far-reaching consequences for political debates: women's bodies and their claims were made structurally invisible while fetuses were (literally!) made more and more visible. Furthermore, the accusation of abortion as murder acquired "physical evidence" through the graphic "proof" of the photograph of the fetus.

Through talking about abortion, feminists in the 1970s and in the 1980s achieved a reconfiguring of the notions of "autonomy" and "self-determination"—issues that were central to both the feminist movement in particular and Western society more generally. "Abortion" therefore stood as a placeholder for a variety of essential feminist demands. These demands negotiated feminist claims in a very groundbreaking way. Since the political was also recognized outside classical political structures, feminists shifted the boundaries of the political sphere. Of course, the traditional and the extraparliamentary fields are linked to each other and form, in the words of Judith Butler, "contested zones of politics."[49] These contested zones include, as I have shown, the logic of the political sphere—its metaphors and rules of what can and cannot be spoken about. This concept might be useful in helping us to understand how debates over abortion intervened in the relationship between established political actors and social movements. Abortion belonged to these zones of contestation in which feminist claims and critique were negotiated and feminist "values [were] under contestation."[50] Within this zone it was possible to expand "the field of the sayable"[51] and to enlarge the field of the political.

When women finally got the right to vote, Swiss feminists made use of the popular initiative as a regular means of influencing legislation in order to reform abortion legislation in addition to their extraparliamentary forms of protest. By such protests, the WLM disestablished and renewed the space of the political. This strategy of WLM's activists in Switzerland was characterized by the parallel use of both formal political institutions *and* extraparliamentary protest. It was their aim to examine closely the relationships between human beings and to declare them as political matters. This recognition of the connection between personal experience and social situation is one of the most important legacies of women's liberation.

Leena Schmitter is adjunct researcher at the chair for Swiss History at the University of Bern, Switzerland, and is currently media spokesperson at the largest Swiss trade union. She received her PhD from the University of Bern in 2014. For the past several years she has been working on the women's liberation movement in Europe and the history of feminisms in Switzerland. Her areas of expertise include the history of sexuality and the body, as well as gender studies and feminist theory. She is currently working on a book project on "Crisis and Neoliberalism in Switzerland."

Notes

1. Switzerland introduced women's suffrage on the federal level in 1971. The last canton (Appenzell Inner Rhodes) followed—on the basis of a federal court decision—in 1990.
2. The exact wording is, "Wegen Schwangerschaftsabbruch darf keine Strafe gefällt werden" ("No punishment may be imposed on grounds of abortion"). A popular initiative in Switzerland aims to change the federal constitution. Until 1977 a popular initiative was achieved with 50,000 valid signatures, but since then, 100,000

signatures are required. The increase is due to the fact that since 1971 women also had the authority to sign. Cf. Wolf Linder, Christian Bolliger, and Yvan Rielle, eds., *Handbuch der eidgenössischen Volksabstimmungen 1848–2007* (Bern: Haupt, 2010), 684. For the initiative, cf. Schweizerische Eidgenossenschaft, Bundeskanzlei, *Chronologie Eidgenössische Volksinitiativen, Eidgenössische Volksinitiative "für Straflosigkeit der Schwangerschaftsunterbrechung,"* online version: http://www.admin.ch/ch/d/pore/vi/vis103.html (accessed March 31, 2017).

3. The popular initiative *für die Fristenregelung* ("for abortion on demand") was submitted on January 22, 1976, with 68,000 valid signatures.
4. For the detailed criteria of legal and illegal abortions, see Articles 118–20 of the Swiss Penal Code. With clear 72.2 percent of votes in favor and 27.8 percent against, and a participation in the election of 40.5 percent, the penal code from 1942 was changed in 2002. At the same time an initiative called *für Mutter und Kind* ("for woman and child"), which asked for the complete prohibition of abortion, was rejected clearly with 81.8 percent.
5. The term "fetus" is in quotation marks to point out the discursive construction of the unborn from a historical point of view. Cf. Barbara Duden, "Zwischen 'wahrem Wissen' und Peripherie: Konzeptionen des Ungeborenen," in *Geschichte des Ungeborenen: Zur Erfahrungs- und Wissenschaftsgeschichte der Schwangerschaft,* ed. Barbara Duden, Jürgen Schlumbohm, and Patrice Veit (Göttingen: Vandenhoeck & Ruprecht, 2002), 13. For the historicity of the fetus see: Barbara Duden, "The Fetus on the 'Farther Shore': Toward a History of the Unborn," in *Fetal Subjects, Feminist Positions,* ed. Lynn Marie Morgan and Meredith W. Michaels (Philadelphia: University of Pennsylvania Press, 1999), 13.
6. See especially the works of Barbara Duden—among others, Barbara Duden, *Der Frauenleib als öffentlicher Ort: Vom Missbrauch des Begriffs Leben* (Frankfurt am Main: Mabuse, 2007), 6f.
7. For the conceptualization of politics see "*The "Personal" as a Political Matter?"*
8. Judith Butler, *Undoing Gender* (New York: Routledge 2004), 175.
9. The FBB was the biggest women's liberation movement group in the German-speaking part of Switzerland and existed from 1969 until 1988. Its name literally means "women's liberation movement."
10. Leaflet, "Eine Frau die abtreiben will, wird immer abtreiben!" ("A Woman Who Wants an Abortion Will Always Have an Abortion"), [1973], SAZ, Ar 465.10.1, Mappe 2.
11. "Für die Freigabe der Abtreibung," *Emanzipation,* no. 1 (January 1985): 3.
12. *Tages-Anzeiger,* no. 112 (May 18, 1978).
13. *Fraue-Zitig,* no. 12 (July–September 1978): 37.
14. Ibid., 36.
15. Ibid.
16. The literal translation is "Das Private ist Politisch" which would be translated as "The private is political."
17. Susan Moller Okin, "Gender, the Public and the Private," in *Political Theory Today,* ed. David Held (Cambridge: Polity Press, 1991), 68.
18. Joan W. Scott, "Gender: A Useful Category of Historical Analysis," *American Historical Review* 91, no. 5 (1986): 1067.

19. Ibid., 1067f.
20. Ibid., 1070.
21. Brigitte Studer, *1968 und die Formung des feministischen Subjekts* (Wien: Picus Verlag, 2011), 32.
22. Ibid., 24.
23. Citation in the original: "Frausein und dazu stehen ist für mich politisch; wie ich lebe, wie ich mit meinem Körper umgehe und mit meinen Beziehungen; wie ich mit anderen Frauen bin." *Fraue-Zitig,* no. 18 (1980): 15.
24. FBB, "Recht auf den eigenen Bauch," *Focus* 50 (March 1974): 25f., SAZ, Ar 65.11.1, Mappe 4.
25. Cf. Leena Schmitter and Kristina Schulz, "Skandalisierung—Enttabuisierung—Politisierung: Reproduktionspolitik und Mobilisierungsstrategien der Neuen Frauenbewegung in Grossbritannien und der Schweiz," *Ariadne—Forum für Frauen- und Geschlechtergeschichte* 60 (2011): 32–33.
26. Anna Dorothea Brockmann, "'Leibhaftige Risiken': Die Herausforderung weiblicher Selbstbestimmung durch pränatale Diagnostik," in *Gläserne Gebär-Mütter. Vorgeburtliche Diagnostik: Fluch oder Segen,* ed. Eva Schindele (Frankfurt am Main: Fischer Taschenbuch Verlag, 1990), 239.
27. Citation in the original: "Vielleicht stehen wir schon kurz davor, die Loslösung der Reproduktion vom Körper der Frau zu erleben.... Das 'weibliche Wesen', mit seiner Fähigkeit, Leben zu geben, das in allen patriarchalischen Gesellschaften vom Mann als 'urweibliche Natur' vorgestellt wird, scheint nun bezähmbar und damit kontrollierbar zu werden. Das Bestreben der Männer, über den weiblichen Körper zu bestimmen, ist so alt wie das Patriarchat selbst. Schritt für Schritt wurde den Frauen Kontrolle und Wissen über den eigenen Körper genommen. Heute sind wir gerade im Bereich der Medizin von Männern abhängig, ausgesetzt den von ihnen entwickelten Technologien." Anita Fetz, "Reproduktionstechnologien: Den Preis bezahlen die Frauen," in *Gene, Frauen und Millionen: Diskussionsbeitrag zu Gen- und Fortpflanzungstechnologien,* ed. Anita Fetz, Anita Koechlin, and Ruth Mascarin (Zürich: Rotpunktverlag, 1986), 19.
28. Citation in the original: "Weder beim Schwangerschaftsabbruch ... noch bei der Pränatalen Diagnostik ... ist heute die Selbstbestimmung der Frauen gewährleistet. Die PD schafft neue wirtschaftliche und soziale Zwänge, sogenannt 'minderwertige' Föten abzutreiben, während gleichzeitig moralische Zwänge ausgeübt werden, sogenannt 'gesunde' Föten unter keine Umständen abzutreiben." Letter from Rita Lanz to Barbara Speck, "Inhalte für das Flugblatt vom 8.3.1989 zum Thema Widerstand gegen Gen- und Reproduktionstechnologien, inkl. Pränatale *Diagnostik*", Zürich," December 19, 1988, SAZ, Ar 201.168.1, Akten 1985–1991.
29. Fetz, "Reproduktionstechnologien," 15.
30. Ibid., 15.
31. Cf. Leena Schmitter and Annemarie Sancar, "Freiwillige Familienplanung? Eine bevölkerungspolitische List!," in *Die unheimlichen Ökologen: Sind zu viele Menschen das Problem?,* ed. Balthasar Glättli and Pierre-Alain Niklaus (Zürich: Rotpunktverlag, 2014), 87–95.
32. Cf. Fetz, "Reproduktionstechnologien," 24f.

33. Ibid., 19.
34. Cf. Rosalind Pollak Petchesky, "The Body as Property of Feminist Re-vision," in *Conceiving the New World Order: The Global Politics of Reproduction,* ed. Faye D. Ginsburg (Berkeley: University of California Press, 1995), 387.
35. The paradox lies in the fact that there very well were social "undesirables": fetuses/embryos that were (with a certain probability) identified as disabled. Women's choice was double-edged: Mothers were responsible for causing social problems and burdening society with an economic encumbrance: "If you choose to have a disabled child you are responsible for all its needs." Maria Barile, "New Reproductive Technology: The Dichotomy of My Personal and the Political," in *Misconceptions: The Social Construction of Choice and the New Reproductive and Genetic Technologies,* vol. 1, ed. Gwynne Basen, Margrit Eichler, and Abby Lippman (Quebec: Maple Pond, 1993), 169.
36. Citation in the original: "Wenn wir die Folgen der Pränataldiagnostik auf das Selbstbestimmungsrecht abschätzen wollen—entscheiden wollen, ob sie eine Erweiterung oder eine Einschränkung bedeutet—geht es nicht um einen Entscheid gegen den Embryo als Individuum sondern um den Entscheid über das Ganze, die Schwangerschaft an und für sich. Das Selbstbestimmungsrecht aus feministischer Sicht beschränkt sich nicht auf eine freie Wahlmöglichkeit unter den Angeboten einer patriarchalen Gesellschaft. Es muss sich in einem weiteren Rahmen mit der Forderung nach mehr Entscheidungsfreiheit aller Frauen vereinbaren lassen." Barbara Fischer (Demokratische Juristinnen und Juristen Schweiz, DJS/Democratic Jurists Switzerland), quoted in Schweizerische Eidgenössische Kommission für Frauenfragen, ed., *Viel erreicht—wenig verändert? Zur Situation der Frauen in der Schweiz. Bericht der Eidgenössischen Kommission für Frauenfragen* (Bern: 1995), 4.
37. Statement of the Swiss Federal Council, in *Neue Zürcher Zeitung,* 27.8.1998, quoted in Danièle Lenzin, *Die Sache der Frauen: OFRA und die Frauenbewegung in der Schweiz* (Zürich: Rotpunktverlag, 2000), 158.
38. The new technologies produced pictures that differed very much from the anatomical pictures from the sixteenth to eighteenth centuries. Cf. Duden, "The Fetus on the 'Farther Shore,'" 20; Duden, Schlumohm, and Veit, *Geschichte des Ungeborenen;* and Barbara Duden, *Die Anatomie der Guten Hoffnung: Bilder vom ungeborenen Menschen 1500–1800* (Frankfurt am Main: Campus, 2003).
39. "Tagebuch eines Embryos," in *Memopress* 3, ed. Emil Rahm (Hallau: 1976), in: SAZ, Ar 437.50.9, Organisationen und Aktionen gegen Abtreibung. *Memopress* was an "anti-Semitic world conspiracy paper, whose ideology remembers too far brown times" [i.O.: "ein antisemitisches Weltverschwörungsblatt, dessen Ideologie allzusehr an braune Zeiten erinnert"]. Jürg Frischnkecht, Peter Haffner, Ueli Haldimann, and Peter Niggli, *Die unheimlichen Patrioten: Politische Reaktion in der Schweiz. Ein aktuelles Handbuch. 5. Aufl. mit Nachttrag 1979–84* (Zürich: Limmat Verlag, 1984), 417.
40. Cf. Duden, "The Fetus on the 'Farther Shore,'" 15.
41. See also Duden, *Der Frauenleib als öffentlicher Ort,* 22–33.
42. One of the visualizations is even called "spaceman."
43. Meredith Michaels and Lynn Marie Morgan, "Introduction: The Fetal Imperative," in Morgan and Michaels, *Fetal Subjects, Feminist Positions,* 4.

44. Frauenbefreiungsbewegung (FBB), leaflet: *Zur Abtreibungskampagne* [no Date], in: AGoF, 601, Privatarchiv Ursula Streckeisen, Schachtel 6: Aktivitäten, Frauenbefreiungsbewegung, 1978–1983, Dossier 24–01.
45. Handwritten note, *Das Privat[e] ist politisch Thesen,* [no Date, no author], in: SAZ, Ar 465.11.1, Akten 1968–2007, Dossier 2.
46. Brockmann, "Leibhaftige Risiken," 245.
47. Barbara Duden, "Die Geschichte vom öffentlichen Fötus," in *Paragraph 218—zu Lasten der Frauen: Neue Auskünfte zu einem alten Kampf,* ed. Susanne von Paczensky et al. (Reinbek bei Hamburg: Rowohlt, 1988), 41–53.
48. Cf. Frischknecht et al., *Unheimliche Patrioten,* 375–83.
49. Butler, *Undoing Gender,* 175.
50. Ibid.
51. Citation in the original: "Feld des Sagbaren." Siegfried Jäger, *Kritische Diskursanalyse: Eine Einführung* (Münster: Edition DISS, 2009), 130.

Bibliography

Unpublished Sources

Gosteli Stiftung—Archiv zur Geschichte der schweizerischen Frauenbewegung, Worblaufen (AGoF)

AGoF, 601, Privatarchiv Ursula Streckeisen, Schachtel 6: Aktivitäten, Frauenbefreiungsbewegung, 1978-1983, Dossier 24–01.

Swiss Social Archive, Zürich

SAZ, Ar 437.50.9, Organisationen und Aktionen gegen Abtreibung.

SAZ, Ar 465.10.1, Mappe 2.

SAZ, Ar 465.11.1, Akten 1968-2007, Dossier 2.

SAZ, 02.1*2 ZA, Schwangerschaftsabbruch, Abtreibung: Allg. & Ausland.

SAZ, Ar 65.11.1, Mappe 4.

Published Sources

Brockmann, Anna Dorothea. "'Leibhaftige Risiken': Die Herausforderung weiblicher Selbstbestimmung durch pränatale Diagnostik." In *Gläserne Gebär-Mütter. Vorgeburtliche Diagnostik: Fluch oder Segen,* edited by Eva Schindele, 239–259. Frankfurt am Main: Tischer Taschenbuch Verlag, 1990.

Fetz, Anita. "Reproduktionstechnologien: Den Preis bezahlen die Frauen." In *Gene, Frauen und Millionen: Diskussionsbeitrag zu Gen- und Fortpflanzungstechnologien,* edited by Anita Fetz, Anita Koechlin, and Ruth Mascarin, 9–26. Zürich: Rotpunktverlag, 1986.

Literature

Barile, Maria. "New Reproductive Technology: The Dichotomy of My Personal and the Political." In *Misconceptions: The Social Construction of Choice and the New Reproduc-*

tive and Genetic Technologies, vol. 1, edited by Gwynne Basen, Margrit Eichler, and Abby Lippman, 167–70. Quebec: Maple Pond, 1993.

Butler, Judith. *Undoing Gender.* New York: Routledge, 2004.

Duden, Barbara. "Die Geschichte vom öffentlichen Fötus." In *Paragraph 218—zu Lasten der Frauen: Neue Auskünfte zu einem alten Kampf,* edited by Susanne von Paczensky et al., 41–54. Reinbek bei Hamburg: Rowohlt, 1988.

———. "The Fetus on the 'Farther Shore': Toward a History of the Unborn." In *Fetal Subjects, Feminist Positions,* edited by Lynn Marie Morgan and Meredith W. Michaels, 13–25. Philadelphia: University of Pennsylvania Press, 1999.

———. "Zwischen 'wahrem Wissen' und Peripherie: Konzeptionen des Ungeborenen." In *Geschichte des Ungeborenen: Zur Erfahrungs- und Wissenschaftsgeschichte der Schwangerschaft,* edited by Barbara Duden, Jürgen Schlumbohm, and Patrice Veit, 11–48. Göttingen: Vandenhoeck & Ruprecht, 2002.

———. *Die Anatomie der Guten Hoffnung: Bilder vom ungeborenen Menschen 1500–1800.* Frankfurt am Main: Campus, 2003.

———. *Der Frauenleib als öffentlicher Ort: Vom Missbrauch des Begriffs Leben.* Frankfurt am Main: Mabuse, 2007.

Duden, Barbara, Jürgen Schlumohm, and Patrice Veit, eds. *Geschichte des Ungeborenen: Zur Erfahrungs- und Wissenschaftsgeschichte der Schwangerschaft.* Göttingen: Vandenhoek & Ruprecht, 2002.

Frischnkecht, Jürg, Peter Haffner, Ueli Haldimann, and Peter Niggli. *Die unheimlichen Patrioten: Politische Reaktion in der Schweiz. Ein aktuelles Handbuch. 5. Aufl. mit Nachttrag 1979–84.* Zürich: Limmat Verlag, 1984.

Jäger, Siegfried. *Kritische Diskursanalyse: Eine Einführung.* Münster: Edition DISS, 2009.

Linder, Wolf, Christian Bolliger, and Yvan Rielle, eds. *Handbuch der eidgenössischen Volksabstimmungen 1848–2007.* Bern: Haupt, 2010.

Michaels, Meredith W., and Lynn Marie Morgan. "Introduction: The Fetal Imperative." In *Fetal Subjects, Feminist Positions,* edited by Lynn Marie Morgan and Meredith W. Michaels, 1–9. Philadelphia: University of Pennsylvania Press, 1999.

Moller Okin, Susan. "Gender, the Public and the Private." In *Political Theory Today,* edited by David Held, 67–90. Cambridge: Polity Press, 1991.

Schmitter, Leena, and Kristina Schulz. "Skandalisierung—Enttabuisierung—Politisierung: Reproduktionspolitik und Mobilisierungsstrategien der Neuen Frauenbewegung in Grossbritannien und der Schweiz." *Ariadne—Forum für Frauen- und Geschlechtergeschichte* 60 (2011): 28–35.

Schmitter, Leena, and Annemarie Sancar. "Freiwillige Familienplanung? Eine bevölkerungspolitische List!" In *Die unheimlichen Ökologen: Sind zu viele Menschen das Problem?,* edited by Balthasar Glättli and Pierre-Alain Niklaus, 87–95. Zürich: Rotpunktverlag, 2014.

Schweizerische Eidgenossenschaft, Bundeskanzlei. *Chronologie Eidgenössische Volksinitiativen, Eidgenössische Volksinitiative "für Straflosigkeit der Schwangerschaftsunterbrechung."* Online version: http://www.admin.ch/ch/d/pore/vi/vis103.html (accessed March 31, 2017).

Schweizerische Eidgenössische Kommission für Frauenfragen, ed. *Viel erreicht—wenig verändert? Zur Situation der Frauen in der Schweiz.* Bern: Report by the Federal Commission for Women's Issues, 1995.

Scott, Joan W. "Gender: A Useful Category of Historical Analysis." *American Historical Review* 91, no. 5 (1986): 1053–75.
Studer, Brigitte. *1968 und die Formung des feministischen Subjekts.* Wien: Picus Verlag, 2011.

Part II

Sharing Words

Introductory Remarks

Silja Behre

How to write about femininity? How to find the right words to describe experiences of oppression and alienation? How to speak about women's bodies? How to write about women's sexuality?

Albeit in different manners, these questions are at the center of the four chapters assembled in this second part. Its title—"Sharing Words"—refers to this search for a language that is able to catch *la condition féminine.* "Sharing Words" also alludes to the women's movement claim to find a common language, to produce a set of ideas, which is crucial in order to mobilize groups. Thus, "Sharing Words" emphasizes the role of language in collective identity building processes.

But "Sharing Words" also implies "Contesting Words": Who is legitimate to speak up for the women's cause? Which language has to be chosen to reach the female public? Does feminist literature necessarily have to be written in a theoretic language? What does "feminism" mean? How to subvert relations of domination by the means of language?

Indeed, the four chapters evolve the question of language and symbolic power. Or, to paraphrase French sociologist Pierre Bourdieu, they all deal with symbolic struggles for the legitimate vision of the social world. These symbolic struggles oppose women to forms of masculine domination. But they are also led within the women's movement and have been part of it and the feminist discourse for the last four decades. The four chapters analyze the social role of "words"—as designations, as literary practice, in theories, and in novels—within the French-, German-, and Portuguese-speaking world in the 1970s and 1980s. The transnational perspective of this collection allows it to bring out the similarities in their struggle: the common issues, but also the hierarchies within the women's movements in as well as beyond national contexts.

Sylvie Chaperon's chapter takes the reader to Paris. It analyzes the conflictual relationship between Simone de Beauvoir and the French women's liberation movement (*Mouvement de Libération des Femmes,* MLF). She shows how the designations as *momone* (the MLF on Simone de Beauvoir) and *les bonnes femmes* (Simone de Beauvoir on the MLF) reflect hierarchies and parallels when it comes to the legitimacy of speaking in the name of the women. Indeed, the image of Simone de Beauvoir as the icon of French feminism hides the difficult dialogue between the author of *The Second Sex* published in 1949 and the MLF of the 1970s. While Simone de Beauvoir first understood the women's struggle as a part of the class struggle, the mostly younger women used different categories to analyze the female condition in society. This theoretical disagreement is, following Sylvie Chaperon, caused by the "generational gap" and Simone de Beauvoir's "halo of glory." She lent her name, her texts, her symbolic capital to the movement's purposes, but kept a relative distance when it came to active commitment. For some women, such as the lawyer Gisèle Halimi, it was just this symbolic capital, the prestige that guarantees media coverage, and its attendant publicity that would be helpful for the women's cause. Other agents of the MLF criticized the focus on the famous and wanted to emphasize "the testimony of ordinary women." As Chaperon puts it, Simone de Beauvoir was led by "a desire to remain above the fray." Nevertheless, her position in the intellectual field structured the French women's movement's internal struggles. That a dialogue in both directions became possible was, as Chaperon argues, due to Simone de Beauvoir's intellectual open-mindedness. Even though the relationships among the women writing on everyday sexism in Beauvoir's *Les Temps Modernes* stayed mostly formal, the younger women's style developed and "matured" under Beauvoir's influence while Beauvoir herself showed her relaxed and humorous side. *Momone* and *les bonnes femmes*: Sylvie Chaperon shows how these designations represent the symbolic power relations between the French women's movement and Simone de Beauvoir. Both wanted to change power relations. And both were deeply involved in symbolic power relations that were difficult to overcome.

While women in France were searching for a view on feminism beyond the icon of Simone de Beauvoir, women in Switzerland created a magazine as well as a women's publishing house in order to speak in their own name(s) and to find a voice of their own. In her chapter, which takes us to the Zurich of the 1970s and 1980s, Kristina Schulz analyzes these "literary practices as collective self-discovery." As she argues, they were more than the "superficial decorative ornament" and were instead "constitutive for the WLM as a social movement." Inspired by Roger Chartier's understanding of texts as products and producers of social reality, Schulz also puts the question of effects and impacts of the WLM. She presents two examples of literary practice aiming at social change by the means of language: the women's journal *Frauezitig* and the publishing company *eFeF.* Both were projects that created collective identity-building. At the same time and despite their collective approach, they had to deal with subtle forms of social inclusion and exclusion caused notably by language and social-economic reasons. Not only was the magazine's language criticized by women lecturers as being too theoretic, but the women involved in the magazine, as well as in the publishing house and similar projects, like women's bookstores, also had to invest time and money and were by thus a socially homogeneous, well-educated, and economically secure group. As in the case of the French movement, the question of the legitimate speaker goes together with the tension between individual and collective action, characteristic of social movements. When it comes to the possible cultural effects of the women's movement, Kristina Schulz underlines that the women's literary initiatives had effects beyond their social function within the women's communities. As she argues, they introduced "feminist perspectives" into the literary culture and by thus subverted schemes of perception.

While the first two chapters deal with symbolic concurrences and forms of inclusion and exclusion within the women's movements in specific national contexts, Ana Margarida Dias Martins discusses forms of symbolic domination beyond national contexts in her chapter on Portuguese feminist literature "on the Edge of Europe." She describes the reception of works of feminist literature in Portuguese by other women's movements and the academy as an ambiguous process of support and appropriation. The first example, a collective work of three authors entitled *Novas Cartas Portuguesas* and published in Portugal of the 1970s, was censored by the regime. In the book, the "Three Marias" (Maria Isabel Barreno, Maria Teresa Horta, Maria Velho da Costa) assemble all kinds of literary material, from fictitious to theoretical, to describe the women's situation in Portugal. Their condition is, as Dias Martins argues, not only defined by the geographical margins but also in relation to the dominant (French) feminist discourse. Although the "Three Marias" gained important support by Simone de Beauvoir and other icons of the French WLM, *Novas Cartas* was never fully received, notably due to translation politics, and therefore failed to enter the feminist literary canon. In contrast, the second book, *Borderlands/La Frontera: The New Mestiza,* published in 1987 by Chicana-Texana Gloria Anzaldúa, was canonized as a "classic classroom and theory text." Against the background of the historically based woman figure "Malintzin Ténepal," the author imagines the image of a "utopian New Mestiza." Because both books switch between linguistic registers and literary forms, they challenged "institutionalized language" and are characterized by their "distrust in the power of existing language and theory to represent the political realities." Both works served also, as Ana Margarida Dias Martins shows, as a "'mirror' for the white feminist self." Following Dias Martins, their receptions varied mostly because of the different ways each challenged the reader. It is the constant shifting between different subjectivities that turned *Novas Cartas* into a pioneer piece of feminist literature—notably in relation to Monique Wittig's *Lesbian Amazon. Borderlands/La Frontera* was, as Dias Martins argues, questioned as an "ideal of the female writing subject" and left Monique Wittig with an "inability to deal productively" with the "ambiguous positioning in between several shifting centers and margins" characteristic for *Novas Cartas.* Like Sylvie Chaperon in her chapter on Simone de Beauvoir and the MLF, like Kristina Schulz on the topic of women's literary practices, Ana Margarida Dias Martins reveals the women's struggles for legitimate categories and language as well as the international circulation of ideas behind the scenes of the women's movements. She problematizes the canonization process within the feminist discourse and the image of the women's body as a geographical terrain (*Novas Cartas/Borderlands*), two topics that are also central to the last chapter of this panel.

When it comes to the question of canonized feminist literature in Germany, one has to mention the 1975 published *Häutungen* (Sheddings) by Verena Stefan. As Christa Binswanger and Kathy Davis argue in their chapter on feminist and postfeminist discourse, *Häutungen* is "operating as a kind of shadow" on latest feminist literature in Germany. By comparing Stefan's book with the 2008 library success *Feuchtgebiete* (Wetlands) written by Charlotte Roche, the authors bring out the tensions and changes between two "feminist discourses on women's bodies" in the last thirty years. Finding words to describe women's experiences with their bodies is central to both novels. Stefan felt "speechless" while searching for a language beyond the everyday to describe women's experiences. A generation later, Roche detected that "women have no language for their desire." Yet, Verena Stefan and Charlotte Roche found different answers. Is this caused, as in the difficult dialogue between Simone de Beauvoir and the MLF, by a generational gap?

As Binswanger and Davis argue, both novels are "feminist stories" on "women's sexual empowerment." But while *Häutungen* follows the modernist model of individual emancipation through collective action, *Feuchtgebiete*'s narrative frame is "post"—an example of postfeminist and postmodern writing. In terms of language, Verena Stefan chose a testimonial style, directed to her readers in the form of a collective "we" to become "the embodied voice" of her reader's experiences with masculine domination. This story of liberation passes by the female homosexual experience as a key toward emancipation. In contrast, the main character Helen Memel sketched by Charlotte Roche in *Feuchtgebiete* is not only exclusively heterosexual, but her interest in other women's bodies is wholly, as Binswanger and Davis write, "scientific" and gives another "kind of transgression" that is different from "the same-sex love" in *Häutungen.* Unlike Stefan's heroine Veruschka/Chloé, Helen Memel in *Feuchtgebiete* is without any feminist collective consciousness; she instead suffers from a loneliness that is increased further by her hospitalization, which she tries to overcome by shocking the staff with various bodily excretions. For Christa Binswanger and Kathy Davis, the postfeminist *Wetlands* allows its author to distinguish herself from the "Big Sister" feminism of the 1970s. In the same time, Charlotte Roche needs "the old feminism" to define herself as feminist in the same way the MLF needed Simone de Beauvoir to develop its own language and categories—one could say, as a sparring partner.

The written examples of women's voices presented in the four chapters have to deal with established schemes of perception on femininity and womanhood, thus developing different forms of subversion. In this sense again, following Pierre Bourdieu, they challenge established categories of perception and act politically. They find different strategies to do so—and the chapters bring out clearly the tension between individual and collective action that is characteristic for social movements in general, and to the women's movement and its search for subjectivity specifically. It is this tension that makes them a captivating field of research.

Silja Behre received a PhD in history from Bielefeld University and the École des Hautes Études en Sciences Sociales (EHESS) Paris. Silja was a research assistant at Bielefeld University and a DAAD-Lecturer in Paris. She specializes in the field of transnational intellectual history, memory studies, and the history of social movements. Currently, she works on the topic of Israeli academics in Germany after 1945 at the Franz Rosenzweig Minerva Research Center (Hebrew University of Jerusalem).

Chapter 4

Momone and the *Bonnes Femmes*; or Beauvoir and the MLF

Sylvie Chaperon

Beauvoir and the *Mouvement de libération des femmes* (MLF): this association seems obvious and familiar to us French women, as so many photos, stories, and memories placed them together throughout the 1970s and 1980s, until Beauvoir's burial in the Montparnasse cemetery in Paris. Their long companionship seems so natural as to go without saying, as self-evident. Yet in order to problematize the necessarily complex aspects of this relationship, we must first step back and take a more objective perspective and consider that, on the contrary, their meeting was neither obvious nor self-evident. There were at least two obstacles liable to deter this relationship, or even to prevent it altogether. The first was their age difference, in that it led to a generation gap. The second was the legendary aura, the halo of glory that surrounded Beauvoir and made her difficult to approach, especially for French women. In this chapter I want to tease out the various implications of these two obstacles and explore their value as tools for analysis. Only the years 1970–74 will be taken into account here.

Momone was the nickname that revolutionary feminists gave to Simone de Beauvoir, while she often spoke of them as "*des bonnes femmes* [good ol' women]."[1] This latter term, however, was not customarily used to name revolutionary feminists; it perhaps resulted from a change of heart when feminists (Delphine Seyrig in particular) occupied the editorial office of *Temps Modernes*[2] to protest against the conditions of female prisoners in Rennes. Whatever their origins, these two nicknames, semi-affectionate, semi-ironic, express the deep and yet somewhat distant connections between Beauvoir and the MLF.

A Generation Gap

The generational difference between Beauvoir and the members of the MLF is well illustrated by the example of Claudine Monteil, alias Serre, who, when

Le Deuxième sexe was published in 1949, was in the womb of her young mother, herself aged twenty-seven.[3] The MLF primarily brought together young women of the baby boom generation, or more precisely, women born in the 1940s. Yet that does not mean that it was necessarily homogeneous demographically, as several generations rubbed shoulders within its ranks: in 1970, Françoise d'Eaubonne and Christiane Rochefort were over fifty, Gisèle Halimi was forty-three, Delphine Seyrig, thirty-eight; the future leaders of the MLF (Christine Delphy, Antoinette Fouque, Anne Zelensky, and Monique Wittig) were in their thirties. At sixty-two, Beauvoir was clearly one of the oldest—one or two generations separated her from the actors of the MLF. In that year she published her essay on *Vieillesse* (old age), for which she had visited hospitals and nursing homes and gathered stories.[4] Of all of her books, this one undoubtedly had the least critical success; at the very minimum, it demonstrates that Beauvoir's social concerns had evolved in accordance with her age.

Age in itself does not mean much, however; it is only as a generational marker that it is significant. Historians commonly use the terms "political generation" or "cultural generation" to identify groups of individuals who are imbued with shared values, references, and a common culture because they have gone through one or several events together that have marked them.[5]

Although Sartre and Beauvoir were born at the beginning of the century and participated only briefly in the Resistance, they were part of the Resistance generation.[6] Since Existentialism had affirmed the responsibility of each person in History with a capital H, Sartre and Beauvoir, who had stayed away from politics before the war, became models of committed intellectuals with their quarterly journal and their frequent involvement in the major debates and issues of the century. Beauvoir also embodied the feminist generation that had renewed demands for women's rights and who only began to identify themselves as feminists in the mid-1960s.[7] Yet she guided this generation from afar, without ever getting involved other than through writing, interviews, and book prefaces.

The generation that created the MLF had been formed by the great events of the late 1960s, the Vietnam War, and especially in France, May 1968 and the proliferation of leftist groups.[8] From this political education, this generation gained both a specific political culture and the rejection of revolutionary machismo. The refusal to work with men in the struggle for women's rights very early resulted in a synthesis of both these tendencies, starting with the demonstration at Vincennes near Paris in May 1970 and the story published about it in *L'Idiot international*.[9]

Thus, the generation gap was considerable and was articulated by a different vision of feminist politics. Beauvoir, like many women of the MLF, called herself a "radical feminist," but that term could have very different meanings. In an interview with Francis Jeanson in 1965, Simone de Beauvoir explained, "I am radically feminist in the sense that I radically reduce 'difference' as a fact having any importance in and of itself," adding, "It is not a betrayal of my ideas when others assimilate me with … absolute feminism."[10] Beauvoirian radicalism was thus a theoretical position that reduced the "fact" of sexual difference (in other words, biological) to almost nothing and affirmed the role of society in the construction of sex, or gender as we would say today. This maximum reduction of biological difference between the sexes was accompanied by an affirmation of the unity of the revolutionary struggle. Beauvoir always encouraged women to join men in the common struggle for socialist revolution. From the conclusion of the *Deuxième sexe* through her interviews in 1968, it appears that her position remained constant. Thus, during a lull in activism following the May movement, she was still able to affirm that "the solution to women's issues can only come about on the day when there will be a comprehensive social solution, and the best thing women can do is to take care of something other than themselves. This is what I have tried to do. What I mean is that I deal with political issues, such as the Vietnam War or the war in Algeria, and with much greater willingness and with much more conviction than with the female question itself, which I do not think can be solved within the current framework of society."[11]

In fact, since 1968, Beauvoir and Sartre had drawn closer to leftists who seemed to embody a new revolutionary spirit. In particular, they defended *La Cause du Peuple* (the cause of the people). Beauvoir was also for a time the editor of the *L'Idiot International* published by Jean Edern Allier. In February 1971, she published an article in *J'accuse* about women workers in a factory at Méru, victims of a work accident, without stressing in any way the need for the struggle to be unique to women (apart from a vague reference to abuse by a foreman).[12]

Inversely, the radical feminists of the MLF (who more readily called themselves revolutionaries) argued that women were specifically oppressed and that the struggle against patriarchy was a priority. This position was expressed very early in articles in *L'Idiot International* or the issue of the *Partisans* in 1970, and the theory behind it was clearly outlined in the article "The Main Enemy" by Christine Dupont, alias Delphy.

Thus, while feminists broke politically with leftists, Beauvoir increasingly drew closer to them. There was, therefore, a large political and feminist gap between Beauvoir and the MLF, or at least one of its factions. One might have expected that Beauvoir would be closer to the branch focused on class struggle, as it was much closer to her point of view. Yet this did not happen;[13] or at least, not to the extent it could have.

Paralyzing Notoriety

In addition to the generation gap that illustrated Beauvoir's distance from members of the MLF, her immense fame and the younger generation's admiration or gratitude toward her was another obstacle. It is not necessary here to underline the well-known impact of the *Deuxième sexe* (*The Second Sex*).[14] As Nadja Ringart said, "The *Deuxième sexe* was a fundamental work for us. It is not our only reference, but perhaps the only one that is common to us all."[15] Even for those women who were disappointed by the *Deuxième sexe,* Simone de Beauvoir maintained a considerable aura for other reasons. For example, Cathy Bernheim, then at the Modern Literature Faculty in Nice, found "The Lesbian" chapter, which she had rushed eagerly to read, disappointing. Already well informed on the subject, she expected Beauvoir to take a position and yet only found a compilation of others' ideas. Nonetheless, Beauvoir remained an essential figure in her eyes, as Beauvoir was the epitome of the "woman writer," and Bernheim had read her complete works.[16] For others, it was Beauvoir's character as a philosopher or an essayist that inspired them. Still others admired her way of life, combining freedom, fame, and a fulfilled love life.

In short, Beauvoir was an idol, an icon, a statue on a pedestal, and much more than a person, which did not make it easy to contact her. The stories of women who were intimidated by Beauvoir's renown are countless: "intimidated, nervous, surprised by our own boldness;" such was the state of the women who were waiting for an appointment with Beauvoir to show her a few of their articles.[17] "We were filled with respect," said Catherine Deudon.[18] For her part, Beauvoir did not foster great intimacy either. Her stiffness, her restraint, her coldness at first impressions are legendary. Some attribute it to an unfeeling heart;[19] most others put forward Beauvoir's timidity.

How were these obstacles overcome? Two counterweights played a role: Beauvoir's interest in young people and their deeply shared beliefs on certain issues.

Interest in Young People and Meeting Points

Beauvoir and Sartre always liked to surround themselves with young people. Some of their former students formed a kind of "family," a varied group that mixed together friends, lovers, and intellectual companions. Her female or male lovers were younger than she was, such as the young Bost, Claude Lanzmann, and Sylvie Le Bon, a young philosophy student with whom she had a long and deep relationship starting in 1960.[20] Beauvoir's very easy rapport with young people corresponded to strong traits in her personality: her zest for life, her enthusiasm, her insatiable curiosity, her passion for discovery—in short, this vital force attracted her to those who were generally even more endowed with these qualities than she was. She often explained herself on this point:

> I especially enjoy the company of young people. I am grateful to them for helping me escape the degradation, the alienation that adults consent to. I find their intransigence, their radicalism, their demands comforting and I delight in the freshness of their perspective: for them, everything is new and nothing is obvious.[21]

Moreover, it was Beauvoir who took the first step and asked to meet the young activists of the MLF. "She was the one who wanted to meet us. To see what her heirs were like. The interview was short."[22] This first meeting is very vague in the memory of Anne Zelensky. The meeting was held in Paris at a Montparnasse café at the beginning of the school year in 1970. Before or after the publication of the issue *Partisans* in October? She cannot remember. She was with some other female friends, but which ones? She remembers Antoinette Fouque with certainty.[23] Monique Wittig? Maybe. The rather short meeting left her with no lasting impressions. The aura of Beauvoir, the generation gap, the diversity of the group, all of these factors probably combined to make the first encounter a missed opportunity.

The second meeting was decisive. This time it was initiated by Zelensky and for a specific purpose: creating a manifesto for free access to abortion.[24] Here, Beauvoir was fully in her element: she had called for the decriminalization of abortion in the *Deuxième sexe,* and as for manifestos, she knew all about them! She did not hesitate: "All this seems very good to me. So, what should I do?"[25] In fact, the more traditional aspects of the campaign were criticized during an MLF general meeting: working with the bourgeois paper *Nouvel Observateur,* alternating famous women with ordinary women on the list of the manifesto's signatories, all of this conflicted with the spontaneous and egalitarian creed of the MLF. Yet signatures were quickly gathered and the manifesto, published in April 1971, was a real success in the press. Afterward, things progressed fairly quickly, and more actions were initiated: the founding of the association *Choisir,* chaired by Beauvoir, to protect the anonymous signatories from possible retaliation; plans to continue the mobilization for women's rights with special days denouncing crimes against women; the trial in Bobigny; a Women's Day at a factory in Vincennes; and the creation of the League of Women's Rights.

The column on everyday sexism, which lasted from 1974 until the early 1980s, was another form of privileged collaboration between Beauvoir and the MLF. The purpose of this column, started by Cathy Bernheim and Liliane Kandel with some others (Claudine Serre, Dominique Fougeyrolas, Catherine Deudon, and Annie Elm), was to denounce sexism in the media using humor.[26] Beauvoir was again fully in her element: her editorial work for *Temps Modernes* motivated her, and she enjoyed it from the start, and increasingly so with Sartre's illness. To these reasons we can add the deep similarities that bound her to the young women working on the column. Their insolence and their sense of humor reminded her of the taste for controversy she herself had long demonstrated, for example, in the direct attack on Claude Mauriac (who had well deserved it), from the first pages of the *Deuxième sexe.*[27] Claire Etcherelli, who managed the administrative side of the quarterly and participated in editorial meetings, remembers the atmosphere of the meetings:

> These women's freedom to write overturned many conformist ideas, including those of the magazine and its members. For Beauvoir, reading the column was a moment of pure joy. She appreciated its excesses and was amused by the insolent and punchy style. For example, [I remember a precise image of] the instantaneous pleasure she had in reading the column "Sexism": she raised her head, even her eyes were laughing—a rare moment, as she had lost her slightly stiff reserve that was all too often linked with her public image.[28]

For lack of space, it is unfortunately not possible to discuss in detail the circumstances and characteristics of Beauvoir's support of the journal *Questions Féministes* (Feminist Questions) or Yvette Roudy's term as minister.

Along the way, Beauvoir modified her political positions, which shows both her great intellectual flexibility and her humility, as she abandoned her former position and moved toward those of the revolutionary feminists. She admitted this shift quite publicly in the interview she gave to Alice Schwarzer for *Le Nouvel Observateur.* Furthermore, she donated the money she earned from the interview to rent the Mutualité conference hall in Paris for the demonstration days.[29] Her position now was that the fight for women's rights had to be done separately, admitting that "everything that I have been able to observe, and what has led me to change my views from the *Deuxième sexe,* is that class struggle itself does not emancipate women."[30] Yet she stressed the need for union in the fight: "As for me, my preference is to want to link women's emancipation to class struggle. I believe that the struggle of women, while unique, is linked with the one that they must carry out with men. Therefore, I completely refuse the total repudiation of men."[31] At that time, she was not convinced by the arguments of materialist feminists, particularly the one advanced in *L'Ennemi Principal:*

> I find that analyses that make patriarchal oppression the equivalent of capitalist oppression are not correct. The work of the housewife does not produce a surplus: it is a different condition from that of the worker, from whom the surplus value of his work is being stolen. I want to know exactly what connection exists between the two. All the tactics that women must follow depend on it.[32]

She also more readily employed the term sex "caste" rather than sex "class." On this point her position would later evolve yet again.

In her preface to the 1975 reprint of the *Temps Modernes* special issue "Women Persist"[33] by Gallimard , she highlighted the insights that she owed to young feminists:

> Because I have more or less played the role of a token woman, it has long seemed to me that some of the disadvantages inherent in women's condition should simply be ignored or overcome, there is no need to attack them. What made me understand the new generation of women activists is that there was a sense of shared understanding in their flippant attitude.[34]

In the same text, she recognized the intimate challenges that the fight for women's rights can generate:

> The fight against sexism is not only directed, like the anticapitalist struggle, against the structures of society as a whole; within each one of us, it attacks what is most intimate and what seems the most sure to us. It challenges our desires, our forms of pleasure. We must not shy away from this challenge; overcoming the anguish it may provoke in us, some of our shackles will be destroyed and we will be opened up to new truths.[35]

Participation from Afar

That is not to say, however, that Beauvoir threw herself headlong into the movement. Instead, she established a certain distance and some levels of protection. Most often her involvement remained traditional and honorific: she lent her name and her image more than she gave of her time. She presided over associations or journals, gave interviews, petitioned, and prefaced books. She also knew the importance of being physically present at major events to signal her support: demonstrations, the Bobigny trial, days for denouncing crimes against women, women's days, etc. As for the rest, and contrary to Gisèle Halimi, Christine Rochefort, and Delphine Seyrig, she carefully kept away from general assemblies and the heated debates that stirred up the movement. The MLF's ways of functioning required a lot of patience and free time, and Beauvoir had neither. The meetings always started late and never with the same people, everyone talked at the same time, decisions were slow to be taken, and even then they were always liable to be challenged later. "Simone de Beauvoir, disliking all that commotion, told me she preferred to come to smaller meetings on a specific topic," said Anne Zelensky about the days preparing the conference at the Mutualité.[36] As we have seen, Beauvoir focused on a few select projects in accordance with her skills and interests. One might even ask whether she was aware of the magnitude of the conflicts that repeatedly rippled through the movement. Many of her texts show, if not ignorance of ongoing divisions, at least a desire to remain above the fray.

In any case, clashes arose between the feminists of the MLF and Gisèle Halimi, which were expressed primarily during the general assemblies of *Choisir.* The disagreements became more pointed in 1972 around the preparation of the days denouncing crimes against women and the trial in Bobigny where G. Halimi defended 3 women accused of abortion. Feminists objected to testimony by experts and the great names in science in favor of the testimony of ordinary women, with everyone being treated the same, famous or not. Gisèle Halimi insisted on the testimony of major personalities in order to ensure the media coverage she wanted to generate. She also emphasized the differences between wealthy women and poor women in their lived experience of abortion, while the other feminists wanted to highlight the oppression common to all women. Simone de Beauvoir, in her interview cited above in February 1972, described the upcoming protest days in a way that pleased Gisèle Halimi: "There will be a sort of inquiry committee, consisting of a dozen women, who will interview the witnesses: biologists, sociologists, psychiatrists, doctors, midwives, but especially women who have suffered from the condition currently imposed on women."[37] This was not at all the scene that came to pass during the protest days, held less than three months later, when all the stands, seats, and specialists were sent away, leaving only women all at the same level, literally. This conflict was then transferred onto the strategy that should be used during the public trial of Bobigny. This strategy was put to a vote at the general assembly of *Choisir* on November 4, 1972. Gisèle Halimi remembers:

> When I presented my project, my plan for how the debates would be conducted, the women of the MLF protested strongly. From their point of view, there should not be any famous witnesses, no men, no Nobel Prize winners! Bobigny should be exclusively a women's issue. And no famous women either.[38]

Beauvoir then voted, as did her companions at the MLF, against the involvement of media at the trial as Halimi had planned. Beauvoir did participate in the trial, however, and in her testimony at Bobigny in November 1972 she always seemed to want to reconcile the varying positions. As in the *Deuxième sexe,* she insisted on the injustices of class difference between women in their experience of abortion, but she also stated that "the law oppresses all women, even those who are privileged."[39] Yet one year later she ended up resigning from her office as president of *Choisir* and cut off all contact with Gisèle Halimi.[40]

When Anne Zelensky and her comrades decided to found the *Ligue pour les droits des femmes* primarily to call for an anti–sex discrimination law, they angered feminist revolutionaries such as Liliane Kandel and Cathy Bernheim. The violence of the latter's criticism matched the depths of their disappointment. As Françoise Picq explained, "To accept the rules of the law of 1901 is to abandon the principles of the movement: spontaneity, direct democracy, and the prohibition to speak 'on behalf of all women.'"[41] Beauvoir took no position, and although she chaired the association she had initiated, she also opened the pages of *Temps Modernes* to her stated opponents.[42] In an editorial she wrote for the first column on "Everyday Sexism," in December 1973, she presented the different positions as two parts of the same concerted action:

> A certain number of women, including myself, have decided to create a *Ligue pour les droits des femmes* [women's rights league]. This association has several goals, among them speaking out against any discrimination against women in posters, writings and public speeches. We demand that "sexist insults" also be considered a misdemeanor. In the meantime, every month *Les Temps Modernes* intends to denounce the most egregious sexist insults: that is the purpose of this new column, which begins today.[43]

Was she unaware of conflicts within the MLF? Was this her attempt at reconciliation? The question merits discussion. Françoise Picq thinks that "[Beauvoir] was supporting various and sometimes divergent initiatives without taking part in strategic battles."[44] Although Beauvoir had moved closer to the revolutionary feminists, she did not want to get involved in their internal conflicts.

The relative distance between Beauvoir and the ups and downs of the movement can also be found in the relationships that Beauvoir established with young women in the movement, some closer and friendlier than others.

Uneven Friendships

These shared projects, regular meetings, and occasional dinners brought Simone de Beauvoir and the women of the MLF closer. Beauvoir frequently brought a bottle of whiskey, her favorite drink. The atmosphere was relaxed and happy. Yet participants could not shake themselves free from a certain feeling of deference, and Simone de Beauvoir rarely let her hair down. Françoise Picq, who was not part of Beauvoir's intimate circle as she only dined with her two or three times, emphasizes the distance that endured between Beauvoir and her "girlfriends" and adds: "She was not someone who made people laugh."[45] Catherine Deudon remembers the slightly formal atmosphere of the monthly meetings to discuss the column on everyday sexism: the women had too much respect for Beauvoir, which prevented them from becoming close friends with their host.

Yet all the participants emphasize her humility: she never took on an attitude of authority. Exchanges could be lively, and disagreements significant, but Beauvoir did not try to impose her point of view on others. During the monthly meetings for the column or when working on the special issue, "*Les femmes s'entêtent,*" Beauvoir often expressed her disapproval of texts that had been submitted to her. She defended Greek film director Yannis Papadakis, who was considered macho; she thought an article on motherhood was bad because in her opinion it was not critical enough; she winced at Evelyne Rochedereux's text, "*Les belles histoires de la guena goudou* [The Beautiful Stories of the Lesbian]," which she covered in red ink. Yet each time it was the majority position and not hers that won out. For one group of authors, in order to get their negative film review published, they accompanied it with a letter parodying a shocked reader, which made Beauvoir laugh so hard that she published the letter with the review. Cathy Bernheim remembers having to defend every inch of the text on motherhood because she wanted "the link between women and this particularity [of motherhood], which both oppresses them and ennobles them, to be as explicit as possible."[46]

Over time, through successive mobilization campaigns, privileged relationships were established between Simone de Beauvoir and certain feminists of the MLF: Anne Zelensky, the German journalist Alice Schwarzer,

Christine Delphy, Liliane Kandel, and Cathy Bernheim, among others. As one of them said about her, "It gradually became clear that the choice of contacts Beauvoir fostered within the MLF—whose activists initially came from very different political backgrounds—were by no means due to chance. It was always—as it still is today—about women relying on a materialist analysis of women's situation (and of the world), and absolutely refusing to believe in a 'feminine [biological] nature.'"[47]

These new friendships eclipsed older ones. Dominique Desanti says that during this period, she stopped seeing Beauvoir:

> Then came the years when the secretaries and the feminists of her League began to stand guard around her, [the time of] "Absolute Feminism," the period when Beauvoir was not only loved, but "worshipped." ... And so, it is true that I no longer sought to see her. She had risen out of reach, always surrounded by others, an idol. She had been too close for me to want to go light a candle for her [to worship her] in Church.[48]

Yet, even these new friendships also remained marked by a certain distance. Each relationship had its own tone, its ways of meeting, and its rituals. Simone de Beauvoir and Anne Zelensky met regularly until Beauvoir's death, primarily for the *Ligue pour les droits des femmes.* They worked in complete harmony in the morning: they exchanged news, Beauvoir handed her the mail ("You will answer better than I will"), and she sent Zelensky the journalists who had contacted her. They were in such agreement that Beauvoir even signed her name to articles written by Zelensky. Then they would leave to have lunch at a restaurant. Beauvoir bombarded her with questions about the movement, but mostly about her private life, her loves, and her psychoanalysis: "She loved that." Yet the inverse was not the case, as Anne Zelensky had too much reverence for Beauvoir to ask such personal questions. She still regrets not having had the time to overcome Beauvoir's armor, which softened with age: "She was so strong-headed, so in control ... I considered myself as her spiritual daughter, she was at once an ideal mother and role model of how to live."[49]

Cathy Bernheim also regularly met with Simone de Beauvoir until the end of her life. Throughout the period of working together on the column, she thinks they all changed as a result. Simone de Beauvoir became more free and open in her relationships with women, increasingly allowing herself to say what she thought thanks to the impertinence and the frank nature of the members of the MLF. In turn, the writing and the style of the MLF women matured. Bernheim saw Beauvoir as an older sister, one whom you want to know what she thinks. She loved Beauvoir's "little streak of fancy that unfailingly reconnected us with our childhoods; we were in the playground with Momone."[50]

Beauvoir's feminist friends compare her to a role model, an ideal mother or a sister, but not as a "girlfriend" as they called each other. Of course, *Momone* was a nickname for her that they used among themselves; none of the MLF women ever felt familiar enough with Beauvoir to address her directly as such. In French, *momone* sounds affectionate (like the word for "mommy" spoken by children), but also irreverent (recalling the French *bobonne,* a pejorative word for "housewife," something akin to "soccer mom"). This diminutive for Simone functioned as a sort of antidote to the aura of respect around Beauvoir, it desacralized her stature and brought her down, for a little while, from her annoying pedestal. The French expression *bonnes femmes* used by Beauvoir served as an exact counterpart to her nickname. This term in the feminine plural is rather ambiguous. In Old French the term was complimentary, but it also includes a dose of sexism, for example, in certain expressions such as *les recettes de bonnes femmes* ("the recipes of good ol' housewives") or in *les affaires de bonnes femmes* ("old wives' business"), something akin to the sexism inherent in the English expression "old wives' tales." Should we see this nickname as a sign of Beauvoir's persistent reservations about the women's movement? It is impossible to state with certainty. Unlike the feminists who, in telling their stories to commemorate the movement, recalled the times they shared with their elder Beauvoir, she hardly mentions them at all. In her last volume of memoirs, published in 1972, she purposefully chose to remain impersonal in her descriptions of the MLF, speaking about the group's actions and its ideas. The only authors she mentions were Americans, probably to avoid offending or favoring any of the French women that she regularly spent time with.

Conclusion

This examination has shown the restraint that characterized the relationship between Beauvoir and the MLF. Further research, however, is called for, not only to analyze events after 1974 but also to reintegrate other factions within the MLF that have been somewhat neglected in current historiography. Josette Trat recently noted that the "class struggle" faction has been like the "poor relation" in the histories written on the MLF.[51] Yet this was the group that was politically closer to Beauvoir in 1970. The first texts on the fight for women's rights were published in the leftist press (the women workers from Méru in *J'accuse*; the strike by young mothers of the Collège d'enseignement technique at Plessis-Robinson in *La cause du peuple*). What became of these ties later, when the divisions between the different MLF factions became more pronounced? In addition, the mutual hostility between Beauvoir and "essentialist" feminists has an origin that must be uncovered and analyzed. After all, one of the first feminists to meet Beauvoir was a determined defender of an essentialist point of view: Antoinette Fouque.[52]

Sylvie Chaperon is a professor of modern history at the University of Jean Jaurès (Toulouse). Her research focuses on the history of feminism, in particular Simone de Beauvoir, as well as the history of sexuality. She has published several books, such as: in collaboration with C. Bard (ed.), *Dictionnaire des féministes, France XVIIIe-XXIe siècle,* Paris, PUF, 2017; *Jules Guyot, Bréviaire de l'amour expérimental,* presented by Sylvie Chaperon, Paris, Payot, 2012; *Les origines de la sexologie 1850–1900,* Paris, Payot, 2012; *La médecine du sexe et les femmes: Anthologie des perversions féminines au XIXe siècle,* Paris, La Musardine, 2008; *Les années Beauvoir,* Paris, Fayard, 2000.

Notes

Translated from the French by Cynthia J. Johnson.
This translation and its title cannot be modified or altered without consent of the translator, in accordance with French law.

1. This story is recounted by Claire Etcherelli, "Quelques photos-souvenirs," *Les Temps Modernes* 647–48 (2008): 65.
2. *Modern Times.* A philosophical and political quarterly founded by Sartre and Beauvoir.
3. Claudine Monteil, *Simone de Beauvoir, le Mouvement des femmes: mémoires d'une jeune fille rebelle* (Paris: Éd. du Rocher, 1996).
4. Simone de Beauvoir, *La vieillesse* (Paris: Gallimard, 1970).
5. See *Vingtième Siècle: Revue d'histoire* 22, no. 22. (1989).
6. Olivier Wieviorka, "La génération de la résistance," *Vingtième Siècle: Revue d'histoire,* op. cit.: 111–16.
7. Sylvie Chaperon, *Les années Beauvoir* (Paris: Fayard, 2000).
8. For a recent revision, see Julie Pagis, "Repenser la formation de générations politiques sous l'angle du genre: Le cas de Mai-Juin 68," *Clio 68' révolutions dans le genre,* no. 29 (2009), http://clio.revues.org/index9230.html (accessed November 4, 2010).
9. Cathy Bernheim, Liliane Kandel, Françoise Picq, and Nadja Ringart, *Mouvement de libération des femmes: Textes premiers* (Paris: Stock, 2009).
10. "Je suis radicalement féministe, en ce sens que je réduis radicalement la différence en tant que donnée ayant une importance par elle même" ajoutant "on ne me trahit jamais quand on me tire vers … le féminisme absolu." Jeanson Françis, *Simone de Beauvoir ou l'entreprise de vivre* (Paris: Seuil, 1966), 258.

11. "La solution du problème des femmes ne pourra exister que le jour où il y aura une solution sociale globale et la meilleure chose que les femmes ont à faire, c'est de s'occuper d'autre chose que d'elles. C'est ce que j'ai essayé de faire. Je veux dire que je m'occupe de problèmes politiques, comme la guerre du Vietnam ou la guerre d'Algérie, et beaucoup plus volontiers et avec beaucoup plus de conviction que du problème féminin proprement dit que je ne pense pas pouvoir être résolu dans le cadre de la société actuelle." "La femme entre le défi de la suffragette et la passivité de la femme-objet, Simone de Beauvoir trace la voie de la femme pleinement réalisée." Interview by M. de Barsy, *Pénéla: Connaître et comprendre,* September 1968, cited in Jacques Zéphir, *Le néo-féminisme de Simone de Beauvoir: trente ans après Le deuxième sexe, un post-scriptum* (Paris: Denoël Gonthier, 1982), 36.
12. *J'accuse* 2 (February 15, 1971), "En France aujourd'hui on peut tuer impunément."
13. Françoise Picq, *Les années mouvement* (Paris: Le Seuil, 1993).
14. Catherine Rodgers, *Le deuxième sexe de Simone de Beauvoir: Un héritage admiré et contesté* (Paris: L'Harmattan, 1998), and Liliane Lazar, ed., *L'empreinte Beauvoir: Des écrivains racontent* (Paris: L'Harmattan, 2009).
15. "*Le Deuxième sexe* est pour nous un texte fondamental. Ce n'est pas notre unique référence, mais peut-être la seule qui nous soit commune." Nadja Ringart, "Scénario pour un film condamné," *Les Temps Modernes* 647–48 (2008): 97.
16. Cathy Bernheim, interview with author, May 6, 2010.
17. Liliane Kandel, "Le sexisme et quelques autres ennemis principaux," *Les Temps Modernes* 647–48 (2008): 117.
18. Entretien du 27 avril 2010.
19. Gisèle Halimi, *Ne nous résignez jamais: Comment devient-on féministe* (Paris: Plon, 2009).
20. Simone de Beauvoir, *Tout compte fait* (Paris: Gallimard, 1972): 69–75.
21. "Je me plais particulièrement dans la compagnie des jeunes. Je leur sais gré d'échapper aux dégradations, aux aliénations auxquelles consentent les adultes. Je trouve réconfortants leur intransigeance, leur radicalisme, leurs exigences et je m'enchante de la fraîcheur de leur regard: pour eux, tout est neuf et rien ne va de soi." Idem, 69.
22. "C'est elle qui avait voulu nous voir. Voir à quoi ressemblaient ses héritières en somme. L'entrevue avait été courte." Anne Zelensky-Tristan, *Histoire de vivre: Mémoires d'une féministe* (Paris: Calmann-Lévy, 2005), 54.
23. Antoinette Fouque also mentioned this meeting in her work, *Il y a deux sexes: essais de féminologie: 1989–1995* (Paris: Gallimard, 1995), 34–35.
24. The famous "Manifesto of the 343" to demand legalizing abortion, in which both celebrities and ordinary women openly admitted to having an abortion, thus exposing themselves to prosecution.
25. Ibid.
26. Kandel, "Le sexisme et quelques autres ennemis principaux."
27. He had declared, in *Figaro Littéraire,* that the most brilliant of women only repeated ideas that "came from us." She responded, "It is obviously not the ideas of C. Mauriac himself that the woman speaking with him reflects, given that we have not found a single idea of his ..." Simone de Beauvoir, *Le deuxième sexe* (Paris: Gallimard, 1976): 28.

28. "La liberté d'écriture de ces femmes renversait bien des conformismes, y compris ceux de la revue et de ses membres. La lecture de la chronique était pour Beauvoir un moment de franche gaîté. Elle en appréciait les outrances et s'amusait d'un style insolent et mordant. Instantané par exemple, ce plaisir que lui donne la lecture de la chronique "Sexisme." Elle lève la tête, même ses yeux rient, instantané rare, elle a perdu cette retenue un peu raide qu'on accole trop souvent à son image publique." Claire Etcherelli, "Quelques photos-souvenirs," *Les Temps Modernes,* 647–48 (2008): 62–63.
29. "La femme révoltée, propos recueillis par Alice Schwarzer," *Le Nouvel Observateur,* February 14, 1972, 47–54, reprinted in Francis Claude and Fernande Gonthier, *Les écrits de Simone De Beauvoir: La vie l'écriture* (Paris: Gallimard, 1979): 482–97.
30. "Tout ce que je peux constater, et qui m'a amené à modifier mes positions du *Deuxième sexe,* c'est que la lutte des classes proprement dite n'émancipe pas les femmes."
31. "Moi, ma tendance est de vouloir lier l'émancipation féminine à la lutte de classes. J'estime que le combat des femmes, tout en étant singulier, est lié à celui qu'elles doivent mener avec les hommes. Par conséquent, je refuse complètement la répudiation totale de l'homme."
32. "Je trouve que les analyses qui font de l'oppression patriarcale l'équivalent de l'oppression capitaliste ne sont pas justes. Le travail de la ménagère ne produit pas de plus-value: c'est une autre condition que celle de l'ouvrier à qui on vole la plus-value de son travail. Je voudrais savoir exactement quels rapports existent entre les deux. Toute la tactique que doivent suivre les femmes en dépend." Ibid., 486, 490–91.
33. The French title of this article, "Les Femmes s'entêtent," is a play on words referring to the work of Max Ernst, *Les Femmes 100 Têtes.* The French title of the article could also be understood as "Women Get Stubborn" or "Women Dig In for the Long Fight."
34. "Moi-même, du fait que j'ai plus ou moins joué un rôle de femme-alibi, il m'a longtemps semblé que certains inconvénients inhérents à la condition féminine devaient être simplement négligés ou surmontés, qu'il n'y avait pas besoin de s'y attaquer. Ce que m'a fait comprendre la nouvelle génération de femmes en révolte, c'est qu'il entrait de la complicité dans cette désinvolture." *Les femmes s'entêtent* (Paris: Gallimard, 1975), 12.
35. "La lutte antisexiste n'est pas seulement dirigée comme la lutte anticapitaliste contre les structures de la société dans son ensemble: elle s'attaque en chacun de nous à ce qui nous est le plus intime et qui nous paraissait le plus sûr. Elle conteste jusqu'à nos désirs, jusqu'aux formes de notre plaisir. Ne reculons pas devant cette contestation; par-delà le déchirement qu'elle provoquera peut-être en nous, elle détruira certaines de nos entraves, elle nous ouvrira à de nouvelles vérités." Ibid., 13.
36. Annie de Pisan and Anne Tristan, *Histoires du MLF* (Paris: Calmann-Levy, 1977), 89.
37. "Il y aura une sorte de commission d'enquête, constituée par une dizaine de femmes; elles interrogeront des témoins: des biologistes, des sociologues, des psychiatres, des médecins, des sages-femmes, mais surtout des femmes qui ont souffert de la condition faite actuellement à la femme." Simone de Beauvoir, "La femme révoltée," 497.
38. "Lorsque j'ai présenté mon projet, mon synopsis pour le déroulement des débats, les filles du MLF ont violemment protesté. De leur point de vue, il ne fallait pas de

grands témoins, pas d'hommes, pas de Prix Nobel! Bobigny devait être exclusivement une affaire de femmes. Et de femmes 'non vedettes.'" Gisèle Halimi, *La cause des femmes, précédé de Le temps des malentendus* (Paris: Gallimard, 1992), 94.

39. Association Choisir, *Avortement: une loi en procès. L'affaire de Bobigny, sténotypie intégrale des débats du tribunal de Bobigny (8 novembre 1972)* (Paris: Gallimard, 1973), 126.
40. Some of the impact of this split can be found in issues of the *Nouvel Observateur* from November 12–16, 1973. See Catherine Valenti, *Bobigny: Le procès de l'avortement* (Paris: Larousse, 2010).
41. "Accepter les règles de la loi de 1901, c'est abandonner les principes du Mouvement, la spontanéité, la démocratie directe, l'interdiction de parler 'au nom des femmes.'" Picq, *Les années mouvement,* 203.
42. Pisan and Tristan, *Histoires du MLF,* 71. "L'idée de créer une Ligue pour les femmes est venue de Simone de Beauvoir. Très choquée, notre Simone, par les oublis de la 'Ligue de l'homme.' Elle, si peu 'militante' dans l'âme, là, elle s'est énervée. Elle a proposé l'idée, le titre de l'association, et a acceptée d'être notre présidente. Elle le resterait jusqu'à sa mort."
43. "Un certain nombre de femmes, dont je fais partie, ont entrepris de créer une ligue du droits des femmes. Cette association se propose plusieurs buts et entre autres de s'élever contre toute discrimination faite aux femmes dans des affiches, écrits et paroles publiques. Nous exigerons que les 'injures sexistes' soient elles aussi considérées comme un délit. En attendant, *Les Temps Modernes* se proposent de dénoncer chaque mois les plus flagrantes: tel est le sens de cette nouvelle rubrique que nous ouvrons aujourd'hui. "Préface à la rubrique sexisme ordinaire," *Les Temps Modernes* 329 (1973), cited in Claude and Gontier, *Les écrits de Simone de Beauvoir,* 514.
44. Françoise Picq, "Simone de Beauvoir et la querelle du féminisme," *Les Temps Modernes* 647–48 (2008): 178.
45. Françoise Picq, interview with author, May 4, 2010.
46. "Ce lien des femmes à cette particularité qui les opprime et les magnifie soit le plus explicite." Bernheim interview.
47. "Il apparu petit à petit que le choix des contacts noués par Beauvoir au sein du MLF –dont les militantes, au départ, provenaient d'horizons politiques très divers- n'étaient nullement dû au hasard : il s'agissait toujours –comme aujourd'hui encore- de femmes s'appuyant sur une analyse matérialiste de la situation des femmes (et du monde), et refusant absolument de croire en une 'nature féminine' (humaine)." Alice Schwarzer, *Simone de Beauvoir aujourd'hui: Entretiens* (Paris: Mercure de France, 1984), 14.
48. "Vinrent les années où les secrétaires et les féministes de sa Ligue montaient la garde. Le 'féminisme absolu', le temps où elle fut non plus seulement aimée, mais 'vénérée.' … Et là; c'est vrai que je n'ai plus cherché à la voir. Elle était portée, entourée. Une idole. Elle m'avait été trop proche pour que j'aie envie de planter un cierge." Dominique Desanti, "Un jeune castor: souvenirs," *Les Temps Modernes* 647–48 (2008): 47.
49. "Elle était tellement volontaire, tellement dans la maîtrise." "Je me suis considérée comme sa fille spirituelle, elle était tout à la fois une mère idéale et un modèle de vie." Anne Zelensky, interview with author, May 10, 2010.

50. "Petit brun de fantaisie qui rattache à l'enfance indéfectiblement, On est dans la cour de récréation avec Momone." Bernheim interview.
51. Josette Trat, "L'histoire oubliée du courant 'féministe lutte de classe,'" *Les Cahiers de critique communiste,* Femmes, genre, féminisme (mars 2007).
52. Antoinette Fouque is a contested leader of the MLF who founded a group called Psychoanalysis and Politics and the publishing house *Des femmes.*

Bibliography

Bernheim, Cathy, Liliane Kandel, Françoise Picq and Nadja Ringart. *Mouvement de libération des femmes; Textes premiers.* Paris: Stock, 2009.

Chaperon, Sylvie. *Les années Beauvoir.* Paris: Fayard, 2000.

———. "Beauvoir et le féminisme français." In *Simone de Beauvoir,* edited by Eliane Lecarme-Tabone and Jean-Louis Jeannelle, 277–83. Paris: Editions de l'Herne, 2012.

Desanti, Dominique. "Un jeune castor: souvenirs." 34–47, *Les Temps Modernes* 647–48 (2008).

Etcherelli, Claire. "Quelques photos-souvenirs," 56–66, *Les Temps Modernes* 647–48 (2008).

Fouque, Antoinette. *Il y a deux sexes: essais de féminologie: 1989–1995.* Paris: Gallimard, 1995.

Halimi, Gisèle. *La cause des femmes, précédé de Le temps des malentendus.* Paris: Gallimard, 1992.

———. *Ne vous résignez jamais: Comment devient-on féministe.* Paris: Plon, 2009.

Kandel, Liliane. "Le sexisme et quelques autres ennemis principaux." *Les Temps Modernes* 647–48 (2008).

Lazar, Liliane, ed. *L'empreinte Beauvoir: Des écrivains racontent.* Paris: L'Harmattan, 2009.

Monteil Claudine. *Simone de Beauvoir, le Mouvement des femmes: mémoires d'une jeune fille rebelle.* Paris: Ed. du Rocher, 1996.

Pagis, Julie. "Repenser la formation de générations politiques sous l'angle du genre: Le cas de Mai-Juin 68," *Clio 68' révolutions dans le genre,* no. 29 (2009), http://clio.revues.org/index9230.html (accessed November 4, 2010).

Picq, Françoise. *Les années mouvement.* Paris: Le Seuil, 1993.

———. "Simone de Beauvoir et la querelle du féminisme." *Les Temps Modernes* 647–48 (2008).

Ringart, Nadja. "Scénario pour un film condamné." *Les Temps Modernes* 647–48 (2008).

Rodgers Catherine. *Le deuxième sexe de Simone de Beauvoir: Un héritage admiré et contesté.* Paris: L'Harmattan, 1998.

Trat, Josette. "L'histoire oubliée du courant 'féministe lutte de classe.'" *Les Cahiers de critique communiste.* Femmes, genre, féminisme, mars, 2007.

Vingtième Siècle: Revue d'histoire 22, no. 22 (1989).

Valenti, Catherine. *Bobigny: Le procès de l'avortement.* Paris: Larousse, 2010.

Wieviorka, Olivier. "La génération de la résistance." *Vingtième Siècle: Revue d'histoire* 22, no. 22 (1989): 111–16.

Zelensky-Tristan, Anne. *Histoire de vivre: Mémoires d'une féministe.* Paris: Calmann-Lévy, 2005.

Sources

Association Choisir. *Avortement: une loi en procès. L'affaire de Bobigny, sténotypie intégrale des débats du tribunal de Bobigny (8 novembre 1972).* Paris: Gallimard, 1973.

Beauvoir, Simone de. *La vieillesse.* Paris: Gallimard, 1970.

———. "En France aujourd'hui on peut tuer impunément" *J'accuse* 2 (February 15, 1971).

———. *Tout compte fait.* Paris: Gallimard, 1972.

———. *Le deuxième sexe.* Paris: Gallimard, 1976. [1949]

———. "La femme révoltée," propos recueillis par A. Schwarzer. *Le Nouvel Observateur,* February 14, 1972, 47–54. Reprinted in Francis Claude and Fernande Gontier. *Les écrits de Simone de Beauvoir: La vie l'écriture.* Paris: Gallimard, 1979, 482–97.

———. "Préface à la rubrique sexisme ordinaire." *Les Temps Modernes* 329 (1973).

Jeanson, Francis. *Simone de Beauvoir ou l'entreprise de vivre.* Paris: Seuil, 1966.

Schwarzer, Alice. *Simone de Beauvoir aujourd'hui: Entretiens.* Paris: Mercure de France, 1984.

Zéphir, Jacques. *Le néo-féminisme de Simone de Beauvoir: trente ans après Le deuxième sexe, un post-scriptum.* Paris: Denoël Gonthier, 1982.

Chapter 5

Women and Words

Literary Practices as Collective Self-Discovery

Kristina Schulz

"Our motivation to become publishers was governed by the idea of actually taking action and contributing to a change in power relations."[1] This quote from the mid-1990s comes from one of the founding members of the women's publishing house *eFeF*, the first and only women's publishing company in Switzerland.[2] The declaration expresses a central conviction of the feminist scene in the first half of the 1990s, a conviction that goes back to the women's liberation movement (WLM) of the 1970s: that is, the idea that the ability to intervene in literary and print culture could contribute to overthrowing patriarchy. There is no doubt that literary activities were central to the WLM. What function did they have for individual participants and the movement as a whole? And did they have any impact on wider society?

Experimental literary practices in the WLM characterized its cultural expressions from the beginning. They encompassed many different activities, such as reading, research on women's and feminism's past, storytelling, discussing, writing to creatively express ideas and emotions, organizing lectures of well-known or less well-known authors, producing newsletters, booklets or journals, printing, and opening women's bookshops and women's libraries. Given how central these activities were for the internal mobilization of the movement, it is astonishing how little historians of feminism in Switzerland have paid attention to them.[3] Literary activities were not only the superficial decorative ornament, the colorful embellishment of more "serious" forms of activism, but they should also be understood as constitutive for the WLM as a social movement.

The first part of this chapter will explore certain theoretical and methodological issues surrounding the identification of the cultural outcomes and effects of social movements. The second and third parts will discuss literary activities in the feminist scene in Switzerland—and more precisely in Zurich—between the 1970s and the second half of the 1980s and 1990s in order to document changes over time. My aim is to better understand the role that women's literary practices played in the internal and external mobilization of the WLM. I will argue that those practices had an important integrative function for the movement and were a source of solidarity, but that they also constituted a barrier, keeping away women that lacked the necessary means (in term of education, time, language skills, economic situation) to participate in such activities.

Theoretical Reflections

When thinking about the effects and impacts of the WLM, I was confronted by the very complicated task of how to define what is actually meant by "effects," and especially by *cultural* effects. First, I learned that, in attempting to identify concrete effects of the women's liberation movement, I had to distinguish carefully between the aims and the claims of the movement on the one hand and, on the other hand, what the movement actually achieved or at least set in motion, intentionally or otherwise. Analyzing the aims, claims, and strategies of a social movement, and exploring how activists understood their actions, turned out to be a *condition sine qua non* for the complex enterprise of demonstrating correlations between social movement activity and phenomena of broader political, social, and mental change.

Second, the term "culture" is difficult to define. In her article about "cultural consequences of social movements," Jennifer Earl has discussed the polysemic meaning of culture, which is reflected in the different uses of the term, not least in social movement research.[4] Movement scholars have focused on a range of different topics, such as belief and value systems, rituals, symbols, and various forms of cultural expression. The focus of this chapter is on "women's writing": literary activities that aimed at producing, diffusing, reading, and discussing texts from a women's point of view, with the aim of promoting self-discovery and raising women's consciousness. I have chosen not to define strictly any properties of so-called "women's literature"; rather, I am interested in the functions and effects of women's writing in the WLM. More precisely, I understand this exploration as a contribution to a social history of a feminist (counter)culture, its constitutive practices, institutions, and networks.

Furthermore, I wish to enrich this social history of culture with elements of a cultural history of the social. This cultural history perspective seeks to identify collective interpretations of the social order by studying cultural manifestations of individuals or groups at a certain moment in time. Last but not least, this case study is inspired by studies about feminist culture that are based on a broader notion of culture as—in the words of one of the pioneers of cultural studies, Stuart Hall—a "distinct way of life of a group or class."[5] The works of Nancy Whittier and Verta Taylor about lesbian communities, and those of Leila Rupp about movement culture in the international women's movement at the turn of the nineteenth century to the twentieth, have demonstrated that movement culture is fundamental in the formation of collective identities because it gives room for sharing experiences and developing a sense of belongingness and common understanding.[6]

The works of one of the pioneers of a new cultural history of the social, Roger Chartier, have inspired an analysis that aims at understanding the relationship between cultural practices and identity formation. Developed in the productive exchange with Anglo-Saxon representatives of cultural history,[7] his approach seems particularly useful when it comes to identifying the cultural effects of collective practices within a social movement. Chartier's focus is on cultural practices that engage people in the making, diffusion, and reception of literary works. From this point of view, the content of a literary oeuvre is not independent from the conditions under which readers make sense of what they read. According to Chartier, the materiality of a text and the conditions under which it circulates are very important factors. Texts can have different meanings in different social contexts. In other words: the many and various meanings of a text depend on the ways and situations in which it is received. Although Chartier's focus is on early modern cultural history, his approach provides interesting suggestions for the study of contemporary cultural phenomena. The most striking of these is the notion that texts are at the same time products and producers of social differentiation. This has methodological implications for the issues discussed here: first of all, studying the material appearance of a given text may provide information about the public it is written for. Second, studying the materiality of a text may also inform us about the conditions under which it has been produced and the relationship between those who have participated in its production. And third, Chartier argues that group identities ("interpretive communities") may result from literary practices.[8] If we understand literary practices as places and expressions of (collective) social identities, the analysis of these practices of literary production and reception can give us information about the identities that they represent. It is perhaps not texts as such that change society—in his famous book about the cultural origins of the French Revolution, Chartier states that "books do not make revolutions"[9]—but, rather, that the sociability that arises around their production and reception constitutes a new social reality. The following case studies focus on Zurich, one of the most important cities in Switzerland and a center of feminist activities and of the printing industry in the German-speaking part of the country. The main focus is on the movement's mouthpiece *Die FRAueZitig* (dialect for: "women's journal," also called FRAZ) alongside other kinds of publishing and literary activism.

"To Liberate Us from the Damages of the Masculine Colonisation of Our Culture"[10]: FRAZ

FRAZ was produced by a women's collective that was part of the *Frauenbefreiungsbewegung* (FBB) in Zurich, an association that served as social movement organization and coordinated the WLM in several places. On the Swiss level, the journal was an early example of a flourishing movement press of the second half of the 1970s. *De fil en aiguille* appeared in Geneva in 1973 but vanished shortly after. Actually, most other bulletins and newsletters in these early years were ephemeral, and only the ones that were supported by leftist parties or organizations survived longer, such as *Femmes en luttes* (Lausanne, from 1976 to 1981), close to the Maoists; *Emanzipation* (Basel, from 1975 to 1996), which was edited by dissident women of the communist party (*Progressive Frauen Schweiz,* later OFRA); or *Tout va bien,* organ of the radical left in Geneva in which women's groups published occasionally.[11] Also compared to the developments in neighbor countries, *FRAZ* was an early and relatively durable publishing experience. Out of the more than fifty bulletins that appeared in the context of the French WLM between 1971 and 1982, only ten came out before 1975.[12] The two most successful German feminist magazines *Courage* and *Emma* started in 1976 and 1977 only,[13] whereas the first number of *FRAZ* was published in the summer of 1975. It was distributed hand-to-hand in and around the city, especially in places where women would meet, such as the women's community center that had opened in 1974, and women's bars. Initially, the journal appeared on a monthly basis, but this frequency was soon reduced to once every three months.

FRAZ was to "recognize, put into words and impart the desires of all women."[14] The journal provided information about what was new in the WLM, published reports of feminist events, gave space to discussions about feminist theory and everyday politics, reported on self-help and consciousness-raising groups, and reproduced short stories, poems, pictures, and cartoons. The journal itself can be considered to be a product of feminist activism. Its mode of production was collective and aimed to include as many voices from the movement as possible. Therefore, the task of the journal collective was primarily to coordinate contributions from different groups or individuals and to fill the recurring columns such as "News from the Movement" or "Women's Histories" (which later became "Women Write"). Each edition of the journal took a specific topic as a theme, and production was passed around the various member groups of the FBB. For example, the group Women's Shelter prepared the issue about violence and women's shelters, the abortion group the special issue about contraception and abortion, and so on. The journal collective faced a deep crisis in 1981–82 and altered its composition as well as its ways of working. But it kept a decentralized mode of organization that was based on voluntary, unpaid, and informal work.[15]

The mode of organization of *FRAZ* hints at the function that literary activities had in the WLM: women's writing and literary activities stimulated processes of collectivization. Although changes in the composition of the journal group took place, the collective became a fixed institution within the movement. Its decentralized mode of organization was not without conflict, but it reflected the self-understanding of the WLM as a democratic place where, theoretically, every woman would express herself. Producing the journal effected the commitment of groups and individuals to the movement.

Despite its universal aspirations to speak for *all* women, *FRAZ* was situated in a specific local context and social milieu. As much as it was a source of solidarity and provided women a space to express themselves, to share thoughts and sentiments, it seems to have attracted women with a homogeneous set of social characteristics. In 1977 a handful of FBB activists started an internal survey in order to bring out information about the social background of FBB activists and their expectations as to the movement. *FRAZ* published the results of the survey in two parts in summer 1977 and autumn 1978.[16] According to the evaluation of the results, the FBB was composed of one-third women in education and training, one-half in part or full-time employment—quotas far beyond the national average of women in employment[17]—and under 5 percent housewives and pensioners. More than eight out of ten women were under thirty-six and more than seven out of ten did not have children. A total of 87 percent of the women were living in the central areas of the city of Zurich; only 12 percent were coming from the wider agglomeration.

One might object that only women inclined to sociological considerations and reflexive thinking, and disposing of personal autonomy over time and space, did complete the questionnaires and that the survey would have had other results if more activists had responded. But if we consider completing a questionnaire as an act of expressing one's own belonging to the movement, if furthermore we think that the silent mass of women who did not respond to the survey did either not get the questionnaire that was sent by mail and distributed at meetings or was not interested in giving an opinion on the movement (the second part of the question was dedicated to women's expectations to and criticism on the movement), then the evaluation gives a relatively clear idea of who was inside the circles of the more active members and attracted to its public voice, *FRAZ*: young, urban (which here means living in the city of Zurich), well-educated, and professional women. These findings correspond with a recent prosopographical analysis of the Swiss adherents of the 1968 protest movements, WLM included, showing that the majority of the movement's activists had an access to educational privilege.[18]

Interestingly enough the 1977 survey did not ask for the national/ethnic background of FBB members. Even if the social movements of the late 1960s and 1970s in Switzerland—of which women's liberation was part—did not, as in other countries, engage in a discussion around the impact of "race," they were sensible to considerations about global (in)justice.[19] *FRAZ* itself talked at several occasions about "Women in the Third World."[20] Furthermore xenophobia was an important issue of public debate in Switzerland in the 1970s, especially since the Swiss electorate witnessed the xenophobic campaign in favor of the the right-wing popular initiative "against foreign influence," also called—referring to the main leader of the campaign—"Schwarzenbach-Initiative" in 1970. The initiative was rejected, but no fewer than 46 percent voted in favor of it. Considering the impact of "race" or nationality in the composition of the movement would therefore have been an option for the organizers of the survey. But either it did not occur to them because foreigners were the exception in the movement and neither nationality nor ethnicity were considered as a category that "mattered"[21] or they avoided such questions on national origin and ethnicity because they did not want to *make* it a category that "mattered."

Unfortunately data was also not collected about the linguistic background that is so important in Switzerland, where four national languages coexist and where the "Schwiizerdütsch" (Swiss-German dialect) makes it difficult for people from other areas (be it the French, Italian, or Raetho-Rumansh speaking areas of Switzerland or foreign countries) to fully integrate from the point of view of language skills. We can say that literary activities not only were the expression of a socially relative homogeneous movement but that they also served as reinforcement for the boundaries of class, nationality/ethnicity, and, what is important in the multilingual context of Switzerland, of mother tongue.

If the *content* of the journal's content gives us a picture of the various activities and opinions in the movement, then the *form* of its content allows us to draw some further conclusions about the processes of inclusion and exclusion at work as to the production of the journal. Most of the texts were written in standard German, according to the linguistic convention that dialect, which substantially differs from High German, was (and still is) mainly an oral means of expression. Some shorter and personal texts by individuals, such as poems, where nevertheless written in dialect. Many of the texts had an experimental character that included leaving blank spaces through ellipses, aposiopesis, or sudden change of subject matter. This was not only the case for the numerous poems readers sent but also for prose. Such creative features point to the authors' and journal makers' horizon of expectations. For them, writing and collecting were not the only forms of an intense involvement with ideas about and from women: reading, hearing, and discussing were also perceived as crucial in the collective learning process. Thus, participation was very important: the journal collective appealed regularly to its readers to send texts, to take responsibility of one issue, or to join the journal collective. Feminist activists concerned with women's writing (and women's history) were aware of the traditional eighteenth- and nineteenth-century concept of writing as a means of individual and hidden resistance by daughters of the bourgeoisie. They explicitly referred to women's traditional affinity toward writing and reading, as evidenced by the journal collective's special issue "Weiber and Wörter" (Women and Words) in summer 1988. "Many of our readers," it was said in a draft paper, "are at the same time writers. Most women write (especially intimate forms such as diaries and letters) and they have, because of their female education, a very special relationship with writing."[22] But female writing in the 1970s was not perceived as an individual subversion, not as—to take the words of Claudia Honegger and Bettina Heintz—"Listen der Ohnmacht"[23] but, rather, as a form of collective "empowerment." Readers got information about the possibilities of contributing articles ("How does one make the journal?"[24]) and given tips such as, "Instead of marking mistakes by hand, it is better to rewrite the whole line. We can cut out those erroneous passages when we work on the lay-out." Nevertheless, not all readers were enthusiastic about the outcome. In 1978 a reader named "Gabi" complained about the journal's style: "I see myself as a feminist, even if I am not so active and politically involved as you are. I do not swamp my environment with words of foreign origin and technical terms, as to be understood only by some 'elected' people. The way you address us (normal) women is designed to intimidate us. How can we employees, house-wives, waitresses etc. understand the slang of intellectuals, if we do not understand what we read?"[25] She went on criticizing the self-centered character of the journal, which, from her point of view, was limited to dealing with the problems of well-educated women in the city who had no idea what was going on in the countryside where taking the pill still was a "secret to be kept" and where women who undertook paid employment were considered as "greedy chicks."

As the example of the *FRAZ* shows, literary activities had an inclusive and at the same time still an exclusive function within the WLM in Switzerland. Due to the practice of signing an article only with the first name or not at all, we know little about the concrete social/linguistic/ethnical/national background of most of the authors of the journal. But it seems likely that language skills served as one criteria of selection for publication. In some respects, however, the barrier for participation was relatively low: to write, read, take and draw pictures, and to produce the journal technically was considered a collective practice where the lack of language skills of some could be adjusted by others. Writing in High German allowed the integration of women from German-speaking countries or those—Swiss or not—who had learned German as a foreign language at school or university. For some of them, the written culture might have been more easily accessible than the oral culture, which emphasized, due to the use of dialect, the differences between locals and "strangers." The very nature of the printed texts itself was such as to valorize personal experience in preference to stylistically perfect journalistic and literary products.

Women's Bookshops

The women's journal provided information about many other literary activities, such as the setting up of a women's library group, workshops on creative writing, or a theater group in the women's community center. All these activities aimed at opening spaces where women could express themselves freely and discover female history and traditions of thinking, writing, reading and editing. So did the women's bookshops that began to open in several Swiss cities, be it in the French- or German-speaking areas or, with some delay, in Ticino.[26] The first of these enterprises started in Zurich in October 1976. When the women's bookshop opened in the second district of Zurich not far from the city center, its collaborators—a collective of six (in 1978 reduced to four) women who were committed to women's liberation—explained in an interview that they wanted to make books from and about women accessible to a wider public.[27] Some of them worked in the collective because they wanted to be part of a project with other women, and the bookshop project was simply somewhere that they could realize this desire. Others had been professionally involved in producing and selling books before and tried to bring together their interest for literature and their feminist activism. The feminist bookshops wanted to address women who were close to the WLM but also women of the neighborhood. Offering books and advice about new or interesting publications about the "women's question" was one aim of the feminist bookshops. Danièle Lenzin, a member of the alternative bookshop *Atropa* in Winterthur, a smaller city not far from Zurich, recalled that one of the principal motivations to work there was to be able "to sell books that I found to be significant and smart."[28] The Zurich collective produced a biannual newsletter in order to present new publications; it also was involved in book presentations and other literary events that could not take place in the shop itself because of a lack of space, and it offered a book-shipping service all over German-speaking Switzerland. This service was crucial to readers of lesbian literature, as it was not available in ordinary libraries and bookshops, especially in rural areas, and customers did not dare to order it. Another aim was to get customers to think about women's concerns, desires, and emancipation. The women's bookshop in Zurich, in similar ways to its counterparts in Geneva, Lausanne, Lugano, or Baden, understood itself as a meeting and information point, a space of exchange not only for books but also for ideas and opinions: "A center of the cultural life in the city"[29] as well as a contribution to feminist consciousness-raising.

In the first years, those bookshops existed thanks to private investment and donations. Danièle Lenzin spoke about the difficulties of getting the starting capital together: "Somehow it worked out." Founded in 1978, *L'inédite* in Geneva was also based on private investment (in time and money).[30] The Zurich bookshop faced a crisis in 1981 and was overtaken by a new owner who invested private capital in order to save the company. The bookshop collectives were, like *FRAZ,* organized around unpaid and voluntary work and its members were supposed to earn their living elsewhere. Working for the bookshop was still "luxury" in the beginning of the 1980s because the salary was so low.[31] Research on the social composition of the bookshop collectives still has to be done, but the requirement for un- and low-paid labor—hence for resources as to time and money—suggests that class had an impact, as did language skills and the location to/in the city centers.

To summarize, we can say that in the 1970s women's writing was a central element of the WLM and contributed to collective identity formation by fostering processes of identification; providing meeting places, organizational structures, networks, and movement organs; enabling discussion of previously taboo subjects such as female sexuality, lesbianism, and abortion; and, by that, giving space to a female expert culture. Female writing both strengthened the movement internally and made it visible to the external world. The women's journal as well as the bookshops served as interface between "insiders" and the movement's environment. Such activities contributed to the expansion of unifying ideas and concepts that were important to the collective identity of the movement. By purpose or not, the literary activities were also a means of social homogenization of the movement. Mobilizing processes of social movements have per se an ambiguous character:

they need to address people in very concrete situations, but by doing so, they may miss the needs of other. The WLM could not escape from that.

These features of female writing were characteristic of the 1970s. Such texts written by female authors replaced the texts, which had been popular in the pre-1968 era, written about women by men, as, for example, the *Kinsey Report* on female sexual behavior (1953), August Bebel's *Women and Socialism* (1879), or Wilhelm Reich's works on the *Sexual Revolution* (1966). They also differed from what was traditionally perceived as "women's literature": popular fiction or advice literature on childcare, household, or marriage counseling. Women were now interested in literary activities that would reflect women's perspectives, rather than men's. Studying literary activities in the second half of the eighties reveals another shift in women's writing. The history of the women's publishing company *eFeF* demonstrates these changes well.

The women's publishing company *eFeF*

During the late 1970s and the 1980s, several nonconventional publishing houses came into existence in Switzerland that were willing to give a voice to critical authors—be it historians or sociologists, poets or storytellers—who would not have a chance to get published in the traditional editorial landscape. *Limmat Verlag* was founded in 1975 and made its appearance with a volume on the Swiss labor movement; the same year, *Zoé* opened in Geneva; *Rotpunkt* ("Red Spot") emerged in 1976 on the initiative of the *Progressive Organisationen Schweiz,* a young left-wing party; *Chronos—Verlag für Geschichte* ("Editing House for History") was brought to life in 1985 by young academics belonging to a new generation of critical historians. It was the time when also more classical publishing houses, such as, for the German-speaking public, *Fischer,* established women's series ("Die Frau in der Gesellschaft"), started to reprint "emancipative" literature like Simone de Beauvoir's *Le deuxième sexe* or Virginia Woolf's *A Room of One's Own* in cheap paperback versions and published promising works of feminist thinkers like Luise Pusch's *Deutsch als Männersprache.* Smaller publishers were skeptical about this new discovery of women as consumers of books. They had more idealistic motives, even if they could not escape from business logics.

The women's publishing company *eFeF* was officially founded in 1988 and still exists 25 years later. Its most successful sale was the new edition of *Frauen im Laufgitter* (literally "Women in Playpens"), a near-forgotten work about the situation of women in Swiss society. The first edition of this book by Iris von Roten was published at the end of the 1950s, but at the time it received extremely negative reviews. When it appeared in a new edition in

1991,[32] it became a best seller that gave its publishers financial independence for some years.

The founding of the women's publishing company (men were not invited to participate) was preceded by several years of preparation. I interviewed one of the founding members, Heidi Lauper, who had then been a thirty-year-old student of German philology. She remembered sitting at a kitchen table with Brigitte Ebersbach, a fellow student from Germany, and talking about the idea again and again. Lauper had studied for some years at the Free University in West Berlin and observed the local feminist scene closely. When she returned to Bern in 1983, she became engaged in feminist activities and soon had the idea of opening a publishing house for women. At the same time, women in the arts and in academia were becoming increasingly aware of discrimination against them, as, despite their growing number and capacities, their research remained unknown, and their manuscripts unnoticed. In 1983 the association *Women, Feminism, Research* (*FemWiss*) was launched. *FemWiss* arranged several workshops that centered on women's scientific writing and organized the national conference "From Manuscript to Publication," which took place in Bern in 1986. It was here that Heidi Lauper and Brigitte Ebersbach met women with experience of how to run a publishing company. In 1987 five women founded *eFeF* (standing for "five women"), and in 1988 the publishing company was officially registered. The first two books came out in autumn 1988: a travel report and an investigation into women struggling for education.[33]

The collaboration with women in academia remained very important for *eFeF* as some members of the company were also engaged in *FemWiss.* Soon, *FemWiss* started a series within *eFeF* entitled "Schriftenreihe feministische Wissenschaft" that aimed to introduce a feminist perspective in scientific work. Apart from these scientific works, the publication of *eFeF* was many and varied, and included (auto)biographies, travel reports, works focused on women of other cultures, and, rather sporadically, collections of stories or poems. Several women interviewed claimed that it was difficult to find fictional texts that would satisfy the publisher's quality standards. Many manuscripts were returned unpublished to their authors. The editorial and layout standards were also high: "We did not want to give the expression of a handmade outfit. We wanted to have a professional appearance, to leave our own little world and go right to the center of the publishing business."[34]

In the first years of *eFeF,* none of the women engaged in the publishing company were paid. Enthusiasm and income from other jobs were the basis on which collective publishing activities were founded. In 1989 the company underwent its first financial crisis. Shortly after, some of the founding members left the company, declaring that the principle of unpaid work was no longer acceptable to them. In the mid-1990s the publishing company was completely restructured and left in the hands of Lilian Studer, a philologist, who served as executive director until 2001. At that time the responsibility for company—which for several years had been in the red—went to Doris Stump as main editor. She was a sociodemocratic politician and author of several books about female writers in Swiss literature. As a politician, Stump was fighting for a nondiscriminatory language in public administration.

What does this short history of a publishing company reveal about the literary activities of feminist activists since the mid-1980s? First, it is important to state that the publishing company operated in a social context that was, strictly speaking, no longer that of a social movement. The cycle of mobilization that brought the WLM into life changed its face at the end of the 1970s. It left behind networks of rather specialized projects, groups, and associations that would eventually collaborate at certain moments but that were not involved in a continued collective mobilization process. I would argue that *eFeF* was one of them. Its mode of organization and ideals came from the WLM of the 1970s, especially in its use of direct democracy in decision-taking, use of volunteer labor, and emphasis on female autonomy. The feminist networks of the seventies were also important for the company's day-to-day-business of finding authors or collaborators, accessing markets, and placing advertisements. But in contrast to female writing in the 1970s, for the publishing company, the search for a female identity was no longer a central concern. The aim of publishing texts written by women was to make them accessible to a wider public that was not necessarily entirely female. "We wanted," said one of the company members, "to make public what women write, how they think and act—yesterday and today."

Compared to the literary activities of the 1970s, the publishing company was much more professional. Its collaborators were bound by professional ethics, which were influenced by opinions of the dominant male culture as to what constituted "good literature" and a "good book." To want to express oneself as a woman was not a sufficient reason to be considered for publishing. The company's overall aim was to show the diversity of female literary expression in the past and in the present, to provide women's knowledge and expertise, to foster the exchange of information, and to rediscover feminist foremothers in order to strengthen women's self-confidence.

Conclusion

Literary activities were critical for the WLM's collective identity-formation process. Female writing and its associated cultural practices were perceived as collective activities and provided spaces were women could meet, think, and discuss. Those spaces, against their intention, were not open to every woman the same way. They assumed a great deal of economic independency, autonomy over time, and language skills. Still, the barrier was set low: the collective approach could, to a certain degree, help to compensate a lack of time, language skill, or other element. Over time, a shift took place in the perception of the role that female writing should play in the larger project of women's liberation. Whereas in the 1970s female writing was primarily associated with self-discovery and consciousness-raising within the women's liberation movement, the literary activities of the late 1980s aimed to communicate the diversity of women's creativity and knowledge to a wider public.

To conclude, I wish to discuss five aspects related to the question about the function of female writing for the WLM and its impact.

First, this essay has argued that female writing contributed to the formation of feminism as a social movement in the 1970s. As producers, distributors, and readers of texts by and about women, feminists took part in community-building processes. Building groups and networks around female writing allowed women to both mentally conceive of themselves as political subjects and to become publically visible as a collective social force. This was also the case on a transnational level.

Second, feminists involved with these writing and publishing practices brought some important and long-forgotten texts by women to light and built a corpus of feminist reference works that ranged from Anaïs Nin to Doris Lessing, Iris von Rothen, and Simone de Beauvoir. In doing this, the WLM inscribed itself in a long-standing tradition of female writing that gave a historical dimension to their fight.

Third, the spontaneous and informally constructed publishing, reading, and writing communities aimed to include women regardless of their social origin. For example, the members of the journal collective—as well as those of *eFeF*—tried to keep the prices of their literary products as low as possible by refusing payment. The use of the women's library in the Zurich Women's Community Centre was free in order to grant wider access to literary products/books and periodicals. However, it was mostly younger, well-educated, and childless women from nonimmigrant backgrounds that joined the movement and in particular its literary activities. Despite of an explicit all-welcome-policy, participation required certain education and language skills and accessibility was therefore limited.

Fourth, the establishment of a small number of women's publishing groups has allowed women's writing, in the long term, to enrich the publishing landscape. Traditional publishing houses have also adapted their literary program to the new demand and created women's book series, mostly in the form of cheap paperback editions. Overall, literary works written by women have become more visible and accessible, even while representatives of the feminist book scene reproach commercial publishing houses for being interested in financial gain.

Fifth, whether women as authors have found more literary appreciation than before is still open to debate. Additionally, it is also unclear whether Swiss literary institutions—such as the *Solothurner Literaturtage*—have become more accessible to women. But it seems clear that female writing has entered the domain of the university, developed new scholarly perspectives, and defined new objects of investigation, especially in the humanities. Feminist linguistic and literary criticism is now found even in the guidelines for institutional language. The close connection between women in academia and feminist publication activities, so crucial from the very beginning of the women's liberation movement, has clearly had significant impact here.

Of course the transformation of perception that the WLM caused was only made possible by changes that had taken place in society as a whole: the higher level of women's education, the slow but growing female participation in the Swiss workforce, and changes in demographic patterns. In this, the literary activities of women's liberation were a result of the very same processes that they tried to make sense of; they attempted to understand these changes, not least by looking back to older female writers and literary traditions. "When you look through the lens of feminism," said one of the founders of *eFeF*, "the horizon is getting wider." To have brought feminist perspectives into the academy, print culture, the language of public institutions, and literature is, without doubt, a direct effect of the literary activism of the WLM.

Kristina Schulz, PhD, is Senior Lecturer for Contemporary History and Migration History at the University of Bern. She is a specialist of Western feminist history in comparative perspective and is the author of a book on the French and German WLM: *"Der lange Atem der Provokation": Die Frauenbewegung in der Bundesrepublik und in Frankreich (1968–1976).* Together with Leena Schmitter and Sarah Kiani she published a source and archive guide about the Swiss women's liberation movement in 2014. With Magda Kaspar she is currently preparing an audio archive and interactive website about the feminist movement in Switzerland from the 1970s to the present (*Women's Movement 2.0*).

Notes

1. The "Porträt des eFeF Verlag" stems from the private archive of Heidi Lauper. It is not dated but must have been written around 1994, just before Liliane Studer took over the publishing house in 1995.

2. In fact there was a previous "one-woman enterprise" run by Brigit Keller, but this never became professional.
3. The Swiss women's liberation movement has been mainly studied from local perspectives. Literary activities so far have only been looked at in passing. See for exemple: Ruth Ammann, *Politische Identitäten im Wandel: Lesbisch-feministisch bewegte Frauen in Bern 1975 bis 1993* (Nordhausen: Traugott Bautz, 2009); Leena Schmitter, *"Sex Wars": Feminismus und Pornographie in der Deutschschweiz (1975–1992)* (Nordhausen: Traugott Bautz, 2010); Carole Villiger, *"Notre ventre, leur loi!" Le Mouvement de Libération des Femmes de Genève* (Neuchâtel: Editions Alphil, 2009); Julie De Dardel, *Révolution sexuelle et mouvement de libération des femmes à Genève (1970–1977)* (Lausanne: Antipodes, 2007). For an overview, see Kristina Schulz, "Neue Frauenbewegung in der Schweiz: Vorwort zum Themenschwerpunkt," *Schweizerische Zeitschrift für Geschichte* 57 (2007): 237–42.
4. Jennifer Earl, "The Cultural Consequences of Social Movements," in *The Blackwell Companion to Social Movements,* ed. David Snow, Sarah Soule, and Hanspeter Kriesi (Oxford: Blackwell, 2004), 509–30.
5. See Colin Sparks, "Stuart Hall, Cultural Studies, and Marxism," in *Critical Dialogues in Cultural Studies,* ed. David Morley and Chen Kuang Hsing (New York: Routledge, 1996), 71–102.
6. Verta Taylor and Nancy Whittier, "Analytical Approaches to Social Movement Culture: The Culture of the Women's Movement," in *Social Movements and Culture,* ed. Hank Johnston and Bert Klandermans (Minneapolis: University of Minnesota Press, 1995), 163–87; Leila Rupp and Verta Taylor, "Loving Internationalism: The Emotion Culture of Transnational Women's Organizations (1888–1945)," *Mobilization* 7 (2002): 141–58.
7. Robert Darnton's works (and mostly *The Great Cat Massacre and Other Episodes in French Cultural History* [New York: Basic Books, 1984]) have been particularly important for Roger Chartier; cf. Pierre Bourdieu, Roger Chartier, Robert Darnton, "Dialogue à propos de l'histoire culturelle," *Actes de la Recherche en Sciences Sociales* 59 (1985): 86–93. The list of works about the history of books and printing culture is endless; for an overview cf. Leslie Howsam, "Old Books and New Historians: An Orientation on Book and Print Culture" (Toronto: University of Toronto Press, 2006). Interestingly enough, most of the authors concentrate on the early modern period. Because of Switzerland's multilingual situation, regional studies, often focused on one editor, have been given precedence before all-encompassing overviews. Concerning the development of the editing industry in the French-speaking part of Switzerland, cf. François Vallotton, *L'édition romande et ses acteurs 1850–1920* (Geneva: Slatkine, 2001).
8. Roger Chartier, "Popular Appropriations: The Readers and Their Books," in *Forms and Meanings: Texts, Performances and Audiences from Codex to Computer* (Philadelphia: University of Pennsylvania Press, 1995), 83–97; Roger Chartier, *The Order of Books: Readers, Authors, and Libraries in Europe between the Fourteenth and Eighteenth Centuries* (Cambridge: Cambridge University Press, 1994).
9. Roger Chartier, *The Cultural Origins of the French Revolution* (Durham, NC: Duke University Press, 1992).
10. "Zur Befreiung von maskulinen Kolonisationsschäden an unserer Kultur," *FRAZ* 12 (1978): 7.

11. Rare exceptions were part of the lesbian movement, such as *Lesbenfront* (Zurich, 1975–83), which became *Frau ohne Herz* (1984–95), and *Clitt 007: Concentré Lesbien Irréstiblement Toxique* (Geneva 1981–86). For a complete account of the feminist press in Switzerland, see Kristina Schulz, Leena Schmitter, and Sarah Kiani, *Frauen in Bewegung: Die Schweiz seit 1968. Dokumente. Analysen. Archive. Bibliographie* (Baden: hier + jetzt, 2014).
12. Chantal Bertrand-Jennings, "La presse des mouvements de libération des femmes en France de 1971 à 1982," in *Féminité, Subversion, Ecriture,* ed. Suzanne Lamy and Irène Pagès (Toronto: Les editions du remue-ménage, 1983), 15–49.
13. In contrast, the *Frauenzeitung: Frauen gemeinsam sind stark* was edited in turn by women's liberation groups all over West Germany from 1973 on. Whereas the similarity in the title suggests a direct relation between the Swiss Frauezitig and the German Frauenzeitung, I was not able to find further evidence, such as direct contacts or personal links.
14. "Warum eine Zeitung," *FRAZ* 1 (1975): front cover.
15. The *Frauezitig* preceded the *FRAueZitig* (also, FRAZ), which appeared until recently. After the 1981 crises, the journal stabilized itself as "Organ from and for Swiss Feminists," and no longer as the institutional mouthpiece of the FBB in Zurich.
16. "FBB intern. Fragen und Gedanken zum heutigen Stand der FBB," *FRAZ* 8 (1977): 21–22, and 10 (1978): 30–32. The number of FBB members was estimated around four hundred. Slightly over one-third of the questionnaires (126) were returned filled out.
17. As of 1977, 40.5 percent of all women (from fifteen years on) in Switzerland were employed (six hours or more/week), most of them in low-qualified part-time jobs. Source: Bundesamt für Statistik: Brutto- und Standartisierte Erwerbsquoten nach Geschlecht, Nationalität, http://www.bfs.admin.ch/bfs/portal/de/index/themen/03/02/blank/data/03.Document.100672.xlsA (accessed January 1, 2014).
18. Renate Schär and Nuno Pereira, "Soixant-huidardes helvétiques : Etude prosopographique," *Le mouvement social* 239 (2012): 9–23.
19. Konrad J. Kuhn, *Entwicklungspolitische Solidarität: die Dritte-Welt-Bewegung in der Schweiz zwischen Kritik und Politik 1975–1992* (Zurich: Chronos, 2011); Nicole Peter, "'Die Utopie ist ein Teil der Wirklichkeit': Implikationen des schweizerischen Drittweltdiskurses der 1960er Jahre," in *1968–1978: Ein bewegtes Jahrzehnt in der Schweiz,* ed. Janick Marina Schaufelbuehl (Zurich: Chronos, 2009), 137–46.
20. Quoted here from *FRAZ* 8 (1977): 6–17.
21. Schär/Perreira's collected data show that more than 90 percent of the 1968 protest movement in Switzerland was of Swiss nationality.
22. "Weiber und Wörter—Frauen machen Literatur in der Schweiz. Konzept der FRAueZitig Nr. 26" (June–September 1988), SozArch, AR 465.20.6.
23. Claudia Honegger and Bettina Heintz, *Listen der Ohnmacht: Zur Sozialgeschichte weiblicher Widerstandsformen* (Frankfurt: Europäische Verlagsanstalt, 1981). Might be translated as "Cunnings of the powerless."
24. Back cover of the first number of the *FRAZ* 1 (1975): 16.
25. *FRAZ* 11 (1978): 46. The following quotes come from here.
26. The women's bookshop *Clexidra* opened in Lugano in 1989. Many activists from Ticino were oriented toward Milano where a literary scene developed within a broad feminist subculture. Cf. Anna Rita Calabrò and Laura Grasso, *Dal movimento*

femminista al femminismo diffuso Storie e percorsi a Milano dagli anni 60 agli anni 80 (Milano: F. Angeli, 1985).
27. "Frauenbuchladen," *FRAZ* 5 (1976): 17–18.
28. Danièle Lenzin, interview with author, June 5, 2012, in Bern. Interestingly enough, *Atropa*—which was named after a toxic plant causing delirium and hallucinations—was a mixed but decisively alternative project with a large feminist offer.
29. Ibid., 18.
30. "Librairie L'inédite: Bonnes feuilles," *Le Courrier,* March 3, 2007.
31. This was confirmed in several interviews I made with members of women's bookshops' collectives in the course of 2012–14 in Zurich and Bern. On this aspect see also Lucy Delap, "Feminist Bookshops, Reading Cultures and the Women's Liberation Movement in Great Britain, c. 1974-2000," *History Workshop* 81 (2016): 171–196.
32. Iris von Rothen, *Frauen im Laufgitter: Offene Worte zur Stellung der Frau* (Zurich: eFeF, 1991).
33. Verein Feministische Wissenschaft, *Ebenso neu als kühn: 120 Jahre Frauenstudium an der Universität Zürich* (Zurich: eFeF, 1988).
34. Heidi Lauper, interview with author, January 12, 2012, in Bern.

Bibliography

Ammann, Ruth. *Politische Identitäten im Wandel: Lesbisch-feministisch bewegte Frauen in Bern 1975 bis 1993.* Nordhausen: Traugott Bautz, 2009.

Bertrand-Jennings, Chantal. "La presse des mouvements de libération des femmes en France de 1971 à 1982." In *Féminité, Subversion, Ecriture,* edited by Suzanne Lamy and Irène Pagès, 15–49. Toronto: Les editions du remue-ménage, 1983.

Bourdieu, Pierre, Roger Chartier, and Robert Darnton. "Dialogue à propos de l'histoire culturelle." *Actes de la Recherche en Sciences Sociales* 59 (1985): 86–93.

Calabrò, Anna Rita, and Laura Grasso. *Dal movimento femminista al femminismo diffuso Storie e percorsi a Milano dagli anni 60 agli anni 80.* Milano: F. Angeli, 1985.

Chartier, Roger. *The Cultural Origins of the French Revolution.* Durham, NC: Duke University Press, 1992.

———. *The Order of Books: Readers, Authors, and Libraries in Europe between the Fourteenth and Eighteenth Centuries.* Cambridge: Cambridge University Press 1994.

———. "Popular Appropriations: The Readers and Their Books." In *Forms and Meanings: Texts, Performances and Audiences from Codex to Computer.* Philadelphia: University of Pennsylvania Press, 1995, 83–97.

Dardel, Julie de. *Révolution sexuelle et mouvement de libération des femmes à Genève (1970–1977).* Lausanne: Antipodes, 2007.

Darnton, Robert. *The Great Cat Massacre and Other Episodes in French Cultural History.* New York: Basic Books, 1984.

Delap, Lucy, "Feminist Bookshops, Reading Culture and the Women's Liberation Movement in Great Britain, c. 1974-2000." *History Workshop* 81 (2016): 171–196.

Earl, Jennifer. "The Cultural Consequences of Social Movements." In *The Blackwell Companion to Social Movements,* edited by David Snow, Sarah Soule, and Hanspeter Kriesi, 509–30. Oxford: Blackwell, 2004.

Honegger, Claudia, and Bettina Heintz. *Listen der Ohnmacht: Zur Sozialgeschichte weiblicher Widerstandsformen.* Frankfurt: Europäische Verlagsanstalt, 1981.

Howsam, Leslie. *Old Books and New Historians: An Orientation on Book and Print Culture.* Toronto: University of Toronto Press, 2006.

Kuhn, Konrad J. *Entwicklungspolitische Solidarität: die Dritte-Welt-Bewegung in der Schweiz zwischen Kritik und Politik 1975–1992.* Zurich: Chronos, 2011.

Peter, Nicole. "'Die Utopie ist ein Teil der Wirklichkeit': Implikationen des schweizerischen Drittweltdiskurses der 1960er Jahre." In *1968–1978: Ein bewegtes Jahrzehnt in der Schweiz,* edited by Janick Marina Schaufelbuehl, 137–46. Zurich: Chronos, 2009.

Rothen, Iris von. *Frauen im Laufgitter: Offene Worte zur Stellung der Frau.* Zurich: eFeF, 1991.

Rupp, Leila, and Verta Taylor. "Loving Internationalism: The Emotion Culture of Transnational Women's Organizations (1888–1945)." *Mobilization* 7 (2002): 141–58.

Schär, Renate, and Nuno Pereira. "Soixant-huidardes helvétiques: Etude prosopographique." *Le mouvement social* 239 (2012): 9–23.

Schmitter, Leena. *"Sex Wars": Feminismus und Pornographie in der Deutschschweiz (1975–1992).* Nordhausen: Traugott Bautz, 2010.

Schulz, Kristina. "Neue Frauenbewegung in der Schweiz: Vorwort zum Themenschwerpunkt." *Schweizerischen Zeitschrift für Geschichte* 57 (2007): 237–42.

Schulz, Kristina, Leena Schmitter, and Sarah Kiani. *Frauen in Bewegung: Die Schweiz seit 1968. Dokumente. Analysen. Archive. Bibliographie.* Baden: hier + jetzt, 2014.

Sparks, Colin. "Stuart Hall, Cultural Studies, and Marxism." In *Critical Dialogues in Cultural Studies,* edited by David Morley and Chen Kuang Hsing, 71–102. New York: Routledge, 1996.

Taylor, Verta, and Nancy Whittier. "Analytical Approaches to Social Movement Culture: The Culture of the Women's Movement." In *Social Movements and Culture,* edited by Hank Johnston and Bert Klandermans, 163–87. Minneapolis: University of Minnesota Press, 1995.

Vallotton, François. *L'édition romande et ses acteurs 1850–1920.* Geneva: Slatkine, 2001.

Verein Feministische Wissenschaft, *Ebenso neu als kühn: 120 Jahre Frauenstudium an der Universität Zürich.* Zurich: eFeF, 1988.

Villiger, Carole. *"Notre ventre, leur loi!" Le Mouvement de Libération des Femmes de Genève.* Neuchâtel: Editions Alphil, 2009.

Sources

"Weiber und Wörter—Frauen machen Literatur in der Schweiz. Konzept der FRAueZitig Nr. 26" (June–September 1988), SozArch, AR 465.20.6.

"Weiber und Wörter—Frauen machen Literatur in der Schweiz. Konzept der FRAueZitig Nr. 26" (June–September 1988), SozArch, AR 465.20.6.

Interview with Heidi Lauper, January 12, 2012, in Bern.

Interview with Danièle Lenzin, June 5, 2012, in Bern.

Chapter 6

Lesbian Vertigo

Living the Women's Liberation Movement on the Edge of Europe

Ana Margarida Dias Martins

In "The Invention of French Feminism: An Essential Move," Christine Delphy argues that French feminism was invented to legitimate the introduction on the Anglo-American scene of a specific brand of essentialism.[1] "French theory," Delphy argues, was constituted "as a 'whole' by a series of rhetorical maneuvers that use distortion and generalization, imperialism, and exoticism."[2] In her analysis of the relevance of national boundaries for the fabrication of this "whole," the critic outlines the ideological features of what she considers to be a construction (a biased version of reality) and an invention (a series of highly contentious theoretical statements) proposed under the guise of "French feminism." To Delphy, French feminism does not correspond to feminism from France, but rather to "a body of comments by Anglo and non-French writers" who conferred prestige on the *psy et po* faction of the French *Mouvement de Libération des Femmes.*[3]

Delphy's essay does not contemplate the consequences of this arguably biased politics of quotation for the marginal female voices that have been taken under the wing of those very subjects whose work was essentialized and endorsed by many Anglo-American feminists. If disparate theoretical ideas have been appropriated, labeled as "French" and as "feminist," and decontextualized by Anglo-American critics, where does that leave us in relation to those marginal subjects who have been object, at times, of "French feminist" appropriation? Are we to conclude, in the light of Delphy's analysis, that Portuguese-speaking women, such as Clarice Lispector from Brazil and the Three Marias from Portugal, whose work was enthusiastically and often imperialistically endorsed by canonical names such as Hélène Cixous and Monique Wittig respectively, are the objects of a double process of exoticization?[4] If this is the case, then surely national boundaries should not be discarded as easily as Delphy suggests, for they reveal the central role of supposedly marginal nations in confirming the theory boundaries of the white, or French and Anglo-American, women's liberation movement (WLM). In attempting to draw a line between "real" feminism from France and essentialism, Delphy minimizes the role of national boundaries in the fabrication of this "body of comments," stating that "inasmuch as there are, in feminism as elsewhere, definitional problems for borderline cases, these problems are always situated, precisely for this reason, at the margins, they do not touch on the core."[5] Here, Delphy not only defines "real" feminists as being above definitional problems but she also locates them spatially, by implying that they do not inhabit the margins.

In this essay, I want to suggest that what passes as "real feminism" in Delphy's article—the critic feels for Monique Wittig's work—is not above definitional problems. I contend that both the "invention" of French feminism and the supposedly "original" feminism from France have produced two distinct ideals of the female writing subject that could be said to police the entrance of marginal female voices into the feminist center(s) of canonical titles and theories: the bisexual mother epitomized by the work of Hélène Cixous, and the Lesbian Amazon championed by Monique Wittig.[6] In what follows, I propose to measure the impact of the latter female writing ideal from a Portuguese viewpoint by thinking through the relations of domination and subordination triggered by the second-wave community and experienced in Portugal, a small country situated in the Westernmost margins of Europe.[7]

The 1970s saw *Novas Cartas Portuguesas,* a book collectively written by Portuguese writers Maria Isabel Barreno, Maria Teresa Horta, and Maria Velho da Costa, censored by the Portuguese right-wing regime and fiercely defended by national and international feminist voices of the second wave.[8] The three women escaped jail terms of up to two years due to the support of Portuguese intellectuals, but it was mainly because of the involvement of prominent members of the French feminist movement, such as Simone de Beauvoir, Marguerite Duras, and Christiane Rochefort, who first publicized the case to a wider audience. The international crowds supporting the book and the Three Marias, as they came to be known, were, at best, fragmentary readers and, at worst, nonreaders of the text's transgressions. This was because no published translations of the book from the original Portuguese were available in the first two years of its notoriety. One consequence of this was the consolidation of the notion that Portuguese feminism was a simple variation of white feminisms. Another consequence was the emergence of a Portuguese nonfeminist discourse highlighting, as a reaction to reductive liberal feminist readings of *Novas Cartas,* what was specifically Portuguese and antifascist (i.e., nonfeminist) about the book.[9]

As several critics have argued, neither of these perceptions fully accounts for the kind of margin and center Portugal became in relation to the multiple and shifting feminist and linguistic cores and peripheries of the feminist community, which Delphy aims, in part, to account for in her article.[10] Building on this body of work, I want to further question dichotomic understandings of *Novas Cartas* by arguing that this publication, which solidified the development of a Portuguese feminist consciousness in the early 1970s, may have actively contributed to questioning the boundaries of what Delphy terms "real" feminism from France.

Graça Abranches has noted that "we [in Portugal] have much to learn from others, in other multiple locations. And much of our strength has come—and is coming—from non-paternalistic and non-imperialistic international cooperation."[11] In seeking to preserve the nonimperialistic "simultaneously other focus when reading Portuguese literature" defended by Abranches, I shall take as a case in point two foundational texts that stand today as cornerstones of Portuguese and Chicana literary history and feminist thought: the already mentioned *Novas Cartas*, and *Borderlands/La Frontera: The New Mestiza,* published by Chicana-Texana Gloria Anzaldúa in 1987.[12] My aim in drawing this comparison is twofold. As I problematize the view that *Novas Cartas* simply confirms white feminisms, I also ask what led to the theoretical canonization of Anzaldúa's text, and to the political reification of the Marias' publication, within the feminist community. It suits my purpose in this context to think in terms of obligations, agreements, and implicitly accepted sanctions for those who fail to conform to a community's sets of consensus regarding hegemonic subjects. My goal, therefore, is to focus on these women's honoring and dishonoring of some second-wave contract obligations, which may have aided the process of canonization (Anzaldúa) and subjection to the margins of theory-making (the Three Marias) by more central, canonical feminist voices.

As I compare Portuguese and Chicana traditions of writing resistance against more centralized feminist theory-making, I position the reception of *Novas Cartas* and *Borderlands* in relation to one canonical model of the idealized Lesbian writing subject that emerged in the late 1970s following the split of the French *Mouvement de Libération des Femmes* and the ensuing appropriation of its psychoanalytical-oriented French feminist faction by Anglo-American critics: the Lesbian Amazon promoted by Monique Wittig in clear opposition to the bisexual mother championed by Hélène Cixous. While both writing models view women's relation to the body as central in the fight to overcome oppression, they differ considerably in their perceptions of one's relation to the female body. As noted by Ann Rosalind Jones,

Cixous and Wittig "share a common opponent, masculinist thinking [and Western culture as fundamentally oppressive], but they envision different modes of resisting and moving beyond it."[13] In "The Laugh of the Medusa," Cixous proclaims a turn to *féminité* as a challenge to male-centered thinking. To Cixous, writing the body involves not only writing as a mother—"There is always within her at least a little of that good mother's milk"—but also a return to a lost bisexuality on which "every subject not enclosed in the false theatre of phallocentric representationalism has founded his/her erotic universe."[14] It is by defending a return to this model of bisexuality, "which doesn't annul differences but stirs them up," that Cixous concludes: "woman is bisexual."[15] In contrast with the "bisexual mother" ideal's view of the world, and against its tendency to delve deep into an analysis of female difference, another faction of the MLF put forward an equally radical understanding of the idealized feminist subject, which questioned the very notion that there are men and women. Monique Wittig's materialist approach illustrates this particularly well, calling for a total refusal of an original position written in the language of domination, and refining the ideal of the Lesbian Amazon in her creative and critical writings. As Wittig argues, "a materialist feminist approach shows that what we take for the cause or origin of oppression is in fact only the mark imposed by the oppressor: the 'myth of woman,' of women."[16] If, according to Cixous, the sexual contract may be broken only by rescuing the feminine and using it as a space of subversion, for Wittig the sexual contract is heterosexuality itself, and therefore needs to be assaulted from what she terms a Lesbian point of view: "Lesbian is the only concept I know of which is beyond the categories of sex (woman and man), because the designated subject (lesbian) is not a woman, either economically, or politically, or ideologically. For what makes a woman is a specific social relation to a man."[17]

I delineate these two conceptualizations of the writing subject not as fake *versus* truthful representations of feminist thinking but as two distinct idealizations, which involve some degree of essentialism. In her openly partial reading of the difference between these two models, Diane Crowder urges us to choose: "Women's culture could thus become a retreat from the battle or it could become the most potent weapon we have against oppression. We must choose or risk floundering on this hidden conceptual schizophrenia."[18] Choose in these terms, however, and you will risk throwing away the Lesbian with the heterosexual bathwater. Crowder's black and white call for choice denounces, I submit, a dangerous hunger for purity in this domain that could be said to keep marginal feminist voices out of the centers of feminist theory for being either too "other" (i.e., Lesbian) or not "other" (i.e., lesbian) enough.

Novas Cartas and *Borderlands* revisited

Linda Kauffman has famously argued that *Novas Cartas* was not easily absorbed by the canons of feminist theory precisely because it was deemed too "other" by second-wave feminists.[19] As a radical site of theory shaped by the experiences of three women living on the edge of Europe and of the dominant feminist discourse, *Novas Cartas* is indeed very difficult to describe with the standard critical terminology. The book presents many different kinds of material. In it, various international feminist discourses of the time are acknowledged, problematized, and woven together with other epistemological sources: invented letters spanning a period of three centuries written by a host of fictitious Anas, Marias, Marianas, and Maria Anas, historical documents, poems exchanged between the three authors, prose essays on the condition of women through time, personal *bilhetes* (notes), and reflections on the role of men in shaping the condition of women. Various Western theoretical approaches to women's oppression by patriarchal ideologies rub shoulders with legends, witchcraft beliefs, invented stories, and popular myths. One Maria tells the Native American myth of *Mãe dos Animais* (Mother of Animals), in which a woman is abandoned by her tribe when her pregnancy threatens to slow down their migration (23); another Maria invents a letter penned from the perspective of a man struggling with the experiences of the Portuguese Colonial War in Africa (218); another Maria calls attention to the pitfalls of the legacies of Marxist feminism, which to her mind places too much emphasis upon class relations in the economic sphere and neglects female experiences outside the labor market (88). Precise bibliographic citations from feminist theorists coexist with the telling of imprecise stories that lack detail, denouncing academic language's mask of neutrality: "lembro-me apenas destas coisas, sem nomes nem detalhes, mas lembro aquilo que me interessa."[20] The constant shifts between the personal and the collective, and between various literary genres, are communicated via an untranslated mix of Portuguese, French, and English.

In this respect, *Novas Cartas*'s performance as a border tongue challenging institutionalized languages resembles "the serpentine movement" of *Borderlands*'s text, published fifteen years later.[21] As a spiritualist and a PhD doctorate at the time of writing *Borderlands,* Anzaldúa, the self-proclaimed border-woman, uses both Western and non-Western theoretical and philosophical approaches in her writing: "I know things older than Freud, older than gender."[22] As noted by Sonia Saldivar-Hull in her study on Chicana feminism, Anzaldúa's feminism "exists in a borderland grounded in, but not limited to geographical space, ... in a space not acknowledged by the dominant culture."[23] Anzaldúa's insistence on negotiating multiple contradicting and ambiguous subject positions between the Mexican and the Anglo borders reveals a lucid perception of subordination issues on the ground. In *Borderlands*'s highly experimental and fragmented textual surface, the constant code-switching between English, Spanish, Nahuatl, and Chicano English, among other tongues, defies linear understanding and may be read as a political statement, representing a clear break between the phonetic, phonemic, and morphologic systems of the main languages (English and Spanish).[24] Anzaldúa displays a thoughtful mediation between English and Spanish through ironic translations, which work as an explicit critique of how prominent groups reinforce domination through language. For example, the title of chapter 7, "La conciencia de la mestiza," is not the exact equivalent to "Toward a New Consciousness." The writer's translation "terrorism," together with her linguistic *mestizaje,* stresses women's oppression for their illegitimate tongues: for speaking subaltern languages, such as Spanish and Chicano English, for speaking the dominant language (English), and simply for speaking their minds.

The political rationale behind each book's fragmentation lies in the Three Marias' and Anzaldúa's distrust in the power of existing language and theory to represent the political realities they are concerned with. As Anzaldúa puts it, "For a people who are neither Spanish nor live in a country in which Spanish is the first language; … for a people who cannot entirely identify with either standard (formal, Castilian) Spanish nor standard English, what recourse is left to them but to create their own language?"[25] In the case of the Three Marias, linguistic and textual fragmentation also reveals a preoccupation with the limits of what can be achieved through writing: "Mas o que pode a literatura? Ou antes: o que podem as palavras?"[26] This reveals a preoccupation with the material realities of real-life experiences and also with class issues, as the three authors acknowledge that trading with the written word is a luxury not all can afford and that might simply lead to further abstraction. As Hilary Owen argues, the three women share a "fear of mysticizing [language] for its own sake to the exclusion of the problems of reality."[27] Anzaldúa and the Three Marias could thus be said to respond—although in distinct ways—to a similar desire to create, in the midst of their *povo/pueblo* (people), new domestic audiences with whom they may share images of feminist possibility in the context of the material realities of their communities. In this respect, *Novas Cartas* and *Borderlands* effectively merge identity politics and political praxis, so that the emphasis on "who we are" does not replace the issue of "what needs to be done" but rather determines how things will be done.[28]

It is precisely in "how things are done" that the most striking point of comparison between these two foundational texts may be found, as attested by my initial response to both as "literature" rather than "theory." Working against the tendency in dominant academic discourse to homogenize reading habits, the books demanded innovation in this reader's search for theory. As noted by Saldivar-Hull, because we are often unable to "recognize anything that is different from what the dominant discourse constructs," we have to "look in non-traditional places for our theories: in the prefaces to anthologies, in the interstices of autobiographies, in our cultural artifacts."[29] Indeed, by extending the borders of what is considered legitimately political, the authors encourage Portuguese and Chicana feminists to theorize—and to look for theory—in places and manners not always legitimized by Anglo-American and French feminisms.

In the light of the above it is understandable that the international reception of *Novas Cartas* and *Borderlands* should figure as one important aspect that brings them together. Both books were enthusiastically embraced by second-wave feminists, as well as criticized along similar lines. Between 1972 and 1974–75, *Novas Cartas* was uniformly consumed internationally as a shiny symbol of sisterhood and feminist unity. This was a logical response to the context of Portuguese censorship that threatened the Marias with prison sentences of up to two years. It was also very much a result of the lack of available translations of *Novas Cartas* from the original Portuguese, which may have contributed to feeding the official metaphor of "absolute reciprocity" between Portuguese and Anglo-American/French feminisms, as acts of nonreading or fragmentary reading became the common way in which international audiences first got in touch with the Marias' work.[30]

The impulse to treat the text as a "mirror" for the white feminist self also characterizes *Borderlands*'s international reception. According to Yvonne Yarbro-Berejano, two potentially problematic areas in the reception of *Borderlands* are "the isolation of this text from its conceptual community and the pitfalls in universalizing the theory of mestiza or border consciousness."[31] One way in which white feminists have dealt with *Borderlands* has been to read it "as one looks in a mirror."[32] *Borderlands* has been perceived as offering a spectacle of the struggles experienced by Chicanas "for the voyeuristic delectation of European American readers."[33] Furthermore, the label "essentialist" has been fired at both *Novas Cartas* and *Borderlands,* despite both texts' commitment to the construction of multiple subject positions. A 1975 review of *Novas Cartas* published in *Red Rag: A Magazine of Women's Liberation,* for example, argues that the book "founders on its lack of analysis, its ahistoricism, its heterosexist assumptions, and … the middle-class situation of its writers."[34] The representation of the indigenous in *Borderlands,* on the other hand, has evoked very critical responses from Chicana/o and non Chicana/o readers. The text's focus on the Native woman and the privileging of the pre-Columbian deity Coatlicue is seen as an essentialist and elitist move that "obscures the plight of present day Native women in the Americas."[35]

Nevertheless, although *Borderlands* has been dismissed as indulging in the quest for lost origins and criticized for appropriating an indigenous heritage that does not belong to Chicanas, this did not impede the relatively quick implementation of the book as a classic classroom and theory text. As Saldivar-Hull puts it, *Borderlands* "signaled a new visibility for academic programs on the study of the U.S.–Mexico border area," inspiring the publication of a number of anthologies and other academic publications, and bringing to light "a remapped academic topography with the border as the organizing trope."[36] In fact, the first edition of *Borderlands* was repeatedly printed. When its second edition came out in 1999, it included an academic validation stamp in the form of a critical introduction signed by Saldivar-Hull, associate professor of English at UCLA, signaling Chicana feminist studies as a legitimate field of scholarship. In comparison, the Portuguese edition of *Novas Cartas* fell on stony ground, remaining out of print throughout most of the 1980s and 1990s, until *Dom Quixote*'s edition came out in 1998. If the universalist (international feminist) type of readings did not provide wholly adequate tools for dealing with the theoretical experimentations of *Novas Cartas,* neither did the nationalist (Portuguese nonfeminist, antifascist) type of reading, which failed to address the complex dialogues and conflicts enacted between the Three Marias and their various feminist audiences, both national and international.[37] With the appearance of the first official translations of *Novas Cartas* into French and English in 1974 and 1975 respectively, the metaphor of absolute reciprocity was replaced by one of anachronism, as (mainly Anglo-American) critics described *Novas Cartas* in their reviews as an old-fashioned feminist text. For example, in February 1975 the *Washington Post* published a review of *Novas Cartas* titled "Alien Porn" by William McPherson, who observed, "That women have been oppressed, and may be especially oppressed in macho Latin cultures, is no longer news sufficient to justify a book."[38] This trend led to the marginalization of the work on a theoretical level, consolidating a view of the Lusophone cultural sphere as an anachronistic feminine space for political action, entirely disconnected from the centers where feminist theory is made. The first Portuguese annotated edition featuring an academic introduction to the text by Amaral and two prefaces penned by Maria de Lourdes Pintasilgo appeared only in 2010. In sum, *Novas Cartas* has been only sporadically studied at undergraduate level and researched as an early example of queer and feminist theory texts in Portugal.[39] Anzaldúa's text, on the other hand, is generally understood as being representative of American studies, Chicano/a studies, cultural studies, ethnic studies, feminism, literary studies, critical pedagogy, women's studies, and queer theory; it was "named one of the 100 Best Books of the Century by both *Hungry Mind Review* and *Utne Reader*" and has contributed to "critical and cultural theory across disciplines."[40]

In this context, Kauffman's assertion that *Novas Cartas* was too other to be absorbed by the canons of feminist theory could be said to be only the tip of the iceberg. Other literary "things" deemed ahead of their time and characterized by extreme fragmentation and excess have been branded as belonging to canons, albeit alternative ones. This is the case of Anzaldúa's *Borderlands*, whose performing discourse mixes lyric and prose, myth and autobiography, the personal and the academic, reason and spirit, Spanish and English, past and present. What do these very different success stories tell us about the idealized subject at the heart of the second-wave feminist contract?

Lesbian Vertigo: Mariana and Malintzín

A more attentive comparative look at *Novas Cartas* and *Borderlands* reveals that the distinct success stories I am concerned with here may be intimately related to the kind of writing subject each one chooses to celebrate. *Novas Cartas* and *Borderlands* may be read as culturally and historically distinct attempts to free two female figures, Mariana Alcoforado and Malintzín Ténepal respectively, from the original position of "valued" transgressors. Each book engages in a revision of locally grounded, cherished national beliefs by drawing on these two paradigmatic figures of femininity who have played important roles in Portugal's and Mexico's historically and geopolitically distinct nation-making processes, as valued "original victims."[41] The Three Marias set out to reappropriate Mariana Alcoforado from a Portuguese tradition of representation that had imprisoned her in the crystal cage of femininity as the symbol of the abandoned weeping woman. Mariana Alcoforado, a Portuguese nun living in Beja (Alentejo region in Portugal), is the protagonist of *Lettres Portugaises,* the seventeenth-century text that supplied the starting point for *Novas Cartas.*[42] First published in 1669 by Claude Barbin in Paris, *Lettres Portugaises* is a collection of five letters written in French from the perspective of Mariana and addressed to the Chevalier de Chamilly, her French lover. The letters, set at the time of Portugal's struggle for independence from Spain, were supposedly translated from the original Portuguese, which was never found. It is now accepted that these letters, which speak of the nun's suffering after being abandoned by her lover, were originally penned by a French male writer, Gabriel Joseph de Lavergne de Guilleragues, and not by a real Portuguese nun. Nevertheless, Soror Mariana's letters, specifically their content and style, contributed toward the invention of a much-celebrated gendered national myth—that of the female victim abandoned by her lover—that has since dictated conceptions of feminine sensibility and female suffering/passiveness in Portugal. As noted by Anna Klobucka, "Barreno, Horta e Velho da Costa descobriram na história da freira portuguesa um repositório aparentemente inesgotável de fontes para o seu objectivo principal, um levantamento dos padrões míticos e factuais, contemporâneos e históricos, que moldaram as vidas e as obras das mulheres portuguesas."[43] The choice and development of Guilleragues's character Mariana Alcoforado by the Three Marias thus serves to disrupt traditional views of femininity that have helped to imagine the Portuguese community and the female subject at the heart of that community.

Anzaldúa, on the other hand, grounds the fragmented methodology of her book in the history of the Americas, bringing to light pre-Columbian female deities and, with them, a utopian New Mestiza vision framed by the historical figure of Malintzín Ténepal (also Coatlalopeuh or Malinche). Malintzín was sold to the Mayans by her mother so as to increase the social status of her brother, and she was later given to Hernán Cortés as a gift, along with several other women.[44] Because of her linguistic skills, she worked as an interpreter and guide for the Spaniards. Named as *la lengua* (the tongue) by Cortés and other Spanish conquerors, Malintzín not only translated for the Spaniards but also bore their children. She was, as a result, transformed into Virgen Guadalupe's monstrous double. As argued by Norma Alarcón, "Malintzín may be compared to Eve, especially when she is viewed as the originator of the Mexican people's fall from grace and the procreator of a 'fallen' people."[45] In *The Labyrinth of Solitude* (1990), Octavio Paz transforms Malintzín into Mexico's historically grounded originator, a primeval mother of sorts, accepted by the community despite her treacherous sexual and linguistic behavior.[46] In doing so, Alarcón suggests, Paz paradoxically "displaced the myth of Guadalupe, not with history, but with a neomyth, a reversal properly secularized yet unaware of its misogynistic residue."[47] In *Borderlands,* Anzaldúa rescues Malintzín from the periphery of the patriarchal order, using her name(s) to create new meanings and rehearse a female coming to consciousness in the present. From signifying the Mexican people's primeval mother/goddess/whore, Malintzín is raised from the ashes as the mother of *mestizaje* and as the ultimate rebellious Indian-mestiza: "The dark skinned woman has been silenced, gagged, bound up in servitude with marriage, bludgeoned for 300 years, sterilized and castrated in the twentieth century. For 300 years she has been a slave, a force of cheap labor, colonized by the Spaniard, the Anglo, by her own people.... Battered and bruised she waits ... Coatlalopeuh waits with her."[48]

One crucial difference between Mariana and Malintzín is that, contrary to the latter, Mariana is not simply confined to the position of the colonized woman. Rather, as argued by Owen, she suffers from vertigo as the colonizer's wife who is "tired of pedestal existence."[49] Throughout the book, Mariana steps up and down her pedestal, oscillating between multiple border positionalities not only as a colonized subject but also as the colonizer's lover, wife, mother, and daughter. In this respect, the distance between Mariana and Malinztín is dramatic, since the former inevitably "invokes the complicity of the Portuguese feminine in the colonial project."[50] Owen's reading of the metaphor "woman as land" in *Novas Cartas* is enlightening. Rather than reproducing Kauffman's more essentialist equation of colonial status in Mexico and Portugal, she demonstrates how Mariana is trapped within *Novas Cartas*'s at times essentialist metaphorical systems that define "woman as land." Owen quotes the following passage by Kauffman to make her point: "Woman is thus the conquest even of those who are themselves colonized, whether in Mexico or Portugal. Men in love seek not a face but a mirror; it is that narcissism, that mystification and manipulation that the Marias set out to dismantle."[51] With this quote, Owen signals the tendency, in international criticism, to elide the multiple shifting and, at times, competing cores and peripheries that *Novas Cartas* enacts. As Owen contends, "the Mari/ana 'complex' which the three Marias build is simultaneously subject of colonial desire, the woman who waits, the land barren and longing and also the object of 'colonizing' desire, the feminine aspired to and conquered, fertilized and found."[52] With Malintzín, Anzaldúa also engages in a negotiation of her multiple contradicting and ambiguous subject positions, but she does so always as a colonized Indian lesbian woman. Through testimonial writing, what she calls "auto-historia," Anzaldúa invokes several subjectivities in her fight against a monochromic "I" responsible for the reinforcement of Western binary models, such as the Self-Other and Object-Subject formations. She does this so as to reflect upon the condition of Chicanos in Anglo culture, of women in the Hispanic culture, and of lesbians in the straight world.

In this regard, Mariana inhabits a much more challenging original position for she crosses several competing borders simultaneously: not only between various colonized conditions but also between colonizer and colonized. The sense of vertigo produced by the Three Marias' back-and-forth and up-and-down movement, that is, between the consolidation of an essentialist colonial otherness and the disruption of the boundaries of heterosexuality on which the concept of the Portuguese nation rests, could be said to be in tension with the two idealized subjects that were about to be produced by the MLF and its North-American (mis)interpretations, as delineated above. On the one hand, Mariana is clearly at odds with Cixous's model because she does not represent a retreat into a feminine world. In fact, one of the greatest challenges put forth in *Novas Cartas* is precisely the destabilization of both male and female positions, and the questioning of the seemingly "natural" division of the sexes, as defended by Amaral.[53] In this respect, Mariana's point of view is much closer to the "Lesbian point of view," which would later be developed by Wittig in her 1980 essay where she elaborates the famous statement that *on ne nait pas femme.*[54] As noted by Brad Epps and Jonathan Katz, Wittig's "lesbian point of view" does not correspond to an essentialist attempt to reconfigure society in a separatist way. Rather, it demonstrates that the division between male and female, "with its basis in heterosexual reproduction, is in fact artificial, that is to say, political."[55] Similarly, in "When Lesbians Were Not Women," Teresa de Lauretis reads Wittig's statement as one that "fire[s] the imagination" and "has the power to open the mind and make visible and thinkable a conceptual space that until then had been rendered unthinkable by … the hegemony of the straight mind."[56] For De Lauretis, the Lesbian in Wittig's work is not necessarily a lesbian, but "a different kind of woman" who inhabits this new conceptual space as an "eccentric" subject: "I called the subject eccentric not only in the sense of deviating from the conventional normative path but also eccentric in that it did not center itself in the institution that supports and produces the straight mind, that is, the institution of heterosexuality."[57] This view is echoed by Judith Butler, who notes that to distinguish between bodies that are lesbians and bodies that are not is clearly the wrong way to read Wittig's concept of the Lesbian: "The Lesbian body is precisely the site for the dismemberment and recrafting that is at the same time a peculiar act of re-inscription, a destruction and a reimagining, a reworking of the culturally-sedimented body towards its unanticipated future."[58] It follows that the "Lesbian point of view" does not aim to describe the world from an authoritarian minority viewpoint but rather intends to fracture the whole male/female framework by means of a continuous process of disidentification and displacement, a back and forth between the old and the new that leads to the inevitable splitting of the self—"J/e"—as often found in Wittig's creative writing. De Lauretis describes this movement, back and forth, as "leaving or giving a place that is known, that is 'home'—physically, emotionally, linguistically, epistemologically—for another place that is unknown … a place from which speaking and thinking are at best tentative, uncertain, unauthorized."[59] Such displacement enables a position of resistance "that is not outside but rather eccentric to the socio-cultural apparati of the heterosexual institution."[60]

Contrary to Anzaldúa, the three Portuguese authors do not explicitly choose the homosexual route as a way to face the issues they are concerned with. Nevertheless, they articulate, to my mind, something akin to a "Lesbian point of view," by producing a writing that is able to fracture not only the male/female framework but also the oppressed/oppressor formation according to what Owen terms as the "Mari/ana complex," the slash here revealing the kind of negotiation, or refusal and engagement, at work in *Novas Cartas* that is so typical of Wittig's creative writing. The Three Marias knew, eight years before Wittig destabilized the meaning of Simone de Beauvoir's words, "one is not born a woman but becomes one," that received knowledge could be displaced and dismembered by exercising repetition with a difference. They knew that if they repeated the opening words of *Lettres Portugaises*—"Considère, mon Amour" (Consider, my Love)—with a difference—"Considerai, irmãs minhas" (Consider, my sisters)—they would shift the emphasis from the word *Amour* to the word *irmãs,* creating a sudden destabilization, a shock that is continuously repeated throughout the book, rocking the very foundations of the heterosexually defined myth of the abandoned weeping woman. Barreno, Horta, and Velho da Costa's treatment of the myth of Mariana Alcoforado thus effectively transforms her into an eccentric subject of sorts: although she is not entirely outside the heterosexual apparatus of colonial Portugal, she nevertheless occupies a decentered, or eccentric, position by renegotiating, as both a multiply oppressed subject and as the colonizer's lover, "the all-too-familiar-inside" of the political regime called heterosexuality.[61] Mari/ana is a Lesbian *avant la letter*—her (re)creation by the Three Marias predates Wittig's theory—because she cultivates a critical distance in relation to heterosexuality while problematizing the division of the sexes.

As a Lesbian *avant la lettre,* however, Mariana contributes to a more nuanced—less "pure" and less singular—understanding of Wittig's "Lesbian point of view."[62] This is because Mariana suffers from vertigo, the sensation of whirling arising from her position(s) as both subject and/or object of colonial desire. The agitation produced by Mariana's vertigo (up-and-down movement between the positions of colonizer and colonized) effectively complicates the simpler swaying (back-and-forth movement, which displaces heterosexuality) of Wittig's disidentified subject, which De Lauretis has compared to "women or lesbians of color such as Trinh T. Minh-ha, Gloria Anzaldúa, Barbara Smith, and Chandra Mohanty."[63] Wittig's theory is adaptable to postcolonial feminisms mainly because what characterizes the eccentric subject is a double displacement—leaving the known for the unknown—that contributes to reconceptualizing subjectivities on the move, and to challenging Western philosophical traditions based on binary positions. Mariana's choice, however, is not simply one between two levels of reality, home and the unknown, or the inside and/or the outside of heterosexuality. For her, the unknown is often too close to home, as Africanized and eroticized descriptions of the Alentejo (Mariana's home region) in *Novas Cartas* suggest, and as "third-world" readings of the book by international feminists confirm. And home has too many dark corners. It is from those dark corners that the three "aranhas astuciosas" weave their webs of discontent, as they brand their assault on the thin air of domesticity.[64]

Conclusion: Mariana's Choice

Mariana's point of view in *Novas Cartas* thus precludes perceptions of a "pure" Lesbian point of view, in the singular. The consequences of this for Wittig's own engagement with the Three Marias' text, as one of the official translators (with Evelyne Le Garrec) of *Novas Cartas* into French in 1974, are yet to be analyzed. While I agree with Epps and Katz that existing critiques of Wittig's insistence on the singular "Lesbian" are often the result of ungenerous readings, I would like to suggest that perhaps a residue of purity is at work in tacit understandings of the Lesbian writing subject, to such an extent that it has rendered Mariana's point of view all too other (i.e., too Lesbian, and not lesbian enough) to be allowed into the canons of feminist theory texts, whether mainstream or alternative.

In this respect, it is interesting to observe Wittig's own ambivalence about *Novas Cartas*'s ability to assault heterosexual structures, to act as a Trojan horse, and to transform the minority point of view into a universal one. In the translator's note, which Wittig penned with Le Garrec, she starts by defining the book as a symbol: "Ce livre est un symbole. Par son histoire. Par la façon dont nous avons eu l'occasion, nous et d'autres femmes, de l'approcher."[65] To define it as a political symbol, however, amounts to issuing a veiled death sentence, for as Wittig would later write in an essay titled "The Point of View: Universal or Particular?," when a book or a text becomes a symbol or a manifesto for something, it is subjected to disregard: "Taken as a symbol or adopted by a political group, the text loses its polysemy, it becomes univocal. This loss of meaning and lack of grip on the textual reality prevents the text from carrying out the only political action that it could: introducing into the textual tissue of the times by way of literature that which it embodies."[66] Wittig and Le Garrec finally rescue the book from the symbolic limbo to which they had subtly condemned it, noting that "Ce n'est pas simplement un livre écrit par des femmes portugaises et traitant des femmes portugaises. Sa portée est universelle."[67] As Butler argues in her analysis of Wittig's commitment to universality, to universalize here is not to reverse power positions or to set up a new hegemony from a minority position. Rather, to universalize in Wittig's work is to assault the very framework upon which the notions of "universality" and "minority" rest. It is to "pluralize the feminine and the lesbian, to render existing categories of sex obsolete …, to produce a shock for the reader, any reader, and to conduct an assault of some kind."[68] By arguing that *Novas Cartas* is "universelle," then, Wittig and Le Garrec defend that it is, after all, able to act on a reader's pre-established understandings, and that it is able to represent and posit interests and questions that do not yet exist.

In sum, if the translators' note denotes anything other than its authors' political solidarity with the Three Marias, it is an ambiguity as to whether the text is to be taken as a symbol or a universal book, whether or not it is able to act as a Trojan horse and rearrange reality. To my mind, this lack of consensus is symptomatic of Wittig's inability to deal productively with Mariana's ambiguous positioning in between several shifting centers and margins. This reveals a purity residue underlining Wittig's notion of the Lesbian point of view, which inevitably renders the original position of the Lesbian Amazon partially uninhabitable for an ideal subject such as Mariana, but ultimately amenable for Malintzín.

Ana Martins is a Lecturer in Portuguese Studies at the University of Exeter, where she acts as Programme Director of Portuguese. She is the Web Liaison officer for the lusophone pages of the Centre for the Study of Contemporary Women's Writing (CCWW) at the Institute of Modern Languages Research, University of London. She has published on women's writing from Portugal, Mozambique and Brazil. Her research interests lie in postcolonial, transnational and memory studies in lusophone contexts, with a particular emphasis on Portugal's relationship with lusophone Africa and Brazil, and dominant French and Anglo-American theory centres of postcolonial and feminist thought. She is the author of Magic Stones and Flying Snakes: Gender and the Postcolonial Exotic in the Work of Paulina Chiziane and Lídia Jorge (Peter Lang, 2012), co-editor of The Luso-Tropical Tempest: Postcolonial Debates in Portuguese (Bristol University Press, 2012), and co-author of Authentic Recipes from Around the World (Ceredigion, 2015).

Notes

1. I would like to thank Hilary Owen for introducing me to *Novas Cartas Portuguesas* and *Borderlands/La Frontera: The New Mestiza* back in 2000 and 2005 at the University of Manchester. I am deeply indebted to her for her inspiring work, generous reading suggestions, and unwavering support over the years. Some of the ideas developed in this chapter were initially presented at the IV International Conference of the Association of British and Irish Lusitanists (September 9–10, 2011), which was dedicated to the theme *Communities/Comunidades*. The title of the paper was "The Three Marias' Pact and the Feminist Contract."
2. Christine Delphy, "The Invention of French Feminism: An Essential Move," *Yale French Studies* 87 (1995): 216.

3. Ibid., 196. Further references to the movement of the liberation of women will be done in the main text as MLF. Cixous was connected to the *psy et po* faction of the MLF, which defended a valued femaleness and the maternal family model to explain desire in areas excluded from male discourse.
4. See Anna Klobucka, "Hélène Cixous and the Hour of Clarice Lispector," *SubStance* 73 (1994): 41–62. The Three Marias became the common way of referring to three Portuguese women, Maria Isabel Barreno, Maria Teresa Horta, and Maria Velho da Costa, who published a controversial book in 1972 titled *Novas Cartas Portuguesas* (*New Portuguese Letters*), banned by the censors of the Portuguese right-wing dictatorship.
5. Delphy, "The Invention of French Feminism," 219.
6. See Hélène Cixous, "The Laugh of the Medusa," *Signs* 1, no. 4 (1976): 875–93; Monique Wittig, *The Straight Mind and Other Essays* (New York: Harvester Wheatsheaf, 1992); Monique Wittig, "One Is Not Born a Woman," *Feminist Issues* 1, no. 2 (1981): 47–54. Throughout this chapter, the word "Lesbian" shall be used to refer to Wittig's theory as opposed to "lesbian," which will retain its normal English meaning.
7. I shall focus specifically on the French feminist movement due to the fact that the Three Marias' case was first taken up by French feminists in the early 1970s.
8. Maria Isabel Barreno, Maria Teresa Horta, and Maria Velho da Costa, *Novas Cartas Portuguesas,* ed. Ana Luísa Amaral (Lisbon: Dom Quixote, 2010). Further references to this book shall be made in the main text as *Novas Cartas.* This was not the first time that Portuguese women writers faced legal prosecution for writing books that dealt with female sexuality. Six years earlier, Azorean-born writer Natália Correia had been condemned to three years in prison for publishing an anthology of poetry titled *Antologia de Poesia Portuguesa Erótica e Satírica* (1966). In 1971 Maria Teresa Horta had published an anthology of poetry titled *Minha Senhora de Mim,* dealing explicitly with female sexuality, which also had been censored. What made *Novas Cartas* different from these other cases of censorship was the international impact it would achieve following the Portuguese banning of the book.
9. A prominent example of this is Helder Macedo's important 1975 review where the critic takes issue with the commodifiable expression "Three Marias," arguing instead for politically and historically situated readings of the book that value its specifically Portuguese roots. See Helder Macedo, "Teresa, Fátima and Isabel," *Times Literary Supplement* (1975): 1484.
10. See Ana Luisa Amaral, "Desconstruindo Identidades: Ler *Novas Cartas Portuguesas* à Luz da Teoria Queer," *Cardernos de Literatura Comparada* 3, no. 4 (2001): 77–91; Linda Kauffman, *Discourses of Desire: Gender, Genre and Epistolary Fictions* (Ithaca, NY: Cornell University Press, 1986); Hilary Owen, "Um Quarto que Seja Seu: The Quest for Camões' Sister," *Portuguese Studies* 11 (1995): 179–91; Hilary Owen, "New Cartographies of the Body in *Novas Cartas Portuguesas*: The (Counter-) Narrative of the Nation and the Sign of the Voyage Back," *ellipsis* 1 (1999): 73–83; Hilary Owen and Claudia Pazos Alonso, *Antigone's Daughters? Gender, Genealogy and the Politics of Authorship in 20th-Century Portuguese Women's Writing* (Lewisburg, PA: Bucknell University Press, 2011).
11. Graça Abranches, "On What Terms Shall We Join the Procession of Educated Men? Teaching Feminist Studies at the University of Coimbra," *Oficina do CES* 125 (1998): 18.

12. Gloria Anzaldúa, *Borderlands/La Frontera: The New Mestiza* (San Francisco: Aunt Lute Books, 1999). Further references to this book shall be made in the main text as *Borderlands.*
13. Ann Rosalind. Jones, "Writing the Body: Toward an Understanding of 'L'Écriture Féminine,'" *Feminist Studies* 7, no. 2 (1981): 248.
14. Cixous, "Laugh of the Medusa," 881, 884.
15. Ibid., 884.
16. Wittig, "One Is Not Born a Woman," 104.
17. Ibid., 53.
18. Diane Crowder, "Amazons and Mothers? Monique Wittig, Hélène Cixous and Theories of Women's Writing," *Contemporary Literature* 24, no. 2 (1983): 143.
19. Kauffman, *Discourses of Desire,* 307.
20. "I remember only these things, without names or details, but I remember what is important to me." Barreno, *Novas Cartas,* 23. All translations are mine, unless otherwise stated.
21. Yvonne Yarbro-Bejarano, "Gloria Anzaldúa's *Borderlands/La Frontera*: Cultural Studies, 'Difference' and the Unitary Subject," *Cultural Critique* (1994): 17.
22. Anzaldúa, *Borderlands,* 26.
23. Sonia Saldivar-Hull, *Feminism on the Border: Chicana Gender Politics and Literature* (Berkeley: University of California Press, 2000), 67.
24. Nahuatl is a language spoken by the Aztecs and belongs to a large group of languages spoken by tribes of Western North America. Chicano English refers to all the English spoken by Chicanos. See http://www.indians.org/welker/nahuatl.htm.
25. Anzaldúa, *Borderlands,* 77.
26. "But what is the power of literature? Or better: what can words do?" Barreno, *Novas Cartas,* 197.
27. Owen, "Um Quarto que Seja Seu," 76.
28. Saldivar-Hull, *Feminism on the Border.*
29. Ibid., 46.
30. Ana Margrida Dias Martins, "*Novas Cartas Portuguesas*: The Making of a Reputation," *Journal of Feminist Scholarship* 2 (2012): 24–39.
31. Yarbro-Bejarano, "Gloria Anzaldúa's *Borderlands,*" 7.
32. Ibid., 8.
33. Ibid., 15.
34. *Red Rag: A Magazine of Liberation,* "*New Portuguese Letters* by Maria Isabel Barreno," 1 (1975–76): 30.
35. Yarbro-Bejarano, "Gloria Anzaldúa's *Borderlands,*" 12.
36. Anzaldúa, *Borderlands,* 12 (introduction by Saldivar-Hull). See Héctor Calderón and José David Saldívar, eds., *Criticism in the Borderlands: Studies in Chicano Literature, Culture and Ideology* (Durham, NC: Duke University Press, 1991); Emily Hicks, *Border Writing: The Multidimensional Text* (Minneapolis: University of Minnesota Press, 1991); Alfred Arteaga, ed., *An Other Tongue: Nation and Ethnicity in the Linguistic Borderlands* (Durham, NC: Duke University Press, 1994); Carl Guttierrez-Jones, *Rethinking the Borderlands: Between Chicano Culture and Legal Discourse* (Berkeley: University of California Press, 1995).
37. See Martins, "*Novas Cartas Portuguesas*: The Making of a Reputation," 33.

38. William McPherson, "Alien Porn," *Washington Post,* February 2, 1975, 139 in Martins, "The Making of a Reputation," 26.
39. According to Amaral, what is queer about *Novas Cartas* is the recognition that language "is the space of excess in our discourse, always threatened by the hegemonic, whether cultural, universal or national." See Amaral, "Desconstruindo Identidades."
40. Ana Louise Keating, ed., *Entre Mundos/Among Worlds: New Perspectives on Gloria Anzaldúa* (New York: Palgrave Macmillan, 2005), xvi, 3.
41. Norma Alarcón, "Traduttora, Traditora: A Paradigmatic Figure of Chicana Feminism," *Cultural Critique* 13 (1989), 60.
42. Gabriel Joseph de Lavergne Guilleragues, *Lettres Portugaises* (London: Harvill Press, 1996).
43. "Barreno, Horta and Velho da Costa found in the story of the Portuguese nun an apparently inexhaustible repository of sources for their main goal, which was to gather mythical and factual, contemporaneous and historical patterns that have shaped the lives and work of Portuguese women." In Anna Klobucka, *Mariana Alcoforado: Formação de Um Mito Cultural* (Lisbon: Imprensa Nacional-Casa da Moeda, 2006), 144.
44. Adelaida del Castillo, "Malintzín Tenepal: A Preliminary Look into a New Perspective," in *Chicana Feminist Thought: The Basic Historical Writings,* ed. Alma M. Garcia (New York: Routledge, 1997), 122–26.
45. Alarcón, "Traduttora, Traditora," 58.
46. Octavio Paz, *The Labyrinth of Solitude,* trans. Lysander Kemp, Yara Milos, and Rachel Phillips Belash (London: Penguin, 1990).
47. Alarcón, "Traduttora, Traditora," 65.
48. Anzaldúa, *Borderlands,* 44.
49. M. Angelou, "Family Affairs," in *And I Still Rise* (London: Virago, 1986), 92, cited in Owen, "New Cartographies of the Body," 46.
50. Owen, "New Cartographies of the Body," 51.
51. Kauffman, *Discourses of Desire,* 292.
52. Owen, "New Cartographies of the Body," 50.
53. Amaral, "Desconstruindo Identidades."
54. Wittig, "One Is Not Born a Woman."
55. Bradley Epps and Jonathan Katz, "Monique Wittig's Materialist Utopia and Radical Critique," *GLQ: A Journal of Lesbian and Gay Studies* 13, no. 4 (2007): 435–36, 424.
56. Teresa De Lauretis, "When Lesbians Were Not Women," in *Monique Wittig: Theoretical, Political and Literary Essays,* ed. N. Shaktini (Urbana: University of Illinois Press, 2005), 51–52.
57. De Lauretis, "When Lesbians Were Not Women," 52.
58. Judith Butler, "Wittig's Material Practice: Universalizing a Minority Point of View," *GLQ: A Journal of Lesbian and Gay Studies* 13, no. 4 (2007): 530–31.
59. De Lauretis, "When Lesbians Were Not Women," 53.
60. Ibid.
61. Epps and Katz, "Monique Wittig's Materialist Utopia and Radical Critique," 425.
62. For a critique of Wittig's "Lesbian point of view," see Diana Fuss, *Essentially Speaking: Feminism, Nature, and Difference* (New York: Routledge, 1989).
63. De Lauretis, "When Lesbians Were Not Women," 53, cited in Epps and Katz, "Monique Wittig's Materialist Utopia and Radical Critique," 430.
64. "Astute spiders," Barreno, *Novas Cartas,* 34.

65. "This book is a symbol. For its history. For the way in which we and other women approached it." Barreno, Maria Isabel, Maria Teresa Horta, Maria Velho da Costa, *Nouvelles Lettres Portugaises,* trans. Monique Wittig and Eveline Le Garrec (Paris: Seuil, 1974), 7.
66. Monique Wittig, *The Straight Mind and Other Essays* (New York: Harvester Wheatsheaf, 1992), 63.
67. "This is not simply a book written by Portuguese women about Portuguese women. Its tone is universal." Barreno, *Nouvelles Lettres Portugaises,* 10.
68. Butler, "Wittig's Material Practice," 521.

Bibliography

Abranches, Graça. "On What Terms Shall We Join the Procession of Educated Men? Teaching Feminist Studies at the University of Coimbra." *Oficina do CES* 125 (1998): 1–21.

Alarcón, Norma. "Traduttora, Traditora: A Paradigmatic Figure of Chicana Feminism." *Cultural Critique* 13 (1989): 57–87.

Amaral, Ana Luisa. "Desconstruindo Identidades: Ler *Novas Cartas Portuguesas* à Luz da Teoria Queer." *Cadernos de Literatura Comparada* 3, no. 4 (2001): 77–91.

Anzaldúa, Gloria. *Borderlands/La Frontera: The New Mestiza.* San Francisco: Aunt Lute Books, 1999.

Arteaga, Alfred, ed. *An Other Tongue: Nation and Ethnicity in the Linguistic Borderlands.* Durham, NC: Duke University Press, 1994.

Barreno, Maria Isabel, Maria Teresa Horta, and Maria Velho da Costa. *Nouvelles Lettres Portugaises.* Translated by Monique Wittig and Eveline Le Garrec. Paris: Seuil, 1974.

———. *Novas Cartas Portuguesas,* edited by Ana Luísa Amaral. Lisbon: Dom Quixote, 2010.

Butler, Judith. "Wittig's Material Practice: Universalizing a Minority Point of View." *GLQ: A Journal of Lesbian and Gay Studies* 13, no. 4 (2007): 519–33.

Calderón, Héctor, and José David Saldívar, eds. *Criticism in the Borderlands: Studies in Chicano Literature, Culture, and Ideology.* Durham, NC: Duke University Press, 1991.

Castillo, Adelaida del. "Malintzín Tenepal: A Preliminary Look into a New Perspective." In *Chicana Feminist Thought: The Basic Historical Writings,* edited by Alma M. Garcia, 122–26. New York: Routledge, 1997.

Cixous, Hélène. "The Laugh of the Medusa." *Signs* 1, no. 4 (1976): 875–93.

Crowder, Diane. "Amazons and Mothers? Monique Wittig, Hélène Cixous and Theories of Women's Writing." *Contemporary Literature* 24, no. 2 (1983): 117–44.

De Lauretis, Teresa. "When Lesbians Were Not Women." In *Monique Wittig: Theoretical, Political and Literary Essays,* edited by Namascar Shaktini. Urbana: University of Illinois Press, 2005.

Delphy, Christine. "The Invention of French Feminism: An Essential Move." *Yale French Studies* 87 (1995): 190–221.

Epps, Bradley, and Jonathan Katz. "Monique Wittig's Materialist Utopia and Radical Critique." *GLQ: A Journal of Lesbian and Gay Studies* 13, no. 4 (2007): 423–54.

Ferreira, Ana Paula. *A Urgência de Contar: Contos de Mulheres dos Anos 40.* Lisbon: Caminho, 2002.

Greene, Gayle, and Coppélia Kahn, eds. *Changing Subjects: The Making of Feminist Literary Criticism.* New York: Routledge Library Editions: Women, Feminism and Literature, 2012.

Guilleragues, Gabriel Joseph de Lavergne. *Lettres Portugaises.* Paris: Chez Claude Barbin, 1669.

Guttierrez-Jones, Carl Scott. *Rethinking the Borderlands: Between Chicano Culture and Legal Discourse.* Berkeley: University of California Press, 1995.

Hicks, Emily. *Border Writing: The Multidimensional Text.* Minneapolis: University of Minnesota Press, 1991.

Jolly, Margaretta. *In Love and Struggle: Letters in Contemporary Feminism.* New York: Columbia University Press, 2008.

Jones, Ann Rosalind. "Writing the Body: Toward an Understanding of 'L'Écriture Féminine.'" *Feminist Studies* 7, no. 2 (1981).

Kauffman, Linda. *Discourses of Desire: Gender, Genre and Epistolary Fictions.* Ithaca, NY: Cornell University Press, 1986.

Keating, Ana Louise, ed. *Entre Mundos/Among Worlds: New Perspectives on Gloria Anzaldúa.* New York: Palgrave Macmillan, 2005.

Klobucka, Anna. "Hélène Cixous and the Hour of Clarice Lispector." *SubStance* 73 (1994): 41–62.

———. *The Portuguese Nun: Formation of a National Myth.* Lewisburg, PA: Bucknell University Press, 2001.

Macedo, Helder. "Teresa and Fátima and Isabel." *Times Literary Supplement,* December 12, 1975: 1484.

Martins, Ana Margarida Dias. "*Novas Cartas Portuguesas*: The Making of a Reputation." *Journal of Feminist Scholarship* 2 (2012): 24–39.

McPherson, William. "Alien Porn." *Washington Post,* February 2, 1975: 139.

Owen, Hilary. "Um Quarto que Seja Seu: The Quest for Camões' Sister." *Portuguese Studies* 11 (1995): 179–91.

———. "New Cartographies of the Body in *Novas Cartas Portuguesas*: The (Counter-) Narrative of the Nation and the Sign of the Voyage Back." *ellipsis* 1 (1999): 73–83.

Owen, Hilary, and Claudia Pazos Alonso. *Antigone's Daughters? Gender, Genealogy and the Politics of Authorship in 20th-Century Portuguese Women's Writing.* Lewisburg, PA: Bucknell University Press, 2011.

Paz, Octavio. *The Labyrinth of Solitude.* Translated by Lysander Kemp, Yara Milos, and Rachel Phillips Belash. London: Penguin, 1990.

Red Rag: A Magazine of Liberation. "*New Portuguese Letters* by Maria Isabel Barreno, Maria Teresa Horta and Maria Velho da Costa", 1 (1975–76): 30.

Roth, Benita. *Separate Roads to Feminism: Black, Chicana and White Feminist Movements in America's Second Wave.* Cambridge: Cambridge University Press, 2004.

Saldivar-Hull, Sonia. *Feminism on the Border: Chicana Gender Politics and Literature.* Berkeley: University of California Press, 2000.

Vertigo (DVD). Directed by Alfred Hitchcock. Universal Home Video, 2005.

Wittig, Monique. "One Is Not Born a Woman." *Feminist Issues* 1, no. 2 (1981): 47–54.

———. "The Point of View: Universal or Particular?" *The Straight Mind and Other Essays.* New York: Harvester Wheatsheaf, 1992.

Yarbro-Bejarano, Yvonne. "Gloria Anzaldúa's *Borderlands/La Frontera*: Cultural Studies, 'Difference' and the Unitary Subject." *Cultural Critique* (1994): 5–28.

Chapter 7

Sexy Stories and Postfeminist Empowerment

From *Häutungen* to *Wetlands*

Christa Binswanger and Kathy Davis

This chapter explores shifts in feminist and postfeminist discourse on sexuality using two influential novels about women's sexual agency and empowerment as a case in point. Both were written in Germany more than thirty years apart and became international bestsellers, and both were proclaimed as provocative critiques of societal norms surrounding women's sexuality.[1] *Häutungen*[2] (literally 'shedding') by Verena Stefan appeared in 1975 at the peak of the New German Women's Movement. It was published by a feminist publisher and went on to become a seminal feminist text about women's sexuality and sexual empowerment, selling more than 150,000 copies within the first three years and being translated into many languages.[3] *Feuchtgebiete* (or *Wetlands*) by Charlotte Roche was published three decades later in 2008, in the midst of what has been called postfeminism.[4] Written in a confrontational, humoristic, and arguably pornographic manner, this semiautobiographical novel focuses on a young woman's exploration of her body and sexuality. *Wetlands* has been heralded as a new feminist manifesto that breaks with the "old" feminism of the 1970s and speaks to young women of today.[5] Both texts focus on women's bodies and sexuality as a site for women's sexual empowerment and both present heroines who use their own embodied experiences to engage with repressive cultural norms. Further, both are concerned with encouraging women to explore their bodies, to discover and act upon their sexual desires. We argue that both present models for an active, knowledgeable female sexual subject—a subject embedded in the Western, post-Enlightenment culture from which both texts have emerged. Yet while sharing some similarities, the books also contain marked differences. They often offer radically different perspectives on women's embodiment and sexual pleasure. Whereas Stefan draws upon the notion of "authentic voice" in her critique of sexism and the commodification of women's bodies,[6] Roche uses pornography and abjection to transgress normative representations of the female body. The authors address their (largely female) audiences differently, with each engaging in specific exclusions and inclusions with regard to gender, race, and class. The books are highly dissimilar in the ways that female sexual subjectivity and empowerment are constructed, with Stefan proposing a collective of "we feminists," while Roche addresses her readers as autonomous individuals. For Stefan, feminism is the solution to women's sexual disempowerment, while for Roche, feminism is part of the problem.

It is interesting to see how many resonances there are between the two texts with many of the earlier feminist critiques of sexuality that had informed *Häutungen,* operating as a kind of shadow in Roche's *Wetlands*—as a textual trace that she at once takes up and fights against. At the same time, the texts replay many of the discontinuities and fissures in feminist discourse on sexuality during the past three decades. Since the 1970s, feminists have been concerned with the body and with women as desiring sexual subjects. The notion that women should wrest control over their bodies and sexualities from a repressive patriarchal social order has always been the lynchpin of feminist sexual politics. For example, the transnational classic of second-wave feminism, *Our Bodies, Ourselves,* criticized cultural and scientific discourses that treated women's bodies and bodily functions as dirty, unruly, and shameful.[7] It encouraged women to explore their bodies in order to discover their own specific needs and desires, initiating a self-conscious process that literally involved women reappropriating their bodies in all their sensual concreteness, from physical sensations, smells, and tastes to embodied sexual experiences. "Taking back the body" became the slogan that shaped a collective feminist body/politics. *Häutungen* belongs to this tradition as a prototypical feminist story about women's sexual empowerment in the context of the feminist movement of the 1960s and 1970s.

While the themes of celebrating the physicality of the body, sexual desire, and agency are also present in *Wetlands,* the narrative distances itself from feminism. *Wetlands* is an example of what is often referred to as post-feminism—a historical and generational shift involving changing interests, practices, and identity projects of women who came of age after second-wave feminism.[8] As Rosalind Gill puts it, postfeminism is a cultural sensibility across a range of spheres (including the body, sexuality, and agency) in which feminist and antifeminist elements are entangled in an ironic and sometimes playful way.[9] *Wetlands* resonates with this particular reading of post-feminism. In the text the body is a central concern—and, indeed, almost an obsession. Sexuality is celebrated; once the "object" of the male gaze or the "victim" of pornography, women within postfeminist discourse are sexual subjects who are "forever up for it." "Being oneself" is promoted, whereby the emphasis is on individual choices and self-empowerment. Postfeminism is about following one's own desires, the only constraint being how to "please oneself." Sexual confidence is "cool," and part of this coolness entails being able to laugh at sexism. Postfeminism specializes in an ironic attitude that "sees through" attempts at manipulation and turns them on their head. Postfeminism is sometimes treated as "beyond" feminism, either negatively, for example, as an expression of the current backlash against feminism in the media and popular culture,[10] or positively, among academic feminists as part of the necessary epistemological break that has occurred in the wake of feminism's encounter with difference, the deconstruction of the universal "we," and the acknowledgment of the variety of women's experiences and struggles for empowerment.[11] However, many contemporary feminist scholars have argued that postfeminism is, in fact, not "beyond" feminism at all.[12] As Angela McRobbie has suggested, postfeminism needs and, indeed, presupposes feminism. It has to invoke feminism in order to relegate it to the past and to initiate "a new regime of sexual meanings based on female consent, equality, participation, and pleasure, free of politics."[13] For this reason, postfeminism remains firmly tied to the very discourses of feminism that it seeks to deny. It is precisely this tension—the tension between feminist and antifeminist themes—that characterizes postfeminism. In McRobbie's view, the challenge is to understand how postfeminism speaks to women's struggles for (sexual) empowerment while challenging the silencing of feminist critiques of the ways sexuality remains embedded in gendered relations of power.

Here we take up this challenge, using these two texts as a starting point for exploring how feminist discourse on women's bodies, sexual pleasure, and empowerment has changed over the last three decades. We begin by paying particular attention to how each text might be considered a feminist story. We then compare the narratives, showing how *Wetlands* takes up and recycles but also rearticulates and transforms some of the themes initiated in *Häutungen.* Conclusions will be drawn concerning shifts in feminist and postfeminist thinking about women's embodiment, sexuality, and agency, as well as how each text enables or circumvents critical perspectives on sexual empowerment.

Häutungen, Authenticity, and the Female Sexual Self

Verena Stefan, a physical therapist, was born in 1947 in Switzerland. She left Bern in 1968 to go to Berlin. There, she cofounded the group Brot & Rosen and coauthored the first edition of *Frauenhandbuch Nr. 1*[14]—the German equivalent to *Our Bodies, Ourselves.*[15] *Häutungen* (1975), her first novel, was the most read example of German feminist *Erfahrungsberichte* ("reports of experience") in the 1970s and the most broadly discussed text in female reading circles and self-awareness groups.[16] It achieved cult status among second-wave feminists.[17] Stefan narrates her life, locating it in everyday experiences of women of her generation. The book is written as a coming-of-age story with its major turning point triggered by the protagonist's accumulation of denigrating sexual experiences with men in a male-dominated society. Freeing herself from male affirmation and engaging in female friendship and erotic same-sex experiences become the motor for her emancipation and, ultimately, lead to her transformation as sexual subject. The metaphor of "shedding" (*Häutungen*) describes this process—a process that resonated with what many women of her generation and class were experiencing across Western Europe as well as other parts of the world.[18]

The narration reflecting daily life in Berlin is fragmented and intertwined with flashbacks to childhood and adolescence in Switzerland. Stefan makes use of varying registers, from pamphlet language to poetry, focusing on her protagonist's emotional processes. Nature is used as a source for metaphors to express "true" female feelings, bodily sensations, dreams, and fantasies. The plot is organized in four chapters. The first chapter is narrated by Verushka in the first person. It depicts her as a "woman of average intelligence, twenty-three years of age."[19] She works as a physical therapist in Berlin where she is initially involved in a heterosexual relationship with Dave, a Black Panther activist. Later she takes up with the Marxist activist, Samuel, and moves into a flat with him. At the same time, she has her first erotic experiences with a woman, Nadjenka. By the end of the first chapter, she decides to turn away from men and embarks on a life of loneliness and sexual abstinence. Chapter 2 is marked by Verushka's self-questioning and her retreat to working in a women's group. In chapter 3 she re-enters the world of female same-sex desire and passion, and, in the chapter that follows, the process of shedding takes place. To underline this process, the author changes the narrative perspective from "I-Verushka" to "she-Chloe," a new name that is connected to the process of writing her story and, by implication, of gaining a new sense of the self. Chloe gives voice to her own experiences, creating her own language to express them not only as her own but also as a result of a collective feminist consciousness. Thus, *Häutungen* provides both a platform for lesbian separatism and an independent space for all women to find their "true sexual selves," regardless of their sexual orientation.[20]

Häutungen was not only a very personal account but also the product of a collective effort. Looking back at the book, Stefan noted in 1994, "*Shedding* is in fact the offspring of a collective political process. … The oppressed were no longer exclusively other people, the exploited working class and inhabitants of the so-called third world, but also us women."[21] The gesture of women giving voice to their own perspectives was clearly directed against some of the men on the left who had labeled the "women's question" as a "secondary contradiction."[22] The first and most extensive part of the book consists of narratives about sexual experiences with men as marked by agency and dominance on the part of men and passiveness and taking over of the perspective of male pleasure on the part of women. The following excerpt is particularly revealing:

> One of them kissed passionately, madly, so that I
> felt teeth, nothing but teeth –
> and I kissed passionately, madly.
> Another kissed gently and thought anything else
> adolescent and immature –
> and I kissed gently, mature.
> One of them likes my legs together, another spread
> and prone, another open and wrapped round his back –
> and I kept my legs together or spread and prone or open and
> wrapped round his
> back.
> One of them wanted to keep going all night, another
> could only get it on once –
> And I kept going all night long or could only get
> it on once.
> …
> I now found myself looking for a human man.[23]

Here Stefan sets out to rewrite the heterosexual script by articulating women's desire for an equal partner of the opposite sex as well as the need to overcome previously learned lessons of passivity. The text seeks to put an end to women being the sole object of male-dominated sexual scripting and of having to automatically adapt to male needs and desires. *Häutungen* claimed to represent the authentic voice of femininity, thereby speaking to a wide range of female readers. This authenticity was rhetorically constructed as a contiguity of voice and body. According to Warner, "voices in testimonies … have an affective function of persuasion, insofar as the reader's emotional responses to the conveyed personal experiences might bring them around to new ways of thinking and treating the individuals whose collective marginalization and oppression are represented."[24] The authenticity of the embodied experiences of the "I" in the excerpt cited above is created by the testimonial-like description of the author's different sexual encounters with men. The need for change is created through the repetition of the female voice unquestioningly doing what a man wants her to do. The author draws her readers into her experience through the use of "we"—as in, "we know," "we act and react accordingly"—thereby enabling them to identify with the text and respond affectively. It was this rhetorical move that allowed *Häutungen* to become more than a personal testimony, coming to stand in for women's collective experience of becoming sexual subjects.[25] Female readers could identify with the person who was telling the testimonial-like story in the book to the extent that they often addressed Stefan when she appeared in public as the embodied voice of their experience and as the representative of the women's movement.[26] That *Häutungen* has been a key text for understanding women's sexuality is attested by the hundreds of letters that Stefan received as well as the critical acclaim the book garnered in the media.[27] It played an important role in the collective belief within the German women's movement of the seventies that sexual scripts among men and women could be changed. In *Häutungen* Stefan also initiated the search for a new language—a language different from the one that had been imposed upon women by men: "No places on my body … correspond to these … brutal designations. *Clitoris* has nothing in common with this part of my body which is called clitoris."[28] Criticizing the history of language and literature, Stefan attempted to go beyond merely neutralizing sexist language to find words that could capture the "new experiences" related to sexual intimacy with other women.

Stefan indicates that when "I wanted to write about sensations, experiences, eroticism among women I went completely speechless. That's why I removed myself as far as possible from everyday speech and tried to find new ways through poetry."[29] Stefan's emphasis on women's ability to change the heterosexual script by including explicit depictions of female same-sex relationships was important for German feminist literature. As Levin notes, her belief in empowerment through developing a new kind of feminist literacy "certainly takes seriously the claim that the 'personal is political,' pouring that idea into aesthetic moulds."[30] In her move to get rid of sexism by concentrating on women's bodily experience and pleasure in sexual encounters, Stefan put the female body outside the reach of men.[31] She turned to nature as a source of authentic female embodiment. By exploring the female body and its true sexual sensations, by rejecting sexual encounters with men in favor of same-sex experiences, and by looking for a new language as a way for women to overcome their speechlessness about their own bodies and sexuality, *Häutungen* could be heralded by a broad range of female readers as providing the feminist path toward liberation from patriarchal suppression. This move was enormously influential, with nearly all the leading daily newspapers printing reviews, both laudatory and critical. The text was even called "the contemporary women's bible."[32] Although some of Stefan's contemporaries questioned the aesthetic quality of the text,[33] most welcomed her decisive critique of sexism and her search for new, authentic self-expression and true female sexual embodiment.

Wetlands, Sexual (Un)inhibition, and Shock

Charlotte Roche, the author of *Wetlands,* was born in England to a white, middle-class family (her father was an engineer, her mother a politically active artist). She later moved to Germany, where she went to secondary school, sang in a girls' garage rock group, and undertook self-mutilation, drug experiments, and shaving her head. She gave up school to act and her performances appeared regularly on YouTube, where, for example, she may be seen stripping and exposing her armpit hair. Roche later became a presenter on VIVA, the German equivalent of MTV, and she made her name on a late-night talk show where she invited celebrities like Quentin Tarantino, Uma Thurman, and Kylie Minogue to talk about their sexual fantasies. In 2004, she won the prestigious Grimme Prize for television. Unlike Stefan, who was virtually unknown before the publication of *Häutungen* catapulted her to fame, Roche was already a well-known celebrity when she published her first book, *Feuchtgebiete* (or *Wetlands*) in 2008.[34] The book draws upon Roche's own experiences as a rebellious teenager. She was, like eighteen-year-old Helen Memel, the heroine in her book, the child of divorced parents, and she remembers entertaining the fantasy that her parents might someday be reunited. However, unlike the heroine of her book, she regards herself as far less daring than Helen, thereby making the book more fictive than autobiographical.

The book is narrated by Helen, who has been hospitalized after suffering an anal lesion during an intimate shaving incident. The entire book takes place on the proctology unit of a hospital where Helen is recovering from surgery. During her stay, Helen—who is in pain and bored out of her mind—entertains herself by remembering various sex acts and developing creative ways to masturbate (she uses anything from avocado pits to the showerhead in the bathtub to her father's barbeque tongs), by experimenting with her bodily fluids, and by playing pranks on hospital workers and visitors. Helen will eat anything: vaginal fluids (which she calls smegma), her own menstrual blood as well as that of a friend, semen, piss, pus, puke, snot, scabs, and even the secretions from her anal wound. As she puts it, "I am my own garbage disposal. Bodily secretion recycler."[35] The book contains many accounts of her hemorrhoids (which she affectionately refers to as her cauliflower) as well as her delight in having anal sex. She discusses genital shaving, enemas, the nuances of having sex during menstruation, and a dizzying array of positions and practices, usually involving multiple penetrations. Her biggest triumph is always being able to have an orgasm during anal intercourse. "I can come with just a cock up my ass, not being touched anywhere else. Yep, I'm proud of that."[36] While Helen clearly prefers to have sex with men (and, following Oedipal logics, her father is not exempt from her fantasies), she also makes regular trips to brothels to—as she puts it—"study pussy." Her preference is the black hooker since "black women have the reddest pussies" compared to the "pussy pink next to light pink skin that is a lot more boring."[37] Helen rejoices that this particular hooker is even more sexually daring than Helen herself, something that allows her to feel like she's "doing something unbelievably taboo, something crazy."[38] While Roche presents Helen's sexual encounters with women as transgressive, it is a very different kind of transgression than the same-sex love promoted in *Häutungen.* Helen's desire for women is never expressed as anything other than a scientific interest in women's genitals or as a thinly disguised colonial fascination with black women's sexuality.[39]

Perhaps the most striking feature of *Wetlands,* however, is Helen's delight in engaging in outrageous and shocking performances. She enjoys walking the corridors in her hospital gown with her ass (including bloody ass plug) exposed and leaving her used tampons in the hospital elevator. She provokes the hospital staff and taunts her male nurse, asking him to take her (anal) portrait. As she puts it, "In any room, I have to be the most uninhibited of everyone present."[40] When the long-suffering hospital cleaning woman expresses disgust at Helen's carefully choreographed messes, Helen takes revenge by getting her into trouble with the head nurse, thereby showing that her crusade against the "cleanliness police" supersedes any consideration of the working conditions of underpaid and overworked cleaners. In a strange reversal, she manages to position herself as the victim of the hospital worker's "resentment over cleaning up after filthy patients."[41] Helen's sexual and scatological antics take up much of the novel, structuring it as a series of performances. For example, she describes how she masturbates with the showerhead in the bathtub, aiming the water at "the spot a guy with a long cock can hit in certain positions … I fold my arms behind my head—both hands are free because my pussy holds the shower head all by itself—close my eyes, and hum 'Amazing Grace.'"[42] Told with humor and a heavy dose of irony, these performances are interspersed with flashbacks of earlier sexual encounters. Helen situates herself as a disinterested observer, intent on cataloguing her acts and finding ever more creative ways to shock. However, there is also another storyline. This involves Helen's traumatic childhood in which her mother attempts suicide with Helen's little brother. Helen finds them lying on the kitchen floor when she comes home from school. Further trauma is detailed relating to her parents' divorce and remarriage to different partners. Throughout the book, Helen engages in a desperate struggle to bring her parents together at her hospital bed—a struggle that dramatically ends in her horrific, but ultimately unsuccessful, act of self-mutilation. Alone and despondent, she renounces her family, and along with it, her "Bad Girl" identity, and leaves the hospital with the only person who seems to care about her, her male nurse. They ride off into the sunset on his bicycle. *Wetlands* is thus not just a pornographic account, it is also a novel about loneliness, despair, and alienation.[43] The heroine is, by her own admission, "numbingly lonely."[44] Underneath the joyously subversive facade lurks an anguished young woman. Her predicament will seem familiar—working mothers, emotionally absent or ineffectual fathers, divorce are all products of the transformations that have occurred since the 1970s and, in part, as a result of second-wave feminism. Helen's loneliness and alienation resonate with the distress experienced by many young women. Her strategies for alleviating her anguish—her outrageous antics as well as her self-abuse—are not unlike the practice of self-harm (in the form of cutting, self-starvation) employed by many white, middle-class young women as a means to gain control over their circumstances. *Wetlands,* as a text and in its reception, provides a contemporary example of how feminism is taken up and, simultaneously, resisted. Its success with European and North American women indicates its appeal, addressing a broader set of concerns around gender, embodiment, and sexuality. However, Roche's relationship with feminism is contradictory. She has repeatedly insisted in the media that she is a feminist. Given the current backlash against feminism, this is itself a daring act for a young woman in a context where feminism is often treated as "the F-word." Roche refers to her brand of feminism as "feminism of the body that has to do with anxiety and repression and the fear that you stink, and this for me is clearly feminist, that one builds confidence with your own body."[45] While she views her book as a "manifesto" that takes up the emancipatory principles of the 1960s and 1970s that have not "arrived properly," she is critical of feminism, claiming that hers is not a feminism "in the political sense."[46] Moreover, she has repeatedly locked horns with Germany's most well-known feminist Alice Schwarzer, the editor of the famous feminist magazine *Emma,*[47] and has made frequent disparaging references to the "old feminism" of the 1970s, which she presents as dowdy and moralistic. The protagonist seems to be intent on shocking feminists of the "Alice Schwarzer era" with her deliberately irreverent or "politically incorrect" statements. Feminism is transformed into the "Big Sister" whose disapproval only intensifies the secret pleasures of the book's protagonist. Feminism allows her to play the disobedient daughter.[48] In addition to representing a contradictory relationship toward second-wave feminism, *Wetlands* presents an identity project that is deeply ambivalent. It is an identity project in which the heroine is both a rebellious bad girl and a vulnerable motherless child. She is both mockingly provocative and deeply distressed, desiring to be in control at all times but ultimately realizing that—as the heroine puts it—"everything's pointless and I can't control things."[49] In the final analysis, it may be exactly this ambivalence that has had so much resonance with privileged, young white women at this particular juncture in late modernity. Their ambivalence about their bodies and sexualities, the contradictions of an ideology of individual choice in a neoliberal context of increasing precarity and global inequalities, and, last but not least, the necessity of having to distance oneself from anything "old," including feminism, may be at the heart of *Wetlands*' extraordinary success.

Feminist Stories

At the outset, we suggested that both *Häutungen* and *Wetlands* are feminist stories. Both focus on women's bodies and sexuality as a site for women's sexual empowerment. Both present protagonists who use their own embodied experiences to engage with repressive cultural norms. Both are concerned with encouraging women to discover and act upon their sexual desires. Both present models for an active, knowledgeable female sexual subject. While they address many of the same concerns, they do so, however, in ways that are very different. In Stefan's view, women's bodies have been appropriated by men. If women are to find their authentic selves, they will have to "break free of men."[50] They have to overcome their dependency on male approval within the sexual encounter, an encounter that is aimed at fulfilling men's expectations and ignoring the needs and pleasures of the female partner. Male-dominated social structures and institutions have inscribed women's bodies in ways that have to be unlearned in order for a woman to become a truly embodied female sexual self. Women's groups and collective efforts enable the female subject to gain a new self-understanding and to achieve an embodiment as an independent sexual self beyond the male gaze. Roche is also critical of the social constraints on women's embodiment. Against the backdrop of a media-saturated culture,[51] she laments the fact that women's bodies are defined by a popular culture that is obsessed with hygiene. Women's bodies have been sanitized by the media with its emphasis on airbrushed models, deodorants, and perfume. Women have become insecure about their bodies, experiencing them as repulsive and dirty. Roche's project entails recovering precisely those aspects of embodiment that have been most reviled, the female body's "leakiness," that is, all that is dirty, unruly, and excessive.[52] Rather than turning to self-discovery, she urges women to poke fun at the hygienic order by becoming willfully monstrous, embracing the abject body, to renegotiate the conditions of their embodiment, and to "reclaim" their bodies under their own terms.[53]

In addition to providing critiques of women's embodiment, both authors problematize women's sexuality. For Stefan, sexual intercourse, as commonly practiced, "is an undertaking too inconsequential to create happiness, to learn something about the other person and oneself, to communicate with each other."[54] Similarly, orgasm has been blown out of proportion: "Everything else is forgotten, including the question of what orgasm actually is and what significance it might have for human understanding."[55] She situates women's sexuality in a relational economy of self and other, whereby there is a need to discover other, "new" forms of bodily encounter "beyond orgasm," which will enable both communication and self-understanding. By becoming experts on their own bodies, overcoming taboos of touching, and exploring their sexual desires, women can begin the long, demanding, and never-ending journey for new ways of experiencing female sexuality, a journey that culminates in same-sex intimacy. The "new" female sexuality is marked by reciprocity and softness. This shift enables women to understand themselves as sexual selves, always changing and open to new ways of becoming. It is this self-reflective move that frees women from patriarchal suppression and allows them to become sexual subjects. For Roche, the problem with women's sexuality is not men. Nevertheless, she believes that women have a disturbed relationship with their sexuality. They want to be sexy—and, indeed, have to be sexy in a culture obsessed with sex.[56] However, the obsession many women have with cleanliness, with excretions, with bodily hair, runs counter to their ability to enjoy sex. She insists on raising precisely those issues that are not normally talked about in public—masturbation, sexual fantasies, masochism, and the relationship between pain and pleasure. According to Roche, unlike men who have a whole range of names for their sexual organs as well as different ways of talking about what state of arousal they are in, "women have no language for their desire. I think a lot of women don't masturbate simply because they don't know how to talk about it."[57] Roche encourages women to live out their fantasies, however abject.

While Stefan problematizes heterosexuality, Roche has been criticized for being unabashedly heterosexual, and even heteronormative.[58] For her, sexual desire is, first and foremost, about novelty, about women finding new and different ways of pleasing themselves. The enemy is, therefore, not heteronormativity per se, but rather anything that is normative or linked to shame or inhibition. Her project is to transgress the borders of "normal" sexuality, whether her protagonist is having sex with a woman or exalting in her ability to climax during anal penetration "without being touched anywhere else." In this sense, Roche's perspective on sexuality can be seen as transgressive and even queer. However, she also suggests that the critique of gender, heteronormativity, and other relations of power, which has been the hallmark of the feminism propagated by Stefan and others, can be discarded, once and for all, and replaced by a vision of women as sexual agents, free to pursue their own desires whatever they may be. *Wetlands* resonates with postfeminism[59] in that it takes up critical notions of second-wave feminism and transforms them into a more appealing and less overtly political version for a contemporary audience. For example, *Wetlands* might be understood as feminist in its refusal of repressive norms of feminine hygiene. Its insistence on naming what is normally shrouded in shame may be experienced by some as liberating. Its uninhibited delight in transgression and celebration of women's unfettered agency may open up a space for the exploration of non-normative sexualities. At the same time, however, it presents a highly ambivalent perspective. Without the explicit critique of gender and power so central to Stefan's text, Roche leaves heteronormativity as an unproblematized escape hatch, implying that it is always possible for women to retreat into the safety of the romantic heterosexual script. Both Stefan and Roche make a strong case for women's sexual agency. However, their vision of what constitutes female sexual subjectivity differs markedly, and each version entails specific and problematic exclusions. For Stefan, the authentic female subject speaks for all women because, in her view, all women are oppressed by the patriarchy and, therefore, are united by this common experience. Her feminist sexual subject embarks upon sexual encounters that transgress the patriarchal script of inequality that history, culture, and society have inscribed in heterosexuality. An imagined female community of equal women, looking for new authentic bodily experiences, forms the ground for this "new" sexual subject and, simultaneously, provides the basis for Stefan's feminist utopia.[60] Stefan's focus on how sexism shapes encounters between the sexes in everyday life remains unreflective with regard to other hierarchies of power based on racialization or class.[61] Her conviction that sexism runs deeper than racism or class struggle—a fairly common position in second-wave feminism—neglects the entanglement of racism and sexism in women's sexuality. Similarly, her statement that women across the globe are sexually oppressed by men and that this oppression transcends any other context of belonging is problematic when read against situated analyses of how power works in local contexts. Roche's text avoids some of these pitfalls, although her interest in "black pussies," as described earlier, comes perilously close to colonial fascination for black sexuality. Unlike Stefan, Roche does not posit a specifically female subject, nor does she speak problematically of women as a collectivity. *Wetlands* is devoid of any suggestion that women might be the objects of male fantasies or gendered structures of power. Roche's protagonist is emblematic of a new femininity organized around self-confidence and autonomy. She is the sexualized subject *par excellence* whose only aim in life seems to be discovering new ways to act upon her body, new ways to reinvent herself. For Roche, being an agent requires little beyond finding new ways to shock, whereby the specific content of the action is of little consequence. It is a subversive strategy, which does not require the agent to worry about class privilege or racism.[62] In fact, the only requirement is that her actions be novel, entertaining, and without inhibition. At the same time, Roche does not deny women's vulnerabilities. These vulnerabilities, however, remain caught in the logic of their autonomous and abject desires. For example, she shows how it is possible to suppress physical pain and discomfort, as long as it has been freely chosen or is the result of one's own actions. In a similar vein, she rejects any notion of connection with others, remaining focused upon her protagonist as isolated and self-sufficient sexual subject.[63] Roche does not reject heterosexual romance and even implies that it can provide an answer to her heroine's loneliness—and here she is far more sanguine about its positive effects on women's well-being than Stefan. Still, as a solution it remains tantalizingly vague—no more than a promise. Roche's model of female subjectivity is, therefore, considerably less utopian than Stefan's. It provides a contradictory and ambivalent combination of autonomy and dependence, agency and vulnerability, and transgressiveness and conventionality. It is perhaps precisely this combination of recalcitrant sexual subject and vulnerable lost child that is at the heart of *Wetlands*' appeal. Both texts draw upon feminist critiques of a normative order that demeans the female body and curtails women's sexuality. Both encourage women to actively explore their sexuality and discover what gives them pleasure. While both stories are transgressive, this transgression has different implications for thinking about women's sexual empowerment.

Toward a Critical Perspective on Sexual Empowerment

Since the last quarter of the twentieth century, feminist and queer theorists have been concerned with developing critical perspectives on sexual empowerment in an increasingly sexualized culture.[64] We will now turn to how the "sexy stories" that have been the subject of this chapter might be viewed as emblematic of the shift in critical thinking on women's sexual empowerment from the modernist frame of second-wave feminism to a more postmodernist—and perhaps postfeminist—frame. In accordance with a modernist frame, Stefan constructs a plot in which her heroine "escapes" from oppression and "finds" empowerment by articulating her authentic female sexuality. Female sexuality is a clear-cut category, a "truth waiting to be discovered."[65] Telling her story allows a woman to articulate her sexual experience as authentic, thereby finding her "voice" as sexual subject. This new language can then be mobilized to create a feminist "we"—a "we" that transcends the personal experience of the individual women to become political, a means of collective empowerment. In contrast, Roche follows a postfeminist logic when she disregards notions of a specifically feminine or authentic sexuality in favor of a fragmented and ever-changing identity. She cultivates a transgressive space where bold and provocative "bad girls" can explore their sexual desires. Her heroine is frivolous and hedonistic, intent on breaking rules and finding creative ways to shock. For Roche, writing in the postmodern era, there is no feminist "we." While her heroine may be admired, she is not necessarily regarded as the "voice" of women's authentic experiences with sexuality. Her transgression is "beyond" the political.[66] Indeed, Roche's mode of narration creates a reflexive gap between representation and identification. Her second narrative of the abandoned and vulnerable child is interwoven with the narrative of the transgressive female agent, offering the reader different and highly ambivalent possibilities for identification. Roche creates a model for an identity project that combines sexual agency and outrageous acts of transgression with experiences of vulnerability, alienation, and loneliness. It is precisely this refusal to flatten out contradictions that makes the text subversive.

While both *Häutungen* and *Wetlands* provide perspectives on sexuality and women's sexual agency as well as offer possibilities for subversion for their readers, the question remains whether they also suggest a critical feminist perspective on empowerment. The search for critical feminist perspectives has always been plagued by the uneasy search for a "we," for an "imagined community" that is both impossible and yet part of what fuels the necessary flames that keep feminist debates going. Inclusion never works without exclusion, making it essential that feminists ongoingly reflect their claims to a particular standpoint or perspective. Despite its rejection of the old feminist "we," postfeminism has not changed the fact that relational economies of self and other remain crucial.[67]

While *Häutungen* invites a critical reading in terms of its exclusions along the axes of race and class, the metaphor of empowerment as a constant process of shedding continues to provide possibilities for thinking critically about relations between the sexes. Stefan's perspective demands an ongoing self-reflection, of articulating, interrogating, and rethinking processes of change. This is, we would argue, the key to any critical feminist approach to sexuality. It is in this respect that *Wetlands* leaves us empty-handed. While Roche opens up the possibility for exploring the desires and fears of a younger generation of women, she precludes an exploration of the rifts that divide feminists and postfeminists on the issue of sexuality as well as the ways in which the stories of previous generations have contributed to the self-understanding of the generations that have followed. In this sense, Roche's text is a missed opportunity. However, even more problematic is her adolescent gesture of total refusal, which precludes the very possibility of reflection. It is difficult to be critical of Roche's text without appearing antisex, moralistic, and—worst of all—out of touch and obsolete. Ultimately, the foreclosure of reflexivity and self-critique is what makes *Wetlands*—as well as Roche's mode of transgression—unsuited as a critical feminist perspective on sexual empowerment.

Christa Binswanger is senior lecturer (ständige Dozentin) and director of the Gender and Diversity department at the University of St. Gallen in Switzerland. In her ongoing research project, "Sexuality and Gender: Sexual Scripts as Palimpsests," she investigates gendered sexual scripts in selected German literature from the late 1950s to 2014. Her main research areas are: gender, queer, and affect studies; critical sexualities studies; intersectionality, diversity, and inclusion; care economies. Her most recent publication: Angelika Baier, Christa Binswanger, Jana Häberlein, Yv Nay, Andrea Zimmermann, eds., *Affekt und Geschlecht: Eine einführende Anthologie* (Wien: Zaglossus, 2014).

Kathy Davis is senior research fellow in the Sociology Department at the VU University in the Netherlands. Her research interests include sociology of the body, intersectionality, traveling theory and transnational practices; biography as methodology,; and critical and creative strategies for academic writing. She is the author of many books, including *Reshaping the Female Body* (Routledge, 1995), *Dubious Equalities and Embodied Differences* (Rowman & Littlefield, 2003), and *The Making of* Our Bodies, Ourselves*: How Feminism Travels across Borders* (Duke, 2007). Her most recent book is *Dancing Tango: Passionate Encounters in a Globalizing World* (NYU Press, 2015).

Notes

This is the slightly shortened version of a paper published in *Feminist Theory* in 2012: Christa Binswanger and Kathy Davis, "Sexy Stories and Postfeminist Empowerment: From *Häutungen* to *Wetlands*," *Feminist Theory* 13, no. 3 (2012): 245–63.

This work was supported by the SNSF grant PMPDP1_128987. We also would like to thank Nina Lykke and Barbro Wijma, who headed a program in November 2009 at the Centre of Gender Excellence (GEXcel) at Linköping University, where we met and took up this dialogue on the two books. We have purposely left one title in German and provided the translated English title of the other. While we are aware of the problems surrounding the hegemonic position of English with regard to language politics and translation issues, we want to show that these books are not merely local products but became, in different ways, influential outside the German-speaking community.

1. See, for example Tobe Levin, *Political Ideology and Aesthetics in Neo-Feminist German Fiction: Verena Stefan, Elfriede Jelinek, Margot Schroeder* (Ann Arbor, Michigan, University Microfilms International, 1979) on the history and reception of *Häutungen*, and Christina Scharff, "The New German Feminisms: Of *Wetlands* and *Alpha-Girls*," in *New Femininities: Postfeminism, Neoliberalism and Subjectivity*, ed. Rosalind Gill and Christina Scharff (Basingstoke: Palgrave, 2011), 265–78 on *Wetlands*.
2. Verena Stefan, *Häutungen. Autobiographische Aufzeichnungen. Gedichte. Träume. Analysen.* (Munich: Frauenoffensive, 1975).
3. *Häutungen* was edited and published by the collective *Frauenoffensive* with—as they put it—"no advertising or attention from a media establishment." See Tobe Levin, "Afterword," in *Shedding and Literally Dreaming*, ed. Verena Stefan, trans. Johanna Steigleder Moore, Beth E. Weckmueller, Johanna Albert, and Tobe Levin (New York: The Feminist Press, 1994), 151–76. Nevertheless, the book's success was extraordinary, and it received considerable attention from the mainstream and alternative media. By the end of 1977, 150,000 copies had been sold, and in 1985 the book was still a German best seller. See Christiane Rasper, "Verena Stefan," in *Frauenliebe. Männerliebe. Eine lesbisch-schwule Literaturgeschichte in Porträts*, ed. Alexandra Busch and Dirk Linck (Stuttgart und Weimar: Metzler, 1997), 409. By 1994, 300,000 German copies had been sold, and *Häutungen* had already been translated into seven European languages as well as Japanese. In the United States, a second translation into English was published in 1994. Levin, "Afterword," 151–52.
4. Charlotte Roche, *Feuchtgebiete* (Cologne: Dumont, 2008) and the translation: Charlotte Roche, *Wetlands*, trans. Tim Mohr (London: Fourth Estate, 2009). *Wetlands* can be situated among a recent spate of international sex best sellers such as Catherine Millet, *La Vie Sexuelle de Catherine M.* (Paris: Éditions du Seuil, 2001) and Virginie Despentes, *Baise-Moi*, trans. Bruce Benderson (New York: Grove Press, 2003) in France; Heleen van Royen and Marlies Dekker, *Stout* (Amsterdam: HvR, 2007) in the Netherlands; and Inga Muscio, *Cunt* (Berkeley, CA: Seal Press, 1998) in the United States. While these books differ in content and ideology, they share a provocative and explicit focus on women's sexuality that, for many, borders on the pornographic.
5. See Sallie Tisdale, "Graphic Novel," *New York Times*, April 19, 2009. By 2008, more than a million copies of *Feuchtgebiete* had been sold in Germany. It was the only German book to appear at the top of the Amazon global best-seller list (Nicholas Kulish, "Germany Abuzz at Racy Novel of Sex and Hygiene," *New York Times*, June 6, 2008). As of this writing, it has been translated into twenty-seven languages, including most European languages.

6. See Chantelle Warner, "Speaking from Experience: Narrative Schemas, Deixis, and Authenticity Effects in Verena Stefan's Feminist Confession Shedding," *Language and Literature* 18, no. 1 (2009): 7–23.
7. Boston Women's Health Book Collective, *Our Bodies, Ourselves* (Boston: New England Free Press, 1971).
8. See, for example: Rosalind Gill, "Postfeminist Media Culture: Elements of a Sensibility," *European Journal of Cultural Studies* 10, no. 2 (2007): 147–66; Rosalind Gill and Christina Scharff, eds., *New Femininities: Postfeminism, Neoliberalism and Subjectivity* (Basingstoke: Palgrave Macmillan, 2011); Angela McRobbie, "Postfeminism and Popular Culture," in *Interrogating Postfeminism: Gender and the Politics of Popular Culture,* ed. Yvonne Tasker and Diane Negra (Durham, NC: Duke University Press, 2007), 27–39; Christina Scharff, *Repudiating Feminism* (Farnham: Ashgate, 2012); Yvonne Tasker and Diane Negra, eds., *Interrogating Postfeminism: Gender and the Politics of Popular Culture* (Durham, NC: Duke University Press, 2007) for critical discussions about what is at stake with postfeminism.
9. Gill, "Postfeminist Media Culture," 149–61.
10. Susan Faludi, *Backlash: The Undeclared War against Women* (London: Chatto & Windus, 1992); Imelda Whelehan, *Overloaded: Popular Culture and the Future of Feminism* (London: The Women's Press, 2000).
11. Anna Yeatman, *Postmodern Revisionings of the Political* (New York: Routledge, 1994); Ann Brooks, *Postfeminisms: Feminism, Cultural Theory and Cultural Forms* (London: Routledge, 1997).
12. Gill, "Postfeminist Media Culture," 147–66; McRobbie, "Postfeminism and Popular Culture," 27–39.
13. McRobbie, "Postfeminism and Popular Culture," 34.
14. Brot & Rosen, *Frauenhandbuch Nr. 1.* (Berlin: Verlag Frauen im Gerhard Verlag, 1974) *Brot & Rosen* (Bread & Roses) was propelled by the idea that women had to learn more about their bodies. They also fought for women's right to contraception and abortion.
15. Levin, "Afterword," 151.
16. 'The emphasis in the dominant German autobiographical genres such as *Erfahrungsberichte* (reports of experience) and *Verständigungstexte* (literally, texts of identification) was not simply on documentation but on the subjective expression of underrepresented lives. Minority and women writers were encouraged to "give voice" to their experiences. Voice, in the sense emphasized by these social movements, was inextricably connected with questions of agency—who speaks, who does not get to speak, and in what forms and contexts' (Warner, "Speaking from Experience," 9.) See also Sigrid Weigel, *Die Stimme der Medusa: Schreibweisen in der Gegenwartsliteratur von Frauen* (Reinbek: Rowohlt, 1989), 103; and Sabine Puhlfürst, *Mehr als bloße Schwärmerei: Die Darstellung von Liebesbeziehungen zwischen Mädchen/jungen Frauen im Spiegel der deutschsprachigen Frauenliteratur des 20. Jahrhunderts* (Essen: Die Blaue Eule, 2002), 225. In line with this, Stefan assumed that finding a new language to express authentic female experiences would be central to the political project of changing the conditions under which women lived (Stefan, *Häutungen,* 3.)
17. Rasper, "Verena Stefan," 409.

18. *Häutungen* is the most successful book of a number of German female confessional "reports of experience," such as Karin Struck, *Klassenliebe* (Frankfurt am Main: Suhrkamp, 1973) and Margot Schröder, *Die Vogelspinne: Monolog einer Trinkerin* (Munich: Frauenbuchverlag, 1982), which are a continuation of self-confession as a typically female genre (see Weigel, *Die Stimme der Medusa,* 94f.). These are comparable with other personal narrative texts such as Erica Jong, *Fear of Flying* (New York: Holt, Rinehart and Winston, 1973) and Anja Meulenbelt, *De schaamte voorbij: Een persoonlijke geschiedenis* (Amsterdam: Van Gennep, 1976).
19. Verena Stefan, *Shedding and Literally Dreaming,* trans. Johanna Steigleder Moore, Beth E. Weckmueller, Johanna Albert, and Tobe Levin (New York: The Feminist Press, 1994), 29. Unless noted, we use the English translation from 1994, with the caveat that the translation does not do full justice to the German text, which is linguistically highly innovative and experimental in the way it represents ruptures in normativity. It is precisely these ruptures that are, we argue, difficult to translate (see also Warner, "Speaking from Experience," 21.)
20. As Levin notes, "Stefan brought to the cause the most coherent lesbian separatist viewpoint, without however making her vision incompatible with radical feminist insights" (Levin, *Political Ideology and Aesthetics,* 43.) *Häutungen*'s lesbianism therefore can be interpreted as a metaphor of a "phantasmatic space" (see Teresa de Lauretis, *The Practice of Love* [Bloomington: Indiana University Press, 1994], empowering for women of all sexual orientations. Most interestingly, Stefan's turn to female same-sex intimacy has only rarely been taken up by contemporary reviews. See Puhlfürst, *Mehr als bloße Schwärmerei,* 224.)
21. Verena Stefan, "Cacophony," trans. Tobe Levin, in *Shedding and Literally Dreaming,* ed. Verena Stefan, trans. Johanna Steigleder Moore, Beth E. Weckmueller, Johanna Albert, and Tobe Levin (New York: The Feminist Press, 1994), 140.
22. Levin, "Afterword," 156.
23. Stefan, *Shedding and Literally Dreaming,* 25–26.
24. Warner, "Speaking from Experience," 8–9.
25. Ibid., 13.
26. Stefan, "Cacophony," 138.
27. Levin, "Afterword," 158f.; Stefan, "Cacophony," 139.
28. Stefan, *Häutungen,* 3. This citation and some citations that follow are translated by Christa Binswanger (CB).
29. Ibid., 4, trans. CB.
30. Levin "Afterword," 158.
31. Levin points out that the German context insisted much more on an exclusion of men from the feminist movement than the Anglo-American feminist movement (see ibid., 156).
32. See Puhlfürst, *Mehr als bloße Schwärmerei,* 225.
33. Classen and Goettle critiqued Stefan's return to nature as a "confusion of anemone and amazon." Brigitte Classen and Gabrielle Goettle, "Häutungen, eine Verwechslung von Anemone und Amazone," in *Die Überwindung der Sprachlosigkeit: Texte aus der neuen Frauenbewegung,* ed. Gabriele Dietze (Darmstadt: Luchterhand, 1979), 55f.
34. Roche's second novel, *Schossgebete,* was published in 2011. Charlotte Roche, *Schossgebete* (Munich: Piper, 2011). Again, sex scenes are an expansive part of the narra-

tive, whereas this time Roche focuses on the psychological repercussions of a horrific family trauma. While the book has received critical and commercial acclaim, it has not had nearly the same impact as *Wetlands.*

35. Roche, *Wetlands,* 120–21.
36. Ibid., 2.
37. Ibid., 125–26.
38. Ibid., 116.
39. See Scharff, *Repudiating Feminism,* 114–15 for a thoughtful analysis of the embedded heteronormativity in Roche's book.
40. Roche, *Wetlands,* 101.
41. Ibid., 163.
42. Ibid., 19.
43. The book has been compared to J. D. Salinger, *The Catcher in the Rye* (Boston: Little, Brown and Company, 1951), a coming-of-age narrative about the adolescent Holden Caulfield. Holden comes from a broken home and has been sent to a boarding school where he is desperately lonely. He feels alienated in a world where people are all—in his vernacular—nothing but "phonies." He, too, tackles his alienation by running away.
44. Roche, *Wetlands,* 123.
45. Kulish, "Germany Abuzz at Racy Novel of Sex and Hygiene."
46. Philip Oltermann, "Interview: Charlotte Roche," *Granta,* May 10, 2008.
47. *Wetlands* has been the subject of considerable controversy in Germany, where the positions tend to be mobilized along generational lines. See, for example, Thea Dorn, *Die neue F-Klasse: Wie die Zukunft von Frauen gemacht wird* (Munich: Piper Verlag, 2006); Meredith Haaf, Susanne Klingner, and Barbara Streidl, *Wir Alphamädchen: Warum Feminismus das Leben schöner macht* (Hamburg: Hoffmann and Campe, 2008); and Jana Hensel and Elisabeth Raether, *Neue deutsche Mädchen* (Reinbek: Rowohlt, 2008).
48. This is, of course, a fairly standard practice within third-wave feminism as well as postfeminism. See Gill, "Postfeminist Media Culture," 147–66.
49. Roche, *Wetlands,* 203.
50. Stefan, *Shedding and Literally Dreaming,* 35.
51. Kathleen Rowe Karlyn, "Scream, Popular Culture, and Feminism's Third Wave: 'I'm Not My Mother,'" *Genders Online Journal,* no. 38 (2003).
52. Margrit Shildrick, *Leaky Bodies and Boundaries: Feminism, Postmodernism, and (Bio) ethics* (London: Routledge, 1997). See also Mary Douglas, *Purity and Danger: An Analysis of Concepts of Pollution and Taboo* (London: Routledge & Kegan Paul, 1966) for the classic rendition of why bodily fluids are potentially terrifying.
53. Roche's position resonates with the argument made by Jane Juffer, *At Home with Pornography: Women, Sex, and Everyday Life* (New York: New York University Press, 1998) that pornography can be domesticated by women in the privacy of their homes, whereby they make use of it whenever and however it suits them. In her view, the problem with pornography is not that it fundamentally victimizes (as for example Andrea Dworkin and Catharine MacKinnon have argued) women but rather that it should be accessible to women to do with as they like in the service of their own sexual pleasure.

54. Stefan, *Shedding and Literally Dreaming,* 44.
55. Ibid., 43.
56. *Wetlands* has resonances with Ariel Levy's work on raunch culture. See Ariel Levy, *Feminist Chauvinist Pigs: Women and the Rise of Raunch Culture* (London: Simon & Schuster, 2005). While Levy is more critical, both show how the obsession of young women with "raunch" does not necessarily go hand in hand with sexual enjoyment.
57. Oltermann, "Interview: Charlotte Roche."
58. Scharff, "The New German Feminisms," 265–78.
59. While Roche would probably not use the term herself, *Wetlands* resonates with post-feminist notions of individual identity, a heightened interest in consumerism and popular culture, and a focus on sexuality and sexualization. Karlyn, "Scream, Popular Culture, and Feminism's Third Wave, para. 20.
60. This utopian view of a unified and equal female community was later problematized by the author herself—see for example Stefan, "Cacophony," 136f.
61. An example of this is when she describes the protagonist's sexual involvement with Dave, a black man living in precarious financial circumstances in Berlin. She suggests that he is "more sexy" than white men, thereby engaging in the familiar strategy of othering through the hypersexualization of blackness. She unproblematically employs an analogy between sexism and racism when her protagonist becomes angry with Dave's selfish sexual behavior and concludes that "Dave fought against the tyranny of whites over blacks and yet continuously recreated the tyranny of men over women." Stefan, *Shedding and Literally Dreaming,* 21.
62. The most telling example is Helen's behavior toward the overworked cleaning woman who makes the mistake of expressing disgust at having to clean up Helen's playfully constructed messes. Helen has no problem relegating her to the ranks of the "cleaning police," thereby legitimating her subsequent punishment by the head nurse.
63. A telling example of this is Helen's sterilization, a voluntary act that marks her coming of age as an adult and eliminates any possibility of maternity.
64. Feona Attwood, "Sexed Up: Theorizing the Sexualization of Culture," *Sexualities* 9, no. 1 (2006): 79.
65. Ibid., 80.
66. Ibid., 79.
67. Shildrick argues for the need to overcome the distance between self and other within relational economies. While she also addresses the monstrous and leaky body—not unlike Roche—she articulates an urgent need for overcoming the separation of self and other in an ethical sense. Margrit Shildrick. *Embodying the Monster: Encounters with the Vulnerable Self* (London: Sage, 2002), 103.

Bibliography

Attwood, Feona. "Sexed Up: Theorizing the Sexualization of Culture." *Sexualities* 9, no. 1 (2006): 77–94.

Binswanger, Christa, and Kathy Davis. "Sexy Stories and Postfeminist Empowerment: From *Häutungen* to *Wetlands.*" *Feminist Theory* 13, no. 3 (2012): 245–63.

Boston Women's Health Book Collective. *Our Bodies, Ourselves.* Boston: New England Free Press, 1971.

Brooks, Ann. *Postfeminisms: Feminism, Cultural Theory and Cultural Forms.* London: Routledge, 1997.

Brot & Rosen. *Frauenhandbuch Nr. 1.* Berlin: Verlag Frauen im Gerhard Verlag, 1974.

Classen, Brigitte, and Gabrielle Goettle. "Häutungen, eine Verwechslung von Anemone und Amazone." In *Die Überwindung der Sprachlosigkeit: Texte aus der neuen Frauenbewegung,* edited by Gabriele Dietze, 55–59. Darmstadt: Luchterhand, 1979.

Despentes, Virginie. *Baise-Moi.* Translated by Bruce Benderson. New York: Grove Press, 2003.

Dorn, Thea. *Die neue F-Klasse. Wie die Zukunft von Frauen gemacht wird.* Munich: Piper Verlag, 2006.

Douglas, Mary. *Purity and Danger: An Analysis of Concepts of Pollution and Taboo.* London: Routledge & Kegan Paul, 1966.

Faludi, Susan. *Backlash: The Undeclared War against Women.* London: Chatto & Windus, 1992.

Gill, Rosalind. "Postfeminist Media Culture: Elements of a Sensibility." *European Journal of Cultural Studies* 10, no. 2 (2007): 147–66.

Gill, Rosalind, and Christina Scharff, eds. *New Femininities: Postfeminism, Neoliberalism and Subjectivity.* Basingstoke: Palgrave Macmillan, 2011.

Haaf, Meredith, Susanne Klingner, and Barbara Streidl. *Wir Alphamädchen: Warum Feminismus das Leben schöner macht.* Hamburg: Hoffmann and Campe, 2008.

Hensel, Jana, and Elisabeth Raether. *Neue deutsche Mädchen.* Reinbek: Rowohlt, 2008.

Jong, Erica. *Fear of Flying.* New York: Holt, Rinehart and Winston, 1973.

Juffer, Jane. *At Home with Pornography: Women, Sex, and Everyday Life.* New York: New York University Press, 1998.

Karlyn, Kathleen Rowe. "Scream, Popular Culture, and Feminism's Third Wave: 'I'm Not My Mother.'" *Genders Online Journal,* no. 38 (2003).

Kulish, Nicholas. "Germany Abuzz at Racy Novel of Sex and Hygiene." *New York Times,* June 6, 2008.

Lauretis, Teresa de. *The Practice of Love.* Bloomington: Indiana University Press, 1994.

Levin, Tobe. *Political Ideology and Aesthetics in Neo-Feminist German Fiction: Verena Stefan, Elfriede Jelinek, Margot Schroeder.* Ithaca, NY: University Microfilms International, 1979.

———. "Afterword." In *Shedding and Literally Dreaming,* edited by Verena Stefan; translated by Johanna Steigleder Moore, Beth E. Weckmueller, Johanna Albert, and Tobe Levin, 151–76. New York: The Feminist Press, 1994.

Levy, Ariel. *Feminist Chauvinist Pigs: Women and the Rise of Raunch Culture.* London: Simon & Schuster, 2005.

McRobbie, Angela. "Postfeminism and Popular Culture." In *Interrogating Postfeminism: Gender and the Politics of Popular Culture,* edited by Yvonne Tasker and Diane Negra, 27–39. Durham, NC: Duke University Press, 2007.

Meulenbelt, Anja. *De schaamte voorbij: Een persoonlijke geschiedenis.* Amsterdam: Van Gennep, 1976.

Millet, Catherine. *La Vie Sexuelle de Catherine M.* Paris: Éditions du Seuil, 2001.

Muscio, Inga. *Cunt.* Berkeley, CA: Seal Press, 1998.

Oltermann, Philip. "Interview: Charlotte Roche." *Granta,* May 10, 2008.
Puhlfürst, Sabine. *Mehr als bloße Schwärmerei: Die Darstellung von Liebesbeziehungen zwischen Mädchen/jungen Frauen im Spiegel der deutschsprachigen Frauenliteratur des 20. Jahrhunderts.* Essen: Die Blaue Eule, 2002.
Rasper, Christiane. "Verena Stefan." In *Frauenliebe. Männerliebe. Eine lesbisch-schwule Literaturgeschichte in Porträts,* edited by Alexandra Busch and Dirk Linck, 409–13. Stuttgart und Weimar: Metzler, 1997.
Roche, Charlotte. *Feuchtgebiete.* Cologne: Dumont, 2008.
———. *Wetlands.* Translated by Tim Mohr. London: Fourth Estate, 2009.
———. *Schossgebete.* Munich: Piper, 2011.
Royen, Heleen van, and Marlies Dekkers. *Stout.* Amsterdam: HvR (Foreign Media Books), 2007.
Salinger, Jerome David. *The Catcher in the Rye.* Boston: Little, Brown and Company, 1951.
Scharff, Christina. "The New German Feminisms: Of *Wetlands* and *Alpha-Girls.*" In *New Femininities: Postfeminism, Neoliberalism and Subjectivity,* edited by Rosalind Gill and Christina Scharff, 265–78. Basingstoke: Palgrave Macmillan, 2011.
———. *Repudiating Feminism.* Farnham: Ashgate, 2012.
Schröder, Margot. *Die Vogelspinne: Monolog einer Trinkerin.* Munich: Frauenbuchverlag, 1982.
Shildrick, Margrit. *Leaky Bodies and Boundaries: Feminism, Postmodernism, and (Bio)ethics.* London: Routledge, 1997.
———. *Embodying the Monster: Encounters with the Vulnerable Self.* London: Sage, 2002.
Stefan, Verena. *Häutungen: Autobiographische Aufzeichnungen. Gedichte. Träume. Analysen.* Munich: Frauenoffensive, 1975.
———. *Shedding and Literally Dreaming.* Translated by Johanna Steigleder Moore, Beth E. Weckmueller, Johanna Albert, and Tobe Levin. New York: The Feminist Press, 1994.
———. "Cacophony." Translated by Tobe Levin. In *Shedding and Literally Dreaming,* edited by Verena Stefan; translated by Johanna Steigleder Moore, Beth E. Weckmueller, Johanna Albert, and Tobe Levin, 136–47. New York: The Feminist Press, 1994.
Struck, Karin. *Klassenliebe.* Frankfurt am Main: Suhrkamp, 1973.
Tasker, Yvonne, and Diane Negra, eds. *Interrogating Postfeminism: Gender and the Politics of Popular Culture.* Durham, NC: Duke University Press, 2007.
Tisdale, Sallie. "Graphic Novel." *New York Times,* April 19, 2009.
Warner, Chantelle. "Speaking from Experience: Narrative Schemas, Deixis, and Authenticity Effects in Verena Stefan's Feminist Confession Shedding." *Language and Literature* 18, no. 1 (2009): 7–23.
Weigel, Sigrid. *Die Stimme der Medusa: Schreibweisen in der Gegenwartsliteratur von Frauen.* Reinbek: Rowohlt, 1989.
Whelehan, Imelda. *Overloaded: Popular Culture and the Future of Feminism.* London: The Women's Press, 2000.
Yeatman, Anna. *Postmodern Revisionings of the Political.* New York: Routledge, 1994.

Part III

Identities at Stake: Gender, Race, Class

Introductory Remarks

Lucy Delap and Thierry Delessert

As the essays in this collection suggest, a new generation of scholars has contributed to the maturing historiography of late twentieth-century feminism. Earlier generations of activists continue to produce rich memoirs and reflections; younger scholars and activists have linked the women's liberation movement (WLM) to earlier or subsequent phases of feminism and woven its history into the larger narratives of historical change. The essays in this volume offer an opportunity to take stock of the movement within the larger narratives of British, European, and social-movement history, tracing the comparative and transnational impact of feminism as a social movement, policy innovator, and shaper of public opinion and mores. The chapters in this section look at some central areas of conflict within post-1968 feminism—race, class, and gender.

Christine Bard sketches the relationship between political lesbianism and the *Mouvement de libération des femmes* (MLF) in France. She makes clear that the MLF was at the forefront of contemporary lesbian visibilities in the country. A vivid lesbian subculture had existed in the 1920s, but the combined effects of World War II, the German occupation, and the Vichy Regime destroyed homosexual ways of life and culture. The weakness of political feminism after the war further contributed to the continuing invisibility of lesbians in public life. It was only in August 1970 that homosexual women reappeared in public, by marching—together with heterosexual women's activists—for women's liberation during a demonstration at the Arc de Triomphe in Paris. This protest was small in numbers, but widely reported by the mass media. It became the founding event of the MLF in France.

The participating lesbian women had strongly influenced the decision to create a women-only movement, and they also affected the rapid split with the French Revolutionary Gay Liberation Front (*Front homosexuel d'action révolutionnaire,* known as FHAR) in 1971. Both developments promoted an emerging female homosociability within the MLF, as well as some activists' personal embrace of homosexuality. As Bard states, these conditions contributed to a new appropriation of the word "lesbian" within the MLF. In the second half of the 1970s, lesbianism became one of the most important ways in feminist circles to express both a cultural and a political identity. In France, a long-lasting lesbian movement was not established outside the MLF, and the debates about the causes of lesbian oppression led to a critical rupture in 1979 between groups representing different theoretical positions and strategic decisions. On the one hand were the "essentialists," a group of women influenced by psychoanalysis and who officially claimed "MLF" as a trademark for the newly founded bookshop and editing enterprise. On the other hand were the "radicals," whose materialist analysis of women's oppression had its origins in Marxist thought. Both groups argued within a revolutionary framework (revolution of perception via psychoanalysis versus revolution of the material order). Neither had strong connections to the gay movement, which had become steadily more reformist.

After François Mitterrand came to power in 1981, three different outlets for lesbian activism existed: within the MLF, in gay and lesbian groups, and in lesbian-only groups. These last groups proliferated during the 1990s, and, in the process, a national network of lesbian groups was established. This network occasionally supported campaigning for gay and lesbian rights, but it was more concerned with establishing a "queer" critical perspective on heterosexism and the binary sexual order. Beyond the history of feminism as a social movement, Bard's chapter allows us to understand the important impact that lesbianism had on French feminist theories, especially in their subsequent denunciation of patriarchy, psychoanalytical phallocentrism, and social heterosexism.

Marica Tolomelli and Anna Frisone examine the Italian WLM and its distinctive dialogue with the Italian left. The strength of Marxist thought and social protest in Italy around and after 1968 not only led to attempts to critique and transcend class struggle as a site of women's political empowerment but also to attempts to work productively within Marxist politics. The authors chart feminist attempts to broaden Marxist concepts of productive labor and critique the gender division of labor so often taken for granted by the Left.

While Tolomelli and Frisone are skeptical of the influence that either strategy had within the conservative Italian social context, the impact of these feminist initiatives was profound; *Lotta Continua*, a mixed-sex Italian revolutionary group, produced high-profile and sometimes extremely angry accounts of how women and feminists fared in Italian politics. While not always successful at integrating gender justice concerns into Italian revolutionary politics, *Lotta Continua* was extremely influential in shaping the British revolutionary group Big Flame, whose members went on to shape feminist and antisexist men's activism well into the 1980s. Italian feminists were also notably successful in exploiting state benefits and existing labor institutions to gain opportunities for women to debate and study. Tolomelli and Frisone describe the "150-hour courses" that developed through the Italian trade union movement. These grassroots initiatives drew on the feminist practices that had developed in consciousness-raising groups, and they also resemble the women's studies courses that were becoming visible within European and American universities in the 1970s and 1980s. The study groups read the American text *Our Bodies, Ourselves* and gave voice to the concerns of working-class women. The authors argue that Italian feminism developed in a distinctively oral fashion, with face-to-face debate prioritized over print publications. This reduced the barriers to participation that the less educated found so troubling in other national contexts, but the lack of written material poses a challenge for historians, who find that there may be fewer traces left of this relatively informal and lightly documented feminist politics.

Natalie Thomlinson focuses on a parallel debate—the relationship between feminism and race politics—in a contrasting national context, England. While Italian feminism was relatively untouched by debates about race, English feminism experienced wrenching, painful controversies over the extent to which white feminists were inclusive of, or even aware of, Black[1] concerns. The resulting identity politics, where political consciousness was understood to be a direct result of personal experiences of oppression, resulted in seemingly damaging and competitive efforts to demonstrate possession of the necessary attributes (female, Black, working class, disabled, lesbian, etc.) that would grant political authority. Thomlinson charts the longstanding presence of Black feminism and women's activism from the outset of the British WLM, and Black feminists' frustration at the exclusion of their concerns. While white women sought abortion rights, Black women found themselves subject to unwanted abortion and sterilization. While white women protested their isolation and vulnerability to violence in the home, Black women prioritized their precarious, exploitative experiences with the labor market and the problems of police harassment.

Thomlinson's contribution lies in acknowledging the force of the Black feminist critique, but she seeks to look beyond the accusations of racism that, it has been argued, split the British feminist movement at the end of the 1970s. Instead, she notes the existence and (qualified) successes of multiracial collectives that were experimented with in the 1980s. The painful racial interactions of these years were not a sign of disintegration of feminism but were a symptom of much greater integration of Black feminist perspectives within the WLM. The case study of *Spare Rib* magazine and its divisions over race that emerged in a controversy over anti-Zionist and anti-Semitic ideologies both provides a sense of how fraught and irresolvable racial politics were in this period and also points to the sustained efforts to set up more inclusive and diverse feminist institutions. Like Tolomelli and Frisone's account of the trade union movement, Thomlinson also highlights the significance of existing institutions for hosting and funding feminist initiatives. In the British case, local government provided funding and venues for many multiracial women's collectives and sustained some feminist activism despite the hostility of central government under the Conservative Party after 1979.

Finally, Lucy Delap analyzes the development of an antisexist and feminist men's movement inspired by the British WLM of the 1970s. Men's groups participating in this venture published numerous antisexist magazines and participated in 'men's groups'. The chapter points in particular to the difficulties of male feminists as a small and marginalized minority within a largely patriarchal society. Unlike in France—and many other European countries—some UK women's liberation groups remained open to men until the late 1970s. Delap sketches two types of male supporters of British second-wave feminism. The first group consisted of gay activists who did not feel represented by an increasingly commercialized male homosexual scene, in which prejudice against bisexuals and even misogyny was commonplace. Such men constituted a substantial minority within male feminist activism. The second major group of antisexist men were hard to characterize in terms of sexuality. Some had occasionally tried sexual relations with other men, but more as an experiment within the spirit of the sexual revolution rather than because of deeply felt personal desires. Some men adopted celibacy in order to escape social norms; others continued to pursue heterosexual relationships but with considerable anxiety. All in all, the number of feminist groups in the UK that were mixed sex was small. But they attracted men who learned about feminist theories at university, especially in the younger institutions founded as part of the educational expansion from the late 1950s onward, many of which later became pioneers in the growth of gender studies (see chapter 2 of this book). Such students—male and female—became proponents for a new sensibility of what is now termed "gender justice." Those who stayed in academia developed critical analyses of patriarchy. Furthermore, feminist men, some of whom were politicized by their female partners and friends, played an active role in the dissemination of feminist texts and knowledge, especially in the political and cultural environments of the far left.

When those British women's liberation groups that had remained mixed for some years finally decided to adopt the principle of "women only" in the late 1970s, men's groups were forced to think about the necessity and meaning of male-only consciousness-raising groups. The shift to homosociality contributed on the one hand to a clarification of feminist or female identities and formations. But it also led to alienation between feminist men and women on the other. Nevertheless, Delap's chapter shows that we should not mistake the British men's movement for the rise of "masculinism," resolutely opposed to any form of feminism. Masculinist groups represented (and still represent) only a small minority of men, despite their success in building groups and organizations by transmitting their idea of the "New Man" in popular journals from the 1990s.

Taken together, these studies suggest that the WLMs had many internal divisions, and, as a result, their fragmentation led them to the brink of disintegration: the MLF imploded over the lesbian question, the Italian movement were challenged by considerations of class struggle which resisted a gendered analysis; feminist collectives in Britain in the 1980s were confronted with race issues, and the British women's movement was, at least in the very beginning, much more concerned with the "problem of men" than the retrospective construction of feminist memory might indicate. Nevertheless, such negotiations and conflicts, too often used against feminism as examples of the movement's weakness and decline, can also be read as the pluralization of feminist ideas and gender theories, visible *throughout* WLM activism. These chapters demonstrate the ability of feminist activists to work in different settings, and their longstanding acknowledgment of what has now come to be termed intersectional issues. As such, the WLM had a legacy for those feminists who, from the early 1990s (in the United States) and the early 2000s (in diverse European contexts) on, relaunched feminist debates (and activism), building on—under others—key concepts like diversity and intersectionality. In this light the impact of women's liberation on the contemporary movement sector and on subsequent feminist mobilization can hardly be overestimated.

Thierry Delessert, who holds a PhD in political science, is a historian. He is currently part-time lecturer and postdoctoral researcher at the Centre for Gender Studies at the University of Lausanne and also research assistant at the School of Public Health of the Free University of Brussels. His research domains mainly focus on the history of homosexuality in Switzerland.

Lucy Delap is a lecturer in modern British history at the University of Cambridge and Fellow of Murray Edwards College. She works on the history of child sexual abuse and is deputy director of History & Policy. She has published widely on the history of feminism, gender, labor, and religion, including the prize-winning *The Feminist Avant-Garde: Transatlantic Encounters of the Early Twentieth Century* in 2007, *Knowing Their Place: Domestic Service in Twentieth Century Britain* in 2011, and, with Sue Morgan, *Men, Masculinities and Religious Change in Twentieth Century Britain* (2013). She is currently working on a history of modern feminism titled *Feminism: A Useable History* (Penguin Books, forthcoming).

Notes

1. The capitalization of the term "Black" reflects contemporary practice, and indicates the politicized nature of this category in comparison to the loose ethnic concept of "whiteness," which remained relatively unexamined in the context of the 1970s and 1980s.

Bibliography

Bolt, Christine. *Sisterhood Questioned? Race, Class and Internationalism in the American and British Women's Movements, c. 1800s–1970s*. London: Routledge, 2004.

Evans, Elizabeth. *The Politics of Third Wave Feminism: Neoliberalism, Intersectionality, and the State in Britain and the US*. Basingstoke: Palgrave Macmillan, 2015.

Chapter 8

Lesbianism as Political Construction in the French Feminist Context

Christine Bard

For better or for worse, feminism and lesbianism are often linked together. There is something like a logical continuum in loving women and defending them, in fighting both sexism and homophobia. For reactionaries, they are one and the same perversion, against nature and dangerous for the social order. Yet, while feminist and lesbian struggles can be on the same side, they can also go separate ways. But first one must get to a mutual understanding about terms—open receptacles with varied and varying contents—and try to take into account the rejections of imposed terms operated by feminists and also the reassigning of meaning constantly at work, as well as the endless quarrels as to the meaning of "feminism" and "lesbianism." So as to avoid all anachronisms, it is worth going through this history from a chronological point of view.

After the denial of the homosexual issue in first-wave feminism, the *Mouvement de libération des femmes* (MLF) in France became the favored laboratory of a new political identity: lesbianism. Despite the creation of separate lesbian groups and an increasingly offensive radical lesbianism, women's liberation as a project remained very important for lesbians. The parallel development of gay and lesbian activism does not contradict this statement.

Feminist Movement and Female Homosexuality before 1970: The Stage of Denial

It was not until 1970 that "a movement began giving lesbians the possibility of existing as a social group."[1] The MLF (also called simply "the Movement") became "a decisive political space"[2] for them. From here it is interesting to bring into mind what preceded *l'année zéro*[3] (zero hour).

At the end of the nineteenth century, feminism in France was greatly resisted. The family, governed by the Napoleon Code, was not easy to reform: its hierarchic organization was supposed to guarantee the social order, and fecundity became a necessity in a France with Malthusian practices and gripped by the anguish of "depopulation." Political power was exclusively in men's hands until 1944. But the mixed record of French feminism, symbolized by this late entry of women into citizenship—should not hide the cultural dynamic of women's emancipation. In their associations, magazines and newspapers, and their various works, feminists shook up sexual roles and gender identities, a contestation that was amplified by their adversaries' caricatural echo. The conditions were thus created for a new collective existence of homosexual women. Their lot was definitely connected to that of women in general, and the main stake was access to, in terms of social position, an independent life.

This period was, however, marked by a strong stigmatization of homosexuality that had to deal, in addition to moral censorship, with a growing medical body, particularly psychiatrists. Sexuality, in general, was confined to secrecy in the private sphere, except when it was judged dangerous for the public order. Feminine homosexuality was thus not very visible. It was occasionally tolerated as long as it remained hidden. In feminist circles it was at best taboo and at worst the subject of fears and reprobation. This was particularly true in France where the silence was heavier than in Great Britain or in Germany. Feminists, except a very few—among them Madeleine Pelletier (1874–1939), who analyzed and criticized compulsory heterosexuality—wanted to give a reassuring image of themselves and emphasized their role as mothers in the private and the political space.[4] Was this because the promotion of femininity in France was stronger than elsewhere? In the refusal of any masculinization of women there was undoubtedly a condemnation of what is today called lesbian visibility. Thus, feminists disapproved of Pelletier, theoretician of an "integral" feminism advocating women's virilization and militant chastity.[5] They also contested the masculinization often associated with certain sports (see, for example, their conflict with French athlete Violette Morris during the public debate on "the right to wear slacks" in 1930).[6] They were very disapproving of the 1920s fashion with its lesbian "signs" (androgynous look, bobbed hair, tailored suits, etc.).[7] Yet in the feminist movements of Europe and North America, there were couples of women's activists who maintained what was called a "romantic friendship," which meant as much as a strong emotional but platonic relation. Madeleine Pelletier describes this type of relationship in her novel, *La femme vierge* (The Virgin Woman). Between the two world wars, female couples were stigmatized, even in "progressive" movements fighting for sexual reform. The figure of the New Woman, independent, college educated, single, was more scandalous than ever and often diabolized as the "virile lesbian." There were no female couples of friends on the French scene. Visible lesbians with feminist sensibilities could only be found outside of organized feminism, in the informal sociability of the cultural and artistic fields: the Parisian bookshop owners such as Adrienne Monnier and Sylvia Beach, for example.[8]

The feminist eclipse, from the late 1930s to the 1960s, was not beneficial to lesbians. The silence was even heavier before the publication of *The Second Sex,* the famous and daring book by Simone de Beauvoir, in 1949. Devoting a whole chapter to "The Lesbian" was shocking.[9] In her own way, Simone de Beauvoir fought against prejudice, above all by asserting that homosexuality had to do with a choice made in situation; she created a way of thinking (oneself), open to the social and political. Between the lines, she suggested that living a lesbian life was a 'feminist' choice and not only a sexual preference. This conception still runs afoul of those who think that one is "born" lesbian. Nevertheless, Beauvoir did not avoid some clichés that are today held against her, however anachronistic these critiques might be.[10]

In the late 1960s "the collective identification as lesbians was fragile,"[11] but May 1968 would change the terms, with a political contestation of the established order extending to the sexed and sexual order. "Arcadie," a mixed homophile movement directed by André Baudry, suddenly looked gray because of its moderation and caution.[12] Dissidents founded the *Front homosexuel d'action révolutionnaire* (Revolutionary Action Homosexual Front, FHAR) in spring 1971. This mixed gay and lesbian movement focused on sexual liberation through consciousness-raising, debates, and practices. At the outset, "dykes" outnumbered "gays." However, the appeal that the feminist combat sent out to homosexual women, as well as the differences between a male and a female homosexual culture—which became regularly manifest at the Paris Beaux Arts general meetings—quickly masculinized the FHAR without, however, chasing all the women. Some of them would remain in the 1970s gay groups, far from the MLF. They had some feminist sympathies, but they preferred mixed gay and lesbian organizing. Women disappointed by the FHAR joined the MLF.

As of the Arc de Triomphe demonstration on August 26, 1970 that became the founding act of the MLF, heterosexuals constituted the minority among the women present. It is important to emphasize this today, even if the dichotomy "homosexuelle"/"hétérosexuelle" is anachronistic, as is the term "lesbienne." At the time, lesbians did not refer to the term "heterosexual" and they did not speak of themselves as "lesbians," but when, occasionally, they had to speak about their sexual orientation they preferred the term "homosexual." "We didn't talk about lesbianism," witnessed those who had lived through the 1950s and 1960s to Claude Lesselier, historian and activist, founder of the lesbian archives in Paris (*Archives, Recherches et*

Cultures lesbiennes).[13] The feminist activist and sociologist Christine Delphy confirmed in 1981 that "heterosexuality" did not exist in 1970: "It was just considered 'sexuality,' in all simplicity. It is the Movement, the action of lesbians within it, action enabled by the very logic of feminism, that created a reversal of perspective."[14]

The Becoming Homosexual in the MLF during the 1970s

In a context of "sexual liberation," the MLF was organized for women only, offering a new form of relationship between women: *sororité* (sisterhood).[15] Christine Delphy made a point of the "homo-erotic ambience, such pleasure and validation of our being-together..., being with intelligent women who laughed all the time, who wanted to change the society... This joy, this feeling of love for and interest in the others, heterosexual women felt it also; it was not exclusive."[16] For many, homosociality had a homosexual dimension in such a context. Yet the closet did not open immediately, as reveals an often-mentioned anecdote: Catherine Deudon explained to the group she had started to attend in the early 1970s that she was homosexual and wanted to know if others in the group were: "Almost everyone was." For several years, "no one would think of situating oneself in a meeting by stating 'I am homosexual.' "It wasn't said. We were all women,"[17] explains Liliane Kandel, sociologist and activist. *Les "Gouines rouges"* (the "Red Dykes"), a Parisian group that started in 1971, disappeared rather quickly.[18] In Lyon, it was not until 1976 that the lesbians of the MLF got organized.[19]

"How great it felt to be women and not dirty lesbians," says Liliane Kandel in order to describe the feelings of those for whom the ambience in the MLF constituted a shelter from everyday-life homophobia. Many young activists refused labels. "A yellow star, that was enough for the century; we're not going to stick a rose triangle on," explains Kandel, who had lived through the stigmatization as a Jewish child in Bucharest in the 1940s.

The early period of the MLF was characterized by a fusional unanimity, undoubtedly supported by the reference to universalism, so important in French political culture. The songs sung at demonstrations celebrated unity: "We have all had abortions/We are all abortionists/ We are all prostitutes/ Lesbians and frigid/We are freeing society/We are freeing sexuality."[20] As Liliane Kandel said, forming a "Women's Movement" was already a challenge while at the same time fighting an essentialist and differentialist vision of the woman being. And recognizing over and above all the differences of emotional and sexual choices was nearly impossible.

In the early 1970s, lesbianism was neither a political priority of the women's movement nor even on the list of demands. A self-identity as "lesbian" was still unusual among homosexual feminist activists. It is true that pressure was brought to bear on homosexual women to remain discreet, especially in relation to the media. In addition, the more a women's group had a reforming strategy, the more its image was sacrificed to an upstanding heterosexuality (whereas it undoubtedly counted as many homosexuals in it).

The MLF created new ways of being a homosexual woman. For many activists, one was not born homosexual, one became it. And this becoming was expressed as a political choice. The result was a certain idealization of homosexuality and a very strong desire to harmonize private life and activist convictions. Where the MLF existed, heterosexual women became homosexual or bisexual. In 1977 Anne Zelensky attested under the pseudonym of Anne Tristan to this experience, revealing the mechanisms of her "conversion" to homosexuality.[21] Like her feminist friends, she considered the personal to be political and had her homosexual coming out in and thanks to the MLF. After a "painful cleansing," she went through a "rebirth," adopting a new sexual identity: homosexual but not lesbian. Such euphoria of discovery went along with a psychological destabilization. The relationship of those sexual liberation adventurers with psychoanalysis raises many research questions that are still to be explored. Some rejected therapy, while others, though blaming the phallocentric premises and sexual normativity of psychoanalysis, found it a helpful way to remain "authentic" (a decisive value for Beauvoirians) and to put into perspective the moral imperatives of the world in which they lived. The idealization of homosexuality followed by the probable disenchantment was hard to admit, even with hindsight. The loss of illusions was the price to pay for those who had recourse to therapy. The MLF, in any case, enabled many women to experience a homosexual or bisexual coming out. Also, one must not forget the historical conditions under which it became possible to envisage alternative ways of life: women's autonomy was helped by their massive access to higher education and their firm entry into the job market; rebellious women's voices were present in the 1970s culture and media; contraception and abortion constituted possible choices. The 1970s counterculture that radical feminism was fully part of valorized free ways of life and extended the carefree time of youth and its many different experiences that could be shared and discussed in short-lived or long-lasting communities. Being gay in this context was far more than a "preference" or a sexual "orientation," It was constructing an identity and, in doing so, being part of constructing a collective identity. "The most beautiful life is the one that one spends creating oneself, not procreating." This aphorism by Natalie Clifford Barney (1876–1972), American poet living in Paris, was again in fashion.

A new vision of feminine homosexuality came in the forefront. The most obvious new aspect was its political expression, which went along with a new name: lesbianism. American women were the first to publish on this issue; they started already in the mid-1970s. Their message soon circulated all over the Western world: lesbians were taking their destiny into their own hands, redefining the word "lesbian" and making a banner out of a stigma, an act of resistance in itself. "Feminism is the theory; lesbianism the practice" was the slogan.

The lesbian sociability was favorable to romantic encounters, as it offered multiple occasions to get into contact: meetings, conferences, consciousness-raising groups, parties, vacation, and others. The "decolonization" of women first of all concerned the body, sexuality, and the exploration of a "feminine eroticism," different from that of men. Basic elements of common sexual morality were questioned, such as the heterosexual monogamist couple or the idea of lifelong fidelity. Sexual practices were considered as part of a counterculture. Based on a rejection of "all genital" and on a contestation of penetration (even women to women penetration with or without digital devices; those practices were suspicious of imitating heterosexual practices), they were to take into account the erogeneity of the body as a whole. Lesbians wanted to find out about female desire and seduction and to challenge usual criteria of beauty. New health principles went hand in hand with an ecologist / environmentalist contestation of consumer society. Beliefs in the virtues of natural medicine corresponded with rejecting the power of health professionals over women's bodies. Tampons and sanitary napkins were rejected by some in favor of natural sponges. Self-defense techniques such as Wen-Do were also sought after. Discussions on everyone's private life led to a collective exploration of the constraints imposed since childhood that justified the lesbian "choice." Among these constraints was the imposition of the feminine genre by the family and at school (especially prohibiting pants and "boys' games"). Women in consciousness-raising groups got to know firsthand about sexual violence and the trauma that resulted from it.

The explorers of feminist homosexuality also had queries about feminism. They were caught between the egalitarian path that Beauvoir championed and the differentialist way "psych & po" (psychoanalysis and politics), a group led by a psychoanalyst, Antoinette Fouque. This identitarian feminism fostered an identitarian lesbianism, a particularity of which was to keep itself as far away as possible from the gay movement. From this point of view, in a way, all women were lesbian, and all began by loving a woman, their mother.

These new homosexual identities produced new divisions: with "heterosexual" women and with lesbians who did not identify themselves as feminist. It also separated women who were homosexual before becoming feminist from those who became it in the MLF. Their experiences were different. For Liliane Kandel, the former "had an uneasy past, in the closet," while those in the latter group benefited from the newly gained openness and made an activist's "career" out of being a lesbian. There was a pivotal scene during a conference at the famous Paris meeting hall *La Mutualité* on May 13 and 14, 1972, denouncing crimes against women. Repression against homosexuality was one of the themes discussed. A tract was handed out, which said: "Women who refuse the roles of wife and mother, the time has come, from the bottom of silence, we have to speak out." During the meeting, lesbians went on stage, hand in hand, and declared: "We have come out in the light of day." Still, for those who had been homosexual since the 1950s and 1960s, being homosexual was not necessarily a joy every minute of the day or a way of "finding oneself." It was not a choice, rather a destiny, and not always easy to live with.

As time went on, some of the differences faded. Outside the "enchanted circle of the Movement," as Christine Delphy put it, the "had becomes" learned firsthand about lesbophobia in their families, at work, in the street. However, one difference remained insurmountable: the outdated conception of "roles" within lesbian partnerships still at work in some pre-1968 couples. Catherine Deudon underlines that "butch" and "fems" were hardly tolerated by lesbians in the MLF who considered themselves "above roles," "beyond patriarchy." They kept the nightclubs, with their "picturesque gloominess" in a bad memory: "I would have died to see myself in this nagging image with its chain bracelets, ties, and 3-piece suits," she remembers.[22]

Did feminists who defined themselves as heterosexual feel "guilty" because of their taking part in a heterosexual gender order? And what about tabooing bisexuality, banal in practice, absent in theory? The uneasiness was clear—as expressed by the defensive tone in a tract by the group *Femmes mariées* (Married Women): "Are all husbands such pitiless tyrants that rape us every night and then leave us as the oppressed to be welcomed into the bosom of the MLF?"[23] Can we therefore conclude that lesbians had such an importance within a movement whose main topic was free abortion on demand? Or should one simply observe the intellectual and political influence of some movement leaders who, without situating themselves explicitly as lesbians, were obviously so? They were definitely perceived as an avant-garde, a category that commanded respect during those left-wing years and brought life back to the old Leninist principle.

The Turn of the 1980s: Toward Lesbian Autonomization?

The MLF was from the beginning a victim of lesbophobic jibes and insults. Such verbal and sometimes physical attacks have to be taken into account to understand the formation of the lesbian movement and the defensive, aggressive, sometimes paranoiac and self-destructive attitudes among the activists. The violence activists were confronted with had an effect on the internal structure of the movement: it fostered the creation of a collective identity of women who, at certain moments, not only fought against the discrimination of homosexuals but against all forms of gender discrimination. We will not go as far as to say that lesbophobia "made" the lesbian in the modern and feminist meaning of the term, but it contributed to it.

According to Christine Delphy, the name of the first lesbian and feminist group, *Les "Gouines rouges,"* was chosen after a bearded activist exclaimed while they were selling the periodical, *Le Torchon brûle,* "Well, the red dykes." At the time, it could not be seen as the resurgence of an accusation as old as feminism (this history was not yet written). But not much attention was paid to this association of antifeminism and lesbophobia.

In the United States, Ti-Grace Atkinson, one of the first great early feminists took the insult seriously. Women, she observed, distinguished between feminism, a "political" position, and lesbianism, a "sexual" position, but "men" saw lesbianism as "the ultimate political position of women."[24] "When the enemy drops its grenades on an area you think is not important for your defense system, it is necessary to investigate."[25] Called lesbian and struck by the defensive reactions of other activists, she worked out an original position, applying a class analysis to sexual groups that enabled her to define lesbianism as a political commitment.

Lesbophobia, the word, was still lacking and was not used in France until the late 1990s, thanks to the *Coordination lesbienne nationale* (National Lesbian Coordination). The more general term "homophobia" was then not very common. In the 1970s, racism or discrimination against homosexuals was discussed but without the nuances of sex or gender. In fact, gayphobia occupied more media space than lesbophobia. Fighting against homophobia began in the late 1970s. In June 1977 people took to the streets against Anita Bryant who wanted to penalize homosexuality in the United States. A feminist tract was distributed: "Homosexual repression affects all women." Liliane Kandel remembers: "Not many straights came out.… We demonstrated for their right to abortion and they did not raise their little finger for us."

The first lesbian group, the *"Gouines Rouges,"* appeared in Paris in 1971, was part of the MLF : the *"Gouines rouges"* attracted loosely about one hundred women. Too early? In this constitutive stage of a social movement of women it was difficult to organize as a separate group on the basis of a feminist homosexual identity. Thus, at the beginning of 1973, the *"Gouines rouges"* disappeared, but its radicalism permeated elsewhere, in meetings and demonstrations of the movement. In 1975 a lesbian group reformed in Paris and this time the word "lesbian" appeared clearly ("Group of Feminist Lesbians"), and took on a "revolutionary" connotation. The group challenged "society in its most fundamental aspects: the family, the child, reproduction, the economy." Its rapid dissolution revealed some instability, but as of the mid-1970s, Paris no longer had the monopoly: in the big cities, somewhere between homosexual liberation groups and women's groups, lesbian groups and activist newspapers were created.

In 1979, in a Parisian meeting on "lesbianism and feminism," the discomfort of some lesbians in the movement came to a head: "negation," "guilt," "pseudo acceptation," being used as "fieldwork training," being held to silence in the name of "priorities" or under the pretext of "not wanting to frighten the mass of women," marginalization of the debate on sexuality, and separation of the right to homosexuality from the global combat for the right to dispose of one's body… such were some of the criticisms that were expressed."[26] Shortly after, in February 1980, Monique Wittig published "La pensée straight" in *Questions féministes,* a recent journal (1977) developed by sociologist Christine Delphy that nourished materialist feminist theory. The following May, the article "One Is Not Born Woman" stated that "lesbians are not women" because they did not belong to the category "women" as constructed by patriarchy. A collective called *Lesbiennes radicales féministes* (Radical Feminist Lesbians) was formed that criticized the journal for ignoring both lesbianism and criticism of heterosexual power. In June the group *Lesbiennes de Jussieu* (Lesbians of Jussieu—a Parisian University) organized an autonomous demonstration and a meeting in which feminism was accused of "collaboration" with the "class of men." Blaming heteropatriarchy led to blaming "heterofeminism." Lesbianism alone was considered being able to resist "heteroppression." "All our 'affectivity' is directed toward women, for women, with women: nothing for the oppressor. We refuse femininity.… We refuse to 'humanize' the oppressor.… We want neither to make a pact nor collaborate because we know the price to pay: the loss of our living abilities, the betrayal of our class.… All women should become lesbian, that is: stand together, resistant and not collaborators."[27]

Once this political choice was made, sexuality and the possibility of desire would fall into place (literally: "inscribe themselves," *s'inscrivent toutes seules*). This formulation—incomprehensible for nonfeminist lesbians and for lesbians who had always been lesbian—refers to an experience that many activists underwent by attending the feminist movement and that changed their lives. The choice of words nevertheless remains curious. The word "s'inscrire" seems like a lapsus, revealing its origin from an intellectual discourse. This declaration can also be seen as a kind of denial of the subconscious, a dream of self-control. Shortly afterward, in April 1981 the *Front des lesbiennes radicales* (Radical Lesbian Front) was formed. It split up in the summer of 1982, a failure one can attribute to the external hostility and to internal conflicts. Other groups then took up the flame, gathering together French and Belgian women.

How can radical lesbianism's emergence be explained? Its formal novelty, its vocabulary enhanced by Marxism (class, class consciousness, class betrayal), and its references to the Occupation (resistance, collaboration) hark back to a context that was favorable to political radicalization. But also the campaign to criminalize rape, led in the second half of the 1970s and which succeeded with the revision of the penal code in 1980, radicalized arguments against patriarchy. The Aix-en-Provence trial in 1978 was, in this regard, a pivotal moment in the feminist struggle against rape. The two Belgian campers who had been raped and who took the case to court were lesbian and talked openly about their sexual orientation in front of the media and activist groups in order to raise public awareness. At the same moment, a very controversial placard circulated in feminist groups, showing the picture of a man and commenting, in the subtitle: "This man is a man. This man is a rapist."

Simultaneously conflicts erupted within in the MLF. In 1979 Antoinette Fouque registered the signum "MLF" as a trademark, which split her group "psych & po" (that was meant to become the "registered MLF"—MLF *déposé*) and the great majority of feminist activists (MLF *non déposé*).[28] The movement suffered. Furthermore the MLF lost those activists for whom the gains made on contraception and abortion were sufficient. The reformist openings that were on the horizon with the expected election of the Left did not suit everybody and provoked more radical attitudes. The vocabulary employed referred to the "re-awakening of Jewish memory" and the "return of repressed Vichy"[29] and introduced a highly emotional tone, which, in turn, had an impact on the events. What also came to light at this point was that women homosexual deportations during the Vichy Regime had been previously concealed. Whereas some feminists used these recent findings to argue against women's oppression in a general way, others perceived those heavy emotional accusations as inappropriate analogy.

The rise of radical lesbianism also affected the journal *Questions féministes.* Its editorial board split over the question of how to embrace radical feminist and radical lesbian concerns. The editorial board recomposed itself, and the journal changed its name to *Nouvelles Questions féministes* after a lawsuit that was related to the conflict. The editorial to the first number of the re-founded journal explained its position: there was an understanding about the eruption of "homosexual anger" that for centuries had been buried impotently. However, there was a strong resistance against idealizing lesbians, as if they were "revolutionary without even trying, and thriving to boot." From the editorial board's point of view, lesbian relations were not "an island": "Society does not stop at the bedroom door; it goes in with us, with each one of us. And suffering is probably as much, or even more than by social persecution, caused by the fact that in the lesbian relationship each of us is also the outside world—patriarchy, heterosexuality—for the other woman, that brings about this rage."[30]

Lesbian separatism led to controversy; for example, in 1981 *La Revue d'en face* devoted a rich issue to "Heterosexuality and Lesbianism." It reflected not only the shock that Wittig's positions produced but also intellectual resistances to the increasingly pronounced distinction between "homosexual" women and "lesbians." Catherine Deudon, for example, wanted to destroy sexual categories and thus categories of sexual practices. She denounced the inflation in radicalism that presented lesbianism as a "more radical" feminism. And she continued to hold to the word "homosexual," thereby denying any political content inherent in the word "lesbian." "Even though I'm a homosexual, I have no desire for this chauvinistic, sexist lesbian Nation."[31]

Nevertheless, the word "lesbian" began to take hold over the word homosexual, to signify the difference with masculine homosexuality, and to emphasize the feminine nature of this experience. It also made it possible to conceive of a wider identity than homosexual that "reduced everything to sexuality, whereas lesbian went further; it assumed the defense of rights. And also the sound was nicer."[32] Even more numerous, apparently, were those who found the word too strong, too direct. So in 1982, women from Rennes baptized a convivial group project *Femmes entre elles* (Among Women). Anne Zelensky, president of the *Ligue des droits des femmes* (League of Women's Rights), did not approve of the word "lesbian" and found "homosexuality" just as "unyielding." Why? Because of the "horror of oppressive sexual labels," which did not suit her because they had "a bad connotation in society," and she refused to use them.[33] Thus, she preferred paraphrases such as "loving a woman," or "love between women." Then there were those who, like Cathy Bernheim, called themselves "gay," *gaie* (French feminine form), or *gai* (French masculine form).

"For Lesbians Only"? Plural Ways for Lesbian Activism since the 1980s

Lesbianism found its ideological matrix in the feminism of the 1970s, and the feminist movement continued to leave its marks on lesbianism when lesbians started to fight separately. Lesbianism became more and more visible in society and culture,[34] and it entered a phase of definite autonomy from 1981 to 1984, in the general climate of disenchantment in activism. Where feminism bottomed out, lesbianism was about to soar in a very dynamic way. Some lesbians remained in the feminist movement, a movement that was suffering but not dying. They were by now very visible and numerous. Others, in contrast, joined lesbian-only groups, and still others remained in gay groups.

The *Mouvement d'information et d'expression des lesbiennes* (Movement of Lesbian Information and Expression, MIEL) was formed in 1981, the monthly *Lesbia* in 1982 (by Christiane Jouve and Catherine Marjollet), the Lesbian Archives in 1984. The word "lesbian" took on an activist meaning that was not necessarily feminist. The MIEL realized that lesbians started to leave women's groups while the use of the word "lesbian" increased, with this definition by the MIEL: "An affirmation of our identity, affirmation toward greater visibility. In relations among women, this visibility should not express itself uniquely in a sexual or emotional life but equally by challenging and fighting sexist and patriarchal society and the compulsory heterosexuality that it conveys."[35] The MIEL was thus considering itself part of the feminist movement; it set up shop in the women center at the Cité Prost in Paris.

It is impossible to measure the exact influence of lesbians in the feminist movement since the end of the 1970s, but what is sure is that it has been strong. The fight for the criminalization of rape can be seen from this perspective. It produced a distance with gay activists who preferred to contest "bourgeois justice" and thought that sexual violence was overestimated and not specific.[36] Pedophilia, also a subject of discord, was still defended by some in the 1970s.

On the other hand, the fight over the age of sexual consent, differentiated since Vichy (fifteen for heterosexuals, eighteen for homosexuals), was a federating subject that feminists became involved in. The lawyer Gisèle Halimi invited François Mitterrand to a meeting of her association, *Choisir,* in April 1981 at which the presidential candidate made the commitment to do away with the discriminations if he was elected. As a parliamentarian that came in with the pink wave, Halimi led a tough parliamentary battle, tougher than that for the abolition of capital punishment. In spite of resistance from the upper house of Parliament, the Penal Code was finally revised in July 1982, in accordance with European recommendations.

When, in the early 1980s, conflicts between radical and moderate lesbians emerged, a new lesbian current came into existence that centered around certain places, groups, informal networks of *Lesbia* readers, minitel users (a French precursor of the World Wide Web), and festive events. Coming out became easier. Structures for conviviality and consumption were developing, often faithful to lesbian activist commitments, like at the Bagdam Cafée (a 1988–99 lesbian-only Toulousan place).

There was also a certain look. While homosexual feminists of the 1970s did not try to stand out in terms of clothes—they were baba-cool, "like everyone!" of the 1980s—the lesbian look took over: more or less masculine, pants and doc martens, short hair, knapsack, no make-up. One can hardly *not* notice the break with the valorization of the feminine dear to many 1970s feminists.

Lesbian affirmation at this stage was more cultural than political. More and more lesbians did not hesitate to challenge the feminist movement's lacks. The example of the Creteil International Women's film festival, attended by many lesbians (the audience award is often given to a lesbian-themed film), was telling: this gap between programming choices and public taste explains the 1989 birth of a separatist lesbian film festival, When Lesbians Make Films (later called *Cinéffable*).

Quietly, lesbian groups grew in the 1990s, making a federating structure possible and desirable. In 1995 the organization of the Beijing World Conference on Women showed the inexistence of lesbians for public authorities. The *Coordination lesbienne nationale* will later provide with a greater lesbian representation, a branch of associative activism that stand in the shadow of its gay "older brother." Lesbophobia made it possible to gather and legitimize lesbian separatism by pointing out the misogyny and/or lesbophobia in the gay world. Difficult though to avoid the accusations of "ghetto" and the often poorly understood separation of lesbians at the Homosexual summer universities (that started up again in Marseille in 1999) and lesbian studies conferences (since 1999 in Toulouse).

Obvious for the 1970s generation, Lesbian separatism was no longer so obvious. As of the 1990s, mixing became important both in the feminist and in the gay and lesbian movement. This can be explained first by a decline in feminist influence. The utopic dimension of Luce Irigaray's and Monique Wittig's works was far from the real stakes perceived by the lesbians (and gays) of the 1990s.[37] For example, in the 1980s Irigaray, philosopher and psychoanalyst, toned down her thinking on love between women as the foundation of a different feminine subjectivity (see *Spéculum de l'autre femme,* 1974). Young lesbians did not seem interested in the idea of freeing women's body and sexuality from the framework of "phallocentric economy." Where was Wittig leading her readers/admirers? If, as she said for the first time in 1978, "lesbians are not women," how could the relationship between feminism and lesbianism be envisaged? And the (common?) fight against oppression? Was being lesbian only a metaphor? Wittig, like materialist radical feminists, thought that sexed identities maintained women's oppression and that the aim of feminism was to eliminate "sexual difference." The disappearance of both heterosexuality and homosexuality was on the agenda. Such a deconstruction dangerously threatened sexual identities that were not only denaturalized but doomed to disappear. Could it—such as the foundations of a house—support a lesbian-feminist movement? Without a doubt, there was a heavy discrimination at work between those with the intellectual and cultural background for being able to relate to that kind of thinking and the others. And feminist or lesbian theory was, for a good number of young people, a daunting confusion. Between a too "brainy" and/or too politicized feminism and a convivial and festive gay/lesbian activism, the choice was clear. Consumerist habits also endangered quite precarious places like the women center *La Maison des femmes* in Paris (1982 to 1995) that gathered feminist groups and lesbian associations (MIEL, Wen-do group, *Lesbiennes Internationales,* Utopia, *Lesbiennes féministes,* Lesbian Archives as of 1997, etc.). MIEL evenings where one could eat casually for ten francs did not please women who preferred a certain standing. Other feminist places, conversely, were too bourgeois and matronly to attract new generations. Mingling and integration were easier in the gay atmosphere: the supply grew more diversified in the 1990s with the opening of subsidized gay and lesbian centers offering many commercial resources.

During the terrible ravages of the AIDS epidemic, new groups like Aides or Act-Up had an active minority of women. Prevention measures specifically for lesbians were seemingly copied from practices for gay men. "Gay Pride" became "Lesbian and Gay Pride," and then "Lesbian, Gay, Bisexual, Transgender Pride" (LGBT). The organizers of the event recognized the diversity of its partisans; lesbian groups were present but not too visible among the noisy and colorful floats. In these marches that brought homosexuality out of the shadows and in the fight for the PACS (civil union), gay men dominated incontestably. Their activist power was reinforced by their financial (business, sponsors) and even territorial power (the quartier *Le Marais* in Paris, some streets in major cities) to such an extent that the asymmetry with women was remarkable, and certainly inevitable. The depolitization of the period nevertheless brought the sexes together, in particular the young who were not familiar with feminism. The autonomous lesbian approach, for example at *Cinéffable,* appeared narrow-minded.

How far did the term "lesbian" recede in the way lesbians refer to themselves? Women were appropriating the term "gay." Leaders who were supposed to be representative of activist lesbian circles were now being referred to as "historical lesbians," modeled on "historical feminists" (does the assonance with hysterical explain the expression's success?). Thus far, that, in some local mixed (gay and lesbian) associations, a shift occurred (the fronts were reversed): men with a feminist culture and women who did not know anything about it and rejected it, often by an anti-intellectual reflex. When the former denounced sexism, the latter did not "see the problem." Among students where gay and lesbian group dynamics have been strong since the late 1990s, mixing both sexes is a given, for example in fighting homophobia.[38] The *transpédégouine* (transfagdyke) members of the *Panthères roses* (Pink Panthers), acting against "the moral order, patriarchy, sexism, racism, etc.,"[39] embodied mixed (*i.e.* gay and lesbian, going as far as androgynous fusion) groups. They also humorously express this discomfort concerning these categories (differences between the sexes, differences in sexualities). Even in lesbian separatist groups, the transgender issue has brought about a change. Once criticized for not having experienced oppression as woman or lesbian, lesbian transsexuals are now included. So *Cinéffable* makes it a point to say that gender is a declarative act: the festival of lesbian films is thus open to "anyone, in whatever state, who declares herself a women."[40]

Mixing is also highlighted in queer theory. Like all activist movements, lesbian feminism/feminist lesbianism has its "political correctness" to which one is sensitive in these times. Feminist idealization of lesbianism has certainly had some censorship effects on the violence among women, on sexual fantasies, or on the desire for motherhood.[41] It points out, in a way, lesbian historiography, which, obviously, is not without activist interests: the feminist approach to the past remains dominant, with the assumptions that follow from that on lesbian identity. Historian Marie-Jo Bonnet's work, centered on the lesbian *eros* as resistance to patriarchy, attests to it.[42]

The 1990s saw the emergence of the criticism of feminists' "puritanism," whether lesbian or not, accused of having "desexualized" women. Out of fear of sex. To preserve the advantageous status of eternal victim. Out of intellectual routine. Out of the inability to desacralize sex. Anthropologist and also activist since 1960 in the San Francisco gay and lesbian community, Gayle Rubin was one of the first people to defend sexualities that bother feminists: prostitution, pornography, S&M, etc.[43] Her "pro-sex" position was particularly followed by the queer movement that developed in the 1990s on campuses and activist places in the United States and then in other countries. In France, Marie-Hélène Bourcier brought these very critical positions from the other side of the Atlantic, positions regarding the lesbian-feminist culture, accused of having stigmatized certain sexual practices judged phallocentric, of having rejected the popular lesbian strongly gendered (butch/femme) culture, of having cut all ties with lesbians active in mixed gay and lesbian groups, and having stigmatized the "Jules" (The French equivalent for "butch," this word has fallen out of fashion since the 1980s).[44] This "queer" current brought generations together: like FHAR in its time, it was against the normalization of homosexuality (that the PACS of the 1990s followed by marriage for all and the debates on same-sex parenting in the 2000s were beginning to make concrete); it drew on Wittig, a central figure, and did not refrain from a certain antifeminism, taking up, sometimes by not paying attention to it, the arguments of radical lesbianism of the 1980s.

Loosely structured, radical lesbianism subsisted as a style of life. Some discrete rural communities still try nowadays to keep themselves away from the "mixed" world. Intellectual input remains. The anthropologist Nicole-Claude Mathieu has become a reference for sex and gender categorizations. Monique Wittig, far from France's heated discussions among lesbians,[45] settled in the United States in the mid-1970s. She published, among other books, *The Straight Mind and Other Essays* (Beacon Press, 1992). Although there was a conference devoted to her in 2001 in France,[46] she does not have a strong influence. But theoretical work in the current of political lesbianism continues. In 2003 *Lesbianisme et féminisme: Histoires politiques,* edited by Natacha Chetcuti and Claire Michard (L'Harmattan), was published, which gathered articles reflecting the historical network of the most well-known activists, who are often, in addition, intellectuals or artists. It includes many Quebec contributions (the journal *Amazones d'hier, lesbiennes d'aujourd'hui,* published as of 1982, played a major role). This volume shows a timid generational renewal with two sociologists under fifty: Jules Falquet and Natacha Chetcuti, one of the few highly visible scholars working on feminine homosexuality in France. In 2003 Monique Wittig died. Her sister Gille died a few years later. Michèle Causse passed away in 2010; Danielle Charest in 2011. Audiovisual or artistic expression would give a younger image to political lesbianism, for example, the lesbian teleweb, *VidéObstinées,* created in 2008.

* * *

What is the relation between feminism and lesbianism? This is a common question today, and it is not easy to answer. By covering so many ways of living, thinking, speaking, and being active, the history of political lesbianism is so rich as to be unsettling. It becomes more complex by cross-referencing and diversifying the documentary sources and by taking into account the participants and not only theoretical texts or the history of constituted groups. Things become even more complicated if we reject anachronism and seek the meaning or the primary and successive meanings of key words. Thus we can draw on currents and cultures that today have disappeared, or are not very well known or marginalized.

Speaking of feminism and lesbianism in the singular is a mystifying and even dangerous fiction for the pluralistic activist forces that embody these abstractions. It is thus not possible to tell a linear story in which lesbianism, resulting from 1970s radical feminism, separated from feminism to affirm itself in an autonomous strategy. Retracing the multiple entanglements between feminists and lesbians has shown that lesbianism continues its way as well in the feminist movement as in the gay and lesbian movement and, last but not least, in the rewritings of its history.[47]

Christine Bard is professor of history (Université d'Angers). She has published a dozen books in the field of gender history, including works about feminism, antifeminism, skirt and trousers, the *garçonne* fashion, and synthesis on women in France during the twentieth century. She is the president of Feminist Archives and the founder of the virtual museum on women's history, MUSEA. She is the head of a research program on sexist and homophobic discriminations (GEDI).

Notes

1. Catherine Gonnard, "L'amante de la veuve du Soldat inconnu," *Politique, la revue,* no. 5 (1997): 23.
2. Claudie Lesselier, "Féminisme, lesbianisme, hétérosexualité," *Politique, la revue,* no. 5 (1997): 35.
3. That is 1970. "Liberation des femmes année zéro" is the title of a special issue of *Partisans,* July 1970. See Françoise Picq, *Libération des femmes: Les Années-Mouvement* (Paris: Seuil, 1993).
4. See Christine Bard, *Les Filles de Marianne: Histoire des féminismes 1914–1940* (Paris: Fayard, 1995).
5. See Christine Bard, " La virilisation des femmes et l'égalité des sexes," in *Madeleine Pelletier (1874–1939): Logique et infortunes d'un combat pour l'égalité,* ed. Christine Bard (Paris: Côté-Femmes, 1992), 91–108.
6. See Christine Bard, *Une histoire politique du pantalon* (Paris: Seuil, 2010).
7. See Christine Bard, *Les Garçonnes: Modes et fantasmes des Années folles* (Paris: Flammarion, 1998).
8. See on these two women, Laure Murat, *Passage de l'Odéon* (Paris: Fayard, 2003); and more generally, Florence Tamagne, *Histoire de l'homosexualité en Europe (Berlin, London, Paris, 1919–1939)* (Paris: Seuil, 2000).
9. Sylvie Chaperon, *Les Années Beauvoir 1945–1970* (Paris: Fayard, 2000), 169–202.
10. See Sylvie Chaperon and Christine Delphy, eds., *Cinquantenaire du Deuxième Sexe* (Paris: Syllepse, 2002).
11. Claudie Lesselier, "Les regroupements de lesbiennes dans le mouvement féministe parisien: position et problèmes, 1970–1982," in *Crise de la société, féminisme et chan-*

gement, ed. by Groupe d'études féministes, Université de Paris VII (Paris: Revue d'en face/Tierce, 1991), 89.

12. Julian Jackson, *Arcadie: La vie homosexuelle en France de l'après-guerre à la dépénalisation* (Paris: Autrement, 2009).
13. Claudie Lesselier, "Formes de résistances et d'expression lesbiennes dans les années 1950–1960 en France," in *Homosexualités: expression/répression,* ed. Louis-Georges Tin (Paris: Stock, 2000), 105–18.
14. Éditorial (editorial board made up of Christine Delphy, Claude Hannequin, and Emmanuèle de Lesseps), see Christine Delphy et al., "Éditorial," *Nouvelles questions féministes,* no. 1 (1981): 9.
15. See Kolly Bérangère, *La sororité, une société sans société: modalités d'un être-politique* (Philosophy thesis, Université de Paris I, 2012).
16. Christine Delphy, interview with author, February 1, 2001. Quotations from Christine Delphy in the following text refer to this interview.
17. Liliane Kandel, interview with author, January 25, 2001. Quotations from Liliane Kandel in the following text refer to this interview. Still feminist, Catherine Deudon has published her story along with her photos of the movement years: *Un mouvement à soi 1970–2001* (Paris: Syllepse, 2003).
18. See the life story of Evelyne Rochedereux in Françoise Flamant, *À tire d'elles: Itinéraires de féministes radicales des années 1970* (Rennes: Presses Universitaires de Rennes, 2007).
19. Catherine Guinchard, and Annik Houel, Brigitte Lhommond, Patricia Mercader, Helga Sobota, "L'autre mixité: homosexuelles et hétérosexuelles," in *Crise de la société, féminisme et changement,* ed. Groupe d'études féministes, Université de Paris VII (Paris: Revue d'en face/Tierce, 1991), 73–86.
20. Quoted by Cathy Bernheim, *Perturbation ma sœur* (Paris: Seuil, 1983), 54.
21. Anne Tristan and Annie de Pisan, *Histoires du MLF* (Paris: Calmann-Lévy, 1977).
22. Catherine Deudon, photographer, joined the women's movement in 1971. Source: Written answer to questions asked by Christine Bard, March 12–17, 2001.
23. BMD, MLF file. See also in these homo/hetero relations the study of the Lyon example: Guinchard et al., "L'autre mixité," 74.
24. In Ti-Grace Atkinson, "Lesbianisme et feminisme," article reprinted in *Odyssée d'une amazone* (Paris: Des femmes, 1970), 99–100.
25. Ti-Grace Atkinson, "Justice pour les femmes considérées comme 'contre-nature,'" in *Odyssée d'une amazone* (Paris: Des femmes, 1970), 151.
26. Lesselier, "Les regroupements de lesbiennes dans le mouvement féministe parisien," 95.
27. *Nouvelles Questions Féministes,* "Appel à la Rencontre/Lesbiennes, June 21–2, 1980," no. 1 (March 1981): 77–79.
28. See Association du Mouvement pour les luttes feministes, *Chroniques d'une imposture: Du mouvement de libération des femmes à une marque commerciale* (Paris: Voix Off, 1981).
29. Henri Rousso, *Le Syndrome de Vichy* (Paris: Seuil, 1987).
30. *Nouvelles questions féministes,* "Appel à la Rencontre/Lesbiennes," 14.
31. Catherine Deudon, "Radicale-ment, nature-elle-ment," *La Revue d'en face,* no. 9–10 (1981): 81–83.

32. Conversation with Simone Le Gaillard, Rennes, March 5, 2001.
33. Anne Zelensky, interview with author, June 22, 2001.
34. Lesbian history became visible with Marie-Jo Bonnet's thesis in 1981 (Marie-Jo Bonnet, *Un choix sans équivoque* [Paris: Denoël Gonthier, 1981]). In 1981 the poet Geneviève Pastre published *De l'amour lesbien* (Paris: Pierre Horay, 1981).
35. Mouvement d'Information et d'Expression des Lesbiennes (MIEL), *Être lesbienne aujourd'hui: Le MIEL enquête* (Paris: Miel, 1989), 8.
36. See Frédéric Martel, *Le Rose et le Noir* (Paris: Seuil, 1996).
37. Renate Günther, "Are Lesbians Women? The Relationship between Lesbianism and Feminism in the Work of Luce Irigaray and Monique Wittig," in *Gay Signatures: Gay and Lesbian Theory, Fiction and Film in France, 1945–1995,* ed. Owen Heathcote and James S. Williams (New York: Berg, 1998), 73–90.
38. See, for example, Nolwenn Letanoux, "Le Mouvement homosexuel rennais et le mouvement national, des années 1970 à nos jours" (master's thesis, Université de Rennes II, 2001).
39. *Libération,* "Les Panthères roses peuvent tracter," May 4, 2003.
40. *Clap info,* "When Lesbians Make Their Own Films," May 2003.
41. See Christine Lemoine and Ingrid Renard, eds., *Attirances, Lesbiennes fems, Lesbiennes butchs* (Paris: Éditions gaies et lesbiennes, 2001).
42. Marie-Jo Bonnet, *Qu'est-ce qu'une femme désire quand elle désire une femme?* (Paris: Odile Jacob, 2004).
43. The reception of Gayle Rubin in France came late; the translation of *Thinking Sex* (1984) came out in 2001. See Gayle S. Rubin, and Judith Butler, *Marché au sexe,* trans. Éliane Sokol (Paris: Epel, 2001).
44. Marie-Hélène Bourcier, *Queer Zones: Politiques des identités sexuelles, des représentations et des savoirs* (Paris: Balland, 2001); Marie-Hélène Bourcier, *Queer Zones 2: Sexpolitiques* (Paris: La Fabrique, 2005); Marie-Hélène Bourcier, *Queer Zones 3: Identités, Cultures et Politiques* (Paris: Amsterdam, 2011).
45. See her articles in *Paris-la-politique et autres histoires,* POL, 1999, published a long time after the storm.
46. Marie-Hélène Bourcier and Suzette Robichon, eds., *Parce que les lesbiennes ne sont pas des femmes. Autour de l'œuvre politique, théorique et littéraire de Monique Wittig* (Paris: Éditions gaies et lesbiennes, 2001).
47. The author thanks Brigitte Boucheron, Sophie Camut, Christine Delphy, Catherine Deudon, Françoise Flamant, Michelle Guillon, Liliane Kandel, Anne Lepont, Suzette Robichon, and Anne Zélensky, who provided their accounts. She would like to specially point to the contribution of Catherine Gonnard, Claudie Lesselier, Brigitte Lhommond, and Marie-Jo Bonnet whose articles provide most of the limited documentation on France. A far more complete view of this topic will be given by the doctoral thesis of Ilana Eloit (London School of Economics, Gender Institute), who examines the political and theoretical genesis of lesbian collective identities in France in the 1970s and 1980s and their relation to feminist social movements. The author is grateful to Corinne Bouchoux, Sylvie Chaperon, Ilana Eloit, Françoise Flamant, Florence Rochefort, and Barbara Wolman for reading the text and to Sheila Malovany-Chevallier for her translation. This chapter that expands the text "Féminisme" from the *Dictionnaire des cultures gays et lesbiennes,* edited by Didier

Eribon (Paris: Larousse, 2003) is a modified and updated version of the article "Le lesbianisme comme construction politique," which appeared in Eliane Gubin *et al.*, eds., *Le siècle des féminismes* (Paris: L'Atelier, 2004), 111–26.

Bibliography

Association du Mouvement pour les luttes féministes. *Chroniques d'une imposture: Du mouvement de libération des femmes à une marque commerciale.* Paris: Voix Off, 1981.

Atkinson, Ti-Grace. "Justice pour les femmes considérées comme 'contre-nature.'" In *Odyssée d'une amazone.* Paris: Des femmes, 1970, 151–154.

———. "Lesbianisme et feminisme." In *Odyssée d'une amazone.* Paris: Des femmes, 1970, 99–104.

Bard, Christine. "The virilisation des femmes et l'égalité des sexes." In *Madeleine Pelletier (1874–1939): Logique et infortunes d'un combat pour l'égalité,* edited by Christine Bard, 91–108. Paris: Côté-Femmes, 1992.

———. *Les Filles de Marianne. Histoire des féminismes 1914–1940.* Paris: Fayard, 1995.

———. *Les Garçonnes: Modes et fantasmes des Années folles.* Paris: Flammarion, 1998.

———. "Féminisme." In *Dictionnaire des cultures gays et lesbiennes,* edited by Didier Eribon, 190–193. Paris: Larousse, 2003.

———. "Le lesbianisme comme construction politique." In *Le siècle des féminismes,* edited by Éliane Gubin *et al.,* 111–26. Paris: L'Atelier, 2004.

———. *Une histoire politique du pantalon.* Paris: Seuil, 2010.

Bérangère, Kolly. *La sororité, une société sans société: modalités d'un être-politique.* Philosophy thesis, Université de Paris I, 2012.

Bernheim, Cathy. *Perturbation ma sœur.* Paris: Seuil, 1983.

Bonnet, Marie-Jo. *Un choix sans équivoque.* Paris: Denoël Gonthier, 1981.

———. *Qu'est-ce qu'une femme désire quand elle désire une femme?* Paris: Odile Jacob, 2004.

Bourcier, Marie-Hélène, and Suzette Robichon, eds. *Parce que les lesbiennes ne sont pas des femmes. Autour de l'œuvre politique, théorique et littéraire de Monique Wittig.* Paris: Éditions gaies et lesbiennes, 2001.

Bourcier, Marie-Hélène. *Queer Zones: Politiques des identités sexuelles, des représentations et des savoirs.* Paris: Balland, 2001.

———. *Queer Zones 2: Sexpolitiques.* Paris: La Fabrique, 2005.

———. *Queer Zones 3: Identités, Cultures et Politiques.* Paris: Amsterdam, 2011.

Chaperon, Sylvie. *Les Années Beauvoir 1945–1970.* Paris: Fayard, 2000.

Chaperon, Sylvie, and Delphy Christine, eds. *Cinquantenaire du Deuxième Sexe.* Paris: Syllepse, 2002.

Clap info. "When Lesbians Make Their Own Films." May 2003.

Delphy, Christine, et al. "Éditorial." *Nouvelles questions féministes,* no. 1 (1981): 9.

Deudon, Catherine. "Radicale-ment, nature-elle-ment." *La Revue d'en face,* no. 9–10 (1981): 81–83.

———. *Un mouvement à soi 1970–2001.* Paris: Syllepse, 2003.

Flamant, Françoise. *À tire d'elles: Itinéraires de féministes radicales des années 1970.* Rennes: Presses Universitaires de Rennes, 2007.

Gonnard, Catherine. "L'amante de la veuve du Soldat inconnu." *Politique, la revue,* no. 5 (1997): 23.

Guinchard, Catherine, Annik Houel, Brigitte Lhommond, Patricia Mercader, Helga Sobota. "L'autre mixité: homosexuelles et hétérosexuelles." In *Crise de la société, féminisme et changement,* edited by Groupe d'études féministes, Université de Paris VII, 73–86. Paris: Revue d'en face/Tierce, 1991.

Günther, Renate. "Are Lesbians Women? The Relationship between Lesbianism and Feminism in the Work of Luce Irigaray and Monique Wittig." In *Gay Signatures: Gay and Lesbian Theory, Fiction and Film in France, 1945–1995,* edited by Owen Heathcote and James S. Williams, 73–90. New York: Berg, 1998.

Jackson, Julian. *Arcadie: La vie homosexuelle en France de l'après-guerre à la dépénalisation.* Paris: Autrement, 2009.

Lemoine, Christine, and Ingrid Renard, eds. *Attirances, Lesbiennes fems, Lesbiennes butchs.* Paris: Éditions gaies et lesbiennes, 2001.

Lesselier, Claudie. "Les regroupements de lesbiennes dans le mouvement féministe parisien: position et problèmes, 1970–1982." In *Crise de la société, féminisme et changement,* edited by Groupe d'études féministes, Université de Paris VII, 87–103. Paris: Revue d'en face/Tierce, 1991.

———. "Féminisme, lesbianisme, hétérosexualité." *Politique, la revue,* no. 5 (1997): 35.

———. "Formes de résistances et d'expression lesbiennes dans les années 1950–1960 en France." In *Homosexualités: expression/répression,* edited by Louis-Georges Tin. Paris: Stock, 2000, 105–18.

Letanoux, Nolwenn. "Le Mouvement homosexuel rennais et le mouvement national, des années 1970 à nos jours." Master's thesis, Université de Rennes II, 2001.

Libération. "Les Panthères roses peuvent tracter." May 4, 2003.

Martel, Frédéric. *Le Rose et le Noir.* Paris: Seuil, 1996.

Mouvement d'Information et d'Expression des Lesbiennes (MIEL). *Être lesbienne aujourd'hui: Le MIEL enquête.* Paris: Miel, 1989.

Murat, Laure. *Passage de l'Odéon.* Paris: Fayard, 2003.

Nouvelles Questions Féministes. "Appel à la Rencontre/Lesbiennes, June 21–2, 1980." No. 1, March 1981.

Pastre, Geneviève. *De l'amour lesbien.* Paris: Pierre Horay, 1981.

Picq, Françoise. *Libération des femmes: Les Années-Mouvement.* Paris: Seuil, 1993.

Rousso, Henri. *Le Syndrome de Vichy.* Paris: Seuil, 1987.

Rubin, Gayle S., and Judith Butler. *Marché au sexe.* Translated by Éliane Sokol. Paris: Epel, 2001.

Tamagne, Florence. *Histoire de l'homosexualité en Europe (Berlin, London, Paris, 1919–1939).* Paris: Seuil, 2000.

Tristan, Anne, and Annie de Pisan. *Histoires du MLF.* Paris: Calmann-Lévy, 1977.

Chapter 9

Gender and Class in the Italian Women's Liberation Movement

Marica Tolomelli and Anna Frisone

From the middle of the 1960s and during the 1970s in several Western countries of the world, a new, basic dimension, fundamental for the construction of society, was acknowledged, claimed, and loaded with new significance: gender. From this perspective, gender was at the grassroots level of the existing power and dominance relationships between men and women; gender structured life in the so-called private sphere—the family—as well as in the public sphere, in the political and social arenas of the existing social orders. Gender underlay the social organization of labor, of production and reproduction of resources; gender influenced the education of children and affected the ruling forms of social domination.

Gender, understood as one of the fundamental categories upon which society was structured, acquired its own specific relevance in this period. It became an independent concept, no longer subordinated to other principles with universal ambitions, like class or race.[1] As to the problem of women's subjugation during the nineteenth and twentieth centuries, many circumstances and experiences had already revealed how ineffective class struggle and racial emancipation were.

The women's liberation movements (WLMs) that arose in numerous Western countries from the end of the 1960s were responsible for the growing social and political acknowledgment of gender.[2] In many cases, such as in the United States, in the Federal Republic of Germany, and, in part, also in Italy, the women's movements arose through a separation process from the students' movements of 1968, a revolt, so to speak, challenging the rebels themselves. Women accused their male mates of reproducing the same gender-dominated logic against which they claimed to be rebelling.[3] From this point of view, the building of WLMs can be understood both as a continuance and as a radicalization, i.e. a further deepening of the social criticism introduced by the thinking of the New Left and the students' movements during the 1960s.

In the context of industrialized countries, where the New Left claimed that the proletariat had abdicated from its historic revolutionary undertaking, the women's movements now focused on a new "agent of social change"[4]: women as the oppressed of the oppressed. The core quest for radical social change was understood as the achievement of an authentic liberation, in overcoming any form of cultural, economic, political, and philosophical subordination of women to men.

The Italian Context

The emancipationist women's movement in Italy had a tradition that went back to the period of the *Risorgimento,*[5] flourished during the liberal phase,[6] was oppressed by Fascism,[7] and regained vigor within the democratic political frame of the postwar Republic.[8] Considering it through the different political phases that marked the national history, Andreina De Clementi has argued that since its first formation, Italian feminism developed on the ground of a dual agenda: "real emancipation of women in the socialist-communist tradition ..., and an independence of decision-making hinging on a redefinition of identity and role that cuts across social class."[9] De Clementi views a class-crossing politics as capable of gaining consensus, although the relationship between the dimensions of social belonging (class) and sexual identity (gender) was always in practice a matter of precarious balances and cause of tensions. In the 1960s the formation of the new women's movement occurred in a similar way in other Western countries, but in the Italian context the separation process was double. On the one side, it arose through the separation from the students' movement and its incapacity to overwhelm its gender prejudice; on the other it strengthened its new character by emphasizing the separation from the old emancipationist and equalitarian frame of the socialist workers' movement, as well as the traditions inherited from the liberal age.

The women of *Rivolta femminile,* a group founded in Rome in 1970 that greatly inspired Italian feminism in the following years, elucidated the refusal of equalitarian issues. One of the first public statements of the group was a *Manifesto,* hung up in the streets of Rome in the summer of 1970. Without any preliminary introduction—apart from a short but eloquent quotation of Olympe de Gouges—it declared in few sentences that women had to be considered as "whole" human beings and not in relation to men. In other words, women had to be thought as different from men. The *Manifesto* began with the following words:

> Woman must not be defined in relation to man. This awareness is the foundation of both our struggle and our freedom.
>
> Man is not the model to hold up for the process of woman's self-discovery.
>
> Woman is the other in relation to man. Man is the other in relation to woman. Equality is an ideological attempt to subject woman even further.[10]

In the same period, Carla Lonzi, one of the most prominent theoreticians of *Rivolta Femminile,* wrote a longer text, *Let's Spit on Hegel,* in which she also argued against the modern political concept of equality, as in it she saw just a "juridical principle" through which "those with hegemonic power continue to control those without it."[11] Rather than the principle of equality, Lonzi recognized in the principle of *difference* the key concept for any strategy of subversion of male dominance:

> Difference is an existential principle that concerns the modes of being human, the peculiarity of one's own experiences, goals, possibilities, and one's sense of existence in a given situation and in the situation one wants to create for oneself. The difference between woman and man is the basic difference of humankind. A black man may be equal to a white man, a black woman to a white woman.... Equality between the sexes is merely the mask with which woman's inferiority is disguised. This is the stand of those who, being different, want to effect a total change in the culture that has held them prisoners.[12]

Although a considerable part of the women's movement decided to focus its agency on the development of female subjectivity—through the practice of *autocoscienza* (self-consciousness)—independently from class belonging, in some ways it was constrained to come into contact and dialogue with the class struggle paradigm of social change. The necessity to think of radical social transformations in relation also to a traditional Marxist theoretical frame was due to at least two factors: on one side, the strong weight of orthodox Marxism within the left-wing political culture—represented in Italy by a strong left-wing tradition; on the other side, the revival of acute class conflicts that occurred in the same period in which the formation of the new women's movement took place.

From the end of the 1960s and during the 1970s, Italy was in fact crossed by manifold social protests: after the impressive students' mobilization that culminated in the movement of 1968, the public scene was dominated by the workers' upheavals.[13] These reached a first climax in the so-called *autunno caldo* (hot autumn) of 1969 and lasted for several years thereafter. The workers' mobilization overwhelmed the Italian students' movement and was conducive to its decline. In fact, between the spring and the autumn of 1968 the student movement abandoned its previous willingness to act in full autonomy and independence and switched over to the old paradigm of class struggle that foresaw the involvement of the proletariat in any strategy of radical change.[14] The social frame within which arose the agency of many collective actors, who in the 1970s wanted to overcome the existing forms of domination, was therefore very multifaceted: on the one side, the trade unions made enormous efforts to reaffirm control over the worker's claims for autonomy. On the other, groups of the so-called extraparliamentary left wing challenged the trade unions, trying to radicalize the issues of the workers' protests in order to make any bargain with the counterparts impossible. The strength and the radicalism of the workers' conflicts at the beginning of the 1970s gave new impetus to the old orthodox paradigm of class struggle. Even political groups like *Lotta Continua,* which had been strongly influenced by the ideas of the international New Left, its search for new agents of social change and new strategies, could not avoid coming to terms with the widespread labor conflicts. Besides, the changeover of some radical left-wing groups to the strategy of armed struggle was also strictly connected to workers' conflicts that developed within large industrial plants and gained more and more importance.

Gender and Class: A Fertile Field of Tension

How did the Italian women's movement face up to such a class-focused scenario? Did the worker's mobilization influence the development of feminist thought and agency, or, on the contrary, did the women's movement affect in some ways the cultural horizon of workers' protests and trade unions' politics? The answers to these questions can obviously not be unitary, because of the diversity of ways in which the women's movement faced the class struggle paradigm.

The most radical and utopian part of the women's movement, to begin with, considered that the class-struggle paradigm had already shown its incapacity or its unwillingness to face the gender quest. That was the main argument of Carla Lonzi and the women of *Rivolta femminile* in the already quoted booklet *Let's Spit on Hegel*:

> Women realize the political connection between Marxist-Leninist ideology.… But they don't believe that women are secondary, a consequence of the revolution.… They question the idea that their cause should be subordinated to the class problem.… Subsuming the feminine problem to the classist conception of the master-slave struggle is an historical mistake. In fact, this conception comes out of a culture which dismissed the essential discrimination of humankind, i.e. man's absolute privilege over woman; it creates a new perspective only for men, as it poses the problem only in their terms.… Subordination to the classist perspective means for woman the acceptance of terms borrowed from her own.… Woman is oppressed as a woman, at all social levels; not as a class, but as a sex. This gap in Marxist theory is no accident, nor would it be filled by stretching the concept of class to make room for women as a new class.… By trusting all hopes of a revolutionary future to the working class, Marxism has ignored women, both as oppressed people and as bearers of the future. Its revolutionary theory was developed within the framework of patriarchal culture.[15]

These words express the conviction that, for feminists, it was no more a matter of seeking for inclusion in class struggle. Much more, it was a matter of seeking for a radically new social order, within which women could have a place as human beings in their own right. The text goes on: "The equality available today is not philosophical but political. But do we, after thousands of years, really wish for inclusion, on these terms, in a world planned by others? Would we indeed be gratified by participating in the great defeat of man?" From the point of view of *Rivolta Femminile* it was therefore not worth trying to fight for any balance or compromise between social emancipation and women's liberation. The real challenge lay in the foundation of a new "social contract," in the building of which women had to participate and act as persons in their own right. In the feminist approach the preeminence of the gender struggle was evident and therefore not negotiable. However, such radically differentialistic approaches were not shared by the whole movement.

Other groups sought to develop a new theoretical approach in order to find a satisfying dialectical link between class and gender. They tried to put both categories out of the classical frame of orthodox Marxism and to find, consequently, a way to overwhelm the existing contradiction between class struggle and women's liberation issues. Marxist theory subordinated the liberation of woman to the emancipation of the proletariat and saw the premise for women's emancipation in their integration within the *productive* world, i.e. in their access to the salaried workforce. Marxist feminism, organized in groups like *Il cerchio spezzato* at the University of Trento since the end of the 1960s or *Lotta femminista,* a faction of women coming from groups like *Lotta continua* and *Potere operaio* of the extraparliamentary left wing, turned the thought of orthodox Marxism upside down. Marxist feminism focused upon the so-called nonproductive labor and attempted to enlighten its crucial role for an efficient functioning of the hegemonic capitalist system.[16] *Lotta femminista* contested the distinction between productive and unproductive labor—a distinction assumed also by the institutional left-wing parties. The group did not just claim better employment conditions for women in the existing labor market, it claimed the full acknowledgment of domestic work, i.e. the housewives' right to be remunerated. Moreover, it demanded the transcendence of the gendered division of labor, a division that capitalism had not created but strongly consolidated.[17] The Marxist feminist groups perceived the existing gendered division of labor as a means through which capitalism tried to weaken the internal unity within the working class. In the abatement of both the distinction between productive and unproductive labor on the one side and the gender division of labor endorsed by capitalism on the other, Marxist feminists tried to create a new strategic link between women's liberation and the workers' emancipation movements.

It is difficult to assess the social impact of these groups, but some *success*—in Tucholsky's meaning recalled by Kristina Schulz in the introduction to this volume—cannot be ignored. Class-focusing feminism certainly stimulated awareness of how important so-called unproductive labor was and is for a nation's wealth as well as for a capitalist economy in general. It certainly shed light on women's hidden labor. However, Marxist feminism achieved neither concrete goals nor strong influence on the Italian society. It had to face not only gender prejudices that still pervaded Italian institutions as well as the New Left but also a very conservative society where a traditional family model, based on the subjugation of women to men, was deeply rooted. To remain within Marxist jargon we can say that Marxist feminists had to fight on two fronts at the same time: on the structural level, against the separated organization of productive and unproductive labor, and on the level of the superstructure, against the cultural frames that underlay the gender division of labor. Marxist feminist groups did not really succeed in their attempt to break the ideological frame that underpinned the primacy of the class struggle paradigm. They contested it, but they did not effectively overcome its practical and intellectual significance.

Originating in a less ideological viewpoint, finally other women's groups tried to negotiate class and gender issues within another political field in which the two categories of gender and class came together in a difficult but eventually fertile dialogue: the trade unions. In the 1970s trade unions were in fact the institution that most displayed the willingness to dialogue with external social movements and other informal collective actors. This facilitated the entrance of some topics of the women's liberation movement within these longstanding organizations of the workers' movement. Some outcomes of this permeation process have later been called—both by activists and by historians—*femminismo sindacale* (trade union feminism), a choice of words that illustrates that feminist issues could find resonance within the Italian trade unions. This proved to be one of the most peculiar developments of Italian feminism. As it will be illustrated in the following section concerning the specific experience of the so-called *150 ore,* part of the Italian women's liberation movement influenced the meaning that labor organizations gave to culture and education when they addressed workers in general and female workers in particular. With reference to Giugni and Bosi's six domains of possible impact,[18] we argue that the actual impact—a concrete, external political and cultural impact—of the Italian WLM can be convincingly brought to light only when we abandon the level of general statements and enter history through the tools of empirical research.

Feminism, Trade Unions, and the Experience of the "150 Hours" Courses

The 1970s saw Italian trade unions assert themselves as significant political actors, able to respond to new demands.[19] Since the previous decade and even before the well-known "hot autumn" of 1969, Italian trade unions had been going through a phase of major reforms. These reforms greatly expanded the borders of internal democracy and opened the workers' organizations to requests coming from new collective subjects (such as young unskilled workers and immigrants from Southern Italy). New groups of workers began to replace the previous union delegates through a system of representation that had its base inside every specific factory unit. The main idea of such reforms was that the workers' representation had to be based on a common working experience.[20] The distance between workers and their delegates had to be reduced as did the distance between white- and blue-collar workers. This increasing openness of unions, together with the development of the international second-wave feminist movement, led women within Italian trade unions (both militants and workers) to decide to permeate traditional union politics with a new feminist approach.[21]

Many female trade union members began to think about what "being a woman" meant in the labor world. The feminist slogan "the personal is political" acquired a crucial meaning in the context of the trade unions, because the workers' organizations typically oriented their politics around class struggle, on which all other political concerns—including gender injustice—were forcibly leveled out and therefore belittled. For women in particular (but also on occasion for men) the point of view of class struggle was a partial one that did not suit them: the class contradiction and thus work relationships constituted one single part of their lives, but not the whole. In the first half of the 1970s, throughout Italy, women unionists and workers started to organize informal meetings during work time: they met, for example, in the work canteen, separately from their male colleagues, and felt finally free to discuss needs and problems that had no place on the official bargaining agenda. Shortly after (around 1974–75), women unionists decided to institutionalize their position: they substituted the old and inactive *Female Commissions* and built up new interprofessional and united structures: the *Women's Committees.* The women who promoted these new structures strove to give them an open organization and welcomed women from different contexts: workers, students, teachers, and housewives.[22] In September 1976 metalwork unions organized a national training meeting for female delegates in Fiesole (near Florence); there, women from different Italian regions discovered that similar practices were in process throughout the country and could compare their projects, perspectives, and aims.

Women unionists clearly realized that the experience of work was different for men and women and that, despite the fact that the labor movement was made of different subjects, not all of them had a voice within its organizations. The different appraisal of female and male work was a characteristic feature of capitalist societies based on the nuclear family and on the unquestioned figure of the male "breadwinner." As noticed above, the existing gendered division of labor was generally taken for granted, so the first challenge for women was to persuade their male colleagues, male union representatives, husbands, fathers, and brothers to stand up for women's right to paid employment. Even in years when women were entering almost all jobs, the idea of woman first of all as wife and mother strongly survived, especially in Italy.[23]

Feminist trade unionists had therefore to fight primarily for women employment, for its enhancement through training and career opportunities, and for the recognition of female-specific presence within the unions.[24] Women claimed that unions had to consider people not only as workers but also as citizens. They demanded social services that could help workers (men as well as women) to conciliate work and family duties, they dealt with working hours, and they devoted particular attention to women's health in and out the workplace. Since the strikes of 1969, unions had set up, with teams of young work-medicine doctors, inquiries about harm in the workplace based on questionnaires and discussions conducted among workers.[25] Nevertheless, these enquiries seldom focused specifically on female needs and problems. Women usually worked in more unskilled and arduous workplaces, fell ill, and had problems linked to pregnancy or sexual harassment that at the time they could hardly articulate. At the time, feminist radical collectives had founded independent *consultori*—medical structures devoted to women's health issues—that only in 1975 the state institutionalized in the framework of its National Healthcare System, subsuming their grassroots experience.[26] Echoing the famous book *Our Bodies, Ourselves,*[27] feminists within the unions were motivated to address female health problems, to search for respectable languages and locations to debate sexuality, contraception, abortions and miscarriages, menopause, etc.

A study that we recently conducted into labor feminism in the context of Reggio Emilia highlights some of these trends.[28] Reggio Emilia is a town near Bologna, which represented a minor but traditionally vital place in terms of political and union activity. The investigation was based on trade union archives spanning Bologna and Reggio Emilia and on the archive of the Women Documentation Center of Bologna (in particular, a set of documents gathered in the context of research conducted about the history of the women's movement in Emilia Romagna in the 1970s and 1980s).[29] Researching the second-wave feminist movement often implies various difficulties with regard to the sources: as it happens with other kinds of political activism and movements, the preservation of documents has often been left to the individual will of group members. The case of trade union feminism is slightly different because the *Committees,* although autonomous, were still part of strong and well-organized structures, such as the trade unions. Thus, written material produced by women unionists does exist, but it is not often systematically archived or collected and may be catalogued in ways that obscure women's participation. In fact, trade union archives do commonly preserve documents that show women's activism, but these are usually classified under the labels of professional categories (such as metalworkers, chemists, teachers, and so on). This difficulty in tracing women's activism may be somewhat discouraging, but when one has finally constituted a corpus of relevant sources, the documents fully repay the effort. While general meeting minutes, programmatic documents, and leaflets often lack detail and do not pick up traces of the feminist ferment of the period, the language and the communicative methods adopted by women as traceable in the documents prove to be absolutely unique in the framework of general trade union documentation. Luisa Passerini notes that "the documents show a hybrid language, ranging from expressions such as 'labor' to others more related to the body."[30] Moreover, as to these writings it is important to emphasize the frequent use of the ironic register together with the widespread presence of pictures and particularly of cartoons to illustrate the texts.[31] These stylistic choices were made in order to differentiate female communication from the usual trade union language, often marked by Marxist-influenced stiffness and pompous solemnity. Cartoons, for example, were widely used: the comic artist Francesco Tullio Altan was one of the most popular authors, and the women he drew, slyly commenting on a wide variety of social and political events, appeared on the pages of many union women's publications. Another favorite comic author was the Argentinian Quino with his character Mafalda: a little girl, with deep existential doubts, who feels that she has on her shoulders all the responsibility for the earth's destiny. The choice of using images mirrored the need for intuitive and emotionally significant direct communication or, in other words, a language easily accessible for everybody. Trade union women's writings strove to translate—although they did not fully succeed—women's ways of experiencing the workplace as well as the new belief that personal experiences (and not the abstraction of male politics) were a key both to analyze one's own life and to understand that of others. There was a clear attempt to "transcend" the words to create a meta-language that could better express the complexity and exuberance of women's thinking.

Women's experiences in the labor world (as well as other realms) were marked by their gender disadvantage and needed to be openly discussed. In the second half of the 1970s women of the *Committees* decided to take advantage of a recent trade union achievement in order to push forward their feminist agenda: the right to "150 hours" for education. In 1973, first metalworkers and then other working categories obtained a number of hours—paid by the employer—that could be used to accomplish a wide range of formative projects, such as attending secondary school to obtain a diploma or attending thematic seminars at high schools or university.[32] An interesting intersection with claims and struggles coming from the students' movement of 1968 (antiauthoritarianism, democratizing academic institutes, radical modification of education programs, etc.) is evident here. Thanks to new and more intensive collaboration forms between social and educational institutions achieved by the students' movement, unions succeeded in getting involved in the organization of courses set for workers in public educational institutions. Nevertheless, women had difficulties in attending these classes: their double burden both at work and at home, besides a certain feeling of alienation toward the academic context, made the "150 hours" courses unlikely to appeal. However, from 1976, almost everywhere in the country women who joined the newborn *Committees* issued courses "by women for women," which focused on subjects of specific feminine/feminist interest that female workers could now handle, discuss, and analyze. In an internal union document, probably written in 1978, related to women's courses, their promoters wrote:

> The use that women made of the "150 hours" courses constituted a way to raise the consciousness of our condition; a way to connect the factory's problems with the problems experienced by women because of their social condition, and with the problems of the private sphere. We introduced in the discussion problems completely new for the workers' movement (or hitherto overlooked): problems that produced and still produce conflict (e.g. admitting that the man-woman contradiction is present in the workplace, in the family, and even within the trade unions is certainly something hard). However, facing these problems led to women's personal development and to the enrichment of the unions.[33]

In Reggio Emilia, the "150 hours" courses for women were held at the local professional high school since 1977. At the end of each workshop, despite many bureaucratic difficulties, the women of *Committees* often produced booklets collecting all the lecturers' lessons and also including comments and remarks put forward by the participants: as suggested above, the aim seemed to have been "translating,"[34] as immediately and faithfully as possible, the extraordinary orality that characterized women's political activism on the whole. Indeed, the practices of open discussion and self-narrative were widespread throughout the 1970s women's movement, both within trade union feminism and within feminist radical collectives. The amount of documents available for the study of the second-wave women's movement is usually considered by historians as scarce, and recent efforts have been made to collect other, such as oral, sources. Interviewing women who took part in the movement can be described as creating a kind of *continuum* between the object of investigation and the methodology adopted to conduct it.[35]

What were the specificities of the female educational courses? What seems to emerge from the organization of these courses is a sort of effort to "make up for lost time," and thus address altogether topics and issues usually left aside during the "mixed" courses. The outcome was at the same time exciting and uncertain, because each course provided just a dozen lessons, probably not enough to satisfy women's great "thirst for knowledge." The first course, held in Reggio Emilia between April and May 1977, included twenty-six participants from diverse professional sectors. It was organized as lessons held by "experts" from different fields (union representatives, doctors, university professors, etc.) and collective discussion in small groups. It had a very suggestive title: "Female Workers Regain Culture." The promoters used the word "culture" to signify a wide variety of questions: the social norms governing women's employment, safeguarding health, the historical nature of familial roles and relationships, the social construction of genders and their interaction in the public sphere. One of the main features of the female courses was that women tried to consider themselves as a class-crossing collective subject; thus courses addressed to them didn't deal with labor matters only—the strong link between private and public spheres was always foregrounded. For example, in the report of a metalworkers' delegate, the lack of this kind of analysis is directly linked to the limits of the trade unions' action toward women's labor:

> Just think of the partiality that affected the unions' way of dealing with women's problems, taking into consideration only their condition as workers and never their needs due to their being women in general. [There is] an incapacity of understanding the specificities of women's labor, of abandoning incomplete and only quantitative analysis, of realizing the necessary connections.[36]

Teachers and participants collaborated in developing a curriculum. This participatory procedure was to help working women feel more comfortable with the idea of speaking freely and expressing their thoughts. It was a concrete practice rather than a formal commitment: course promoters tried as best as they could to involve participants in the elaboration of lessons. At the end of each course, participants could express themselves about their experiences during the lessons. A promoter explained, "When we met during the months before the course began, we invariably noticed that one of the main difficulties was to persuade women to speak freely. [We made an effort to] shatter their shyness, [which was due to] years of silence."[37] At first glance, the second course, held in 1978, had a more specific profile. Its title was "Female Worker: Political or Subordinated Subject?"[38] Nevertheless, studying the program in detail, it appears clear that the variety of topics was again broad and encompassed issues like health in the workplace, family structure, labor rights and so on. This time, however, a more precise request came directly from the participating women. The topics they had most appreciated and about which they wished to deepen their knowledge were female health and sexuality. This prioritization underlined the importance of women-specific courses. They allowed female workers to discuss some of their most important concerns and to gather knowledge, for example, about places where they could get help, such as the *consultori* (public health-care centers devoted to sexual health and education), and about the introduction of the law on abortion.[39] Such topics, at the intersection between private life and labor policies, were not likely to become a subject of "mixed" courses. Based on a purely Marxist analysis, class struggle often proved to be blind to gender issues. The instrument of the "150 hours" provided an opportunity for women to express needs and thoughts beyond class consciousness. The third course, "Health in Women's Hands,"[40] took place in 1979. This time women were given the opportunity to consult labor doctors, a gynecologist, and a pharmacist. The questions the participants were most interested in appeared to be health at work, possible risks for pregnancy, contraception, and sexual life in general. The consulted doctors and medical staff—some of them pioneers in the field of industrial medicine—responded to these various questions. Following a holistic approach, they underlined the complexity of influences upon women's bodies throughout their entire lives, including feelings and emotions. One participant noted, "We still have many taboos.... One of these is the shame of admitting that we adopt a contraceptive method. I verified this with my colleagues."[41] During the course, the participants, both working women and female students of the hosting high school, asked for a supplementary lesson dedicated to the subject of sexuality.

As this closer look on the "150 hours" courses in Reggio Emilia shows, labor feminism could develop within the relatively classical frame of trade unionism and make use of its financial and organizational resources. The curricula of the *Committee* of Reggio Emilia were in large part developed not only *for* but *by* women, were successful in addressing working-class women who, so far, had not been much organized in trade unions, and were able to meet their interests and needs.

The "150 hours" women courses had been a short episode among trade unions' mobilizing strategies, but their political and cultural quality was high and their impact on women perceived as extraordinary, as the following three statements of former participants clearly illustrate[42]:

> Luisa: "The use of 150 hour courses was a natural consequence of what we were doing at that time; because we needed to think about ourselves. It had been like ... an intuition! ... We were interested in opening the discussion to as many women as possible."

> Anna: "We started saying: hey, let's use this instrument ... the time. Time is invaluable for women. '150 hours' courses represent a 'place' where women can finally talk about themselves, about their problems, their interests.... Housewives started to come and it was not an easy dialogue among us. But in the end it worked!"

Gloria: "I was a student at University and at those courses I met women from the working class who really learnt there to talk, to reason, to read articles.... People who lacked a basic education who tried to analyze problems from a critical point of view. I was really impressed by them."

Conclusion

The women who were directly involved in feminist projects like the women-only "150 hours" courses certainly learned a great deal from this experience. But the outcome of such projects went far beyond the small circle of those activists. The impact of the Italian women's movement can in fact be seen in at least two dimensions: on the one side the spheres of the existing institutions, within which feminists tried to act against deep gender injustice and obtain important social and political reforms. On the other side the movement pursued radical transformations. In this aspect the most radical and utopian aspirations of the movement could experience and practice new forms of sociability, political practice, social life, education, interpersonal relationships, or new forms of what Hannah Arendt succinctly called *vita activa.*

The relationship between the two categories that stimulated collective action during the 1970s, class and gender, was thoroughly controversial and full of tensions. Nevertheless, we can assert that the gender category definitely achieved a place within the social and political discourse of that period.

Ever since, things changed a lot in Italy, including the economic, political, and social order. The impact of globalization fostered the decline of the class struggle paradigm since the 1980s. The fall of the original political order of the Italian republic paved the way for the rising of a system of power—the Berlusconism—that used the depictions of and policies toward women to undermine many feminist gains. But, as some reactions and recent protests have shown,[43] political and social relationships are objects of permanent negotiation, and the gender dimension will long continue to be one of the main fields of conflict and bargaining in the organization of social life.

Marica Tolomelli is associate professor in contemporary history at the University of Bologna. She attained her PhD in history at the University of Bielefeld. Her main research interests focus on social movements, labor history, and political cultures in the twentieth century; methodologically she privileges comparative and transnational approaches as well as the insights developed by the global history. She is general editor of the online history journal *Storicamente* (www.storicamente.org).

Anna Frisone graduated from the University of Bologna and is now completing her PhD thesis at the European University Institute (Florence). Both her BA thesis and her MA thesis have been published and awarded nation-level prizes. Her main research interests are labor history, gender history, second-wave feminism, and oral history.

APPENDIX

- Trade Unions questions -

"I can't remember if we come before the unemployed and after young people or between the South and retired people."

Figure 9.1. Cgil Enti Locali e Sanità, *Women's Committee,* monographic issue for internal circulation only, [no date]: 4.

- *"Mum, being young I'm an explosive problem."*
- *"I am a problem, that's all!"*

Figure 9.2. Delegates' *Committee* FULC (United Federation of Chemical Workers) Reggio Emilia, *Comunicazione della "scheda di maternità"* (information about the "maternity form"): 3.

Notes

1. Robert W. Connell, *Gender* (Cambridge: Polity Press, 2002). Essential for the historical research remains the contribution of Joan W. Scott, "Gender: A Useful Category of Historical Analysis," *American Historical Review,* no. 5 (1986): 1053–75.
2. Drude Dahlerup, ed., *The New Women's Movement: Feminism and Political Power in Europe and the USA* (London: SAGE, 1986).
3. Heinrich-Boell-Stiftung/Feministisches Institut, ed. *"Wie weit flog die Tomate?" 68erinnen-Gala der Reflexion, Berlin 1999* (Berlin: Boell, 1999); Kristina Schulz, *Der lange Atem der Provokation: Die Frauenbewegung in der Bundesrepublik und in Frankreich 1969–1976* (Frankfurt am Main: Campus, 2002); Sarah Evans, *Personal Politics: The Roots of Women's Liberation in the Civil Rights Movement and the New Left* (New York: Vintage Books, 1980); Luisa Passerini, *Il movimento delle donne,* in *La cultura e i luoghi del '68,* ed. A. Agosti, L. Passerini, N. Tranfaglia (Milan: Franco-Angeli, 1991), 366–80.
4. Charles Wright Mills, "Letter to the New Left," *New Left Review,* no. 5 (1960):18–23.
5. Simonetta Soldani, "Il Risorgimento delle donne," in *Storia d'Italia: Annali,* ed. Alberto Banti and Paul Ginsborg (Turin: Einaudi 2007), no. 22, *Il Risorgimento,* 183–224; Elena Doni et al., *Donne del Risorgimento* (Bologna: Il mulino, 2012).

6. Tiziana Pironi, *Femminismo ed educazione in età giolittiana:Conflitti e sfide della modernità* (Pisa: ETS, 2010); Marina D'Amelia, ed. *Donne alle urne: la conquista del voto. Documenti 1864–1946* (Rome: Biblink, 2006).
7. Victoria De Grazia, *How Fascism Ruled Women: Italy, 1922–1945* (Berkeley: University of California Press, 1992).
8. Anna Rossi-Doria, "Le donne sulla scena politica," in *Storia dell'Italia repubblicana,* vol. 1: *La costruzione della democrazia: Dalla caduta del fascismo agli anni Cinquanta* (Turin: Einaudi, 1994), 780–846.
9. Andreina De Clementi, "The Feminist Movement in Italy," in *Thinking Differently: A Reader in European Women's Studies,* ed. G. Griffin and R. Braidotti (New York: Zed Books, 2002), 334.
10. *Manifesto* di Rivolta Femminile (1970), in Carla Lonzi, *Sputiamo su Hegel e altri scritti,* new ed. (Milan: et al. Edizioni, 2010), 5.
11. Carla Lonzi, *Sputiamo su Hegel* (1970), in ibid., *Sputiamo su Hegel e altri scritti,* 15. English translation from http://www.scribd.com/doc/54105461/Lets-Spit-on-Hegel-Carla-Lonzi.
12. Ibid.
13. Sidney Tarrow, *Democracy and Disorder: Protest and Politics in Italy, 1965/1975* (Oxford: Clarendon Press, 1989); Robert Lumley, *States of Emergency: Cultures of Revolt in Italy from 1968 to 1978* (London: Verso, 1990).
14. Marica Tolomelli, *"Repressiv getrennt" oder "organisch verbundet": Studenten und Arbeiter 1968 in der Bundesrepublik Deutschland und in Italien* (Opladen: Leske und Budrich, 2001).
15. Lonzi, *Sputiamo su Hegel,* 16–18.
16. Fiamma Lussana, *Il movimento femminista in Italia: Esperienze, storie, memorie* (Rome: Carocci, 2012), 170–81.
17. Many of the documents produced by *Lotta Femminista* are available on the website http://www.femminismoruggente.it/index.html.
18. Marco Giugni and Lorenzo Bosi, "The Impact of Protest Movements on the Establishment: Dimensions, Models, and Approaches," in *The "Establishment" Responds—Power, Politics and Protest since 1945,* ed. Kathrin Fahlenbrach, Martin Klimke, and Joachim Scharloth (New York: Berghahn 2012), 17–28.
19. See Aris Accornero, *La parabola del sindacato: ascesa e declino di una cultura* (Bologna: Il Mulino, 1992). See also Paul Ginsborg, *A History of Contemporary Italy: Society and Politics 1943–1988* (London: Penguin Books, 1990). This subchapter has been completely written by Anna Frisone, who reports some findings of her empirical historical research. "Per una storia del femminismo sindacale. Le 150 ore delle donne: il caso di Reggio Emilia" (master's thesis, University of Bologna, 2011).
20. See Bruno Trentin, *Il sindacato dei consigli* (Rome: Editori riuniti, 1980).
21. See Fiamma Lussana, *Il movimento femminista in Italia: esperienze, storie, memorie* (Rome: Carocci, 2012), 113–50.
22. See Anna Frisone, "Vogliamo il pane ma anche le rose," in *Non è un gioco da ragazze,* ed. Giovanna Cereseto, Anna Frisone, and Laura Varlese (Rome: Ediesse, 2009), 225–48.
23. See Perry Willson, *Women in Twentieth-Century Italy* (New York: Palgrave MacMillan, 2010).

24. See Bianca Beccalli and Guglielmo Meardi, "From Unintended to Undecided Feminism? Italian Labor's Changing and Singular Ambiguities," in *Gender, Diversity and Trade Unions: International Perspectives,* ed. Fiona Colgan and Sue Ledwith (New York: Routledge, 2002), 113–31.
25. See the considerations about industrial medicine developed by Christian G. De Vito in his essay, "Tecnici e intellettuali dei 'saperi speciali' nei movimenti degli anni Settanta a Reggio Emilia," in *Tempi di conflitti, tempi di crisi: Contesti e pratiche del conflitto sociale a Reggio Emilia nei "lunghi anni Settanta,"* ed. Luca Baldissara (Rome/Naples: L'Ancora del mediterraneo, 2008), 387–426.
26. Law n. 405 of 1975.
27. Boston Women's Health Book Collective, *Our Bodies, Ourselves* (New York: Simon and Schuster, 1971).
28. See Anna Frisone, *Quando le lavoratrici si ripresero la cultura: Femminismo sindacale e corsi 150 ore delle donne a Reggio Emilia* (Bologna : Socialmente, 2014).
29. *Il movimento delle donne in Emilia-Romagna: Alcune vicende tra storia e memoria (1970–1980),* ed. Centro di documentazione delle donne—Bologna (Bologna: Edizioni Analisi, 1990).
30. Luisa Passerini, *Storie di donne e femministe* (Turin: Rosenberg & Sellier, 1991), 114–15.
31. See some examples, taken from my research, in the appendix.
32. Federazione Lavoratori Metalmeccanici, *Contratto nazionale di lavoro: Per i lavoratori addetti all'industria metalmeccanica privata e alla istallazione di impianti,* April 19, 1973. Federazione Lavoratori Metalmeccanici, *Contratto nazionale di lavoro: Per i lavoratori addetti all'industria metalmeccanica a partecipazione statale,* May 4, 1973.
33. Archivio Storia delle donne Bologna, *fondo Storia del movimento delle donne in Emilia Romagna,* b. 11, f. 1, *Proposte per una discussione sui corsi 150 ore delle donne* (no author or date, but referred to experiences held in autumn 1978).
34. See Passerini, *Storie di donne,* 114: "It clearly appears the essentially oral nature of this process and the difficulty in translating it into a written form."
35. See Frisone, *Vogliamo il pane,* 185–90.
36. Biblioteca Archivio Camera del Lavoro Territoriale Reggio Emilia, Federazione Provinciale—Reggio Emilia, *Le lavoratrici si riprendono la cultura, contenuti del corso monografico "150 ore" sulla condizione femminile svoltosi all'I.P.F. di Rivalta—R. E.,* 1978, 19–21.
37. Ibid., 66–67.
38. Biblioteca Archivio Camera del Lavoro Territoriale Reggio Emilia, Federazione Provinciale—Reggio Emilia, *La donna che lavora: soggetto politico o figura subordinata? Contenuti del seminario monografico "150 ore" sulla condizione femminile svoltosi all'I.T.F. di Rivalta—R. E.,* 1979.
39. Law n. 194 of 1978.
40. Biblioteca Archivio Camera del Lavoro Territoriale Reggio Emilia, Federazione Provinciale—Reggio Emilia, *La salute in mano alle donne, contenuti del seminario monografico "150 ore" tenutosi all'I.P.F. di Rivalta—R. E.,* 1980.
41. Ibid., 42.
42. These quotes stem from interviews conducted in 2008 with women who had participated in the "150 hours" courses. See Frisone, *Vogliamo il pane,* 248–86.

43. "La nuova questione femminile," *Ideazione: I percorsi del cambiamento. Rivista di cultura politica,* no. 2 (2002).

Bibliography

Accornero, Aris. *La parabola del sindacato: ascesa e declino di una cultura.* Bologna: Il Mulino, 1992.

Beccalli, Bianca. "Le politiche del lavoro femminile in Italia: donne, sindacati e stato tra il 1974 e il 1984." *Stato e mercato,* no. 15 (1985): 423–59.

Beccalli, Bianca, and Guglielmo Meardi. "From Unintended to Undecided Feminism? Italian Labor's Changing and Singular Ambiguities." In *Gender, Diversity and Trade Unions: International Perspectives,* edited by Fiona Colgan and Sue Ledwith. New York: Routledge, 2002.

Bertilotti, Teresa, and Anna Scattigno, eds. *Il femminismo degli anni Settanta.* Rome: Viella, 2005.

Boston Women's Health Book Collective. *Our Bodies, Ourselves.* Boston: New England Free Press, 1971.

Bracke, Maud Anne. "Building a 'Counter-community of Emotions': Feminist Encounters and Socio-cultural Difference in 1970s Turin." *Modern Italy,* no. 2 (2012): 223–36.

———. *Women and the Reinvention of the Political: Feminism in Italy (1968–1983).* New York: Routledge, 2014.

De Clementi, Andreina. "The Feminist Movement in Italy," in *Thinking Differently: A Reader in European Women's Studies,* ed. G. Griffin and R. Braidotti, 332–40. New York: Zed Books, 2002.

De Vito, Christian G. "Tecnici e intellettuali dei 'saperi speciali' nei movimenti degli anni Settanta a Reggio Emilia." In *Tempi di conflitti, tempi di crisi: Contesti e pratiche del conflitto sociale a Reggio Emilia nei "lunghi anni Settanta,"* edited by Luca Baldissara. Rome-Naples: L'Ancora del mediterraneo, 2008: 387–426.

Fraire, Manuela, ed. *Lessico politico delle donne: Teorie del femminismo.* Milan: F. Angeli, 2002.

Frisone, Anna. "Vogliamo il pane ma anche le rose." In *Non è un gioco da ragazze,* edited by Giovanna Cereseto, Anna Frisone, and Laura Varlese. Rome: Ediesse, 2009: 179–326.

———. *Quando le lavoratrici si ripresero la cultura: Femminismo sindacale e corsi 150 ore delle donne a Reggio Emilia.* Bologna: Socialmente, 2014.

Ginsborg, Paul. *A History of Contemporary Italy: Society and Politics 1943–1988.* London: Penguin Books, 1990.

Lonzi, Carla. *Sputiamo su Hegel e altri scritti.* New edition. Milan: et al. Edizioni, 2010 [1970].

Lussana, Fiamma. *Il movimento femminista in Italia: esperienze, storie, memorie.* Rome: Carocci, 2012.

Il movimento delle donne in Emilia-Romagna: Alcune vicende tra storia e memoria (1970–1980), edited by Centro di documentazione delle donne—Bologna. Bologna: Edizioni Analisi 1990.

Passerini, Luisa. *Storie di donne e femministe.* Turin: Rosenberg & Sellier, 1991.
Ribero, Aida. *Una questione di libertà: Il femminismo degli anni Settanta.* Turin: Rosenberg & Sellier, 1999.
Spagnoletti, Rosalba, ed. *I movimenti femministi in Italia.* Rome: Savelli, 1978.
Stelliferi, Paola. *Il femminismo a Roma negli anni Settanta: Percorsi, esperienze e memorie dei collettivi di quartiere.* Bologna: Bononia University Press, 2015.
Tolomelli, Marica. *L'Italia dei movimenti: Politica e società nella Prima Repubblica.* Rome: Carocci, 2015.
Trentin, Bruno. *Il sindacato dei consigli.* Rome: Editori Riuniti, 1980.
Willson, Perry. *Women in Twentieth-Century Italy.* New York: Palgrave MacMillan, 2010.

Chapter 10

"Sisterhood Is Plain Sailing?"

Multiracial Feminist Collectives in 1980s Britain

Natalie Thomlinson

Race and ethnicity were difficult issues for second-wave British feminists. A feminist movement that was almost exclusively white was increasingly difficult to justify and sustain in a postcolonial Britain where ethnic minorities formed an ever-increasing proportion of the population. As such, as this chapter will demonstrate, white feminists in Britain were often accused of racism by their Black[1] counterparts, and these debates over race and ethnicity grew ever more complex through the 1980s. An increasing level of interaction between Black and white women within the women's movement resulted in these issues assuming a much greater importance within feminist discourse of this period. The early and mid-1980s saw a blossoming of Black feminism, mixed-race collectives, and renewed activism on the part of antiracist feminists. This is not to say, however, that all white feminists responded to the critiques that were mounted of them; many reacted defensively or simply ignored them. The legacy of these debates—and of identity politics more widely—is a highly contested one. Despite the complexity of the issues at hand, the crisis of the movement that resulted has often been portrayed simplistically as either the result of the racism of white feminists or the misplaced radicalism of Black women.[2] This chapter is an attempt to reconstruct these interactions and debates, coalitions and enmities, in a more subtle and nuanced fashion, allowing us to focus on points of engagement between Black and white feminists to a greater extent than has been allowed for in previous examinations; it also demonstrates that, despite tensions between Black and white feminists, the British women's movement was nevertheless able to salvage something positive from these often bitter debates.

In Britain, the beginnings of the movement commonly termed "second-wave" feminism are often traced back to the first conference of the women's liberation movement held at Ruskin College, Oxford, in March 1970. This and subsequent conferences gave rise to the four demands of the British women's liberation movement (WLM): equal pay, equal education and job opportunities, free contraception and abortion, and free twenty-four-hour childcare. Three more demands were added over the course of the 1970s: an end to discrimination against lesbians, legal and financial independence for women, and the right for women to be free from male violence and the laws that perpetuated it.[3] The orientation of the WLM in Britain was predominantly socialist, although over the course of the 1970s and 1980s radical strains of feminism became increasingly prominent. Whatever their political orientation, however, almost all of these feminists were white, a situation that was increasingly critiqued by Black feminists from the late 1970s. Indeed, given how central the issue of race was to the British women's movement during the late 1970s and into the 1980s, extraordinarily little historical attention has been paid to it. Eve Setch, Jeska Rees, and Sarah Browne have all written area studies of the movement within the UK, concentrating respectively on London, Leeds, and Scotland, but their predominant focus has been either implicitly or explicitly on the debates between (white) radical and socialist feminists within the movement.[4] These debates are undoubtedly important, and it would be futile to attempt to understand the British feminist milieu at this time without reference to this. However, the foregrounding of this issue has had the unfortunate effect of minimizing attention to other categories of difference in the movement, such as age, class, and, most pertinently in terms of this chapter, race. Yet race is central to understanding the form and trajectory of the feminist movement within Britain during these years. As this chapter will demonstrate, the challenges presented to white feminists by Black women created a more racially diverse/aware feminism. Differences of political orientation between Black and white feminists, and the structurally embedded nature of racial inequality in the UK, ensured that racially based divisions between feminists in Britain could not be entirely overcome.

The Black Feminist Critique

Black women's autonomous activism in Britain dates back to the early 1970s, with prominent groups such as Brixton Black Women's Group being formed in 1973 and the founding of the Organisation of Women of African and Asian Descent (OWAAD) occurring in 1978.[5] However, it was the early 1980s that witnessed the most significant growth in Black women's autonomous organizing in Britain,[6] a growth given impetus by the funding provided to such groups by leftist local authorities (particularly the Greater London Council) in the early 1980s. This growth of the Black women's movement led to a greater interaction between Black and white feminists, and indeed the growth of a Black feminist critique of white feminism in this period was in itself a product of this greater interaction. Despite the presence of white feminist antiracist groups in Britain during the 1970s, such activism engendered little comment from Black women's groups.[7] The increasingly vehement criticisms of white feminists that were produced during the 1980s were, rather, the product of a greater shift toward feminism on behalf of Black activists. Such tensions were the product of Black and white feminists attempting to find a modus operandi for working together: they had been less present in the 1970s precisely because there was much less contact between the two.

The prime contention of the Black feminist critique in Britain—as in the United States—was that white British feminists had little concept of the ways in which racism profoundly structured their lives as Black women. Furthermore, they contended, this ignorance was compounded by the white domination of most feminist groups, which created an environment in which Black women's concerns were silenced. Indeed, these concerns around "being heard" within the women's movement often attracted as much attention as the substance of the debates themselves. One prominent British Black feminist, Stella Dadzie, suggested during an interview that

> there was arrogance in the sense that there was no deference to Black women's experience or a sense that they might have something to contribute ... an arrogance that was represented in a lack of a presence, you know, there was no attempt to get us involved, or to ask how we felt, or to bring our perspectives to the table.[8]

Essentially, Black British feminists argued that, if liberation was to be achieved for all women, then all facets of women's oppression—including race and class, as well as sex—had to be taken into account. Crucially, British Black feminists argued that white feminists failed to do this and that many of the analytic categories so long clung to by white feminists could not translate onto the realities of Black women's lives.

These criticisms were often scathing, and they were given space in the increasing numbers of Black women's periodicals that were published in the 1980s. In typical fashion, the London-based Black feminist newsletter *We Are Here* published an article in 1985 claiming that:

> The WLM is racist because it does not take seriously the experiences of non-white women. The WLM does not accept that third world women are subsidising WLM the world over, that third world women have made significant contributions to all progressive

> movements during colonial and pre-colonial times and that a huge amount of oral literature existed for centuries in non-white societies about women. White women do not need to teach us how to protest![9]

Such views were reflected in the now-iconic "Many Voices, One Chant" edition of *Feminist Review* in October 1984. As Valerie Amos and Pratibha Parmar wrote in their featured article "Challenging Imperial Feminism," "white, mainstream feminist theory, be it from the socialist feminist or radical feminist perspective, does not speak to the experiences of Black women and where it attempts to do so it is often from a racist perspective and reasoning."[10] They then went on to discuss critically issues such as the family, sexuality, and the feminist peace movement, their conclusion being that

> For us the way forward lies in defining a feminism which is significantly different to the dominant trends in the women's liberation movement.... True feminist theory and practice entails an understanding of imperialism and a critical engagement with challenging racism—elements which the current women's movement significantly lacks, but which are intrinsic to Black feminism.[11]

What for example—as Amos and Parmar argued—was the use of campaigning for better access to abortion when, as many Black feminists claimed, some Black women in Britain were being forcibly sterilized?[12] It was for such reasons that Black feminists came to critique white feminists as "racist." As such, Black women demanded not just a space within feminist discourse but a fundamental transformation of the terms of the debate.

Multiracial Feminist Collectives

The accusation of racism often resulted in bitter debates that at times paralyzed the movement. However, over the course of the 1980s, working in multiracial collectives became increasingly perceived by both Black and white women as a way of breaking out of the impasse that some of these debates had left feminist activism in. As prominent British-Asian feminist Pratibha Parmar stated in 1986, "there comes a point where you've done enough of building within your own groups and when it's necessary for survival to actually step out of your 'isms', (and this is what it has got reduced to) to make links."[13] This reflected an increasing emphasis on antiracist activism within the wider British left at this point, as has been documented by

Alastair Bonnett and Paul Gilroy.[14] Much of this work was funded by leftist local authorities. Others, however, were independent, particularly the ventures of the feminist press.

However, unsurprisingly, the success of these collectives varied widely. The issues surrounding Black and white women working together were significant enough for the cover of feminist magazine *Spare Rib* in July 1986 to ask the imposing question "Black and White Women—Can We Work Together?" underneath a picture of a white woman and Black woman with their backs turned to each other—but also smiling. The iconography of this cover appeared to be intentionally ambiguous, mirroring the content of the article devoted to the question inside. The article focused on four multiracial collectives around Britain: Sheba Feminist Publishers, Camden Council's Women's Unit, The Third World Women's Working Group, and Birmingham Women's Workshop. The experiences of these four groups were vastly different, and none found working together to be completely unproblematic. Thinking through the experiences of collectives such as these helps us to understand more fully the antagonisms between Black and white feminists during this period. These problems were not just based on theoretical differences but were grounded in the day-to-day realities of trying to make collectives like these work. It also points to the very practical problems that many collectives in this period experienced when they became multiracial. The assumption that Black women could be easily absorbed into the structures of what had been previously all-white ventures proved to be naïve: the accumulation of experience and years of having a certain way of doing things meant that, in reality, white women often retained power in these collectives because they had set the terms. White feminists rarely worked with Black collectives, but Black women often worked with white collectives, because they correctly perceived the advantage of pursuing the access to the resources—and indeed numerical strength—of feminist institutions that were largely white. As well-known Black feminist Linda Bellos wrote in a May 1984 conference paper entitled "Advice to White Collectives Wishing to Employ Black Workers":

> As a political principle I find no advantages to black people to leave the majority of resources and privileges to white people. It is on this basis that I choose to join mixed (black and white) collectives when I wish to, but even where all the women are concerned, including me, are committed to having a mixed race collective, the process of dealing with racism hasn't ended, in a sense its [*sic*] only just begun.[15]

Local Authority Funding Ventures: Camden and Cambridge

Local authority funding was instrumental in sustaining feminist politics in the 1980s. Leftist local authorities in Britain at this point—in particular, the Greater London Council—were keen to fund the radical politics ventures of women and minority communities as a response to the spending cuts imposed nationally by the Conservative government led by Margaret Thatcher. Indeed, many such authorities had feminists on their staff, or serving as elected councilors. Certainly, the willingness of such authorities to fund feminist ventures speaks to the ideological gains that feminism had made within public political discourse in the UK by this point. Many such local authorities provided grants to local ventures, and some developed "women's units" designed to deal with local women's issues, the most well-known being the Greater London Council's Women's Unit, headed by Valerie Wise.[16] Particularly in more ethnically diverse cities, these units became increasingly aware of race and the importance of having a racially diverse committee. The women's unit at Camden Council in north London was one such committee. In a 1986 *Spare Rib* article focusing on multiracial collectives, they were cautiously positive about their achievement in having transformed the women's group from an all-white collective into one that, by 1984, was 50 percent Black.[17] Jude Watson, who was one of the white women originally appointed when the unit was first set up, narrated the reasons for the changes as following:

> In 1984 when we decided to change our work priorities we realized that all the consultation work that the Women's Committee had previously been involved in had been mostly with white, middle class women. Things like public meetings, working groups and so on had mainly involved women who already identified with the Women's Liberation Movement and therefore a lot of women who got involved already had access to the Council. The whole question of accountability and consultation had to be looked at afresh.[18]

Nevertheless, despite being positive overall about the experience of working in the Camden unit—particularly as regards its nonhierarchical structure, which was perceived to make it easier for Black women to join the unit, as they were not subordinate to the white women—some of the Black women at Camden were pessimistic about relationships between Black and white women. Black women's comments included, "In the issues I have been involved in white women have not responded," "I think a lot of black women have given up talking to the white women's movement," and "there is still a terrible lack of communication and change."[19] It was clear that they did not believe that the work they were doing in local government, as important as they felt it to be, was a panacea to the problems of the women's movement. Yet despair did not reign; the fact that they were doing these jobs at all underlines a basic optimism. As one of the Black women workers, Monica, strikingly stated,

> When I think of my own background in Cardiff where black people lived alongside white people for many years and where black and white people have married and set up home together, and fought racism together, I find it difficult to be pessimistic about the possibilities of building solidarity between us.[20]

These complexities became particularly evident in interviews I carried out with women from Cambridge, a small city where by sheer virtue of the population size, Black and white feminists were in frequent contact with each other in local feminist ventures that were largely funded by the city council. The ways in which racism was experienced in diverse subtle ways were expanded on by my interviewees. Discussing the feminist milieu in Cambridge, Jamaican-born Bola*[21]—who evinced a moderate leftist rather than radical politics and was committed to working in multiracial collectives—remembered that

> a covert racism was there, and sometimes … it hurt more than the overt one, because you know what's coming, but when you don't know what's coming …—as I usually say, if you stand in an ant's nest, well you cannot see the ants down there.… But until it bit you—that's the time you know that you [are] standing in the nest.[22]

Similarly, Indian-born Adithi*— who has worked in community groups for over thirty years in the Cambridge area—suggested of the multiracial Cambridge Women's Resource Centre's commitment to antiracism that

> I think it was largely honoured, but I do think that there was … if I look back on it, I think perhaps these issues weren't bottomed out really, issues of race, and … there were tensions … and I'm not sure all the Black women who worked there would feel that it was a wonderful place to work at…[23]

When I asked Adithi where she thought these tensions were focused, she suggested that they were largely centered around "credibility and voice"—that some people were listened to more than others, and that this was to do with race.[24] But when I asked her whether she would then call white feminists "racist," she responded that

> I wouldn't have called them racist as I wouldn't have called them classist. You know, I feel certainly that a lot of the women's groups that I went to were predominantly white middle-class women, so ... but there was a—what I felt was the best bit of the movement is that I feel there was a willingness to share experience, and communicate, and think politically.

She further reflected:

> I think that for any kind of "ism" to be you know—to have a huge impact, it's a way of looking at how that links with power structures. And ... and I don't think the women's movement was sort of made up of women who wielded a lot of power, if you know what I mean.[25]

As Adithi's response suggests, there was a certain ambiguity around what constituted racism in the actions of white women. She clearly believed the Women's Resource Centre in Cambridge to be a less than "wonderful" place to work for ethnic minority women, believing that they suffered from subtle prejudices there. Nevertheless, she was hesitant to apply the epithet "racist" to the women who worked there, mirroring the controversial argument made by some white radical feminists that, as women, they could not benefit from racism in a patriarchal society.[26] Clearly, then, there was a variety of responses by Black women to the debates over racism in the movement, and how successfully multiracial feminist collectives transcended these problems.

Southall Black Sisters and the Network of Women

Not surprisingly, given the manifold dynamics at play in feminist coalition work, unexpected alliances were sometimes formed. One such coalition was the alliance of the Southall Black Sisters (SBS) with various radical feminist groups in the 1980s—most notably Women Against Violence Against

Women (WAVAW)—in an attempt to plan a "semi-permanent" alliance called the Network of Women (NOW).[27] Southall Black Sisters themselves were a predominantly Asian socialist feminist group set up in the Southall, West London—an area with a large concentration of South Asian migrants—in 1979. They quickly became well known both inside and outside of feminist circles for their numerous campaigns and outspoken criticism of both white feminists and the Southall Punjabi community. The aim of this alliance between SBS and WAVAW was to protest against domestic violence, and they hoped to start with a national demonstration and rally against violence against women, an area to which SBS had turned their campaigning energies after the deaths of several local Asian women.[28] Although SBS perceived socialist feminists to be their most natural allies, few got involved: writing in a history of SBS, Rahila Gupta acerbically commented that "most of them seemed to have been absorbed into the Labour Party or lucrative employment."[29] But a focus on domestic violence made for an easier alliance with radical feminists—who were often criticized for their emphasis on patriarchy to the exclusion of race and class—than other issues would have allowed for, and this gave the coalition some initial momentum.

Even allowing for this common interest, however, the success of NOW was still distinctly qualified. SBS attempted to raise the issues of race and class with WAVAW, but, according to SBS/NOW activist Smita Bhide in her write up of NOW's history, "our success was limited. They said 'yes, yes, of course,' but stuck to their anti-men guns."[30] Eventually a rally was held in London's Hyde Park, which three thousand women attended. This was an impressive figure, but—despite the "heartening" appearance of delegations of Black women from Liverpool and Sheffield—the vast majority were white radical lesbians associated with WAVAW rather than the hoped-for rainbow coalition of women from a variety of feminist groups.[31] Furthermore, despite hopes for a long-lasting alliance, no more events were held, partly due to SBS's disillusionment with the process of organizing so many women with different demands, a process that they felt severely diluted the group's original aims.[32] While the alliance of NOW and WAVAW can hardly be characterized as a complete failure, it was still far from an overwhelming success. This points to the often frustrating and exhausting process of coalition-building even among willing feminists. And although shared concerns around male violence allowed for some surprising alliances between white radical feminists and Black socialist feminists, ultimately profound differences in analysis made such alliances difficult to sustain. Radical feminism was simply not as conceptually amenable to Black feminism as was socialist feminism, with its emphasis on the intersection of oppressions, and anti-essentialist thinking.

Spare Rib

One of the most famous and controversial multiracial collectives in the British feminist movement during the 1980s was that at *Spare Rib* magazine. Set up in 1972, *Spare Rib* was by far the most well-known and widely circulated of feminist magazines in Britain, and was seen as something of a mouthpiece for the national movement. In October 1982 the editorial collective—which was, until that point, largely white—invited Black and Third World women to join. This move enlarged the group of women running the magazine significantly so that ethnic minority women comprised 50 percent of the collective.[33] However, a heated debate over Zionism and Israel quickly morphed into a wider controversy that exposed ethnic tensions between Black and white women on the collective.

The catalyst for this debate was an interview conducted in August 1982 by *Spare Rib* collective member Roisin Boyd with a Lebanese woman, a Palestinian woman, and an Israeli anti-Zionist woman. This interview was published with the title "Women Speak Out against Zionism" and given the provocative subtitle, "If a Woman Calls Herself Feminist, She Should Consciously Call Herself Anti-Zionist."[34] The article was staunchly anti-Zionist, anti-Israeli, and arguably anti-Semitic, and included the gratuitously offensive statement that the "Jewish people should thank Hitler because without him the Jewish state would never have been created."[35] However, the main focus of the anger of Jewish feminists was the fact that none of the letters from Jewish women that criticized the article were published.[36] Given that many of the Jewish feminists who wrote in often strongly criticized Israel themselves, many concluded that the main motivation behind the nonpublication of the letters was not anti-Zionism, but anti-Semitism. Supporting this contention was the fact that *Spare Rib* also published several articles and letters that contained innuendos about "Zionist control" of the press, which essentially read like updated versions of the longstanding idea of a Jewish world conspiracy.[37] One Black woman on the collective even complained regarding this debate of "the pressure to devote most of my energy on a single group that can insist on our devotion due to the *great power* that they have" (emphasis mine).[38]

One of the most sensitive aspects of the whole debate, indeed, was the fact that it was mostly the "Women of Colour" on the *Spare Rib* collective who were the most strongly anti-Zionist and who were responsible for most of what was considered the anti-Semitic content and censorship of the publications.[39] Feeling strongly about the issue of the Middle East, and wanting also perhaps to prove their power on the collective, the newly arrived Black women apparently had largely forced the censoring of the letters. And they did this from the position that they, as ethnic minority women, had a greater claim to represent Palestinian interests than the white women on the collective did. However, this initial decision not to publish the letters from the Jewish women obviously did not last—and by making the internal dissent explicit at all and eventually allowing discussion of the issue in the letters page, it became apparent that it was still the white women who ultimately held the balance of power at the collective. Having worked there for much longer, they had more experience in producing the magazine that ultimately gave them a greater degree of control over the its editorial line—and there was also apparently a subconscious assumption at work that as the old guard, they were entitled to control of the collective. As an Asian woman on the collective noted, "The strain for us as Women of Colour is having to constantly assert our experiences and politics against the 'norm,' whilst the white women have difficulty coping with always having their assumptions challenged."[40] Additionally, the "Women of Colour" on the *Spare Rib* collective clearly felt victimized over the accusations of anti-Semitism that were put to them. In response, they turned the accusation on its head, claiming that the white feminists were being racist by ignoring their political analysis. One of the Black women on the collective wrote pointedly, "Try challenging your own racism rather than lecturing Black and Third World women on what your view of racism is."[41] It was these issues about power and control that transformed a debate around Israel into a debate that split the collective down racial lines. Relationships between Black and white women on the collective deteriorated to the extent that the Women of Colour decided to meet separately for a period, producing a special "Black women's issue" in September 1983, soon after this controversy.[42]

Ultimately, the crisis at *Spare Rib* reflected the broader conditions that structured interaction between Black and white feminists during this period. The greater access to power and resources that the white women at *Spare Rib* enjoyed mirrored the broader inequalities between Black and white feminists, and indeed Black and white populations as a whole in the UK, at this point. While the *Spare Rib* collective remained multiracial and committed to representing the issues of ethnic minority women the world over until its closure in 1993, recurring arguments about race and representation in the magazine demonstrated that tensions between Black and white women on the collective were never fully resolved. This reflects the mixed success of multiracial feminist collectives more broadly in Britain during this period.

Conclusion: Impact and Outcomes

Overall, the outcomes presented from the case studies of Black and white women working together are clearly mixed. Evidently these collectives were sometimes productive, and heralded a more integrated feminist politics that addressed issues of race in a way that the women's movement had failed to in the 1970s. Nonetheless, sometimes such ventures were unable to transcend antagonisms between black and white feminists, particularly given the difficulties inherent in Black women joining collectives that had been established by white women. Quite apart from theoretical differences between Black and white feminists, the fact that most feminist institutions that became multiracial had been founded by white feminists inevitably gave rise to day-to-day tensions and power struggles. Few women wanted to appear to be taking part in the "ranking of oppressions." Yet it is difficult to see how—when decisions had to be made at the grassroots level about where to allocate resources, time, and money—this could translate into reality. Such pressures, as well as national debates, shaped the daily interactions of Black and white feminists. In the final analysis, it was perhaps too utopian to expect multiracial feminist collectives and coalitions to be able to fully transcend the racism of the society of which they were a part: it is an irony of social movements that they are doomed to be shaped by the very paradigms they hope to contest. The great expectations of some feminists only compounded the bitterness felt when such projects failed to work, despite the real practical and ideological gains that, in retrospect, we can see such ventures brought to feminism. Nevertheless, this period witnessed the formation of multiracial coalitions and collectives that saw white and Black women working together politically in ways that would have been unimaginable even ten years earlier. We can thus see that these collectives and coalitions *did* have a significant impact on the women's movement in the UK. Although such coalitions enjoyed varying degrees of success, ultimately working together on a regular basis unsurprisingly enabled Black and white feminists to understand each other better. Multiracial activism has continued in British feminism ever since, as documented recently by Line Nyhagen Predelli and Beatrice Halsaa.[43] While much remains to be done, it is clear that this shift in feminist praxis was in large part due to the efforts of the women examined in this chapter.

Natalie Thomlinson is Lecturer in Modern British Cultural history at the University of Reading, having taught previously at the universities of Sussex and Wolverhampton. She is a historian of feminism, gender, and race in twentieth-century Britain and has recently published her first monograph, *Race, Ethnicity and the Women's Movement in England, 1968–1993* (Palgrave Macmillan, 2016).

Notes

The majority of the material for this essay is taken from chapter 5 of my book, *Race and Ethnicity in the Women's Movement in England, 1968–1993* (Basingstoke: Palgrave Macmillan, 2016).

1. I capitalize "Black" in this chapter to reflect its contemporaneous British usage as a political term including those of Asian—as well as African and Afro-Caribbean—descent.
2. See Julia Sudbury, *Other Kinds of Dreams: Black Women's Organisations and the Politics of Transformation* (London: Routledge, 1998), particularly pp. 199–220, for an analysis that, although in many ways thorough and excellent, overplays the racism of white feminists without seeking to understand what it was that made it difficult for white feminists to always respond adequately to the Black feminist critique. Perhaps surprisingly, Line Nyhagen Predelli and Beatrice Halsaa apparently accept unquestioningly her analysis in *Majority-Minority Relations in Contemporary Women's Movements* (Basingstoke: Palgrave Macmillan, 2012), 166–67. Conversely, many memoirs of white feminists are largely hostile to identity politics, as are the interviewees in film made by Vanessa Engle, *Angry Wimmin* (BBC: 2006), one of whom (Al Garthwaite) claimed that she could not think of a single positive thing that identity politics had achieved, a clear denial of the validity of the Black feminist critique and its positive impact upon feminism. Perhaps the most thoughtful and evenhanded treatment to these debates is given by Heidi Safia Mirza in her introduction to *Black British Feminism: A Reader* (London: Routledge, 1997), 1–28.
3. Beatrix Campbell and Anna Coote, *Sweet Freedom* (Oxford, 1982), 16–18.
4. Eve Setch, "The Face of Metropolitan Feminism: The London Women's Liberation Workshop 1969–1979," *Twentieth Century British History* 13, no. 2 (2002), 171–90; "The London Women's Liberation Workshop 1969–1979: Organisation, Creativity, Debate" (PhD diss., Royal Holloway, University of London, 2000); Jeska Rees, "'Are You a Lesbian?' Challenges in Recording and Analysing the Women's Liberation Movement in England," *History Workshop Journal* 69 (Spring 2010): 177–87; "A Look Back at Anger: The Women's Liberation Movement in 1978," *Women's History Review* 19, no. 3 (2010), 337–56; "All the Rage: Revolutionary Feminism in Britain, 1977–1983" (PhD diss., University of Western Australia, 2007); Sarah Browne, "'A Veritable Hotbed of Feminism': Women's Liberation in St Andrews, Scotland, c.1969–c.1979," *Twentieth Century British History* 23, no. 1 (2011), 100–23; Sarah Browne, "The Women's Liberation Movement in Scotland, 1967–1979" (PhD diss., University of Dundee, 2009).

5. See Sudbury, *Other Kinds of Dreams,* 1–21 for more information on Black women's autonomous organizing in Britain.
6. See Sudbury, *Other Kinds of Dreams,* for more comprehensive information on this.
7. Apart from the scathing commentary provided by BBWG on All-London Anti-Racist Anti-Fascist Committee (of which WARF was a part), *Speak Out* 2 (undated, c. 1978): 2–3.
8. Stella Dadzie, interview with author, February 24, 2011, transcript p. 9.
9. 'Artusha, *We Are Here: Black Feminist Newsletter* (September 1985), unpaginated.
10. Valerie Amos and Pratibha Parmar, "Challenging Imperial Feminism," *Feminist Review* 17 (Autumn 1984), 3–19: 12–13, 4.
11. Ibid., 17–18.
12. Ibid., 12–13.
13. "Can Black and White Women Work Together?" *Spare Rib* 168 (July 1986): 19.
14. See Alastair Bonnett, *Radicalism, Anti-Racism and Representation* (London: Routledge, 1993) for an in-depth analysis of this activism. Gilroy heavily critiques municipal antiracism in *There Ain't No Black in the Union Jack: The Cultural Politics of Race and Nation,* 2nd ed. (London: Routledge, 2002), 177–94.
15. Linda Bellos, "Advice to White Collectives Wishing to Employ Black Workers," Papers of Stella Dadzie, Dadzie 1/8/4, Black Cultural Archives, London.
16. Although the activities of these left-wing councils in radical politics are well-known, they still await their historian. More information can be found in Lucy Robinson, *Gay Men and the Left in Post-war Britain: How the Personal Became Political* (Manchester: Manchester University Press, 2007), 143–44, about the GLC's funding of various radical groups and the political motivations behind this funding, and Loretta Loach, "Is There Life after the GLC?" *Spare Rib* (March 1986): 10–11. Sudbury in *Other Kinds of Dreams* also provides much information on the funding opportunities provided by local councils to Black and ethnic minority women's organizations in the 1980s and 1990s, particularly pp. 126–27.
17. "Can Black and White Women Work Together?" 20.
18. Ibid., 20–21.
19. Ibid., 21.
20. Ibid.
21. * Indicates pseudonym.
22. Bola C., interview with author, February 8, 2012, transcript p. 12.
23. Adithi, interview with author, March 12, 2012, transcript p. 12.
24. Ibid.
25. Ibid., 28–29.
26. See chapter 4 of Natalie Thomlinson. *Race, Ethnicity and the Women's Movement in England, 1968–1993* (Basingstoke: Palgrave Macmillan, 2016), for more detailed information on this.
27. Smita Bhide, "N.O.W. or Never," in *Against the Grain: A Celebration of Survival and Struggle,* ed. Southall Black Sisters (London: Southall Black Sisters, 1990), 30–36.
28. These women were Krishna Sharma, Balwant Kaur, and Mrs. Dhillon and her five children. See Southall Black Sisters, *Against the Grain,* for more information on the tragic circumstances of these deaths.

29. Rahila Gupta, "Autonomy and Alliances," in Southall Black Sisters, *Against the Grain,* 55–61.
30. Bhide, "N.O.W. or Never," 33.
31. Ibid., 35.
32. Ibid., 30–32, 36.
33. See Editorial, *Spare Rib* 130 (May 1983): 4, for more information on this enlargement of the collective.
34. "Women Speak Out against Zionism," *Spare Rib* 121 (August 1982): 22–23.
35. Ibid., 22.
36. This accusation was articulated by Adi Cooper, Karen Goldman, Rosalind Haber, Francesca Klug, Judy Keiner, and Sally Lawson in a letter to *Spare Rib* 131 (June 1983): 26, and in similar letters to other feminist publications.
37. See, for example, Letters, *Spare Rib* 134 (September 1983): 46, and Letters, *Spare Rib* 135 (October 1983): 4.
38. *Spare Rib* Editorial Collective, "Sisterhood … Is Plain Sailing," 25.
39. However, it is also important to note that the debate did not split the movement simply down Black and white lines. Some Black women did support Jewish women, as evidenced by a letter from the prominent Black feminist and author Barbara Burford to the *London Women's Liberation Newsletter* 319 (June 7, 1983), unpaginated. Additionally, it was a white woman on the collective, Roisin Boyd, who had produced the article, "Women Speak Out against Zionism," that was at the root of the controversy.
40. "Farzaneh" quoted in "*Spare Rib* … See How We Run," *Spare Rib* 131 (June 1983): 7.
41. *Spare Rib* Editorial Collective, "Sisterhood … Is Plain Sailing," 25.
42. Ibid.
43. See Predelli and Halsaa, *Majority-Minority Relations in Contemporary Women's Movements,* for a comprehensive overview of contemporary Black-white feminist relations in the UK, Norway, and Spain.

Bibliography

Amos, Valerie, and Pratibha Parmar. "Challenging Imperial Feminism." *Feminist Review* 17 (Autumn 1984): 3–19.

Baker, Adrienne. *The Jewish Woman in Contemporary Society: Transitions and Traditions.* London: Macmillan, 1993.

Bonnett, Alastair. *Radicalism, Anti-Racism and Representation.* London: Routledge, 1993.

Browne, Sarah. "The Women's Liberation Movement in Scotland, 1967– 1979." PhD diss., University of Dundee, 2009.

———. "'A Veritable Hotbed of Feminism': Women's Liberation in St Andrews, Scotland, c.1969–c.1979." *Twentieth Century British History* 23, no. 1 (2011): 100–23.

———. "Can Black and White Women Work Together?" *Spare Rib* 168 (July 1986): 18–25.

Engle, Vanessa, dir. *Angry Wimmin.* BBC: 2006.

Gilroy, Paul. *There Ain't No Black in the Union Jack: The Cultural Politics of Race and Nation.* 2nd ed. London: Routledge, 2002.

Predelli, Line Nyhagen, and Beatrice Halsaa, *Majority-Minority Relations in Contemporary Women's Movements.* Basingstoke: Palgrave Macmillan, 2012.
Mirza, Heidi Safia, ed. *Black British Feminism: A Reader.* London: Routledge, 1997.
Rees, Jeska. "All the Rage: Revolutionary Feminism in Britain, 1977–1983." PhD diss., University of Western Australia, 2007.
———. "'Are You a Lesbian?' Challenges in Recording and Analysing the Women's Liberation Movement in England." *History Workshop Journal* 69 (Spring 2010): 177–87.
———. "A Look Back at Anger: The Women's Liberation Movement in 1978." *Women's History Review* 19 (2010): 337–56.
Setch, Eve. "The London Women's Liberation Workshop 1969–1979: Organisation, Creativity, Debate." PhD diss., Royal Holloway, University of London, 2000.
———. "The Face of Metropolitan Feminism: The London Women's Liberation Workshop 1969–1979." *Twentieth Century British History* 13, no. 2 (2002): 171–90.
Southall Black Sisters, ed. *Against the Grain: A Celebration of Survival and Struggle.* London: Southall Black Sisters, 1990.
Spare Rib Editorial Collective. "Sisterhood ... Is Plain Sailing." *Spare Rib* 132 (July 1983): 24–27.
———. "*Spare Rib* ... See How We Run." *Spare Rib* 131 (June 1983): 6–8, 30–31.
Sudbury, Julia. *Other Kinds of Dreams: Black Women's Organisations and the Politics of Transformation.* London: Routledge, 1998.
Thomlinson, Natalie. *Race, Ethnicity and the Women's Movement in England, 1968–1993.* Basingstoke: Palgrave Macmillan, 2016.

Archival Papers

The Papers of Stella Dadzie, Black Cultural Archives, London.

Periodicals

The London Women's Liberation Newsletter
Spare Rib
We Are Here: The Black Feminist Newsletter
Speak Out: The Newsletter of Brixton Black Women's Group

Chapter 11

Uneasy Solidarity

The British Men's Movement and Feminism

Lucy Delap

The British women's liberation movement (WLM) worked to promote novel kinds of activism and public protest. Its methods of protest and consciousness-raising (CR) led activist women to call into question much about their political, emotional, and cultural status quo. Historians have only recently begun to chart the British movement, and have investigated the WLM's local, national, and transnational characteristics, its innovative methods of doing politics, its disputes, and its theoretical advances.[1] Understandably, the movement has been read as "by women, for women," with a stress on the evolving development of women-only spaces and separatist strategies. This stress on autonomy and self-authoring was a wider characteristic of the rise of identity politics, evident not only within feminism but also in movements for disability rights and gay liberation. Political activism became more oriented to grassroots, local struggles, with a particular emphasis on the power of lived experiences to inform political consciousness.[2] Nonetheless, this characteristic has led to an inward-looking focus on the movement and its more committed activists, resulting in neglect of the powerful presence and impact women's liberation had in broader circles.

My concern in this chapter will be to look at the inclusivity of the "feminist" identities developed in this period and the impact of feminist initiatives on those not usually included in its boundaries, through an examination of men's relationship to feminism.[3] I will investigate the impact of the British WLM on men who were sympathetic to its ideas, who participated in its activism, or who changed their lives in response to its demands, willingly or unwillingly. Most late twentieth-century men were extremely reluctant to term themselves feminists, despite some having strong convictions of gender justice. They talked and wrote instead of their commitment to an antisexist or pro-feminist position; smaller numbers spoke of "men's liberation." These men are not representative of wider public opinion or reception, but they do offer us a richly documented and observed set of sources that can illustrate the personal and emotional impact of feminist critiques, as well as attempts to formulate new masculinities in a period when postwar full employment and nuclear family stability could no longer be taken for granted.

The British WLM was initially open to men's participation; men were present in its early groups, conferences, and marches. Nicholas Owen has charted the diminishing acceptability of men's presence throughout the 1970s. While there were always men who sought to join feminist campaigns and contribute to newsletters, women activists became less willing to accommodate them and more critical of their motives. From 1973 the national WLM conferences were women-only, and most CR groups followed suit. These decisions were not taken lightly, and they continued to prompt sharp and painful debates over how best to engage with men. Socialist feminist elements of the WLM were largely sympathetic to men's involvement. Prominent feminist activist Sheila Rowbotham wrote widely of the need to include men and allow them space to redefine themselves. Nonetheless, she regretted their tendency to "nervous hostility or benevolent patronage" when participating in women's groups.[4]

The growing radical and revolutionary tendencies within women's liberation were more critical. Marches, conferences, and women's centers were all spaces of contention over men's presence. For heterosexual women, and mothers of sons, this often created deep dilemmas over their own feminist identities, particularly once agendas such as "political lesbianism" became widely debated in 1979.[5] Owen concludes that the "question of men" in the WLM was "startlingly divisive," and unresolvable. Reviewing the publications of the women's movement, he concludes that by the late 1970s most feminists believed men to be "unrescuable."[6] James Hinton's account of late twentieth century Britain concurs, and illustrates the resistance to change amongst men who lived through the upheavals of women's liberation.[7] This chapter offers a less pessimistic picture while remaining alert to the small-scale nature of men's feminist activism. It juxtaposes historical accounts from women with more emphasis on the voices and texts of the men's movement itself, and by extending its narrative frame into the 1980s and beyond, it looks at the continuing efforts among men to respond to the feminist challenge.

My interest in who can call themself a feminist, and what this might mean for their lives or political practices, stems from a broader sense of the controversies over "who could be a feminist" in earlier periods. Though the term "feminist" was first used tentatively in the late nineteenth century, it was around 1910 and 1911 that it began to be widely available to activists. "Feminist" became used alongside "suffragist"; "feminism" supplemented or displaced talk of "the women's movement" that had been more common in earlier decades. "Feminism" initially referred to the more radical or avant-garde elements of the women's movement, though it swiftly gained a wider popular, transnational purchase, and could be understood as referring to the entire women's movement.[8] It was a term that had been deliberately coined to recognize and encourage men to participate in struggles for gender justice.[9] Men had already proved enthusiastic and committed as activists for women's suffrage, and they contributed to early feminist publishing.[10] While the prominent American feminist Charlotte Perkins Gilman wanted to term men's contributions "masculism," she acknowledged in 1914 that their participation was essential to what she called "the larger feminism."[11]

This early twentieth-century inclusivity toward men did not establish them as participants in struggles for gender justice for all time. Both men's ability to see themselves as participants in feminism, and the term "feminist" itself, have gone in and out of fashion throughout the twentieth century. This chapter charts a contemporary historical moment where men's "feminism" was foregrounded, and problematized anew, through innovations in feminist thinking and practice after 1968.[12] Examining the boundaries and inclusivity of feminism enables us to chart its ability to take on new meanings and connotations over time, as well as to examine the limits to its fluidity. It sheds light on the sentiments of urgent need, emotional trauma, and self-hatred experienced by men who had become aware of the patriarchal and homophobic organization of their everyday life and were struggling to create a personal and collective masculine identity that was not rooted in denial and avoidance. Examining their troubled relationship to feminism can help elucidate the changing nature of masculinity in the later twentieth century and determine the scale of impact that the WLM had on British society. This chapter charts antisexist men's attempts to negotiate what has been described as the "impossible" relationship between men and feminism.[13]

The Creation of a Men's Movement

While many men in the post-1968 era responded to feminism with humor, irritation, or indifference, a minority came to see feminism as setting them challenges, or meeting their deep psychic needs. Few, however, found this comfortable. Paul Atkinson (born 1949), who went on to cofound the antisexist men's magazine *Achilles Heel,* recalled, "For me it was passionate, it was a very passionate—it meant an awful lot, so I kind of fought it, and argued with it."[14] The demands feminism made on men produced numerous upheavals within the lives of individual men, but was by no means always destructive. The inspiration of the WLM resulted in the creation of a network of men's CR groups, conferences, and periodicals, largely populated by men who had connections to the political Left, from the Labour Party to smaller Marxist groups such as the International Socialists or Big Flame. Taken together, this activism amounted to what was controversially termed a "men's movement." To take a single indicative location, Sheffield, a moderately sized northern British city, recorded in 1980 an initiative called SMASH (Sheffield Men Against Sexual Harassment), coordinated by MAGIC (the Men Against Gender Injustice Collective). This was a network of thirty activist men meeting in three CR groups and other informal discussion groups. They had plans to found a northern antisexist men's periodical, and brought out *People Against Sexism* in 1986; the group also founded a men's center and produced a nationally distributed discussion pack on sexual harassment, rape, and child abuse.[15]

Sheffield's level of activism was not unusual; local antisexist magazines were published in Manchester, Bradford, Oxford, Cambridge, York, London, the University of Essex, Brighton, and probably many other locations. At least four national periodicals were established and distributed across the 1970s and 1980s—*Achilles Heel* (1978–97), the *Anti-sexist Men's News* (later MAN), *ASAP: Against Sexism, Against Patriarchy, Men for Change,* and *MANifesto.* However, there is little historical memory, popular or scholarly, about these activities, and few of the textual sources have been archived. In 2012 and 2013, I interviewed thirty-six men born 1934–1964, with the majority clustered in the 1940s, who had significant encounters with feminism, through their employment, their activism, or their intimate lives, as well as three activist women. These interviews, along with the magazines, novels, correspondences, and private papers of "feminist men," often generously shared with me by interviewees, form the archival basis of this research.

Motives and Influences

What kinds of experiences had led men to identify with feminism? Many spoke of their memories of gender-normative peer group pressures at school, and the dissonance this caused. While "softened" versions of masculinity were debated in the decades after 1945, there is much evidence that they did not translate into widely changing practices.[16] Boys born around World War II still widely experienced remote fathers, sexual double standards, and strong pressure to adopt patriarchal identities of provider, or heterosexual initiator. They were socialized into jovial yet emotionally impoverished masculine associational life. For those who had come from families that did not support conventional gender norms, experiences of school and peer group were often painful, and they often developed a strong sense of being an outsider. Harry Christian's 1994 study of antisexist men focused on the psychodynamics of early upbringing—the influence of strong mothers, nurturing fathers, or conversely, of absent or distant fathers.[17] Others who identified as feminists simply failed to instantiate the norms of conventional masculinity; some were physically vulnerable, bookish, or unsuccessful at sports, and this led to gender nonconformity. These early experiences were often motives that worked in interaction with more direct triggers (feminist influence, divorce), discussed below, but remained an important factor perceived by antisexist men as disposing them to feminist commitments.

Sexualities and Celibacy

For those who did not identify as heterosexual, they might also be labeled with an outsider status. Antisexist men sometimes adopted "gay affirmative" as a second form of identity, and the changes in the visibility and acceptability of minority sexualities was an important subsidiary component in the shaping of "male feminism." A substantial minority of men involved in men's groups and activism were non-heterosexual and came to antisexist activism through their sense of being outsiders in heterosexual institutions. Gay circles might also impose their own normative masculinities; some antisexist men talked of the anomie and loneliness produced by the pressures to conform to particular models of gay sociability and appearance within the emerging commercial gay scene.

Politically active gay men sometimes came to read and identify with feminism through their interactions with lesbian women, though these were often tense. Chris Heaume (born 1949), a gay youth worker, described his conversations with lesbian women as "very powerful, you know, right in your face, and you couldn't not think about it.... 'I find the way you behave is objectionable' type conversations, ... it made me think, 'Crumbs, what am I doing here? I have to think differently and behave differently.'"[18] Bi- and transsexual individuals were often particularly isolated by their sexuality, which was either unrecognized within gay and lesbian communities, or was actively excluded. The London Lesbian and Gay Centre, for example, banned bisexual groups for much of the 1980s. Radical feminists also frequently took judgmental and hostile positions on trans- and bisexual individuals. In contrast, men's movement periodicals hosted much discussion of bisexuality, including a special edition of the *Anti-Sexist Men's News* devoted to bisexuality in January 1981 and a "bisexuality" issue of *Man* in 1986. It is clear that a range of "queer" identities were visible and influential.

Although the majority of antisexist men identified as heterosexual, many were experimental in relation to their sexuality and reluctant to be pinned down too sharply to a single sexual identity. Interviewees recalled wearing nail varnish, dresses, and skirts and being open to new sexual experiences while drawing on the new lifestyles of drug taking, collective living, and nonmonogamy.[19] As Big Flame activist Alan Mantell (born 1955) recalled, "I did occasionally sleep with men at Essex, … but it was kind of more cuddly stuff, it wasn't really, it wasn't, it wasn't full on sex."[20] A tongue-in-cheek manifesto, "We Demand New Sex Organs," discussed at a 1975 University of Sussex men's conference, declared:

> We demand:
> 1—detachable pricks, cunts and clitorises which can be readily affixed to any part of the body. (Pricks may be superfluous, all but the reproductive functions being fulfilled by the clitoris.)
> 2—multiple sex organs for each individual, of unlimited size, number, colour and variety
> 3—a new sex organ, on the principle of the nipple on a balloon, that can be alternately concave or convex
> 4—voluntarily controlled tendrils, attached to the sides of both pricks and cunts, combining the best features of fingers, clitorises and tongues, but with improved sensitively and dexterity
> 5—quantities of tendrils to be deployed at will over the entire body surface
> 6—surrogate eyes, to be combined with the other organs at one's own discretion
> 7—electric eel organs capable of passing a mild electric shock through the body or any part of it.
> These are our minimum demands.[21]

But there were limits to this playfulness, and many also recalled their anxious homophobia. Mark Long (born 1950), then unemployed and living in Liverpool, attended his first antisexist men's conference in 1980: "I thought, am I going to become gay as a result of this? I was thinking that. … As a political duty, that's what it felt like … am I actually obliged [laughs] in my entrance fee, almost?"[22] There are clear echoes here of the contemporaneous debate around political lesbianism within the women's movement and limits to tolerance over gay sexuality. Significant numbers of men I interviewed had no direct relationships with gay individuals and found this element of antisexist commitment unsettling. Many antisexist men simply opted out of sex altogether. Feminist statements on the intrinsically oppressive nature of heterosexual relationships made straight men uncertain as to how they could avoid this aspect of patriarchy. There was much discussion of celibacy as a political strategy for men within the movement.[23] As Misha Wolf (born 1949), a student activist and later an *Anti-Sexist Men's Newsletter* organizer, described it in an interview,

> I went through this period, you know, 78, 79, whenever, 80 … thinking about androgyny, um, and being celibate, intentionally celibate, because I, I, I didn't know what—OK, so here's the Hite report and all that, and all my feelings, … churned up feelings and, I didn't know what to do.… I made myself this big badge which said "celibacy is subversive," and I went around with it. On the tube I found it acutely embarrassing.

Celibacy spanned gay and heterosexual communities. Gay housing activist Nick Snow (born 1955) noted, "I had long periods of not being sexual at all, just, by myself. … I wanted to be resistant to kind of being a stereotypical gay man." As Lesley Hall has argued, the anxieties associated with sexual expectations and norms imposed on men are longstanding; the late twentieth century saw for the first time secular, public exploration of celibacy as a male response.[24]

Feminism and the Academy

The influence of higher education was also extremely important in motivating and mediating men's encounters with feminism. The men in my interview set were unusually well educated, with most having an undergraduate degree and many also holding graduate or further professional qualifications.[25] A large minority had attended one of the newly founded universities of the postwar era, such as Keele, York, Kent, and Sussex, where many encountered politicized student bodies and came into contact with the far Left. These were settings where courses in women's studies, or other pedagogical innovations, were widely available.[26] Misha Wolf, who studied for a science degree at Sussex in the early 1970s, was required to do some social science modules, and this gave him insights into feminism and power. Alan Mantell describes how studying sociology at Essex supported his interest in antisexist politics, leading to his final-year dissertation being a study of the men's movement. Dave Baigent (born 1944), a former fire fighter, studied sociology and politics as a mature student in the early 1990s at Anglia Polytechnic University. Having been challenged about his sexist behavior by his peer group of mature women students, he opted for some women's studies modules, which became politically and personally formative for him. He described reading Sylvia Walby's work on patriarchy: "I was thinking, well where's the patriarch? And I thought, that's me ain't it? That is me. That is exactly what I am. I am one of those chauvinist pigs … I really am. So I thought, better put that right." This led to a doctoral study of gender norms within the fire service and a professional career as a gender equality consultant in public services. He also spoke of his homophobia and changed attitudes through academic study: "Soon as I'd done a module on gay politics, it was just … you know, I could be gay."[27] Mike Savage has recently convincingly charted the powerful impact that sociology had, not only in describing but also reshaping postwar Britain, providing new categories and classificatory devices.[28] Women's studies was always a more overtly political, transformative project than sociology, deliberately aiming to change the lives of its students and extend into community settings. Like sociology, its impact was highly significant. Male students found social science and humanities study enormously significant in bringing them to feminist political ideas.

Experimental academic pedagogies, a diverse curriculum, and politically committed individuals within higher education helped inform the political perspectives that led men to feminism. Nonetheless, there were also moments of conflict. Andy Barrow (born 1947) studied for what he described as a "Marxist Feminist MA" at Middlesex Polytechnic. He recalled influential feminist lecturers but also his distaste for the aggressive behavior he associated with feminism: "There were a couple of incidents on the course where young women on—on the course, students on the course, were doing things and behaving in ways that I would have found abhorrent in men.… I remember one of our lecturers saying to one of the women students, 'Oh I didn't see you in my seminar this evening,' and she just turned around and said, 'Fuck off you cunt.'" Dave Baigent found feminist sociologists remote; he commented on one eminent feminist academic: "She didn't even want to talk to me.… I found women quite difficult to approach."[29] Women's studies courses often had complex or conflicting goals—many tutors aimed to provide safe, women-only spaces for the development of feminist theory and applied work in policy, social work, and so on. However, it was also important to uses these courses to reach out to new groups, which might include men. Jeff Hearn, who lectured in the early 1980s on the pioneering "Women's Studies (Applied)" course in Bradford University, described the space in his department as a complex mix of tacitly or overtly women-only spaces that he navigated with varying degrees of success. This "semi-separatist" setting did however bring him into contact with feminist theorists and sparked the formation of a men's group among his colleagues.

Reading Feminism

Other men came to an awareness of feminism through the politicization of their female partners and friends. Many were given magazines or books by women they were close to. Men were not the envisaged audience for most feminist writing, and by the later 1970s many publications were issued as "women only."[30] Nonetheless, feminist polemics and novels were clearly circulating within alternative political movements.[31] The expansion of radical bookshops and publishing houses made women's and feminist writing more widely available. Books such as Doris Lessing's *The Golden Notebook,* Kate Millet's *Sexual Politics,* Germaine Greer's *The Female Eunuch,* and magazines such as *Spare Rib* were immensely significant. As one antisexist activist recalled, "We had read our Friedan and our Greer, our de Beauvoir and our Firestone..."[32] For Mark Long, "*Merseyside Women's Paper* was my biggest source of information, plus networks of friends who were engaged with groups and the like.' Paul Smith (born 1950), another Liverpool activist and Big Flame member, recalled the impact of reading feminist literature: "The book that had the greatest impact on me was Andrea Dworkin's *Woman Hating,* which sort of blew my mind.... I thought, you know, 'these bastards, men' and I was caught by this feeling of ... great grief that I hadn't been informed correctly about the oppression of women, which turned into guilt and shame, terrible guilt and shame."[33] The experience for most men of reading feminist texts, often mediated by intimate relationships with feminist women, was not a comfortable one. Some read feminist texts obsessively and felt an urgent need to redefine themselves as a result; others found their emotional response paralyzing.

The late twentieth-century feminist reading community spanned national borders.[34] The men's movement was similarly influenced by the antisexist and feminist publications from other countries. In Britain, the major influence came from the United States; large numbers of my interviewees had traveled in the States; some had been involved in civil rights activism and learned much from its political repertoires. Many men recalled reading American writers such as Jack Stoltenberg and Jon Snodgrass's 1977 *For Men against Sexism.* American antisexist periodicals (*M. Gentlemen for Gender Justice, Changing Men, Brother, Morning Due, Men Talk, Reaching Out*) were circulating in small numbers. Antisexist men traveled to the United States to observe antisexist activism and connect with their movement. Australian theorists such as R. W. Connell and magazines such as *The Australian Male* were also important, though the personal contacts were fewer. European contacts were more ad hoc, but German and Dutch magazines such as *Mannenkrant, De Man, Superman's Niewsbrief, Mannen, Von Mann zu Mann,* and *Herr*

Mann circulated in Britain and were reviewed in British periodicals. Danish and French antisexist men actively engaged with the British movement, with invitations to form international networks or participate in summer camps.[35] The antisexist men's movement was thus a distinctly international affair.

Many participants in men's groups were also young, and there was clearly a synergy between their stage in the life course and their commitment to activism, living beyond the confines of the nuclear family, and rethinking domestic labor. The majority of the men I interviewed were born in the later 1940s. Most were in their early twenties when they became aware of feminism, and this was a moment in their lives when they could devote significant amounts of time to reading, meetings, and reflection. For some men in the 1970s, experiences of unemployment were also crucial, both practically, in the sense of making time available for antisexist organizing, and also symbolically, in making tangible a sense of failing to live up to conventional breadwinning masculine norms. Many of these mostly young men had few other responsibilities or adopted countercultural lifestyles of squatting, taking drugs, and spiritual or therapeutic experimentation. There were similarities between the flourishing therapeutic innovations of the 1970s and 1980s, such as co-counseling or encounter groups, and the techniques of consciousness-raising used by both women's and men's groups. Squats and other kinds of collective housing encouraged the formation of politically active networks, and as John Davis and Anette Warring have charted, these brought men into contact with feminist women. Collective living arrangements were also sites of conflict over the division of domestic labor, and these tensions sometimes forced men to examine critically their commitment to feminism.[36]

Men's Groups

Men's groups built on the many factors that brought men into contact with feminism by offering experiences of emotional release and bonding among men, which sometimes became unexpectedly motivating. As an early men's group member argued in 1974, "For a lot of men, the impetus to begin has come from women.… But what has come to be called the 'men's movement' soon developed its own dynamics and energies. There have been conferences, attended by groups and by individuals; extraordinary, mind-blowing events where scores of men tried to be kind, loving and creative together."[37] Many antisexist men wrote or talked movingly of the deep significance of learning how to love other men and, in the process, love themselves. Yet this was always a project that elicited guilty feelings. The entire period of antisexist activism, stretching across the 1970s and 1980s, saw continuing efforts to balance the imperative to be "accountable" to women while also developing men's sense of self-worth and self-care. Men's groups equivocated between supporting each other and challenging sexist attitudes. They were sometimes unwilling to acknowledge their own members' complicity in women's oppression, to the frustration of feminists. One member of an Oxford men's group complained of the abstractness the discussions: "We were discussing porn as if it had nothing to do with us."[38]

The conflicting goals of men's groups were brought out acutely at the national level when the 1980 Bristol Men's Conference refused to endorse a set of "commitments" that codified the relationship with the women's movement. Instead, a less demanding "minimum self-definition of the antisexist men's movement" was drafted by filmmaker and *Achilles Heel* editor Paul Morrison. Support for "the women's and gay movement in the struggle against sexism" was pledged, but it was expressed in terms of aspirations rather than specific goals. This compromise statement recognized the political diversity of both the men's movement and women's liberation—it was enormously hard to determine what "accountability" might mean when faced with a whole range of feminist positions. But this political moment could also be read as a loss of nerve.

At the grassroots level, incidents of violence had a similarly divisive effect, whether toward female partners or other members of the group. Alan Mantell dropped out of his men's group when the group leader physically assaulted him while drunk. Mark Long and Paul Smith's Liverpool-based men's group broke up over how to respond when one of their group members assaulted a woman. Some members argued for exclusion, others for antiviolence counseling; the painful debates were irresolvable, and the group "burnt out." The dynamics of men's groups hovered between critical confrontation and warm supportiveness; uncertainty about which option to adopt sometimes led to passivity or seeming complacency about patriarchal practices and attitudes.

Some men's groups developed their own responses to male violence, with initiatives in Bristol and Nottingham involving direct work with violent male offenders. Others turned to the women's movement; a Liverpool-based men's group had been connected with the Liverpool Women Against Violence Against Women and attempted to negotiate an acceptable role for men in relation to the women's movement: "Women were quite angry about their position, kind of supportive of the men coming forward to do something, frustrated that they couldn't get of us what they wanted out of all men …" In turn, antisexist men were "inhibited and nervous about being destroyed for having popped their head over the parapet." The overwhelming memory of encounters between antisexist men and feminist women is ambivalent or negative. Joint meetings of men's and women's groups were described as "fraught or unsatisfactory." As Mark Long concluded, "We may have talked about accountability to the women's movement; I don't recall much practice of it." He described a significant attempt by antisexist men to organize a conference against pornography and sex shops for Liverpool, which produced a long prospectus but failed to translate into an actual event: "It was one of those things where the process was more ... useful than the—well, the result didn't happen."[39]

Initial phases of the women's movement had seen extensive work in mixed-sex groups, but this faded in the later 1970s as difficulties became more evident. Pauline Long and Mary Coghill published their reflections *Is it Worthwhile Working in a Mixed Group?* in 1977, and they acknowledged the pain and emotional dissonance of mixed-sex working.[40] Once the principle of women-only spaces (social, activist, and print cultural) had been established, it became harder for men to access feminist discussions and networks. Many recalled accidentally straying into women-only meetings or social gatherings and being ejected. Other men found that the women-only spaces were de facto, and that masculine presence was resented even if not formally banned. It was hard to navigate the complex boundaries of feminist spaces, at conferences, social events, and in print. Misha Wolf recalled dancing at a gig where the lesbian band Ova were playing; as the sole man present, he was asked not to dance. The feminist bookshop Sisterwrite, based in Islington, was never entirely women only, though certain sections were. Nonetheless, squatting activist Mal Peachey (born 1961) recalled entering the shop with friends in 1983, and "the woman at the end going, 'You! You two! Fuck off! You're not allowed in, fuck off! She can stay!'"[41] Despite most antisexist men's respect for the principle of women-only spaces, these experiences of sometimes violently enforced exclusion made for high levels of anxiety and discomfort when men and women did encounter each other politically.

Conflicts between the sexes, and the widespread adoption of women-only spaces, encouraged more open discussion of the value of men-only spaces within the men's movement. Many men's groups maintained a policy of being formally open to women, feeling that learning from and listening to women was one of the activities that would transform patriarchy. However, others began to argue that like women, men needed safe spaces that would allow them to be honest and discuss topics such as pornography or sexuality without fear of being judged by women. This could sometimes lead to a reevaluation of men's company, though many continued to find emotional disclosure between men embarrassing; for Sam Hilton (born 1964), studying drama in Exeter in the early 1980s, being in a men's group was about finding "that camaraderie with men. And it was, you know it felt like a bit of a joke, it felt like something that you didn't really want to talk about outside of, outside of that. Especially not with the women.... So yes, it was, it was a different way of trying to form male bonds as well."[42] Alan Jones discovered through attending a men's group in the 1970s that "I had developed an appetite for men's company." Paul Atkinson saw this as the discovery of a kind of male energy that "was so powerful ... it was like men who you grew to love, quite strongly, you know, and—as well as sometimes hate ..." While antisexist men of the early 1970s had been focused on their accountability to women, the later 1970s witnessed criticism of what Paul Atkinson saw as men "in a supine position [laughs] in relation to feminism, and apologetic about being men." Atkinson and other men who went on to found the prominent men's magazine *Achilles Heel* in 1978 did so in a spirit of understanding men rather than berating them. The first issues called for men to "delve deeply into our inner lives and to consciously explore and develop our sense of ourselves as emotional, sensual and spiritual beings capable of a whole range of experience which our society on the whole denies to men." Atkinson describes himself as "pissed off" with feminist critique of men, while recognizing the "paradox of ... knowing there was something very true and important in it, but at the same time feeling quite defensive and under attack."[43]

Some activists judged this a refusal of feminism. Jeff Hearn (born 1947), a prominent theorist of masculinities based at the University of Bradford for much of the 1970s feared that some antisexist men lacked an interest in feminism: "They were interested in [feminism], sort of, in a vague way, but not perhaps in much—they were interested more in, like curing themselves, or developing good relations with their father or son ... than actually being sort of ... public political allies to women's movement." A discussion of the role of CR groups by the editorial collective of *ASAP* in 1982 concluded succinctly that "CR groups for women were initially support groups which became more politicized whereas men's CR groups became more sexist as they became more supportive (via male bonding)."[44] During the 1980s there was more prominent talk of "men's liberation" and more evidence of what became known as the "mythopoetic" men's movement. Inspired by the better-developed American version, the spiritual men's movement began to experiment with symbolic and religious rituals. Keith Motherson described in 1981 a men's CR group "followed by an all-male sauna in the sweat lodge the tipi people had made and fired the stones for. Naked bodies, dark, steam, heat, sweat, earth, chanting, touch. Magic purification ritual of brotherhood."[45] Prominent antisexist activist John Rowan published *The Horned God* in 1987, intending to help men "heal their wounds," some of which were presented as having been caused by "radical feminists." In place of accountability toward feminism, there was a distinct stress on men's autonomy. Rowan opened the book combatively: "I suppose women can read this book if they want to, over the shoulder of a man. But it is not intended to enlighten or entertain women." In place of CR techniques, Rowan foregrounded "unconsciousness raising" and getting in touch with the "deep inner male."[46] These approaches should not stand in for the wider British men's movement, which continued to promote a much more critical and feminist agenda. But Rowan's approach was to receive a much higher profile after the publication of the American Robert Bly's best seller *Iron John* in 1990.[47] In public and feminist consciousness, the "men's movement" had become synonymous with attempts to forge men-only spaces and revitalize all-male comradeship.[48]

Retreat from Commitment?

While many of my interviewees were highly skeptical about these developments, their commitment to feminism was also changing over time. As countercultural influences lessened in the later 1970s and antisexist men moved out of their early twenties, some (though not all) found feminism less compelling. Interviewees recalled the changes associated with childcare and the demands of formal employment or mortgages entering their lives. As Paul Atkinson recalled, "I needed to assert something about ... being a man ... you know ... and about being able to make some money, and to have a career, and have some identity around ... work, and profession, that ... that I could stand in the world with."[49] Despite the unconventionality of many antisexist men, they still felt strong pressures to achieve conventional masculine status. This was not simply a matter of the changing life course but also one of the historically specific changes over the course of the 1980s. By the mid-1980s, elements of British society had turned away from countercultural, collective endeavors. The men's movement reflected this in a shift to a more individualized, therapeutic mode of organizing. The energetic production of pamphlets and periodicals, experimental lifestyles, and sartorial subversions all receded. More organized forms of women's centres, housing activism and cooperatives replaced the more anarchic squats and collectives of the 1970s.[50] An active far-Left and a high-profile labor movement had prompted and in some cases supported men's awareness of feminism, but these political affiliations were much less evident by the late 1980s.

Nonetheless, it is an open question how the political change of government in 1979 affected women's (and men's) liberation. As Pat Thane points out, dividing the women's movement into characteristic sixties, seventies, and eighties modes is unhelpful.[51] The 1980s continued to see new men's groups formed that displayed deep commitment to reforming men and meeting women's demands. Punk and gay activism continued to provoke the formation of alternative lifestyles, and the strong presence of articulate, politicized women within these circles continued to demand engagement with feminism. The rise of critical men's studies and the history of masculinities during this decade points to the continuing strength of feminism and antisexism in further and higher education.[52] The academy was a site where men's gender activism remained in touch with the women's movement and continues to produce activist commitments.

Over the 1980s, the periodicals of the men's movement became smaller scale; there was much less grassroots energy and growth of men's groups. The antisexist men had always been reluctant to term themselves a "movement." It was clear that most antisexist men, as well as many feminist women, felt it inappropriate to claim the status of a movement for an "oppressor" group. Many men preferred to talk of their activism as allied with and accountable to the women's movement rather than constituting a movement in its own right. To claim a movement status would appear to invite praise and recognition, which seemed inappropriate in the light of men's ongoing oppression of women. It was also felt that "movement" implied a degree of ideological or institutional unity that was lacking. Liverpool-based antisexist activist Mark Long recalled that "we had the infrastructure in terms of newsletters and groups and events, [but] it never struck me as being coherent."[53] This reluctance became more pronounced in the later 1980s as the idea of a men's movement was usurped by mythopoetic elements and feminists became more hostile. Feminist psychotherapist Susie Orbach commented in an early 1990s magazine interview, "I've always been extremely uptight about the idea of a Men's Movement. What are they liberating themselves from? I would prefer to call it a gender-conscious movement. Using the word 'Movement' seems to me to valorise what men have been up to. Nobody would feel comfortable with the idea of a 'White Movement' and it would be seen as racist. I prefer to see men as distressed, not oppressed."[54]

Perhaps it is not surprising that despite the energy and commitment of antisexist organizing, few men were willing to term themselves feminists. Of the men I interviewed, most responded with ambivalence when asked, "Would you have called yourself a feminist?" Whether born towards the beginning or end of the cohort of interviewees, many continued to deny that men could ever qualify as feminists:

> [Alan Mantell]: ["Feminist"] is a province exclusively—an option only available to women. I would have called myself an antisexist man, yeah, yeah.

> [Misha Wolf]: I find it amazing, … astonishing that people nowadays erm even think about … men calling themselves feminists. … In my day, if some man had said that they were a feminist, we would have laughed.

Others clearly did not think it was an identity they could claim in public, though they might have used it as part of a self-narrative: Colin Thomas (born 1939), a Welsh journalist, confessed in the interview, "I've never said that [I am a feminist], but I'd like to think—yes, I would like to think that." Jeff Hearn noted the historical specificity of how such terms are used: "[In the 1970s] it would be very dodgy to call yourself a feminist." One interviewee commented on his frustration that all women, whatever their level of activism, could use the term "feminist," whereas men who had deep commitments to gender justice were excluded: "[My ex-wife] would have called herself a feminist, although … looking back on it I—I think that, if you're looking at credentials, I—I would have fitted the title far better than she would have done but I used it very guardedly."[55] Others came to use the term after the controversies of the 1970s and 1980s had faded. Chris Tribble (born 1948) would not have used the term in relation to himself or his men's group during his period of activism as a single father in Rochdale, preferring "antisexist" as a moniker. But from a twenty-first-century perspective, he felt that feminism is "still probably the only movement that I would align myself with." There are indeed signs that twenty-first-century feminists take a more inclusive stance, though the significance of this must await a longer historical perspective. A younger generation of British men is more public with its feminism, with attendance at the 2013 UK Feminista summer school reportedly 10 percent male.[56] The reluctance of then British prime minister David Cameron to term himself a feminist in September 2013 suggests a residual discomfort, but it also prompted a furor of responses from men willing to embrace this term, and women keen to include them.[57]

Conclusion

It is all too easy to chart the tensions between men and feminism and assume that the men's movement was a failure, or at least a damp squib. Recovering the extensive history of men's engagement with feminism in this period belies such claims, and recovers the resonance that women's liberation had for a minority of men. This does not lead to a simple celebration of antisexist activism. Clearly, in social movement terms, men's groups were always limited to a minority of men. Alan Jones noted that "we would advertise for members in the town's left-wing bookshop, with surprisingly little response. We occasionally attracted lonely gay men seeking a friend, never any black men, and increasingly became a core of young to middle-aged teachers and social workers."[58] These groups had a strong potential to become inward looking and therapeutic rather than in dialogue with feminism. Nonetheless, the location of Susie Orbach's 1992 critique of the men's movement is significant. She published her reflections in a new periodical titled *Body Politic,* one of a group of new publications of the later 1980s and early 1990s that welcomed joint working between men and women. Edited by a black woman, its first issue declared, "*Body Politic* unashamedly welcomes the new man, and supports those men who are trying to move beyond traditional masculine stereotypes towards a more sensitive, emotional, anti-sexist way of being."[59] As Natalie Thomlinson argues in this volume in relation to race and feminist politics, the 1980s produced controversy and debate about important areas of tension within feminism. Yet this should not distract historical attention from the reality of productive working in mixed-sex and mixed-race collectives, such as the 1986 *People against Sexism* periodical in Sheffield, the York-based *Powercut* "for anti-sexist people," or Oxford's *Sexchange. Body Politic* made no claim to belong to the men's movement, yet its stance should be understood as a legacy of the political distance traveled between the men's groups of the early 1970s and the mixed-sex work of the 1990s. Periodicals and zines flourished in the later 1980s and 1990s and testify to men's continuing engagement with feminist ideas. The relative comfort with which late twentieth-century men engaged with feminism, alongside the growth of men's and gender studies within the academy, has led to a recovery a century later of Edwardian connotations of feminism as an identity that spans the sexes.

Interviewing men about their "feminism" was productive and revealing of the dynamics of a social movement organized not to promote the interests of its participants but to critique and transform existing modes of being. Antisexist men's organizing was often premised on a denial or refusal of a positive identity and the embrace of a negative claim about what they were *against.* That some men found this compelling is testament to the power of feminist critique in the last quarter of the twentieth century. Nonetheless, my interviewees found it hard to align their memories with established narratives of the period, which had little space for masculine refashioning beyond clichéd talk of the "new man." They found it hard to name themselves, and uncertain of their place in history. As Becky Thompson has suggested in relation to white antiracist activism in the United States, "the lack of a precise and subversive terminology speaks to the fact that white people who challenge racism have not yet created the critical mass needed to name ourselves collectively."[60] A politics built on shame and guilt proved to be unsustainable; yet the "beyond guilt" attempts to delineate men's liberation lost the critical link to feminist thought and networks that had sustained men's antisexist activism. The question of how to acknowledge the guilt that can prompt political activism, and yet avoid the excessive psychological damage it can inflict, has no easy answers. The uneasiness of male feminism emerges clearly from the archive, yet this did not prove an impossible relationship. Its legacy is demonstrated in the growing ease with which men engage with feminism, leading to high profile and confident participation by young men in the renewal of feminism that the early twenty-first century is witnessing.

Lucy Delap is a lecturer in modern British history at the University of Cambridge and Fellow of Murray Edwards College. She works on the history of child sexual abuse and is deputy director of the knowledge exchange project History & Policy. She has published widely on the history of feminism, gender, labor, and religion, including the prize-winning *The Feminist Avant-Garde: Transatlantic Encounters of the Early Twentieth Century* in 2007, *Knowing Their Place: Domestic Service in Twentieth Century Britain* in 2011, and, with Sue Morgan, *Men, Masculinities and Religious Change in Twentieth Century Britain* in 2013. She is currently working on a history of modern feminism provisionally titled *Feminism: A Useable History* (forthcoming, Penguin).

Notes

1. Eve Setch, "The Face of Metropolitan Feminism: The London Women's Liberation Workshop 1969–1979," *Twentieth Century British History* 13 (2002); Sarah Browne, "A Veritable Hotbed of Feminism': Women's Liberation in St Andrews, Scotland, c.1969–c.1979," *Twentieth Century British History* 24, no. 3 (2011); Jeska Rees, "A Look Back at Anger: The Women's Liberation Movement in 1978," *Women's History Review* 19 (2010); Natalie Thomlinson, "The Colour of Feminism: White Feminists and Race in the Women's Liberation Movement," *History* 97, no. 327 (2012).
2. Nicholas Owen, "Men and the 1970s British Women's Liberation Movement," *Historical Journal* 56, no. 3 (2013); Fidelma Ashe, "Deconstructing the Experiential Bar: Male Experience and Feminist Resistance," *Men and Masculinities* 7, no. 2 (2004).
3. "Feminist" is presented in quote marks here to acknowledge that not all participants, male or female, identified as feminists, though later commentators might choose to see them in this frame. For some, "women's liberation" was a preferable term. Others simply did not see themselves as feminists, while nonetheless adhering to commitments to gender justice or equality. For purposes of readability, the quote marks will be suspended in the remainder of the essay. This analysis extends the account recently offered by Nicholas Owen, drawing more fully on archival and new oral

history records of men's movement activism. Owen, "Men and the 1970s British Women's Liberation Movement."

4. Sheila Rowbotham, "Women's Liberation and the New Politics," *Spokesman Pamphlet* 17, written summer 1969, published October 1971, first pub. May Day Manifesto Group, p. 26 GCIP CWLA 3/21, Girton Archives.
5. Jeska Rees, "'Are You a Lesbian?' Challenges in Recording and Analysing the Women's Liberation Movement in England," *History Workshop Journal* 69 (2010): 177–87.
6. Owen, "Men and the 1970s British Women's Liberation Movement," 825, 822.
7. James Hinton, *Seven Lives from Mass Observation: Britain in the Late Twentieth Century.* (Oxford: Oxford University Press, 2016).
8. Nancy Cott, *The Grounding of Modern Feminism* (New Haven, CT: Yale University Press, 1987).
9. Lucy Delap, *The Feminist Avant-Garde: Transatlantic Encounters of the Early Twentieth Century* (Cambridge: Cambridge University Press, 2007).
10. Claire Eustance and Angela John, *The Men's Share? Masculinities, Male Support and Women's Suffrage in Britain, 1890–1920* (London: Routledge, 1997); Arianne Chernock, *Men and the Making of Modern British Feminism* (Stanford, CA: Stanford University Press, 2010).
11. Gilman, reported in the *New York Times,* April 2, 1914, 11.
12. Recent critiques of the "waves" metaphor within the history of feminism has led to a reluctance to use "second wave" to identify the women's liberation movement of the 1970s and 1980s (see Nancy A. Hewitt, *No Permanent Waves: Recasting Histories of U.S. Feminism* [New Brunswick, NJ: Rutgers University Press, 2010]). This chapter therefore uses "post-1968 feminism" or the "post-1968 era," aiming to set women's liberation within the context of the upsurge of radical and critical politics that followed the protests of 1968. The AHRC-funded "Around 1968" project, http://www.history.ox.ac.uk/research/project/around-1968-activism-networks-trajectories.html, offers a fuller discussion of this transnational periodization.
13. Stephen Heath, "Male Feminism," in *Men in feminism,* ed. Alice Jardine and Paul Smith (New York: Methuen, 1987), 1.
14. Paul Atkinson, interview with author, March 23, 2012.
15. On grassroots politics in Sheffield, see Daisy Payling "'Socialist Republic of South Yorkshire': Grassroots Activism and Left-Wing Solidarity in 1980s Sheffield." *Twentieth Century British History* 25, no. 4 (2014): 602–27.
16. On new masculinities, see Ferdynand Zweig, *The Worker in an Affluent Society: Family Life and Industry* (London: Heinemann, 1961); Claire Langhamer, "Adultery in Postwar England," *History Workshop Journal* 62, no. 1 (2006); Abigail Wills, "Delinquency, Masculinity and Citizenship in England 1950–1970," *Past & Present* 187 (2005): 157–85; Angela Davis, *Modern Motherhood: Women and Family in England, c. 1945–2000* (Manchester: Manchester University Press, 2012).
17. Harry Christian, *The Making of Anti-sexist Men, Male Orders* (London: Routledge, 1994), 21–25.
18. Chris Heaume, interview with author, May 10, 2012.
19. On broader shifts toward more consumeristic and hedonistic sexual cultures since 1969, see Adrian Bingham, *Family Newspapers? Sex, Private Life, and the British Popular Press 1918–1978* (Oxford: Oxford University Press, 2009).

20. Alan Mantell, interview with author, January 11, 2013.
21. Permanent Damage, London, circa 1975, 7SHR/E/2 Box 9, Women's Library @ LSE.
22. Mark Long, interview with author, June 30, 2012.
23. See for example Paula Tree, "Present Position Paper," London Men's Groups, Newsletter One, undated, circa 1977; John Rowan, "Patriarchy—What It Is and Why Some Men Question It," September 5 1977, 7SHR/E/2 Box 9, Women's Library.
24. Lesley Hall, *Hidden Anxieties: Male Sexuality, 1900–1950* (Cambridge: Polity Press, 1991); Misha Wolf, interview with author, May 31, 2012; Nick Snow, interview with author, May 27, 2012.
25. This effect may partly be down to limits to sampling; the interviewees were selected by asking high-profile figures from contrasting wings of the WLM to identify men who had been active in feminist causes, as well as contacting men directly who emerged from the archival sources as active. Those who had left written records were likely to be the more articulate and educated of the men's movement. Nonetheless, it is clear that the nature of the interview set did predominantly reflect the profile of the men's movement and was not hopelessly distorted by sampling biases. Numerous discussions of how to reach out to wider circles of men were published within periodicals such as the *Anti-Sexist Men's News* and described most male activists as predominantly white and middle class.
26. Elizabeth Bird, "Women's Studies and the Women's Movement in Britain," *Women's History Revew* 12, no. 2 (2003).
27. Dave Baigent, interview with author, December 13, 2011.
28. Mike Savage, *Identities and Social Change in Britain since 1940: The Politics of Method* (Oxford: Oxford University Press, 2011).
29. Andy Barrow, interview with author, May 8, 2012; Baigent, interview.
30. Rees, "Are You a Lesbian?"
31. The underground press of the countercultural movements of the 1960s, for example, began to review feminist writings. The anarchist magazine *Black Dwarf* produced a women's edition, edited by Sheila Rowbotham, in 1969. Similarly, *Bit Times,* the 1970s information element related to the better known *International Times*, produced a women's edition, *Bitwoman,* in December 1973.
32. John Rowan, *The Horned God: Feminism and Men as Wounding and Healing* (London: Routledge, 1987), 18.
33. Paul Smith, interview with author, June 30, 2012.
34. Kathy Davis, *The Making of* Our Bodies, Ourselves*: How Feminism Travels across Borders* (Durham, NC: Duke University Press, 2007).
35. The Paris Men's gathering *Pas Rôle d'Homme,* for example, invited British antisexist men to cofound "a men's anti-sexism network (men's awareness network) at international level. Not an organisation (!), just a network facilitating the exchange of men's group and men's centers' experiences, of the newsletters and the personal contacts." Georges Por, *Men's Groups' Newsletter,* issue 2, 1974, Women's Library.
36. John Davis and Anette Warring, "Living Utopia: Communal Living in Denmark and Britain," *Cultural and Social History* 8, no. 4 (2011).
37. *Men's Groups' Newsletter,* issue 2, 1974 (no page numbers), Women's Library.
38. Howard Edmunds, "How Theorising Can Leave you High and Dry," *Sexchange,* no. 1 (1987): 4.

39. Long, interview.
40. Pauline Long and Mary Coghill, *Is It Worthwhile Working in a Mixed Group?* (London: Beyond Patriarchy Publications, 1977).
41. Mal Peachey, interview with author, July 6, 2012.
42. Sam Hilton, interview with author, March 28, 2012.
43. *Achilles Heel*, no. 1 (1978): 3; Atkinson, interview.
44. Jeff Hearn, interview with author, February 22, 2012; Minutes of ASAP/CAS meeting, September 11, 1982, on Action Against Sexism, *Against Sexism Against Patriarchy—ASAP*, no. 8 (October 1982).
45. Keith Motherson, *MAN: Men's Anti-Sexist Newsletter*, issue 16 (Winter 1981–82): 10.
46. Rowan, *The Horned God*, ix, 2, 18, 109.
47. Robert Bly, *Iron John: A Book about Men* (Boston: Addison-Wesley, 1990).
48. A 1992 American collection published under the title *Women Respond to the Men's Movement* solely discussed the mythopoetic men's movement. Kay Leigh Hagan, ed., *Women Respond to the Men's Movement* (San Francisco: Harper, 1992).
49. Atkinson, interview.
50. Stephen Brooke charts the institution-building work of the Women's Committee (1982–6) within the Greater London Council, but notes the more hostile environment in the later 1980s. Brooke, Stephen. "Space, Emotions and the Everyday: The Affective Ecology of 1980s London." *Twentieth Century British History* 28, no. 1 (2016): 110–42.
51. Pat Thane, "Women and the 1970s: Towards Liberation?," in *Reassessing 1970s Britain*, ed. Pat Thane, Lawrence Black, and Hugh Pemberton (Manchester: Manchester University Press, 2013).
52. Jeff Hearn, "The Personal Is Work Is Political Is Theoretical: Continuities and Discontinuities in Women's Studies, (Pro)feminism, 'Men' and My Selves," *NORA—Nordic Journal of Feminist and Gender Research* 16, no. 4 (2008).
53. Long, interview.
54. Interview with Susie Orbach, by Peter Baker, "What Do Men Really Want?," *Body Politic* 2 (1992): 38–39.
55. Interviews with author, Mantell; Wolf; Colin Thomas, April 5, 2012; Hearn; Barrow.
56. Chris Tribble, interview with author, March 23, 2012; Feminist participation reported in the *Observer*, "Young feminists join together …" August 18, 2013, 7.
57. See for example http://www.thefword.org.uk/blog/2013/09/on_power_voice_ (accessed October 10, 2016).
58. Alan Jones, "On Joining a Men's Group: One Man's Experience," *Powercut* 1 (1991): 11–13.
59. Elsie Owusu, *Body Politic* 1 (1992): 4.
60. Becky Thompson, *A Promise and a Way of Life: White Antiracist Activism* (Minneapolis: University of Minnesota Press, 2001), xxii.

Bibliography

Ashe, Fidelma. "Deconstructing the Experiential Bar: Male Experience and Feminist Resistance." *Men and Masculinities* 7, no. 2 (2004): 187–204.

Bingham, A. *Family Newspapers? Sex, Private Life, and the British Popular Press 1918–1978.* Oxford: Oxford University Press, 2009.
Bly, Robert. *Iron John: A Book about Men.* Boston: Addison-Wesley, 1990.
Browne, Sarah. "'A Veritable Hotbed of Feminism': Women's Liberation in St Andrews, Scotland, c.1969–c.1979." *Twentieth Century British History* 24, no. 3 (2011).
Chernock, Arianne. *Men and the Making of Modern British Feminism.* Stanford, CA: Stanford University Press, 2010.
Christian, Harry. *The Making of Anti-sexist Men: Male Orders.* London: Routledge, 1994.
Cott, Nancy. *The Grounding of Modern Feminism.* New Haven, CT: Yale University Press, 1987.
Davis, Angela. *Modern Motherhood: Women and Family in England, c. 1945–2000.* Manchester: Manchester University Press, 2012.
Davis, John, and Anette Warring. "Living Utopia: Communal Living in Denmark and Britain." *Cultural and Social History* 8, no. 4 (2011): 513–30.
Davis, Kathy. *The Making of* Our Bodies, Ourselves*: How Feminism Travels across Borders.* Durham, NC: Duke University Press, 2007.
Delap, Lucy. *The Feminist Avant-Garde: Transatlantic Encounters of the Early Twentieth Century.* Cambridge: Cambridge University Press, 2007.
Eustance, Claire, and Angela John. *The Men's Share? Masculinities, Male Support and Women's Suffrage in Britain, 1890–1920.* London: Routledge, 1997.
Hagan, Kay Leigh, ed. *Women Respond to the Men's Movement.* San Francisco: Harper, 1992.
Hall, Lesley. *Hidden Anxieties: Male Sexuality, 1900–1950.* Cambridge: Polity Press, 1991.
Hearn, Jeff. "The Personal Is Work Is Political Is Theoretical: Continuities and Discontinuities in Women's Studies, (Pro)Feminism, 'Men' and My Selves." *NORA—Nordic Journal of Feminist and Gender Research* 16, no. 4 (2008): 241–56.
Hewitt, Nancy. A. *No Permanent Waves: Recasting Histories of U.S. Feminism.* New Brunswick, NJ: Rutgers University Press, 2010.
Jardine, Alice, and Paul Smith, eds. *Men in Feminism.* New York: Methuen, 1987.
Langhamer, Claire. "Adultery in Postwar England." *History Workshop Journal* 62, no. 1 (2006): 86–115.
Owen, Nicholas. "Men and the 1970s British Women's Liberation Movement." *Historical Journal* 56, no. 3 (2013): 801–26.
Rees, Jeska. "'Are You a Lesbian?' Challenges in Recording and Analysing the Women's Liberation Movement in England." *History Workshop Journal* 69, no. 177–87 (2010).
———. "A Look Back at Anger: The Women's Liberation Movement in 1978." *Women's History Review* 19 (2010): 337–56.
Rowan, John. *The Horned God: Feminism and Men as Wounding and Healing.* London: Routledge, 1987.
Savage, Mike. *Identities and Social Change in Britain since 1940: The Politics of Method.* Oxford: Oxford University Press, 2011.
Setch, Eve. "The Face of Metropolitan Feminism: The London Women's Liberation Workshop 1969–1979." *Twentieth Century British History* 13 (2002): 171–90.
Thane, Pat. "Women and the 1970s: Towards Liberation?" In *Reassessing 1970s Britain,* ed. P. Thane, Lawrence Black, and Hugh Pemberton. Manchester: Manchester University Press, 2013.

Thomlinson, Natalie. "The Colour of Feminism: White Feminists and Race in the Women's Liberation Movement." *History* 97, no. 327 (2012): 453–75.

Thompson, Becky. *A Promise and a Way of Life: White Antiracist Activism.* Minneapolis: University of Minnesota Press, 2001.

Zweig, Ferdynand. *The Worker in an Affluent Society: Family Life and Industry.* London: Heinemann, 1961.

Part IV

Beyond National Boundaries

Introductory Remarks

Lucy Delap and Thierry Delessert

The following two chapters are concerned with the French and the Russian women's liberation movements (WLM) between 1970 and 1990 and with the German-speaking feminist web community since the 1990s, respectively. Both chapters show how feminism extended the boundaries of the national and developed transnational connections, networks, and identities.

The chapters join a growing literature that demonstrates the global dimensions of feminism in ways that "expand the archives of global feminism."[1] What is commonly called "second-wave feminism"—a term that has received major criticism in the last decade or so[2]—has become an object of research for historians and social scientists around the world. Considering feminist activism through the lens of global history has produced more historically nuanced and sophisticated understanding of what feminism has meant for activists in different countries and cultures.[3] Transgressing the boundaries of the nation-state has also guided scholarly research to feminist activities since the geopolitical shifts and the transformation of global communication through the internet during and since the 1990s. This is especially clear within organized international activism such as the activities around the United Nations Fourth World Conference on Women and the NGO Forum in Beijing in 1995. With regard to the 1970s however, research on less-formalized transnational contacts is still the exception. Kathy Davis and Mary Evans have worked in a very fruitful way on conceptualizing feminism as "travelling theory," showing how ideas move from one context to another and change in the same move due to different conditions of appropriation.[4] The contributions gathered here, in contrast, take groups, not ideas, as a point of departure for a connected history of feminism.

As Kirsten Harting's chapter shows us, the "essentialist" group of the French MLF, known as *Psych et Po* (*Psychanalyse et Politique*), was one of the leading influences on the formation of a WLM in Soviet Russia after the Moscow international book fair in 1976. This movement took place within informal circles of dissident culture in Leningrad, where, starting in 1979, a group of women published the almanac *Women and Russia*. The three main authors—a writer, a poet, and a philosopher—had been arrested several times for participating in human rights movements, and were then forced into exile. The almanac was women only and centered on the situation of the Soviet Union while borrowing French feminists' analyses on phallocracy, the expectation of motherhood for women, and of heteronormativity. If the terms were the same as the Western feminist project, the intellectual contents, however, differed. Phallocracy and patriarchy were considered as consequences of the Soviet authoritarian system, which impacted on society as a whole as well as on dissident groups in particular. The demand for gender equality also differed since the USSR promoted it officially, as it did the right to abortion. Feminist criticism focused mainly on the requirement for Soviet women to work the same hours in paid employment as men while simultaneously being expected to undertake the traditional roles of housewife and mother. Moreover, critics focused on the lack of support provided by the state for childcare, which led to mass abortions in underequipped hospitals. Finally, the rejection of nonconformist gender roles was seen to be the result of the persistence of Slavic traditions and of the Orthodox Church's domination even decades after it was officially banned in the USSR.

The main point of the almanac group's convergence with *Psych et Po* was around criticism of ideas of "essential" femininity. However, it was the question of religion that led to a split in the group that began while they were still in Leningrad and grew during their exile. For the Slavophiles and Orthodox authors searching for "typically" female and Russian characteristics in the prerevolutionary period, femininity could be seen in the Virgin Mary or in Mother Russia. In contrast, for the internationalists of the group, feminine essence was attributed to women's greater sensitivity and ethical conscience, leading them to identify more strongly with pacifism, humanism, and democracy. These ideas, in continuation with the pacifist socialist feminism developed in the first half of the twentieth century, have now seen something of a resurgence in the notion of a cultural "ecofeminism," as Harting argues. The study applies various powerful approaches in order to profile the Russian and the French WLMs, giving some elements of a contextualized comparison, making use of the concept of cross-national diffusion of movement ideas developed by social movement scholars, and exploring the historical contexts that made for specific forms of reception and transformation.

The second chapter in this section reflects on the development of a new site of feminist activism—cyberspace. Johanna Niesyto charts the proliferation of diverse feminist utopian thinking, networking, social media, and subversive online arts experimentation in Germany. This radically open-ended, plural feminist activism is allied to a much sharper political agenda, regarding "net politics" and women's role within technology and net governance. Radical thinking influenced by Donna Haraway's well-known idea of the cyborg as a feminist subject position is presented through parody and irony, a feminist activism that aims to irritate, connect women, and empower women's voices online. A feminist hacker's collective founded in 1988, Haecksen is foregrounded as an example of feminist attempts to subvert and influence the production of software and increase women's presence within net forums.

Cyberfeminism, in Niesyto's account, is potentially a more subversive and transgressive form of activism than earlier feminisms. It is less wedded to existing institutions, such as local/national government or trade unions. It is angrily dismissive of the past and adopts new aesthetics and identities such as "fem-geek." It foregrounds the identity of girlhood, the idea of "pop feminism," and draws on the queer perspectives that have developed in from the 1990s. There are echoes here of zine culture and the riot grrl movement that flourished in the nineties—movements that sometimes termed themselves a "third wave" of feminism. All this seems in sharp contrast to the patient, strategic building up of resources and rights for women—the so-called "prudent revolutionaries" (Brian Harrison) of the early to mid-twentieth century. Niesyto notes the lack of sympathy toward what is perceived as "second-wave feminism" within cyberfeminist circles—this feminist phase is associated with a whinging victimhood. Yet there are more links between these very late twentieth-century developments and feminist history than are at first apparent. Cyberfeminism resembles the angry, ironic, playful feminists associated with early modernism—Mina Loy's 1919 *Feminist Manifesto* resonates with "post-humanist" cyberfeminist approaches, as does the South African/British journalist Beatrice Hastings's creation of many "avatars"—feminist and antifeminist, male and female—in her writings in the early twentieth-century modernist press.[5] The individualism evident in the German cyberfeminist sources resonates with Emma Goldman's anarchist feminism; the attempts to imagine feminist utopias has been a feature of all phases of modern feminism, and indeed is echoed in the "wild wish" of earlier activists such as Mary Wollstonecraft. The "fem-geek" may be a genuinely new subject position, offering new forms of empowerment and subjectivity that are particularly attractive to young women. Yet though the engagement with technology and the internet seems novel, we might remember that feminists have been at the forefront of new technologies, with their eager embrace of the political potential of new developments in the printing and periodical press and the liminal, empowering spaces found within new modes of transport. For all the claims about the new networking potential of the internet, scholarship such as Margaret McFadden's and Christine Bolt's accounts of the deep transatlantic connections forged by nineteenth- and twentieth-century feminists suggests that these strategies have long characterized feminism.

The influence of feminist ideas across borders is central to both chapters; the global German cyberfeminists barely occupy a national milieu, and cyberspace lends itself to an individualist disregard for national borders. Much of the content Nietsyo examines is translated into English. Yet we must also remain aware of the limits of transnationalism; it is a landscape structured by highways of strong influence, but also of dead ends and inhospitable terrain. Or to use Nancy Hewitt's provocative "radio waves" metaphor that has challenged us to rethink the contours of feminist history, transnational feminism offers some channels of clear reception and others of static, interference, or jammed broadcasts. Some elements of feminism fail to travel or are resignified by their emergence in new national contexts. The "Old Boys Network" playfully constructed by German cyberfeminists in 1997 used an English-language term that was shorn of its deep class connotations by its German activists' redeployment. Humor in general, ironic or otherwise, is clearly important as part of the feminist repertoire, yet it does not travel easily and may be read quite differently, or fail entirely, in new contexts. Overall, these chapters offer subtle, complex accounts of the development of feminism and its ability to cross national borders.

Lucy Delap is a lecturer in modern British history at the University of Cambridge and Fellow of Murray Edwards College. She works on the history of child sexual abuse and is deputy director of History & Policy. She has published widely on the history of feminism, gender, labor, and religion, including the prize-winning *The Feminist Avant-Garde: Transatlantic Encounters of the Early Twentieth Century* in 2007, *Knowing Their Place: Domestic Service in Twentieth Century Britain* in 2011, and, with Sue Morgan, *Men, Masculinities and Religious Change in Twentieth Century Britain* in 2013. She is currently working on a history of modern feminism titled *Feminism: A Useable History* (forthcoming, Penguin).

Thierry Delessert holds a PhD in political science, and is a historian. He is currently a part-time lecturer and postdoctoral researcher at the Centre for Gender Studies at the University of Lausanne, and a research assistant at the School of Public Health of the Free University of Brussels. His research domains mainly focus on the history of homosexuality in Switzerland.

Notes

1. Abigail J. Stewart, Jayati Lal, and Kristin McGuire, "Expanding the Archives of Global Feminisms: Narratives of Feminism and Activism," *Signs* 36, no. 4 (2011): 889–914.
2. Cathryn Bailey, "Making Waves and Drawing Lines: The Politics of Defining the Vissicitudes of Feminism," *Hypatia* 12, no. 3 (1997): 17–28; Catherine Harnois, "Re-presenting Feminisms: Past, Present and Future," *Feminist Formations* 20, no. 1 (2008): 120–45; Nancy Hewitt, ed., *No Permanent Waves: Recasting Histories of U.S. Feminism* (New Brunswick, NJ: Rutgers University Press, 2010); Kathleen A. Laughlin et al., "Is It Time to Jump Ship? Historians Rethink the Waves Metaphor," *Feminist Formations* 22, no.1 (2010): 76–135; in favor of a reflexive use of the wave metaphor, especially when speaking of a "third wave": Lesly Heywood and Jennifer Drake, eds., *The Third Wave Agenda: Being Feminist, Doing Feminism* (Minneapolis: University of Minnesota Press, 1997); Rory C. Dicker and Alison Piepmeier, eds., *Catching a Wave: Reclaiming Feminism for the 21st Century* (Boston: Northeastern University Press, 2003); Jo Reger, ed., *Different Wavelengths: Studies of the Contemporary Women's Movement* (New York: Routledge, 2005); and Ednie Kaeh Garrison, "Are We on a Wavelength Yet? On Feminist Oceanography, Radios, and Third Wave Feminism," in *Different Wavelengths: Studies of the Contemporary Women's Movement,* ed. Jo Reger (New York: Routledge, 2005), 237–56.
3. An early account from a movement perspective: *Sisterhood Is Global: The International Women's Movement Anthology,* ed. Robin Morgan (New York: Anchor Press/Doubleday, 1984). Cf. Amrita Basu, *The Challenge of Local Feminisms* (Boulder, CO: Westview Press, 1995); Ilse Lenz, Michiko Mae, and Karin Klose eds., *Frauenbewegung weltweit: Aufbrüche, Kontinuitäten, Veränderungen* (Opladen: Leske + Budrich, 2000); Bonnie G. Smith, *Global Feminisms since 1945* (New York: Routledge, 2000); Suki Ali, Kelly Coate, and Wangui wa Goro, eds., *Global Feminist Politics: Identities in a Changing World* (New York: Routledge, 2000); Bonnie G. Smith, ed., *The Oxford Encyclopedia of Women in World History,* 4 vols. (Oxford: Oxford University Press, 2008); Ann Taylor Allen, Anne Cova, and June Purvis, eds., "Special Issue International Feminisms," *Women's History Review* 19, no. 4 (2010).
4. Kathy Davis and Mary Evans, eds., *Transatlantic Conversations: Feminism as a Travelling Theory* (Farnham: Ashgate, 2011); see also Kathy E. Davis, *The Making of* Our Bodies, Ourselves*: How Feminism Travels across Borders* (Durham, NC: Duke University Press, 2007).
5. Benjamin Johnson and Erika Jo Brown, eds., *Beatrice Hastings: On the Life and Work of a Lost Modern Master* (Warrensburg, MO: Pleiades Press, 2016).

Bibliography

Ali, Suki, Kelly Coate, and Wangui wa Goro, eds. *Global Feminist Politics: Identities in a Changing World.* New York: Routledge, 2000.

Allen, Ann Taylor, Anne Cova, and June Purvis, eds. "Special Issue International Feminisms." *Women's History Review* 19, no. 4 (2010).

Bailey, Cathryn. "Making Waves and Drawing Lines: The Politics of Defining the Vicissitudes of Feminism." *Hypatia* 12, no. 3 (1997): 17–28.

Basu, Amrita. *The Challenge of Local Feminisms.* Boulder, CO: Westview Press, 1995.

Bolt, Christine. *Sisterhood Questioned? Race, Class and Internationalism in the American and British Women's Movements, c. 1800s–1970s.* London: Routledge, 2004.

Davis, Kathy. *The Making of* Our Bodies, Ourselves*: How Feminism Travels across Borders.* Durham, NC: Duke University Press, 2007.

Davis, Kathy, and Mary Evans, eds. *Transatlantic Conversations: Feminism as a Travelling Theory.* Farnham: Ashgate, 2011.

Dicker, Rory C., and Alison Piepmeier, eds. *Catching a Wave: Reclaiming Feminism for the 21st Century.* Boston: Northeastern University Press, 2003.

Garrison, Ednie Kaeh. "Are We on a Wavelength Yet? On Feminist Oceanography, Radios, and Third Wave Feminism." In *Different Wavelengths: Studies of the Contemporary Women's Movement,* edited by Jo Reger, 237–256. New York: Routledge, 2005.

Harnois, Catherine. "Re-presenting Feminisms: Past, Present and Future." *Feminist Formations* 20, no.1 (2008): 120–45.

Harrison, Brian. *Prudent Revolutionaries: Portraits of British Feminists between the Wars.* Oxford: Clarendon Press, 1987.

Hewitt, Nancy A., ed. *No Permanent Waves: Recasting Histories of U.S. Feminism.* New Brunswick, NJ: Rutgers University Press, 2010.

Heywood, Lesly, and Jennifer Drake, eds. *The Third Wave Agenda: Being Feminist, Doing Feminism.* Minneapolis: University of Minnesota Press, 1997.

Johnson, Benjamin, and Erika Jo Brown, eds. *Beatrice Hastings: On the Life and Work of a Lost Modern Master.* Warrensburg, MO: Pleiades Press, 2016.

Laughlin, Kathleen A., et al. "Is It Time to Jump Ship? Historians Rethink the Waves Metaphor." *Feminist Formations* 22, no. 1 (2010): 76–135.

Lenz, Ilse, Michiko Mae, and Karin Klose, eds. *Frauenbewegung weltweit: Aufbrüche, Kontinuitäten, Veränderungen.* Opladen: Leske + Budrich, 2000.

Loy, Mina. *Feminist Manifesto. Modernism: An Anthology of Sources and Documents. E. K. e. al.* Edinburgh: Edinburgh University Press, 1998.

McFadden, Margaret. H. *Golden Cables of Sympathy: The Transatlantic Sources of Nineteenth-Century Feminism.* Lexington: University Press of Kentucky, 1999.

Morgan, Robin, ed. *Sisterhood Is Global: The International Women's Movement Anthology.* New York: Anchor Press/Doubleday, 1984.

Reger, Jo, ed. *Different Wavelengths: Studies of the Contemporary Women's Movement.* New York: Routledge, 2005.

Smith, Bonnie G. *Global Feminisms since 1945.* New York: Routledge, 2000.

———, ed. *The Oxford Encyclopedia of Women in World History.* 4 vols. Oxford: Oxford University Press, 2008.

Stewart, Abigail J., Jayati Lal, and Kristin McGuire. "Expanding the Archives of Global Feminisms: Narratives of Feminism and Activism." *Signs* 36, no. 4 (2011): 889–914.

Chapter 12

Echoes of Ourselves?

Feminisms between East and West in the Leningrad Almanac *Woman and Russia*

Kirsten Harting

Moscow in winter 1976: a boycott of the international book fair rages in protest against the violation of human rights in Soviet Russia. The Parisian feminist publishers *Des Femmes* had arrived nonetheless. "The burden of the forbidden is ubiquitous, virtually tangible, everywhere,"[1] the feminist activist Michèle Idels reports afterward. And yet, the French feminist publishers contact the Soviet women; they converse, the French women pass on books, "and an exchange emerges"—an exchange whose impact becomes visible a few years later: in 1979, Michèle Idels and two fellow activists from the feminist group *Psychanalyse et Politique* (*Psych et Po*) returned to Russia, this time headed for Leningrad. In the informal circles of the dissident culture, a group of women had published a small booklet of texts, the almanac *Woman and Russia.*[2] The "first independent journal destined for women"[3] comprised letters, essays, and poems criticizing the situation of women in Soviet Russia. When the Soviet women showed her the literature that had inspired the collection, Idels recognized the books she had taken with her to Moscow three years before—"books that we distributed and that, from hand to hand, reached them."[4]

Michèle Idels's report of this encounter describes a transfer of Western feminist texts to Soviet Russia in the late 1970s. Although she makes no explicit mention of this, we may well presume that Western feminist ideas were adapted by a faction of Soviet dissident culture, where they gave rise to—or fed into a nascent—feminist consciousness, which materialized in the publishing of the almanac *Woman and Russia.* In January 1980 the headline of the journal of *Psych et Po* read, "The Birth of a Women's Liberation Movement in Soviet Russia."[5] Idels and her comrades report on their trips to Moscow and Leningrad, where they had familiarized the Soviet activists with their "practice of the women's liberation movement."[6] Coverage on the Leningrad women continues in the following month, and particularly so when four of the almanac's contributors are expelled from the Soviet Union in early summer of the same year. The journal *Des femmes en mouvements hebdo* translates and publishes the articles collected in the almanac and calls for international solidarity with the Russian women activists, who designate the beginning of a women's movement in the USSR "which echoes our own."[7]

Across the texts of the almanac, this "echo" of Western feminist ideas dispels into a virtual polyphony of "echoes." More than any other contributor, it is the writer Tatyana Mamonova who analyzes the situation of Soviet women within the conceptual and terminological frameworks familiar from many contemporaneous Western feminist discourses in France, Germany, or the United States, to name but a few.[8] Mamonova criticizes the patriarchal, male-dominated Soviet society whose "phallocracy" oppresses all female values.[9] In other contributions to the almanac, however, the alleged "echo" of Western feminist ideas is not only so faint as to be barely detectable, but those ideas seem to be well-nigh turned on their head: Tatyana Goritcheva's suggestion to the Soviet women, for instance, is to embrace an austere, orthodox lifestyle oriented by the Virgin Mary: "The Mother of God is the incarnated femininity,"[10] declares Goritcheva. Accordingly, she defines chastity before marriage and maternity as the most important features of a woman's life. From the perspective of Western feminism at that time, fighting for women's right to self-determination, bodily and sexual autonomy, including the legislation of abortion and for a profound transformation of societal sex roles, this position must have seemed at best bizarre, downright outrageous at worst.

Who was this group of Leningrad women and what were their motives for writing such texts? Is it correct if the French feminist group *Psych et Po* identified their activities as the beginning of a women's movement aligned with contemporaneous Western feminist movements? In pursuit of these questions, this chapter starts out by briefly sketching the personal, social, and intellectual backgrounds of three major activist-writers and their publishing in exile; second, the almanac will be examined as a feminist text within three intersecting interpretive frameworks: first, its significance for the authors as an independent platform for publishing; second, the degree of import of Western feminist ideas, concepts, and explanatory frameworks as, on the one hand, opposed to, and on the other, enmeshed with specific Russian streaks of feminism; finally, the publishing up to the present of one of the authors, Tatyana Mamonova, who continued her work in exile. It will be hypothesized that although it nods toward Western feminist theory, Mamonova's own writing still displays a distinct Russian variant of feminism, which was later termed "Russofeminism." I will then go on to show how she continued to develop this particular fusion of Eastern and Western feminist thought in European and US exile.

For these purposes the so-called almanacs of the Soviet women written in Leningrad and continued in exile later on will be, on the one hand, considered in the broader context of their social background, the dissident culture and their subsequent lives in exile.[11] On the other hand the almanacs will be studied in terms of their entanglement with Western feminist text at that time.[12] Therefore this chapter studies French feminist journals of the 1970s and 1980s, especially the journal *Des femmes en mouvements hebdo* published by *Psych et Po.*[13]

Social Background: The Dissident Movement

For Tatyana Mamonova, Tatyana Goritcheva, Julia Voznesenskaya, and a couple of other authors of the almanac *Woman and Russia,* the most important social, political, and intellectual formative force of their feminist activism was the Leningrad dissident culture—a sphere of informal contacts between writers, artists, and musicians whose ideas did not conform to official Soviet doctrines.[14] "The almanac *Woman and Russia* sees itself as part of the dissident movement," said Mamonova in an interview with a French feminist journal in 1980, "but it is also a feminist protest against the dissident's phallocracy."[15] Born in 1943, Mamonova joined the informal circles of Leningrad in the late 1960s after several frustrated attempts to advance as a writer in the regime-compliant journal *Aurora* and as an artist in officially sanctioned expositions.[16] Before first learning about Western feminist ideas, she took a vivid interest in Russian women's history and studied the lives of Catherine the Great, Alexandra Kollontai, etc. While working for *Aurora,* she tried in vain to get in touch with the president of the Soviet Women's Committee, the governmentally sanctioned women's organization, and repeatedly applied for membership—to no avail.[17]

But the dissident community, to which she tried to introduce her feminist ideas through publishing her art and poetry, also disappointed her. In an interview with a French feminist magazine, she stated that the majority of dissidents, including the avant-garde, did not take her seriously as an equal: "Gradually, I became aware that the same phallocratic spirit, the same disdain for women, prevailed among the 'conformists' and the 'dissidents' alike. ... Within dissident culture, it is more hidden, more veiled, but existent nonetheless."[18]

Obviously, Mamonova did not feel accepted within the dissident circles because of her gender. This individual experience speaks to the wider gender inequities in Soviet dissident culture explicated by Anke Stefan. Her analysis reveals feminine roles that were largely envisaged to perform the male dissidents' groundwork: typing, passing on information, and generally assisting the male dissident writers and artists—in underground and prison. Hence, women were regarded as "adjuncts" of the (male) dissidents rather than activists in their own right. Clearly, the active, public fight against the official doctrines of the regime was regarded as the terrain—and privilege—of men and as noncompliant with the feminine role.[19]

Like Mamonova, other contributors to the almanac were part of the Leningrad dissident culture as well. Julia Voznesenskaya was one of the central figures in the literary underground circles. Nicknamed the "mother of the poets," she supported young writers, organized lectures and exhibitions in her own apartment, and translated and published texts—which, for the most part, she did not author but distributed for others—as samizdat copies. Inside the dissident community, Voznesenskaya was thus rather known and recognized as a supporter of samizdat poets than as a writer in her own right. Between 1976 and 1979, she was arrested several times because of her participation in the human rights movement and was imprisoned in a labor camp for two years.[20]

Tatyana Goritcheva studied philosophy at Leningrad University and chaired a philosophical-religious seminar in the dissident community from 1974 onwards.[21] Tracing her intellectual career up until today, it can be said that her religious orthodoxy increased after her expulsion from the Soviet Union. But even before, her analytical take on the situation of women was clearly informed by her deeply orthodox faith.

Between Western Terminology and Russian Meanings

The broad-brush sketch of these three women's feminist contributions and identities points us to at least three major dimensions of meaning at play in the almanac *Woman and Russia.* First, the almanac was a platform open to women only. The authors created this opportunity to publish their own texts, which did not meet with any acceptance either in official Soviet culture or the dissident one. Julia Voznesenskaya's letters from prison are a case in point: although she does not theorize Russian women's situation in a systematically feminist way, she takes a decidedly gendered perspective in reporting from the Soviet women's labor camps and criticizing the inhumane conditions the inmates were subjected to. Living in Germany after her expulsion, she continued writing fictional texts, calling herself a "women writer."[22] For Voznesenskaya, but also for the other women, the almanac thus presented an ideal platform to voice their own concerns freely and fashion themselves as self-contained without and beyond male influence. Extending beyond its function as a liberating mouthpiece for its authors, the almanac monopolized a subject matter—women's situation in the Soviet Union—hitherto completely disregarded by men, and therefore it can be read as a strategy to gain its female authors a certain visibility, recognition, and reputation.[23] Looking at the writers' careers in exile, it is probably safe to say that their status as expatriated female dissidents boosted their publicity even on an international level: Mamonova continued publishing the almanac, first in cooperation with *Des Femmes* in Paris, later in New York under the title *Woman and Earth Almanac.* Voznesenskaya wrote a couple of fictional women's books before turning toward religious literature;[24] Goritcheva concentrated on religious literature only, comparing, for instance, religious attitudes in Western Europe to Soviet beliefs and practices.[25]

Hence, the authors of the almanac were, on the one hand, part of Leningrad dissident culture, inasmuch as they were involved in and profited from its structures of informal communication and publication, not least of course in creating and publishing the almanac. On the other hand, the almanac represented a process and product of liberation and emancipation from the male-dominated dissident circles—a feminist protest against them even. There are notable parallels here, for example to French women's movements, which first grew as part of the student movement before splitting off to pursue their own cause.[26] Considering the very short period of the almanac group's activism due to the persecution by the Soviet authorities and the eventual expulsion of its protagonists, the women around Momonova, Voznesenkaya, and Goritcheva can be designated no more and no less than the frail beginning of a social movement of women. Yet for the most part their ideas did not correspond to and even contradicted Western feminist concepts, as will be shown in more detail.

The second semiotic dimension of the almanac is the "echo" of Western feminist ideas, which are most frequently referred to by Tatyana Mamonova. Her analysis of the patriarchal Soviet society where "phallocracy" oppresses all feminine values is evident of her familiarity with Western feminist texts and ideas. Among the almanac group, Mamonova can be seen as the protagonist of the transfer of Western feminist terminology and concepts.

In autobiographical writings dated 1980 as well as in recent ones, she portrays her feminism as a direct response to her experiences as a girl and woman in Soviet society, first in her family regulated by tight patriarchal structures, where Mamonova had to perform the traditional female role of doing all the domestic chores. She recalls early resentment for and resistance against these oppressive structures.[27] A second formative experience was the inhumane conditions in a Soviet maternity hospital where she gave birth to her son; hence her criticism of a society that demands motherhood as a service—("If you are not a mother … you are an old maid or a slut"[28]) and yet disavows any respect for or appreciation of mothers. Mamonova's description of pregnancy and childbirth as a painful and humiliating experience is reminiscent of one of the core critiques advanced by Western feminists at that time: the female body that is not fully inhabited and determined by the agent herself but can be disposed of and objectified at will by a patriarchal society. Third, her bisexuality, which she already lived openly in Leningrad, seems to have influenced her feminist ideas. In the almanac Mamonova demands respect for homosexual lifestyles and the varieties of sexual identities.[29]

While all three authors portrayed in this chapter criticize a society dominated by male values and oppressive of femininity, Mamonova describes the origins of this situation from a Western feminist perspective. She defines patriarchy—meaning in this context the domination of men and masculine values—as the root of societal ills, rather than the "Soviet" social structures criticized by her colleagues, as this chapter will later demonstrate.[30] However, there is a characteristic tension between her application of Western feminist *terminology* and actual intellectual *content*, the latter of which is decisively shaped by her particular experience as a woman in Soviet Russia.

The articles by Tatyana Goritcheva indicate knowledge of Western feminist ideas as well. "One is not born, but rather becomes, a woman," she cites Simone de Beauvoir's famous sentence, but continues in a different way: "which is incredibly difficult in our society of hermaphrodites."[31] In contrast to de Beauvoir, Goritcheva does not take this insight into the social construction of gender as her cue for a forceful critique of oppressive societal roles and values assigned to women but turns it on its head by bemoaning the lack of a clear, intelligible gender order in the Soviet Union.

This leads over to the third important issue related to the almanac, namely its interpretation of femininity and the unequal situation of women in society in a way that obviously differs from most Western feminisms in the 1970s. In interviews and publications after their expulsion, Julia Voznesenskaya and Tatyana Goritcheva, whose texts reflect this difference at its starkest, label this unique variety "our Russian 'feminism'"[32] in response to the obvious perplexity of the French and German feminist interviewers. For Goritcheva and Voznesenskaya, the domination of masculine values in society results from a very different deficiency than that made out by Mamonova: to them, the origins of the inequality between men and women are firmly implicated in the Soviet system and its authoritarian structures. Goritcheva's analysis of the "asexual homo soviéticus"[33] implies that Soviet people are too other-directed and alienated from themselves to develop their "natural" personality, including their sexuality. As a consequence of this denied maturation, men lose their masculinity—"the infantile man"[34]—and women have to abandon all their feminine traits. Voznesenskaya uses the metaphor of the sterilized society whose people had to relinquish not only their sexual identities but also emotions and love in general.[35]

While their colleague refuses the old, prerevolutionary traditions, Goritcheva and Voznesenskaya embrace them as the right path to societal change. For Voznesenskaya, spirituality, self-reflection, and the adherence to Christian values will lead to a renaissance of mythical "old Russia."[36] Goritcheva presents the Virgin Mary as the ideal role model for women: living in chastity until marriage and being a devoted mother. While this conception has an alarmingly antifeminist ring to it, its explication reveals a more critical stance: "Nothing impure could touch her."[37] Rather than as a religious feminine role model, the Virgin Mary should be understood here as a symbolic space, which grants women protection from male (sexual) harassment, abuse, and violence.[38]

The authors' different approaches to explaining the unequal and inhumane conditions women were subject to are part of a wider ideological division in Soviet society about the direction of Russian development. Would Russia adopt the same ideas of progress and development as the West or pursue its own, particular Russian form of development?[39] The Soviet dissident culture accommodated adherents of both movements, often designated as "Slavophiles" and "Westernizers" respectively in research literature.[40] Mamonova does not object to communism as such; indeed, she appreciates the Leninist approach to women's liberation in the 1920s, before the conservative backlash under Stalin reestablished patriarchal traditions.[41] Mamonova is opposed to a strong, rigidly hierarchical Orthodox Church and suffers from "the weight of tradition and fossilized mentalities."[42] With her nod toward Western feminist ideas and her insistence on an international solidarity between feminists in order to "draw women out of their isolation,"[43] she thus represents the Western-orientated stream. Voznesenskaya and Goritcheva instead demand the rebirth of the prerevolutionary Russia glorifying the orthodox lifestyle. Representing the "Slavophile" stream in the almanac, they refuse forms of feminism practiced in Western societies at that time. In their reasoning, their integration into or even adaptation to Soviet society is doomed to fail, for their values and objectives do not correspond to the social realities of Soviet women.[44]

Although the authors analyze societal problems in divergent ways, their ideas of femininity are remarkably similar. All of them follow an essentialist, biologistic approach in tracking what they deem the inherent qualities of women back to their "nature": "It is in a woman's nature that she is self-sacrificing,"[45] Mamonova writes while simultaneously criticizing the abuse of women as birth-giving machines. For Mamonova, a range of secondary qualities can be deduced from this assumed natural predisposition of women, most importantly their pacifist, democratic and humanist character; accordingly, the women's movement can be seen as the harbinger of a fully realized humanism.[46] In a similar vein, Voznesenskaya and Goritcheva underline the spirituality of women. All three activist-writers envision a certain ideal of feminine looks and appearance, as contemplated by Goritcheva through that ideal's antithesis, the "femina sovietica": "a sturdy face, a rough-hewn, priggish countenance, wiry hair and two glass beads instead of eyes."[47] The authors of the almanac agree on the ideal of a "natural," essential femininity that is oppressed in Soviet society. Against this background it becomes understandable why Tatyana Mamonova was acutely interested in the journal *Des femmes en mouvements* published by *Psych et Po*: the Parisian feminist group practiced a variety of "sexual-difference feminism" dedicated to retrieving femininity and "the feminine" in society, especially in literature and art.[48]

This particular idea of "natural" femininity and essential female values like altruism and pacifism that Tatyana Goritcheva calls "our Russian 'feminism'"[49] and that all three women subscribe to can be interpreted as the reflection of a cultural paradigm going back a long way in Russian cultural history. It is the idea of the female in the role of the altruistic protector of the family and the community, which is embodied in the symbolic representation of Rossiya-Matushka, "Mother Russia." In this context—or, one could add, within these confines—women are considered respectable and unassailable beings.[50] According to Norma C. Noonan, this traditional conception of Russian women that was at odds with the actual situation of most women in the Soviet Union created a specific idea of women's liberation in the 1970s and 1980s that also pervades the almanac and that Noonan terms "Russofeminism."[51] In stark contrast to their Western counterparts, the Soviet feminists did not want to equate women completely with men in all societal spheres, they did not need to fight for the legalization of abortion, and they did not need to define and campaign for other female roles than the mother role: in the Soviet Union, all these gains had (officially) already been realized.[52] Voznesenskaya, Goritcheva, Mamonova, and their fellows had thus already experienced what passed as a socialist women's liberation, and they criticized the social obligation to work under equal conditions as men in the public sphere, especially when the traditional conception of wife and mother, which entailed performing domestic work and child-rearing alone—on top of paid employment—remained barely unchanged. They hold the socialist system responsible for the glaring shortage of any public facilities that would relieve working women, such as nursery schools, day care, medical care for mothers and children, but also of consumer goods. For them the disregard of the female body was, for example, illustrated in the maternity and abortion hospitals where women suffered from insufficient birth support and brutal mass abortions.[53] In the light of such experiences—the other side of officially heralded emancipation of women—it seems comprehensible why certain, often more traditional concepts of femininity, such as the reclamation of the mother role as a relief from their "double burden" and the revalorization of "feminine" values and the female body, appealed to many Soviet women.

The Feminine Principle

Despite their shared idea of an essential femininity, their different visions of Russian development and their respective feminist implications led quite soon to the split of the almanac group. Already in Leningrad, Voznesenskaya and Goritcheva created the journal *Maria*[54] that corresponded more closely to religious orthodoxy; as expatriates in Germany and France, they also concentrated their further writings on religious questions. Conversely, Tatyana Mamonova has continued her feminist work until today. Until 1984, she published three further volumes of the almanac in France in cooperation with the feminist publisher *Des femmes* and the rather mainstream house *Denoel/Gonthier.*[55] Then she moved with her family to New York City, where her status as a Soviet dissident feminist imbued her, as in Paris before, with a certain celebrity. In retrospect, Mamonova describes her situation inside the different national feminist movements as "a sensational fighting over the right to claim the discovery of feminism in Russia."[56] Already in 1980 she had participated in the reading tour of the American feminist *Ms.* magazine.[57] Four years later, she contributed an article about Russian women to the anthology *Sisterhood Is Global.*[58] Mamonova was also invited to give guest lectures at high-ranking academic institutions, such as the Bunting Institute in Harvard, the University of Michigan, and the Women's Research Institute at Hartford College for Women. They resulted in her subsequently published books *Russian Women's Studies: Essays on Sexism in Soviet Culture* and *Women's Glasnost vs. Naglost: Stopping Russian Backlash,*[59] in which she discusses women's situation in Russia from the perspective of American women's and gender studies. Mamonova intensified her opposition to the "Slavophile" streams in (Soviet) Russia and especially to their orthodox and homophobic thought. To her, contemporaneous Russian feminism as personified by the *Maria* group "becomes a victim of the illusion of [prerevolutionary, religious] 'revival.'"[60] Although Mamonova ostensibly draws on a rich body of feminist and gender research, merely a low degree of theory and abstraction can be found in her written analyses of Russian women's situation. Reviews criticize Mamonova's personal approach to her material and the limited "logical development or theoretical reflection."[61] Perhaps as a consequence of such reactions, but motivated also by her personal inclination to a more activist and independent way of publishing, Mamonova started the publication of her own periodical *Woman and Earth*[62] in 1993, which she explicitly places in the tradition of the Leningrad *Woman and Russia* almanac. Above and beyond that, she maintains the Woman and Earth Global Eco-Network, or WE.

In Mamonova's work to date, at least two crucial feminist ideas are remarkably consistent. First, there is her permanent emphasis on the international solidarity of women. As early as 1984, in the context of "global sisterhood" demanded by many activist groups of second-wave feminism, she imagined an international feminist union of solidarity with the women in Soviet Russia.[63] Mamonova continues to stress the importance of international solidarity today. According to the mission statements of the *Woman and Russia* almanac and *Woman and Earth,* they pursue two related objectives, which are to prepare and distribute information about radical and ecofeminist thought to the women in Russia and post-Soviet countries and to explain these women's experiences to women in Western societies. Thus, the function of *Woman and Earth* is to provide a connection based on exchange between East and West.[64] It is not too far-fetched to suggest that her concern for internationality and transnational communication of women's experience is a reflection of Mamonova's personal situation as an expatriate from her native country and a long-time stateless person. Although Mamonova described and evaluated her situation in a positive light ("I was very happy being a citizen of the world for all these years"[65]), other statements are telling of her distress, frustration, and disorientation at belonging nowhere:

> In Austria they tell me I'm not Austrian, in France not French, and in America not American. When at one point my friends turned to the Jewish Immigrant Fund for aid for me … it was ascertained that I was not Jewish. To the Soviet Union I am not Russian (or else why would they have exiled me?)—so who am I? Where can I turn?[66]

Transferring this record of experience hypothetically to the development of Voznesenskaya's and Goritcheva's work, it could be assumed that their increasing orthodoxy in exile is a reaction to their expatriate status as well, an alternative way of defining and reclaiming their own identity.

The second pervasive characteristic of Mamonova's feminism until today is the idea of an essential and "natural" femininity, as defined earlier in this article as the shared thought of the Leningrad almanac group. The contributions in her still-running *Woman and Earth* indicate the integration of such an essentialist conception of femininity with more recent ideas of cultural ecofeminism. The starting point of cultural ecofeminism is the deep connectivity between nature and "woman" primarily constituted by the womb and the capacity of bearing children, which is the reason why proponents of cultural ecofeminism attribute to women a higher degree of sensitivity and sense of responsibility for nature and the environment than to men. Stemming from this basic insight, they emphasize and glorify the "natural" female character and women's superior ethics and moral values in comparison with men, most importantly pacifism, humanism, and democratic zeal. Just like the authors of the Leningrad group, cultural ecofeminism obviously proceeds from underlying biologistic concepts of human being and character, as a result of which this stream of feminist thought demands a matriarchal society where feminine values dominate.[67]

Asked about the influences on the development of her own feminist ideas and convictions, Mamonova mentions the anthropologists Ashley Montagu and Elizabeth Gould Davis. In *The Natural Superiority of Women,* Montagu analyzed what he deemed biological and physical—i.e. genetic—characteristics of women, concluding with a firm denial of their "natural" inferiority and a plea for the benefit of the domination of feminine values.[68] Gould Davis analyzed ancient matriarchal societies and contrasted their "pacifist" and "civilized" lifestyle with that of patriarchal societies.[69] A well-known proponent of current ecofeminism is the scholar Riane Eisler, who set the patriarchal model of "dominator model" against the matriarchal model of "partnership culture."[70] Like a number of other contemporary ecofeminists, Eisler frequently publishes in the periodical *Woman and Earth* and significantly shapes its theoretical orientation.

It stands to reason that in France and the United States alike, Mamonova joined in those Western feminist movements that were and are most dedicated to the idea of an essential, positive femininity—what Mamonova today terms "the Feminine Principle"[71]—by first establishing and maintaining close contact to *Psych et Po* in Paris, which practiced a pronounced feminism of difference, and later on by adopting cultural ecofeminist thought in American exile. The genuinely feminine responsibility for nature and society stressed by ecofeminism sits comfortably with the ideas developed by the Leningrad group in 1979, which defined humanism and pacifism as "natural" female values. Until today, Tatyana Mamonova's feminist work is characterized by a discourse that corresponds to a considerable degree to traditional Russian conceptions of femininity and the "feminine mission"—the influential maternal symbol of Rossiya-Mathuska lives on. Against this background,

Mamonova's designation as the most Western-orientated author represented in *Woman and Russia* has to be qualified. On her transnational trajectory from Leningrad to Paris to New York, she has certainly adopted streaks of Western feminist thought, yet she has selected, reassembled, and interpreted them in a way that is strongly reminiscent of her native sociocultural and intellectual context.

Conclusion

So what about the Western feminist "echo" that the French feminist publishers from *Des femmes* had noticed in the almanac *Woman and Russia* in 1980? In this chapter I have tried to demonstrate that this echo was not only faint but always superseded by other localized, culturally and intellectually distinct women's voices. After the expulsion of the authors, the *Maria* group existed only for a couple of months in Leningrad, but then dissolved. Tatyana Mamonova received little response from her colleagues still in Leningrad and continued her feminist work for the Soviet women from exile abroad. Although the background of the extensive media coverage on the "Leningrad feminists" cannot be analyzed in any depth at this point, it is certainly noteworthy that not only *Psych et Po* but also other French, European, and American feminist journals literally competed for the first interview, for the most enthusiastic declarations of "global sisterhood" solidarity, and for publishing rights of the almanac. In any case, this "sensational fighting over the right to claim the discovery of feminism in Russia,"[72] as Mamonova phrases it in hindsight, might well be regarded as an example of the often reported misunderstanding or discordance between feminisms in the East and West.[73] *Psych et Po* were especially preoccupied with promoting their own image as an internationally active, avant-garde feminist network through the support of and solidarity with the Leningrad women, while not being aware of or interested in the distinct cultural and gender identities and experiences of Soviet women.[74] Regarding the disputes and competitions between different feminist groups in France in the 1970s and 1980s (in an ideological way about the definition of feminism but at the same time in pragmatic terms of public recognition and the struggle about followers and supporters), the support, promotion, and incorporation of the Soviet almanac women by *Psych et Po* can be interpreted as a "survival strategy" of their feminist group. Using the analytical framework of Charles Tilly, we can say that *Psych et Po* pursued an "expansive trajectory strategy" by expanding their activism on an international level.[75] Also, the attempt of *Psych et Po* to register the MLF (*Mouvement de Libération des Femmes*) as an association, i.e. to institutionalize their movement, can be seen as an attempt to score another coup of their "expansive trajectory strategy."[76] *Psych et Po* interpreted the almanac *Woman and Russia* from their hegemonic Western feminist perspective, which was manifest in the supposition that women's needs, experiences, and strategies for liberation and equality were monolithic, independent of the manifold localities women were and are embedded in, whether in France or in the Soviet Union. Therefore the almanac *Woman and Russia* and its interpretations are but one example for the transnational empowerment of women through the exchange of ideas and material and moral support, but just as well an example for the misunderstandings between feminists of different cultures.

Kirsten Harting focused on Gender and Women's Studies in the Soviet Union while studying at the University of Bielefeld, the Yaroslavl State Pedagogical University, and Paris Diderot University (2007–2014). She currently works in the field of science communications.

Notes

1. All translations from French to English in this essay are provided by the author and are therefore her sole responsibility. I am grateful to Ronja Waldherr for her great support. Michèle Idels, "Les Éditions *Des femmes* à Moscou," in *Génération MLF 1968–2008,* ed. Antoinette Fouque (Paris: Des femmes, 2008), 199.
2. This essay works with the French translation of the almanac: *Femmes et Russie* (Paris: Des femmes, 1980).
3. Collectif de rédaction, "Appel," in *Femmes et Russie,* 136.
4. Idels, "Les Éditions *Des femmes* à Moscou," 199.
5. *Des femmes en mouvements hebdo,* no. 10 (1980).
6. Ibid., 7.
7. Preface by the editors, in *Femmes et Russie,* 9.
8. Good overviews of the different streams inside the manifold second-wave feminisms with an emphasis on France are provided by: Dominique Fougeyrollas-Schwebel, "Le féminisme des années 1970," in *Nouvelle encyclopédie politique et historique des femmes,* ed. Christine Fauré (Paris: Les Belles Lettres, 2010); Ingrid Galster, "Französischer Feminismus: Zum Verhältnis von Egalität und Differenz," in *Handbuch Frauen- und Geschlechterforschung: Theorie, Methoden, Empirie,* ed. Ruth Becker et al., 2nd ed. (Wiesbaden: VS Verlag, 2004), 45–51.
9. Collectif de rédaction, "Ces bons vieux fondements du patriarcat," in *Femmes et Russie,* 19–26.
10. Tatiana Goritcheva, "Délivrée des larmes d'Eve, réjouis-toi!," in *Femmes et Russie,* 27.
11. The almanacs published in Leningrad and immediately after the expulsion of the authors were translated and published in cooperation with the French feminist group *Psych et Po,* later with the publisher Denoël/Gonthier: *Femmes et Russie* (Paris: Des femmes, 1980); *Des femmes russes* (Paris: Des femmes, 1980); *Maria: Journal du Club*

féministe 'Maria' de Léningrad (Paris: Des femmes, 1981); Tatyana Mamonova, ed., *Voix de femmes en Russie* (Paris: Denoël/Gonthier, 1982). The books published in exile are in the case of Mamonova published by academic publishing houses: Tatyana Mamonova, ed., *Women's Glasnost vs. Naglost: Stopping Russian Backlash* (Westport, CT: Bergin & Garvey, 1994); Tatyana Mamonova, ed., *Russian Women's Studies: Essays on Sexism in Soviet Culture* (Oxford: Pergamon Press, 1989). Her *Woman and Earth Almanac* is published independently: Tatyana Mamonova, ed., *Woman and Earth Almanac* (New York: Woman and Earth Press, 1993–2013). The author had the pleasure to enrich its material by interviewing Tatyana Mamonova in June–July 2013 via e-mail. The author would like to thank Tatyana Mamonova for the captivating and inspiring dialogue. Tatiana Goritcheva continued publishing with the German Catholic publisher Herder: Tatiana Goritcheva, *Von Gott zu reden ist gefährlich: Meine Erfahrungen im Osten und im Westen* (Freiburg: Herder, 1984); Tatiana Goritcheva, *Hiobs Töchter* (Freiburg: Herder, 1988); Tatiana Goritcheva, *Nur Gott kann Russland retten: Aufzeichnungen in bewegten Zeiten* (Freiburg: Herder, 1990). Julia Voznesenskaya continued publishing with Lev Roitman: Julia Voznesenskaya, *Briefe über die Liebe: Von Frauen in Haft und Verbannung* (Munich: Roitman, 1987); Julia Voznesenskaya, *Das Frauen-Dekameron* (Munich: Roitman, 1985).

12. This chapter follows the approaches of cultural transfer and *histoire croisée*: Michel Espagne and Michael Werner, *Transferts: Relations interculturelles dans l'espace franco-allemand (XVIII–XIX siècles)* (Paris: Recherche sur les Civilisations, 1988); Michael Werner and Bénédicte Zimmermann, eds., "Penser l'histoire croisée: entre empirie et réflexivité," in *Les Annales: Histoire, Sciences Sociales* 1, no. 58 (2003): 7–36.
13. The Bibliothèque Marguerite Durand à Paris maintains an archive of feminist journals, also *Des femmes en mouvements hebdo* and *Questions féministes.*
14. Anke Stefan's study of female Soviet dissidents devotes a whole chapter to the authors of the almanac; see Anke Stephan, *Von der Küche auf den Roten Platz: Lebenswege sowjetischer Dissidentinnen* (Zurich: Pano, 2005), and also Cecilie Vaissié, *Pour votre liberté et pour la notre: Le combat des dissidences de Russie* (Paris: Robert Laffont, 1999), 10–12.
15. Martine Storti, "Tatiana Mamonova l'exil pour cause de féminisme," in *F Magazine,* no. 30 (1980): 33.
16. Tatyana Mamonova, "Autobiographie," in *Des femmes russes,* 11.
17. Cf. Anna Köbberling, *Zwischen Liquidation und Wiedergeburt: Frauenbewegung in Rußland von 1917 bis heute* (Frankfurt: Campus, 1993), 72–78.
18. Storti, "Tatiana Mamonova l'exil pour cause de feminism," 33.
19. Cf. Stephan, *Von der Küche,* 494–99.
20. Julie Curtis, "Iuliia Voznesenskaia," in *Women and Russian Culture,* ed. Rosalind Marsh (New York: Berghahn Books, 1998), 173–77
21. Cf. Stephan, *Von der Küche,* 429–30.
22. Voznesenskaya, *Briefe über die Liebe,* 9.
23. Nicole Racine and Michel Trebitsch, "Présentation," in *Intellectuelles: Du genre en histoire des intellectuels,* ed. Nicole Racine and Michel Trebitsch (Brussels: Éditions Complexes, 2004), 28–33.

24. Voznesenskaya, *Das Frauen-Dekameron* and *Briefe über die Liebe.*
25. Goritcheva, *Von Gott zu reden ist gefährlich*; Goritcheva, *Hiobs Töchter*; Goritcheva, *Nur Gott kann Russland retten.*
26. Cf. Kristina Schulz, "Macht und Mythos von '1968': Zur Bedeutung der 68er Protestbewegung für die Formierung der neuen Frauenbewegung in Frankreich und Deutschland," in *1968—Vom Ereignis zum Mythos,* ed. Ingrid Gilcher-Holtey (Frankfurt: Suhrkamp, 2008), 350–57.
27. Cf. Anna Jakovleva, "Tretuja kultura: Feminizm—eta ja.," interview with Tatyana Mamonova, June 6, 2011, http://www.chaskor.ru/article/tretya_kultura__23644 (accessed April 16, 2013).
28. Tatyana Mamonova, "Accoucher dans le monde des hommes," in *Femmes et Russie,* 47.
29. Cf. Tatyana Mamonova, "À propos de la libération sexuelle," in *Des femmes russes,* 75–83.
30. Collectif de rédaction, "Ces bons vieux fondements du patriarcat," 19–26.
31. Tatyana Goritcheva, "Des sourcières dans l'espace," in *Maria,* 55.
32. Goritcheva, *Von Gott zu reden ist gefährlich,* 127.
33. Goritcheva, "Délivrée des larmes d'Ève, réjouis-toi !," 31.
34. Tatiana Goritcheva, "L'homme-enfant," in *Des femmes russes,* 93.
35. Julia Voznesenskaya, "Lettre à trois amis," in *Des femmes russes,* 127–29.
36. Voznesenskaya, "Le mouvement féministe dans notre pays," in *Maria,* 52.
37. Goritcheva, "Délivrée des larmes d'Ève, réjouis-toi !," 28.
38. Cf. ibid., 32–33.
39. Ana Siljak, "Between East and West: Hegel and the Origins of the Russian Dilemma," *Journal of the History of Ideas* 62, no. 2 (2001): 335–58.
40. The term "Slavophile" describes (in the context of the Soviet Union) the struggle for "old," prerevolutionary Russian values and the refusal of the entire Soviet system. However, an intellectual or activist termed "Westernizer" does not necessarily adopt Western ideas and values entirely; see Siljak, "Between East and West," and Harvey Fireside, "Dissident Visions of the USSR: Medvedev, Sakharov & Solzhenitsyn," *Polity* 22, no. 2 (1989): 213–29.
41. Storti, "Tatiana Mamonova: exil pour cause de feminisme," 35.
42. Collectif de rédaction, "Ces bon vieux fondements du patriarcat," 20.
43. Tatyana Mamonova, "The USSR: It's Time We Began with Ourselves," in *Sisterhood Is Global,* ed. Robin Morgan (New York: The Feminist Press, 1984), 688.
44. Cf. Voznesenskaya, "Le mouvement féministe dans notre pays," 41.
45. Collectif de rédaction, "Ces bon vieux fondements," 25.
46. Tatyana Mamonova, "Action et réaction," in *Femmes et Russie 1981,* 231.
47. Goritcheva, "Des sourcières dans l'espace," 59.
48. Fougeyrollas-Schwebel, "Le féminisme des années 1970," 906–57.
49. Goritcheva, *Von Gott zu reden ist gefährlich,* 111.
50. Cf. Christa Ebert, *Frauenliteratur in Osteuropa* (Berlin: Akademie Verlag, 2010), 201–2.
51. Norma C. Noonan, *Russian Women in Politics and* Society (Westport, CT: Greenwood Press, 1996), 85.

52. Cf. ibid., 85–87; see also Ioana Cîrstocea, "'Between the Past and the West': Le dilemme du feminism en Europe de l'Est postcommuniste," in *Sociétés Contemporaines* 3, no. 71 (2008): 7–27.
53. Cf. Carola Hansson and Karin Liden, eds., *Unerlaubte Gespräche mit Moskauer Frauen,* 2nd ed. (Munich: Lev Roitmann, 1986).
54. *Maria: Journal du Club féministe 'Maria' de Léningrad* (Paris: Des femmes, 1981).
55. *Des femmes russes*; *Femmes et Russie 1981*; Mamonva, ed., *Voix de femmes en Russie.*
56. Tatyana Mamonova, e-mail interview with author, June–July 2013, 4.
57. Cf. Chandra Niles Folsom, "Foreword," in Mamonova, ed., *Women's Glasnost vs. Naglost,* x.
58. Cf. Mamonova, "The USSR," 676–89.
59. Mamonova, *Russian Women's Studies*; Mamonova, *Women's Glasnost vs. Naglost.*
60. Tatyana Mamonova, "Regeneration or Degeneration," in *Russian Women's Studies,* 151–60.
61. Heather Jon Maroney, "Review of Tatyana Mamonova, ed., *Russian Women's Studies,*" *Canadian Woman Studies* 4, no. 10 (1989): 101.
62. Mamonova, ed., *Woman and Earth Almanac.*
63. Mamonova, "The USSR," 688–89.
64. Cf. "Mission Statement of Woman and Earth Global Eco-Network since 1979," in *Woman and Earth Almanac* 19 (New York: Woman and Earth Press, 2011): 1.
65. "She's an American Girl: Exiled Russian Dissident Granted US Citizenship after Three Decades Stateless," in ibid., 53.
66. Cf. Tatyana Mamonova, "Solidarity between American and Soviet Feminists," in *Russian Women's Studies,* 166.
67. Christine Bauhardt, "Feministische Ökonomie, Ökofeminismus und Queer Ecologies—feministisch-materialistische Perspektiven auf gesellschaftliche Naturverhältnisse," in *Gender Politik Online* (April 2012): 9–10.
68. Cf. Ashley Montagu, *The Natural Superiority of Women* (New York: Macmillan, 1953).
69. Cf. Elisabeth Gould Davis, *The First Sex* (New York: G. P. Putnam's Sons, 1971).
70. Cf. Riane Eisler, *The Chalice and the Blade: Our History, Our Future* (New York: Harper & Row, 1987).
71. Mamonova, e-mail interview with author, 4.
72. Ibid.
73. A misunderstanding that persisted in the postcommunist era; see Cîrstocea, "Between the Past and the West," and Laura Busheikin, "Is Sisterhood Really Global? Western Feminism in Eastern Europe," in *Ana's Land: Sisterhood in Eastern Europe,* ed. Tanya Renne (Boulder, CO: Westview Press, 1997), 12–21.
74. For further reading on the conflicts inside the French women's movement, see Bibia Pavard, *Les éditions des femmes: Histoire de premières années* (Paris: l'Harmattan, 2005).
75. Charles Tilly and Lesley J. Wood, *Social Movements 1768–2008* (Boulder, CO: Paradigm Publishers, 2009). Here: last chapter: "Future of Social Movements," 148f.
76. Cf. Gill Allwood, *French Feminisms: Gender and Violence in Contemporary Theory* (London: UCL Press, 1998), 29.

Bibliography

Allwood, Gill. *French Feminisms: Gender and Violence in Contemporary Theory* (London: UCL Press, 1998).

Bauhardt, Christine. "Feministische Ökonomie, Ökofeminismus und Queer Ecologies—feministisch-materialistische Perspektiven auf gesellschaftliche Naturverhältnisse." *Gender Politik Online* (April 2012): 9–10.

Busheikin, Laura. "Is Sisterhood Really Global? Western Feminism in Eastern Europe." In *Ana's Land: Sisterhood in Eastern Europe,* ed. Tanya Renne, 12–21. Boulder, CO: Westview Press, 1997.

Cîrstocea, Ioana. "'Between the Past and the West': Le dilemme du feminism en Europe de l'Est postcommuniste." *Sociétés Contemporaines* 3, no. 71 (2008): 7–27.

Curtis, Julie. "Iuliia Voznesenskaia: A Fragmentary Vision." In *Women and Russian culture,* ed. Rosalind Marsh, 173–87. New York: Berghahn Books, 1998.

Davis, Elisabeth Gould. *The First Sex.* New York: G. P. Putnam's Sons, 1971.

Des femmes en mouvements hebdo, no. 10 (1980).

Des femmes russes. Paris: Des femmes, 1980.

Ebert, Christa. *Frauenliteratur in Osteuropa.* Berlin: Akademie Verlag, 2010.

Eisler, Riane. *The Chalice and the Blade: Our History, Our Future.* New York: Harper & Row, 1987.

Espagne, Michel, and Michael Werner, eds. *Transferts: Relations interculturelles dans l'espace franco-allemand (XVIII–XIX siècles).* Paris: Recherche sur les Civilisations, 1988.

Femmes et Russie. Paris: Des femmes, 1980.

Femmes et Russie 1981: Léningrad—Paris. Paris: Des femmes, 1981.

Fireside, Harvey. "Dissident Visions of the USSR: Medvedev, Sakharov & Solzhenitsyn." *Polity* 22, no. 2 (1989): 213–29.

Fougeyrollas-Schwebel, Dominique. "Le féminisme des années 1970." *Nouvelle encyclopédie politique et historique des femmes.* ed. Christine Fauré. Paris: Les Belles Lettres, 2010.

Hansson, Carola, and Karin Liden, ed. *Unerlaubte Gespräche mit Moskauer Frauen.* 2nd ed. Munich: Lev Roitmann, 1986.

Idels, Michèle. "Les Éditions *Des femmes* à Moscou." In *Génération MLF 1968–2008,* edited by Antoinette Fouque. Paris: Des femmes, 2008.

Galster, Ingrid. "Französischer Feminismus: Zum Verhältnis von Egalität und Differenz." In *Handbuch Frauen- und Geschlechterforschung: Theorie, Methoden, Empirie,* edited by Ruth Becker et al., 45–51. 2nd ed. Wiesbaden: VS Verlag, 2004.

Goritcheva Tatiana. *Von Gott zu reden ist gefährlich: Meine Erfahrungen im Osten und im Westen.* Freiburg: Herder, 1984.

———. *Hiobs Töchter.* Freiburg: Herder, 1988.

———. *Nur Gott kann Russland retten: Aufzeichnungen in bewegten Zeiten.* Freiburg: Herder, 1990.

Jakovleva, Anna. "Tretuja kultura: Feminizm—eta ja." Interview with Tatyana Mamonova, June 6, 2011, http://www.chaskor.ru/article/tretya_kultura__23644. Accessed April 16, 2013.

Köbberling, Anna. *Zwischen Liquidation und Wiedergeburt: Frauenbewegung in Rußland von 1917 bis heute.* Frankfurt: Campus, 1993.

Mamonova, Tatyana, ed. *Voix de femmes en Russie.* Paris: Denoël/Gonthier, 1982.

———. "The USSR: It's Time We Began with Ourselves." In *Sisterhood Is global,* edited by Robin Morgan, 676–89. New York: The Feminist Press, 1984.

———. ed. *Women's Glasnost vs. Naglost: Stopping Russian Backlash.* Westport, CT: Bergin & Garvey, 1994.

———. *Russian Women's Studies: Essays on Sexism in Soviet Culture.* Oxford: Pergamon Press, 1989.

———, ed. *Woman and Earth Almanac.* New York: Woman and Earth Press, 1993–2013.

———. E-mail interview with author, June–July 2013.

Maria: Journal du Club féministe 'Maria' de Léningrad. Paris: Des femmes, 1981.

Maroney, Heather Jon. "Review of Tatyana Mamonova, ed., *Russian Women's Studies.*" *Canadian Woman Studies* 4, no. 10 (1989): 101.

Montagu, Ashley. *The Natural Superiority of Women.* New York: Macmillan, 1953.

Noonan, Norma C. *Russian Women in Politics and Society.* Westport, CT: Greenwood Press, 1996.

Pavard, Bibia. *Les éditions des femmes: Histoire de premières années.* Paris: l'Harmattan, 2005.

Racine, Nicole, and Michel Trebitsch, eds. *Intellectuelles: Du genre en histoire des intellectuels.* Brussels: Éditions Complexes, 2004.

Schulz, Kristina. "Macht und Mythos von '1968': Zur Bedeutung der 68er Protestbewegung für die Formierung der neuen Frauenbewegung in Frankreich und Deutschland." In *1968—Vom Ereignis zum Mythos,* edited by Ingrid Gilcher-Holtey, 350–57. Frankfurt: Suhrkamp, 2008.

Siljak, Ana. "Between East and West: Hegel and the Origins of the Russian Dilemma." *Journal of the History of Ideas* 62, no. 2 (2001): 335–58.

Stephan, Anke. *Von der Küche auf den Roten Platz: Lebenswege sowjetischer Dissidentinnen.* Zurich: Pano, 2005.

Storti, Martine. "Tatiana Mamonova l'exil pour cause de féminisme." *F Magazine,* no. 30 (1980): 27–35.

Vaissié, Cecilie. *Pour votre liberté et pour la notre: Le combat des dissidences de Russie.* Paris: Robert Laffont, 1999.

Voznesenskaya, Julia. *Briefe über die Liebe: Von Frauen in Haft und Verbannung.* Munich: Roitman, 1987.

———. *Das Frauen-Dekameron.* Munich: Roitman, 1985.

Werner, Michael, and Bénédicte Zimmermann. "Penser l'histoire croisée: entre empirie et réflexivité." *Les Annales. Histoire, Sciences Sociales* 1, no. 58 (2003): 7–36.

Chapter 13

Cyberfeminism on the German-Speaking Net

Contestation beyond Binary Code

Johanna Niesyto

The motivations and practices of why women have contributed and continue to contribute to computing as well as to the development of the net are manifold: to research, to have fun, to be part of a community, to enhance social change, and/or *to engage in feminist politics on the internet.* While cyberfeminism concerns itself with the participation and engagement of these women, they do not have to self-identify as "cyberfeminists" themselves to use and develop new technologies.

In general, the organization and development of cyberfeminism is strongly intermeshed with that of the internet. In the early net cultures that started to spread in the late 1980s, online bulletin board systems, Usenets, and mailing lists played a crucial role. After the introduction and growth of the World Wide Web since the late 1990s and the early 2000s, "social media" (wikis, blogs, etc.) have extended the participation of these cultures. Principles of coproduction and openness underlie these sociotechnical infrastructures. There is a clear correspondence between the principles of net cultures and factors, dynamics and frames that have encouraged the spectacular growth in cyberfeminism.

This chapter, instead of trying to map the contested discourse of what constitutes cyberfeminism, posits it as a set of *political* self-descriptions that have been put forward in texts, pictures, discourses, and practices on the net and beyond in order to build up and to strengthen the fight for justice and freedom for women taken up by independent grassroots groups and networks since the 1990s. In doing so, different frames of cyberfeminism are identified. Introducing "framing" as "signifying work," Snow and Benford focus on how social movement actors interpret problems and articulate ways of actions and/or solutions. Hence they put into foreground the interpretation efforts of the actors themselves, seeing them "as actively engaged in the production and maintenance of meaning for constituents, antagonists, and bystanders or observers."[1] I analyze the German-speaking web along two different axes within this framework: (1) I elaborate the frames that construct the concept of cyberfeminism, paying particular attention to (2) the transnational (non)references and practices within German-speaking cyberfeminism. Cyberfeminism, in popular understanding, is often reduced to a movement that protests against a "toys for boys" perception of the internet. However, as the title of this chapter suggests, there is a need to look beyond such a binary depiction when it comes to cyberfeminism. It is the primary argument of this essay that cyberfeminism cannot be reduced to a singular concept since the diversity of feminist approaches is digitally adopted, modified, combined, and remixed with online action repertoires. These action repertoires are used in social movement theory to describe actions and tools of contention that are commonly used. In this context, online action repertoires would include e-petitions, hacking, virtual sit-ins, and so on. I use framing theory as an interpretative research method,[2] to analyze and systematize self-descriptions and action repertoires (e.g., in "about us" sections, as well as in online discussions, papers, manifestos, interviews, etc.) from within the German-speaking net. A sample of the feminist websites, blogs, and gateways has been methodologically extracted from the project www.grassrootsfeminism.net, and further sites have been identified online through the snowball method (e.g., blog rolls). Additionally, academic literature and its interpretation of cyberfeminism have been referenced in the analysis. What will be shown is the diversity of approaches with respect to frames that cyberfeminism comprises of and which are rooted in different networks/collectives. These networks may be linked to each other, through both framing and shared personnel. Different online sites and formats can be used for all kinds of feminist actions. Hence, in my exploration, the actors' (symbolic) contribution toward a feminist politics on the internet is taken as the systematization criteria. In doing so the following frames of cyberfeminisms can be identified:

First: Net utopias. In the absence of one singular definition of cyberfeminism, artists and activists frame cyberfeminism as a utopia that is open to diverse interpretations. This idea of net-utopia finds the most prominence in feminist art practices and interventions. This frame calls for contributing to feminist politics on the net by building and developing new utopias, first and foremost in the realms of academic writing and arts.

Second: Networking info-activism. One of the most prominent tropes within the info-activism frame is that of making women visible on the net and amplifying their presence. This frame calls for contributing to feminist politics on the net by using feminist (social) media as tools for spreading and organizing feminist thought and action.

Third: Net politics.[3] Within net politics, cyberfeminism is interpreted as a field in which women actively contribute to the technical and conceptual development of the internet, in which women accompany critically and push forward discussions about net governance as well about underlying restrictions of soft- and hardware. This frame calls for contributing to feminist politics on the net by shaping the internet on a (socio)technological level.

This chapter will present each of these frames by illustrating cases with direct quotations used. Moreover, the cases chosen will be embedded in the histories of the cases themselves. The intention of this chapter is to foreground certain crucial questions: Since when did these frames become visible on the net, to which (academic) discourses are they historically linked to? And which transnational dimension have they developed, or refused? The final section points to the future and also to the start: How do principles of net cultures correspond to cyberfeminism?

Net Utopias

Net utopias as well as dystopias were strongly formulated at the beginning of the 1990s, a time when technical conditions allowed for the birth of the World Wide Web. Against this backdrop many utopias and dystopias nurtured themselves from an understanding of the web as space for produsers,[4] decentralization, and nonlinearity. One of the key actors on the German-speaking net at that time – the Old Boys Network (OBN) – was interested in experimenting with these new possibilities and using them for media activism. The OBN was founded in 1997 in Berlin by Susanne Ackers, Cornelia Sollfrank, Ellen Nonnenmacher, Vali Djordjevic, and Julianne Pierce as the first cyberfeminist alliance.[5]

> OBN stands for Old Boys Network. OBN is regarded as the first international Cyberfeminist alliance.... Since the early days the network keeps changing due to changing members. OBN is a real and a virtual coalition of Cyberfeminists. Under the umbrella of the term "Cyberfeminism", OBN contributes to the critical discourse on new media, especially focussing on its gender-specific aspects.[6]

Also in 1997, the OBN was invited to the Hybrid Workspace in Kassel as a part of the art exhibition "documenta X." This invitation was taken as occasion to call for the First Cyberfeminist International conference. This conference in 1997 forms a crucial marker, because at this point the cyberfeminist movement became visible as an international movement. The OBN as well as the Cyberfeminist International conference underline, by way of their names and self-descriptions, the transnational dimension as a core element of cyberfeminism. Moreover, transnational references are implied as the analyzed contributions are published in English as well as in German.

The first Cyberfeminist International conference showed how the self-images of these "early cyberfeminists" were frequently ambiguous. The press release published by the Old Boys Network declared,

> For eight days this cross-cultural meeting of women has taken place at the 1st CYBERFEMINIST INTERNATIONAL and discussed, debated, workshopped and made presentations.... The 1st CYBERFEMINIST INTERNATIONAL slips through the traps of definition with different attitudes towards art, culture, theory, politics, communication and technology – the terrain of the internet.... The 1st CYBERFEMINIST INTERNATIONAL will spread information about the net behind the net, about net-grammars in business and politics, strategies in communication and networking, translating code into strategies and strategies into code.[7]

This press release captures quite a lot. First of all it shows the refusal of definition. In another published text, the Old Boys Network also replaced definition by a hundred negative definitions of what "cyberfeminism is not."[8] Next to that, the cited press release highlights the cross-cultural approach of the first Cyberfeminist International – many of the thirty-seven participants located themselves in Germany and elsewhere in Europe.[9] The self-image as "translator" between code and strategies is put forward, adhering to cyberfeminism as part of net politics.

The key actor playfully constructs a self-image beyond dichotomies by having chosen the name Old Boys Network. In colloquial language, the term alludes to social and/or business networks of graduated elite male students. Already the preceding manifesto of VNS Matrix – an Australian artists' group – had denied any identity definitions,[10] but it claimed their subversive political power: "We are the virus of the new world disorder / rupturing the symbolic from within."[11] The underlying "net utopia" contains the promise that "the choice is yours in cyberspace – you can be anything you want to be."[12]

One of the cases found in the German-speaking net that further illustrates the frame of "net utopias" and at the same time links to the frame of "net politics" is that of net artist Cornelia Sollfrank. In 1997 she hacked a cyberart competition named "Extension," using a computer program to submit 127 contributions from "women." This perceived nature of participation from women was reported and celebrated in popular media. In the revealing statement published on artwarez.org, in which the frame of "net utopias" is built up by putting emphasis on the ironic game with virtual identities beyond the dichotomy of man/woman,

> Next to raising the probability of winning the prize, with FEMALE EXTENSION the artist tried to take particularly seriously the given topic of the competition 'Internet as material and object'.
>
> Which significance the gender attributions male/female do still have on the internet? Who can verify if a man or a woman is behind an e-mail address? And in how many virtual identities can a single net artistic split herself? FEMALE EXTENSION raises these questions and at the same contradicts prejudices of woman and technology.[13]

In another text, Sollfrank directly calls for utopias:

> We are living in a mental climate which is full of contradictions. Utopian theories promise a post-humanist age which is marked by gender- and body-obsolescence. On the other hand, the individual is still part of the power structures constituted by capital, race and gender. We have to bear with this contradiction, try to attenuate the power and the explosive force of the new utopias, and build new social realities with it.[14]

Cyberfeminism in the time of Donna Haraway's writings sees the net with its tools and protocols as a potentially emancipatory space. Haraway, feminist scholar in the field of science and technology studies, draws up the image of a cyborg as a central figure for female emancipation, as well as an "ironic political myth" that merges body and technology:

> Irony is about contradictions that do not resolve into larger wholes, even dialectically, about the tension of holding incompatible things together because both or all are necessary and true. Irony is about humour and serious play. It is also a rhetorical strategy and a political method, one I would like to see more honoured within socialist-feminism. At the centre of my ironic faith, my blasphemy, is the image of the cyborg. A cyborg is a cybernetic organism, a hybrid of machine and organism, a creature of social reality as well as a creature of fiction....

> It [this chapter] is also an effort to contribute to socialist-feminist culture and theory in a postmodernist, non-naturalist mode and in the utopian tradition of imagining a world without gender, which is perhaps a world without genesis, but maybe also a world without end.[15]

While the figure of the cyborg is contested, irony is seen as the core element in this frame and labeled as the "big narration" of cyberfeminism.[16] Parody and irony are used to trans-code language and perception on the net. In doing so, cyberart irritates and intervenes.[17]

Networking Info-Activism

Since the late 1980s, feminist networking info-activism has gained a foothold on the German-speaking net, first as a part of the *Computernetzwerk Linksysteme (/CL-Netz)* gateway, which understands itself as medium and archive of new social movements; later, the first women network "femnet" emerged from it. For a fee, "femnet" as a mailbox network provided women with an e-mail address and access to information and discussion lists. Soon afterward another mailbox network, "Woman" (Woman Only Mail And News), was launched.[18] Various websites and gateways – like *AVIVA-Berlin,* the Jewish online magazine for women founded by Sharon Adler – followed in the late 1990s and at the beginning of 2000s. From about 2005 even more individual and joint online projects enlarged the German-speaking feminist nets, comprising various communities. While websites, e-zines, or websites such as *Aus Liebe zur Freiheit, Frau Lila,* Genderblog, Genderwiki, Girls Can Blog, *Mädchenblog* (Girls' Blog), and *Mädchenmannschaft* (Girls' Team)[19] gather different actors and partly focus on different subtopics, they jointly contribute to the frame of "networking info-activism." These online sites share the meaning of making women and their topics visible[20] on the net and spreading feminist debates and/or protest. One illustrating example of this frame is provided by the project *Frau Lila*: "The project 'Frau Lila' is a feminist initiative. We want encourage women to speak out, to act politically, to network, to fight for their rights and voices. Even today, we still think emancipation is necessary and up to date."[21]

With the technical development of the social web and its spread in active usage, feminist net cultures developed. "New" possibilities like pingbacks (a method that allows users to link back and authors to keep track of external links to their own contributions), comments, and blogroll (a list of other blogs a blogger is recommending to his/her readers) that extended the technique and practice of hyperlinking were used to create a web of different resources and practices.[22] This is the frame of "networking info-activism," as making feminist politics both visible and an integral part of online discourse becomes evident in these practices of networking.

Networking is not restricted to online spaces. Emerging feminist action and debates can also be observed in conferences dealing with the internet in general. Since 2007 the bloggers' conference "re:publica" has been taking place every year in Germany. While in 2007 cyberfeminism was not discussed, subsequent years have seen a growing interest in questions of cyberfeminism, with the 2010 conference featuring a standalone panel on feminist net culture.[23] In the follow-up to the 2010 "re:publica," a list was published of female speakers who were practitioners and/or researchers in the field of online (social) media.[24] Also in 2010, an event called "Gendercamp" started in Hüll, next to Hamburg.[25] The first Gendercamp called for participation in English and German languages:

> We invite everyone interested in networking at the intersections of queer-feminism and netculture: People that are home in both worlds, queer-feminist folks interested in gaining insight of netculture, net-people who feel like digging into queer, feminism and gender. GenderCamp aims at networking, kicking off projects and giving those who know each other from queer/feminist online communities, discussion boards, mailing lists and the blogosphere the chance to meet in real life. [...] We consider a feminist perspective on society necessary to make visible, criticize and change structural discrimination of women and female persons as well as sexist structures. However, a feminist perspective alone is not enough to focus power relations of the binary system of gender, where two binary genders are organized hierarchically and supposed to desire each other exclusively.[26]

The camp's announcement stresses both the political as well as the networking dimension of cyberfeminism. Similarly, other online sites that frame cyberfeminism as "networking info-activism" emphasize the net as a sociocultural space in which power relations are interwoven as well as deconstructed and changed. In line with this, Zobl et al. introduced three interrelated feminist discourses that fall under the frame of "networking info-activism": (1) do-it-yourself feminism, (2) intersectional perspectives on feminism, and (3) pop feminism, the latter in particular in the context of German-speaking feminist discourse.[27] The blog *Mädchenmannschaft* stands as a good example of pop feminism, especially when we look at the interview with one of the (fe)male editors:

> Our aim is not to complain about the status quo in society; rather we want to point out to particular developments in society, no matter if they are positive or negative. But certainly, pop feminism is very important for us.... Second Wave Feminism really made things better for us as a younger generation but there is far too much attitude of being a victim and of complaining and excluding men. Men are not perpetrators in general, they can be also feminists. We are very positive and we think that feminism makes life more beautiful.[28]

While the Gendercamp opened its participation in English as well as German, most of the affiliated (social) media online sites were in German. There is a transnational element to these debates, with direct references and links to other German-speaking spaces in Austria and Switzerland. Female bloggers and feminists also read feminist sites in other languages, refer to foreign-language debates, link to foreign-language sites, and/or have e-mail contacts with other feminist activists throughout the world.[29] This confirms the results of the research project conducted by Zobl et al. about on- and offline feminist media across Europe: they found that the vast majority of content is published in the native language of the editors.[30] In analyzing their vast amount of empirical data,[31] Zobl et al. at the same time underline the idea of networking across different levels:

> A common feature of the analysed media projects is that they refer to networking discourses through which the affiliation of feminist groups and positions is established. Networking occurs on a local, transnational and virtual level. In fact, this aspect of networking across national borders using the internet proves to be a major difference compared to the more restricted (in terms of geography, time, etc.) communication exchanges that took place during the era of second wave feminism.[32]

Next to Zobl et al.'s documentation of feminist media in Europe or the *Plotki* femzine, some multilingual online projects also include issues such as gender, women, and/or feminism from a transnational perspective.[33]

Net Politics

On similar lines as the frame of "networking info-activism," from the late 1980s onward net politics has taken a feminist stance in the German-speaking nets. In 1988 Rena Tangens and Barbara Thoens founded *die Haecksen,* which is a collaborative collective of the female members of the Chaos Computer Club (CCC). Thereafter, the *Haecksen* have met yearly on the Chaos Communication Congress of the CCC, conducting their own projects and exchanging information, staying in communication via a mailing list. The *Haecksen* strive to culturally recode the traditional picture of a hacker as a male person, meaning that they aim to show that dealing creatively with technology is also common among women.[34] As a term, *Haecksen* is a wordplay pointing to the word *Hexen* (witches) and hacking. Hacking comprises practices and discourses that refer to the active and productive development of technology, in particular software. In this line of thought, hacking can be depicted in a positive way:

> Although hackers hold multiple motivations for producing their software, collectively they are committed to *productive freedom*. This term designates the institutions, legal devices, and moral codes that hackers have built in order to autonomously improve on their peers' work, refine their technical skills, and extend craftlike engineering traditions.[35]

Beyond hacking, the feminist frame of "net politics" constituted by varied practices and discourses highlights the technical and conceptual development of the Internet from a feminist perspective. As with the rather slow inclusion of feminist perspectives on the blogger's conference "re:publica," there are also other platforms on the net that critically discuss the link between women and technology on the German-speaking net.[36] As the link list and blogroll of "femgeeks" suggests, most references beyond the German-speaking net are primarily made to the English-speaking net. This is no surprise, as English-speaking web projects, like the Women's Programme of the Association for Progressive Communication, that fight against gender inequities in the creation, design, implementation, and use of computer communication have been around since the early 1990s.[37] The English-speaking web has also seen the emergence of new feminist projects with a sociotechnological stance. For instance, the Ada Initiative – named after Countess Ada Lovelace, known as the world's first computer programmer – which began in 2011, shows a strong synergy with the "networking info-activism" frame because its primary ambition is a call for women's participation in networks. However, the Ada Initiative also focuses on an involvement in the technical and conceptual development of the internet:

> The Ada Initiative is a non-profit organization dedicated to increasing the participation and status of women in open technology and

> culture. Open tech/culture includes areas like open source software, Wikipedia, and open data, the technologies behind Google, Facebook, and the Internet as a whole. These communities are changing the future of global society, yet *women make up only 2% of the open source community and 10% of Wikipedia editors.* If we want that society to be socially just and to serve the interests of all people, women must be involved in its creation and organization.[38]

Calling for women's involvement, the Ada Initiative builds connections beyond the English-speaking net. For example, in January 2013 the initiative commented on incidents of sexism on the twenty-ninth Chaos Computer Congress and published its comments in German as well as in English.[39] This recent incident shows that women's involvement in hacker cultures cannot be taken for granted but must be won and conceived again and again.

Interlinking Framings

Women such as Rena Tangens, who has become a key figure in the German-speaking net community and has made important contributions to feminist theory and practice on the net, calls for contributing to feminist politics on the net by shaping the internet above all on a (socio)technological level. It would, however, be shortsighted to suggest that her writings and actions might only contribute to the framing of "net politics." She understands herself as an artist who creates projects that link to the "digital world" ("net utopia"). Among other projects, she cofounded the *Haecksen* ("net politics"), and she actively contributes to the frame of "networking info-activism" by publicizing texts online that discuss digital cultures from a feminist viewpoint. Reflecting her experiences as a woman on the net, Tangens argues in her writings that androcentrism is not only observable in the academic world but also on the net. She defines androcentrism as a perception of life from a male perspective that implies the inability to describe or perceive female activities and the life of women. Starting from a feminist critique of androcentrism in sciences, she analyzes androcentric influences on the net, and finds many similarities. For instance, with respect to women in data networks she juxtaposes androcentrism against sexism and points to the emergence and growth of women's projects in the net. She discusses gendered use of language in manuals to call for an inclusive design of interfaces.[40] In one text she summarizes her approach through an anecdote in which the key protagonist is an active female net user called Alice:

> Repeatedly journalists asked Alice if she does not feel exotic, if she is not annoyed being constantly harassed by men, and in general by the vast amount of net pornography. Alice is annoyed: As if there were no questions of higher importance. Here and now we are about saving the world. But Alice also wonders. Why is she meeting only a few women in this new world? Do they want no part of technology, aren't they interested or what keeps them away? … Alice is fascinated by the parallels between sciences and the net. Also on the net, women and topics that concern women are underrepresented. The tools, the software – they pretend to be value free, but often they are only customized for men. After all the whole system is based on the differentiation of 0 and 1.[41]

With art projects – such as films like *Der Druckertreiber* (Printer Driver)[42] – Tangens intervenes in net cultures without proposing a fixed definition but revealing a male-dominated (hacker) culture ("net utopias"). On the level of "info-activism," she has helped develop citizens' networks such as /CL and has used the internet for spreading her feminist thoughts and actions. Referring to the framing of "net politics," she encourages public debates about the development of the internet as well as about privacy and data protection, for instance by being directly involved in the development of networks, such as mailbox program *Zerberus*, as well as by establishing events like the Big Brother Award. In her understanding, cyberfeminism is about women but not only about women:

> There is much to be done! Particularly for women. Staccato: presence on the net, democracy in dialogue, net structures and power relationships, economy and citizen's rights, design of technology. In the broadest sense this all is net politics. And it's not just about women.[43]

Rena Tangens bridges the presented framings by her critique of androcentrism, by looking for its underlying power structures, and by putting forward a broad term of net politics that highlights the political dimension of the three framings "net utopias," "networking info-activism," and "net politics."

A Wish

Instead of a conclusion, I will instead discuss cyberfeminism as political force that is needed on the net: How do the principles of net cultures and factors, dynamics, and frames of cyberfeminism correspond? And why does cyberfeminism need to engage in net politics?

"We reject kings, presidents and voting. We believe in rough consensus and running code." This well-known phrase coined by David D. Clark in July 1992 at the twenty-fourth annual Internet Engineering Task Force conference has become a mantra for those who are particularly interested in working systems. It remains a dominant view of those who are interested in keeping the system running. In order to ensure that this view persists, we need even more and/or louder Ada Initiatives on the German-speaking net who also reach out for alliances on a transnational level. The internet is globally organized; there's a need cyberfeminists to speak up even louder on the discourse about the central questions: What kind of net should we encounter online? What are the goals for which we need the method of rough consensus? Who should keep the system running? How shall we keep the system running? It is a contestation beyond binary codes of 0/1, men/women, structure/content, technology/community…

Freedom and coproduction have always been deeply inscribed in feminist do-it-yourself cultures. In order to strengthen these fruitful interlinkings, cyberfeminists need to pay further attention to the preservation of a free and open internet. It is important to obtain the freedom and power to determine where to go, to get creative, and to decide what to do on the net. Free communication and autonomy are closely interlinked to the feminist politics of enabling liberation and emancipation. In times of commercialization of net platforms and discussions about net neutrality, it has become more crucial than ever for cyberfeminist framings and networks to connect with the movements of free and open software and culture. Global cultural citizenship and universal access are preconditions of struggles for freedom in which power structures can be unveiled, criticized, and creatively transformed. To use the net for feminist action, spreading feminist thought, and, last but not least, developing a critique of the open (e.g., criticizing the apparently missing link between women and Wikipedia), the net needs to also be a space for oppositional politics and counterpublics. It is only at these junctures of intersection that we can begin to discuss questions of visibility, building of inclusive interfaces, and development of new feminist utopias.[44]

Johanna Niesyto, PhD, worked as research fellow in the project "Changing Protest and Media Cultures," which was part of the Collaborative Research Centre "Media Upheavals" and funded by the German Research Foundation. Her field of research covers political cultures, political knowledge coproduction, political consumerism, and political campaigning – with a focus on the internet in general and Wikipedia in particular. She has edited the publication *Political Campaigning on the Web* (with Sigrid Baringhorst and Veronika Kneip, 2009). For her full list of publications, see http://transnationalspaces.net.

Notes

1. David A. Snow and Robert D. Benford, "Master Frames and Cycles of Protest," in *Frontiers in Social Movement Theory*, ed. Adlon D. Morris and Carol McClurg Mueller (New Haven, CT: Yale University Press, 1992), 136.
2. See Maria Di Cenzo, Lucy Delap, and Leila Ryan, *Feminist Media History* (New York: Palgrave Macmillan, 2011), 45ff.; Liesbet van Zoonen, *Feminist Media Studies* (London: Sage, 1996), 133.
3. While introducing this frame of "net *politics*," it is not meant that the master frames "net utopias" and "networking info-activism" comprise less strong references to feminist politics.
4. The term "produsers" was coined to capture user-led, collaborative processes of content creation and to emphasize the interwoven roles of producers and consumers. See Axel Bruns, *Blogs, Wikipedia, Second Life, and Beyond: From Production to Produsage* (New York: Peter Lang, 2008).
5. See Cornelia Sollfrank, "The Art of Getting Organized," unpublished manuscript, n.d.
6. Old Boys Network, "FAQ___Frequently Asked Questions," n.d., http://www.obn.org/inhalt_index.html (accessed March 1, 2013).
7. Old Boys Network, "1st CYBERFEMINIST INTERNATIONAL Media Release," 1997, http://www.obn.org/cfundef/press_eng.html (accessed February 1, 2013).
8. See Old Boys Network, "100 Anti-theses," n.d., http://www.obn.org/reading_room/manifestos/html/anti.html (accessed February 1, 2013).
9. See Old Boys Network, "1st CYBERFEMINIST INTERNATIONAL Media Release."
10. E.g., "Identity explodes in multiple morphings and infiltrates the system at root." VNS Matrix, "Bitch Mutant Manifesto," 1996, http://www.obn.org/reading_room/manifestos/down/vns_bitch_mutant.rtf (accessed March 1, 2013).
11. VNS Matrix, "Cyberfeminist Manifesto for the 21st Century," 1991, http://www.obn.org/reading_room/manifestos/down/vns_cyberfeminist.rtf (accessed March 1, 2013).
12. F. Wilding, "Where Is Feminism in Cyberfeminism?," n.d., http://www.obn.org/cfundef/faith_def.html (accessed March 1, 2013).
13. artwarez.org, "EXTENSION-Wettbewerb gehackt," 1997, http://www.artwarez.org/femext/content/public.html (accessed February 1, 2013); trans. Johanna Niesyto.
14. Cornelia Sollfrank, "Women Hackers," 1999, first published in *next Cyberfeminist International*, http://www.obn.org/reading_room/fs_read.html (accessed March 1, 2013). While I have pointed to shared interpretations, it is also obvious that here, different interpretations exist. E.g., Sollfrank distances herself indirectly from the VNS Matrix when she writes, "I am not assuming that women and technology necessarily have as special and as close a relationship as certain cyberfeminists proclaim.

My clitoris does not have a direct line to the Matrix—unfortunately. Such rhetoric mystifies technology and misrepresents the daily life of the female computer worker" (Sollfrank, "Women Hackers"). VNS had formerly claimed in its manifesto that "the clitoris is a direct line to the matrix" (VNS Matrix, "Cyberfeminist Manifesto for the 21st Century"). Considering her role as "computer worker" (Sollfrank, "Women Hackers."), she calls for women to actively influence the development of hard- and software. In this regard she links to the frame "net politics."

15. Donna Haraway, "A Cyborg Manifesto: Science, Technology, and Socialist-Feminism in the Late Twentieth Century," in *Simians, Cyborgs, and Women: The Reinvention of Nature,* ed. D. Haraway (New York: Routledge, 1991), 149.
16. See Jutta Weber, "Ironie, Erotik und Techno-Politik: Cyberfeminismus als Virus in der neuen Weltunordnung. Eine Einführung," *Die Philosophin. Forum für feministische Theorie und Philosophie* 12, no. 24 (2001): 82ff.
17. See also Heike Weinbach, "Die Auferstehung des Feminismus im Cyber," n.d., http://www.philopraxis-mediation.de/Cyberfeminismus.pdf (accessed March 1, 2013).
18. See Gabriele Hooffacker, "Virtuelle feministische Communities," in *Feminist_ Spaces: Frauen im Netz. Diskurse. Communities. Visionen,* ed. Heinrich-Böll-Stiftung and Feminististisches Institut (Königstein/Taunus: Ulrike Helmer, 2002), 144.
19. The list is arbitrary; the link lists and blog rolls of these and other online sites show how manifold the feminist German-speaking websphere is.
20. Visibility is used here as a political category that is positively connoted, and implies striving for (mutual) recognition. For a discussion of visibility as a political category, see Johanna Schaffer, "Ambivalenzen der Sichtbarkeit: Zum Verhältnis von Sichtbarkeit und politischer Handlungsfähigkeit," in *Medien—Politik—Geschlecht: Feministische Befunde zur politischen Kommunikationsforschung,* ed. Johanna Dorer, Brigitte Geiger, and Regina Köpl (Wiesbaden: VS Verlag, 2008).
21. Frau Lila, "Über uns," n.d., http://fraulila.de/ueber-uns/, accessed April 26, 2013.
22. See Tanja Carstensen, "Gendered Web 2.0: Geschlechterverhältnisse in Zeiten von Wikis, Weblogs und sozialen Netzwerken," *Medien Journal* 2 (2012): 28f.
23. See re:publica, "Feministische Netzkultur," 2010, http://www.youtube.com/watch?v=YQSf8ORaMHY (accessed April 26, 2013); Johanna Emge, "Och nö, hier geht's ja um Feminismus," n.d., http://feminismus-netzkultur.de/republica (accessed April 26, 2013).
24. See Netzfeminismus, "Speakerinnen: Keine Ausreden mehr für frauenlose Panels," n.d., http://netzfeminismus.org/?page_id=114 (accessed April 26, 2013).
25. As it serves networking, the Gendercamp is discussed in the light of the frame "networking info-activism." However, the Gendercamp, with the scope of its participants and topics, also serves the frame "net politics" and is one example of the blurred lines between cyberfeminist framings.
26. Gendercamp, "Ankündigungstext auf Englisch," 2010, http://www.gendercamp.de/networks/wiki/index.AnkuendigungstextEN_ (accessed April 26, 2013).
27. See Elke Zobl, Rosa Reitsamer, and Stefanie Grünangerl, "Feminist Media Production in Europe: A Research Report," in *Feminist Media: Participatory Spaces, Networks and Cultural Citizenship,* ed. Elke Zobl and Ricarda Drüeke (Bielefeld: transcript, 2012), 21–54.

28. *Mädchenmannschaft* editor cited in Zobl et al., "Feminist Media Production in Europe," 44ff.
29. As an example, see A. Schrupp and J. Niesyto, "interview cyberfeminismus #01: antje schrupp," 2013, http://transnationalspaces.wordpress.com/2013/04/19/interview-cyberfeminismus-01-antje-schrupp (accessed April 26, 2013).
30. See Zobl et al., "Feminist Media Production in Europe," 28.
31. Empirical data including various feminist online sites is documented by this research project at http://www.grassrootsfeminism.net.
32. Zobl et al., "Feminist Media Production in Europe," 31.
33. See for example de.globalvoicesonline.org/category/topics/women-gender.
34. See Haecksen, "Wer sind die Haecksen," 2012, http://www.haecksen.org/index.php/Hauptseite (accessed April 28, 2013).
35. E. Gabriella Coleman, *Coding Freedom: The Ethics and Aesthetics of Hacking* (Princeton, NJ: Princeton University Press, 2013), 3, emphasis in original.
36. See for example femgeeks.de, www.fitev.de, www.shegeeks.ch, or www.technixen.net.
37. See Edie Farwel, James Wood, Maureen Peregrine, and Karen Banks, "Global Networking for Change: Experiences from the APC Women's Programme," in *Women@Internet: Creating New Cultures in Cyberspace,* ed. Wendy Harcourt (New York: Zed Books, 1999), 102–13.
38. The Ada Initiative, "Who We Are," n.d., http://adainitiative.org/about-us/ (accessed April 28, 2013), emphasis in original.
39. See the Ada Initiative, "In Arbeit: Das Ende von Sexismus in der Hackerkultur," 2013, http://adainitiative.org/2013/01/in-arbeit-das-ende-von-sexismus-in-der-hackerkultur/ (accessed May 23, 2013).
40. See Rena Tangens, "Ist das Internet männlich? Androzentrismus im Netz," in *Kursbuch Internet: Anschlüsse an Wirtschaft und Politik, Wissenschaft und Kultur,* ed. Stefan Bollmann and Christiane Heibach (Mannheim: Bollmann, 1996), 355–78.
41. Rena Tangens, "Alice im Cyperspace," 2000, http://www.heise.de/tp/artikel/5/5655/1.html (accessed April 27, 2013); trans. Johanna Niesyto.
42. The film is available at media.ccc.de/browse/chaostv/hacker_packen_aus.html.
43. Tangens, "Alice im Cyperspace."
44. The author thanks Nishant Shah for his constructive criticism and linguistic editing of the text, as well as Rena Tangens for her very useful remarks.

Bibliography

The Ada Initiative. "Who We Are." N.d. http://adainitiative.org/about-us/. Accessed April 24, 2013.

———. 2013. "In Arbeit: Das Ende von Sexismus in der Hackerkultur." http://adainitiative.org/2013/01/in-arbeit-das-ende-von-sexismus-in-der-hackerkultur/. Accessed May 23, 2013.

artwarez.org. 1997. "EXTENSION-Wettbewerb gehackt." http://www.artwarez.org/femext/content/public.html. Accessed February 1, 2013.

Carstensen, Tanja. "Gendered Web 2.0: Geschlechterverhältnisse in Zeiten von Wikis, Weblogs und sozialen Netzwerken." *Medien Journal* 2 (2012): 22–34.

Coleman, E. Gabriella. *Coding Freedom: The Ethics and Aesthetics of Hacking*. Princeton, NJ: Princeton University Press, 2013.

Di Cenzo, Maria, Lucy Delap, and Leila Ryan. *Feminist Media History*. New York: Palgrave Macmillan, 2011.

Emge, Johanna. "Och nö, hier geht's ja um Feminismus." http://feminismus-netzkultur.de/republica/. Accessed April 26, 2013.

Farwel, Edie, James Wood, Maureen Peregrine, and Karen Banks. "Global Networking for Change: Experiences from the APC Women's Programme." In *Women@Internet: Creating New Cultures in Cyberspace*, edited by Wendy Harcourt, 102–13. New York: Zed Books, 1999.

Frau Lila. "Über uns." http://fraulila.de/ueber-uns/. Accessed April 26, 2013.

Gendercamp. 2010. "Ankündigungstext auf Englisch." http://www.gendercamp.de/networks/wiki/index.AnkuendigungstextEN_. Accessed April 26, 2013.

Haecksen. 2012. "Wer sind die Haecksen." http://www.haecksen.org/index.php/Hauptseite. Accessed April 28, 2013.

Haraway, Donna. "A Cyborg Manifesto: Science, Technology, and Socialist-Feminism in the Late Twentieth Century." In *Simians, Cyborgs, and Women: The Reinvention of Nature*, edited by Donna Haraway, 149–81. New York: Routledge, 1991.

Hooffacker, Gabriele. "Virtuelle feministische Communities." In *Feminist_Spaces: Frauen im Netz. Diskurse. Communities. Visionen*, edited by Heinrich-Böll-Stiftung and Feminististisches Institut, 133–46. Königstein/Taunus: Ulrike Helmer, 2002.

Netzfeminismus. "Speakerinnen: Keine Ausreden mehr für frauenlose Panels." http://netzfeminismus.org/?page_id=114. Accessed April 26, 2013.

Old Boys Network. 1997. "1st CYBERFEMINIST INTERNATIONAL Media Release." http://www.obn.org/cfundef/press_eng.html. Accessed February 1, 2013.

———. "100 Anti-theses." http://www.obn.org/reading_room/manifestos/html/anti.html. Accessed February 1, 2013.

———. "FAQ___Frequently Asked Questions." http://www.obn.org/inhalt_index.html. Accessed March 1, 2013.

re:publica. 2010. "Feministische Netzkultur." http://www.youtube.com/watch?v=YQSf8ORaMHY. Accessed April 26, 2013.

Schaffer, Johanna. "Ambivalenzen der Sichtbarkeit: Zum Verhältnis von Sichtbarkeit und politischer Handlungsfähigkeit." In *Medien—Politik—Geschlecht: Feministische Befunde zur politischen Kommunikationsforschung*, edited by Johanna Dorer, Brigitte Geiger, and Regina Köpl, 233–48. Wiesbaden: VS Verlag, 2008.

Schrupp, A. and J. Niesyto. "interview cyberfeminismus #01: antje schrupp." *Transnational Spaces*. http://transnationalspaces.wordpress.com/2013/04/19/interview-cyberfeminismus-01-antje-schrupp. Accessed on April 26, 2013.

Snow, David A., and Robert D. Benford. "Master Frames and Cycles of Protest." In *Frontiers in Social Movement Theory*, edited by Adlon D. Morris and Carol McClurg Mueller, 133–55. New Haven, CT: Yale University Press, 1992.

Sollfrank, Cornelia. 1999. "Women Hackers." First published in *next Cyberfeminist International*. http://www.obn.org/reading_room/fs_read.html. Accessed March 1, 2013.

Sollfrank, Cornelia. *The Art of Getting Organized*. Unpublished manuscript, n.d.

Tangens, Rena. "Ist das Internet männlich? Androzentrismus im Netz." In *Kursbuch Internet: Anschlüsse an Wirtschaft und Politik, Wissenschaft und Kultur,* edited by Stefan Bollmann and Christiane Heibach, 355–78. Mannheim: Bollmann, 1996.

———. 2000. "Alice im Cyperspace." http://www.heise.de/tp/artikel/5/5655/1.html. Accessed April 27, 2013.

VNS Matrix. 1991. "Cyberfeminist Manifesto for the 21st Century." http://www.obn.org/reading_room/manifestos/down/vns_cyberfeminist.rtf. Accessed March 1, 2013.

———. 1996. "Bitch Mutant Manifesto." http://www.obn.org/reading_room/manifestos/down/vns_bitch_mutant.rtf. Accessed March 1, 2013.

Weber, Jutta. "Ironie, Erotik und Techno-Politik: Cyberfeminismus als Virus in der neuen Weltunordnung. Eine Einführung." *Die Philosophin: Forum für feministische Theorie und Philosophie* 12, no. 24 (2001): 81–97.

Weinbach, Heike. "Die Auferstehung des Feminismus im Cyber." http://www.philopraxis-mediation.de/Cyberfeminismus.pdf. Accessed March 1, 2013.

Zobl, Elke, Rosa Reitsamer, and Stefanie Grünangerl. "Feminist Media Production in Europe: A Research Report." In *Feminist Media: Participatory Spaces, Networks and Cultural Citizenship,* edited by Elke Zobl and Ricarda Drüeke, 21–54. Bielefeld: transcript, 2012.

Zoonen, Liebeth van. *Feminist Media Studies.* London: Sage, 1996.

Part V

Thinking about Impact and Change: Concepts and Research Strategies

Introductory Remarks

Magda Kaspar

The feminist struggle for women's rights has come a long way, and so has the historiography of feminism. The emergence of oral history as a method for analyzing historical and cultural contexts in the first half of the twentieth century in the United States opened up new possibilities of gaining sources.[1] In addition to existing, mostly written sources, everybody could now record an interview and guarantee its accessibility irrespective of space and time. The oral history method has been greatly important in studies on women's history. In the early 1970s the lack of sources documenting women's lives and its impacts on women's historiography was discussed extensively. The debates over the following years were significant for raising the awareness of the high relevance of producing and archiving the voices of women who had directly or indirectly shaped the political, social, and economic conditions of their time.[2] Consequently, in the last few decades, historiographical research on the feminist movement has flourished. The oral history method created many new sources and collected testimonies, and it inspired a new way of thinking about women's histories. A significant part of what we know about the women's movement was indeed produced by activists themselves and had mainly an autobiographical character, as Elisabeth Elgán noted in her chapter on *Grupp 8*, the largest feminist group in the 1970s in Sweden. She identifies an inconsistency between the self-perception of *Grupp 8* and how it was perceived by others. In their autobiographies, former activists describe a feminist group; however, Elisabeth Elgán's research in the archives paints another picture: that of a mainly socialist group that was, in the first place, dedicated to the class struggle. The struggle against women's subjugation seems to have been, at least initially, subordinated to the commitment to socialism. In that logic, the liberation of women was considered as a quasi-causal consequence of the emancipation of the human being. In the early

1970s the term "feminist" was not popular within *Grupp 8* because it was associated with radical feminism or nonsocialist ideas. Nevertheless, punctually, concrete goals were defined in order to improve the situation of women, like increasing women's work opportunities or better childcare. However, this did not go far enough for those group members who advocated for a more intense debate of feminist concerns. By the end of the decade, various feminist ideas were discussed within *Grupp 8,* although the reconciliation of socialism and feminism led to tensions, internal conflicts, and critics.

Following Pierre Bourdieu, Elisabeth Elgán analyzed the campaigning methods and showed a change in the feminine *habitus* that framed *Grupp 8.* In addition to the change in the group's mode of addressing the public, the situation of women was increasingly described in terms of victimhood. In this process, the public interventions of *Grupp 8* lost a lot of their humoristic character. Nevertheless, the group shaped a new way of being a woman, because it promoted loudness, disorder, and revolt and encouraged women to become financially independent and to live an autonomous life.

Elisabeth Elgán raises the question of the reliability and representativeness of testimonies of former activists. Indeed, memories depend on a variety of interpretative and integrative processes and different factors during the phase of recording and retrieval. These have to be considered in a historical context.[3] The discrepancy between activists' narratives and Elisabeth Elgán's findings in the archives emphasizes the importance of comparing and reconciling different source types and shows us how important a source-critical perspective is.

The subsequent chapter also works with autobiographical narratives: Margaretta Jolly provides insights into the experiences of *Sisterhood and After: The Women's Liberation Oral History Project.* Supported by the British Library, different experts in the history of contemporary feminism and narrative life methods conducted sixty life history interviews with core activists of the women's liberation movement in the UK. In addition to a permanent multimedia archive, they created a website about the movement's history with the aim of reaching secondary school teachers, students, and the broad public.

Desiring to present the most complete picture possible, Jolly noted the challenge of representativeness: to represent a diverse range of voices reflecting the multifaceted nature of the women's liberation movement, their selection methods aimed to capture geographical diversity and to include different ideologies, classes, races, sexualities, and other minority categories To measure the effects of activism, the British team compared the life stories of their interviewees with those of their peer generation and their mothers. On one hand, this method enabled a discussion of how generational effects can influence the activists and, further, the movement itself. On the other hand, political and social movements have macro-level effects and also individual-level effects in terms of the life cycles of the involved activists. Jolly discusses these biographical consequences and personal transformations resulting from activism. In addition to consequences for childhood experiences, alternative sexualities, and a transformation of the image of women's bodies, she raises questions about upward or downward economical mobility and physical and mental health.

Margaretta Jolly and Elisabeth Elgán both discuss a discrepancy between the self-description of the activists and external descriptions given by the public or researchers. While *Grupp 8* activists in Sweden viewed themselves as taking action against the subordination of women, the picture that emerged from the archives showed a group that predominantly followed socialist goals. On the other hand, Jolly's British team had to deal with activists who had a central role in their movements, but disclaimed any kind of leadership.

The chapter closes with the aim of the *Sisterhood and After Project*: to create change through storytelling and political education. The almost 450 recorded, transcribed, and evaluated hours of interviews with former activists make a significant contribution to sources in the field of women's history.

The importance of this is shown in the last chapter in the last part of this book: Karen Offen's summarization of feminism from a long-term and global view leads to the conclusion that our society is at a "generational turning point" where it is important to recollect and reassess sources about the feminist struggle and pass them on to the next generation of historians. She stresses that the importance of preserving and transmitting historical knowledge about women is essential because the loss notably contributed to their subordination.

Karen Offen contends that feminist claims were aimed at the right to vote as well as at social and power demands such as reduced economic injustice and promotion of peace. Therefore, the feminist struggle did not finish once women gained suffrage. She noted that many goals were attained in European countries and the Western world, but not globally. In some parts of the world, neither economical nor educational basics can be assumed, and the history of feminism remains absent in the school curricula of many countries. Variations in women's situations from one country to another make it difficult to measure the impact of feminism globally. In addition to geographical differences, the possibility of evaluation and comparability can also be questioned along the time axis. How can we compare successes considered in the 1970s, like the right to vote, to the slow but important progress in the economic situation of women in the 1990s? Moreover, the evaluation methods differ significantly from law to more social and cultural issues. Karen Offen notes the different time relations of the first and second waves of feminist protest because the former has a timeframe of 150 years and the latter has one of only 40 years. Consequently, it may be too soon to tell whether the last generation's women's movement has had a lasting effect. Nevertheless, she concludes that feminism deserves recognition as a major historical movement and as a major event of the twentieth century and advocates that the history of feminism should be recognized as political history because of the significant difference it makes to the understanding of the past. It is thus important to collect the various types of sources required for documenting the histories of feminism; otherwise, they will be lost as something that happened in the past.

Technical advancements like the voice recorder have enabled new research methods and strategies like oral history and have led to more democratic access to the production of sources. The women's liberation movement and its historiography profited significantly by the oral history method. As Margaretta Jolly notes, activists and researchers of the women's liberation movement are confronted with similar challenges. Like feminist activists, who wanted to take experimental and personal factors into account and discuss questions of representation, researchers of feminist history seem to go the same way. With relatively new methods like oral history, they changed the way of working with sources. Today's technical advancements have led to a global connection of feministic activities. Information can be published with incredible speed on the internet, and vast new sources can be created through manual or automatic archiving processes. Here, the historiography has to react and work on new concepts and methods for how this enormous amount of information can be processed and evaluated and how a movement, which is still ongoing, can be captured.

Magda Kaspar obtained in 2015 her master's in contemporary history from the University of Bern. Her master's thesis investigated the relationships between the women's liberation movement and feminist art in Switzerland. With Kristina Schulz she is currently preparing an audio archive and interactive website about the feminist movement in Switzerland from the 1970s to the present (Frauenbewegung 2.0).

Notes

1. Rebecca Sharpless, "The History of Oral History," in *History of Oral History: Foundations and Methodology* (Lanham, MD: AltaMira Press, 2007), S. 9–32.

2. Sue Armitage, "The Stages of Women's Oral History," in *The Oxford Handbook of Oral History*, ed. Donald A. Ritchie (Oxford: Oxford University Press, 2011), 169–85.
3. Cf. Dorothee Wierling, "Oral History als Bewegung und Disziplin," in *Aufriss der Historischen Wissenschaften*, ed. Michael Maurer (Stuttgart: Reclam, 2005), 81–148; Yvonne Küsters, *Narrative Interviews: Grundlagen und Anwendungen* (Wiesbaden: VS Verlag, 2006).

Bibliography

Armitage, Sue. "The Stages of Women's Oral History." In *The Oxford Handbook of Oral History*, ed. Donald A. Ritchie, 169–85. Oxford: Oxford University Press, 2011.

Küsters, Yvonne. *Narrative Interviews: Grundlagen und Anwendungen*. Wiesbaden: VS Verlag, 2006.

Sharpless, Rebecca. "The History of Oral History." In *History of Oral History: Foundations and Methodology*, S. 9–32. Lanham, MD: AltaMira Press, 2007.

Wierling, Dorothee. "Oral History als Bewegung und Disziplin." In *Aufriss der Historischen Wissenschaften*, ed. Michael Maurer, 81–148. Stuttgart: Reclam, 2005.

Chapter 14

The Myth and the Archives

Some Reflections on Swedish Feminism in the 1970s

Elisabeth Elgán

Much of our understanding of the new feminist groups that arose throughout the Western world in the 1970s is based directly or indirectly upon the activists' own stories. Out of the six books that have been published in Sweden on this topic, two are memories of leading activists; the third is a collection of memories from a group of former feminists and the three remaining are doctoral dissertations, two of these largely using interviews with former activists.[1] I would like to argue here that even if their stories are interesting for today's activists as well as for researchers, they should not be the only source for writing the history of the 1970s new feminist groups.

In writings and in interviews former activists pick up actions and discussions they were involved in, along with more personal narratives about their lives as young women of that time. It is well known that memory is selective, and for many of the former feminist activists the struggle is still ongoing, which certainly plays a part in the way they recall what happened forty years ago. The Swedish autobiographical narratives about 1970s feminism deal a lot with the feelings of joy and power that the new movement brought with it. Some of them describe it as having finally found what they had always been looking for.[2] This rosy picture is reinforced by the media's narrative and aesthetics concerning the new feminist groups of the 1970s. Media in Sweden regularly commemorate these groups using a discourse similar to that of the former activists, accompanied by images of beautiful young women with long hair, arguing or marching. Altogether this gives ground to what I would characterize as a myth about the 1970s new feminists, a myth recalling them as gorgeous and tremendously successful. What they really did and fought for, except for free abortion, is less clear in this discourse.

The doctoral dissertations mentioned above are interesting but are also specialized studies, not concentrating on what the feminist groups did and stood for in general; those dissertations deal with the identity work inside the feminist lesbian groups, the spread of feminist groups around Sweden, and the ideas of these groups.[3] The lack of more comprehensive studies of the new feminist groups leaves those who are interested in Swedish feminist history with the myth of the young women who marched and changed the word.[4] Why they marched, how they organized, which actions they undertook, and which ideas they formulated must be studied empirically, in order to enable us to have an informed discussion about the legacy of the 1970s feminists.

In this chapter, my aim is to show that a study based on the material preserved in the archives paints a picture of the new feminist groups of the 1970s that differs from the one mediated by former activists. While doing so I will also reflect upon the impact of this group.

My focus here will be on the largest of the new feminist groups in 1970s Sweden, *Grupp 8* (Group 8).[5] Its glory days coincide with the 1970s, and at its zenith, about four hundred women belonged to *Grupp 8*.[6] I will concentrate my argument on two aspects: the socialist character of the group and its way of organizing.

The archives of *Grupp 8* are available in the Swedish National Archives, where the material fills about thirty archive boxes. A smaller number of documents, corresponding to four boxes and primarily from *Grupp 8*'s earliest years, are found in the Labor Movement Archives and Library. I will support my arguments with examples from the archives.[7]

Socialism vs. Feminism

Grupp 8 was founded in Stockholm in 1968 as "a socialist group that works against sex discrimination," and it remained a Stockholm-based group.[8] Within the autobiographical writings of former activists this group is often depicted mainly as a feminist group, but the picture that emerges from the archives shows, especially for the first half of the 1970s, an organization that before all underlined its commitment to socialism as the goal of the organization and the class struggle as the way to get there.

Grupp 8 spent several years trying to conceive claims and campaigns that would unify the goal of a socialist revolution with the struggle against the subjugation of women. In repeated statements *Grupp 8* affirmed that only socialism was able to liberate humanity, and thus also women. It's probably this utopian conviction that explains why the group derived most of its analytical tools for understanding the subjugation of women from socialist thoughts.

This definitive choice of socialism as both a framework of understanding and a goal in the struggle against women's subjugation and male-dominated society was not unique to *Grupp 8*. There were groups in most Western countries that embraced this *féminisme lutte des classes* as it is called in French. In her study of the Danish Redstockings, the political scientist Drude Dahlerup shows that the Danish movement embraced both socialist feminism and the more unadulterated feminist current called radical feminism.[9] In Sweden, however, virtually all new feminist groups that arose in the 1970s followed *Grupp 8*'s ideological orientation.

Arising from the distinctly socialist emphasis, *Grupp 8* did not use the term "feminism" for several years in relation to the organization itself. The word was associated with radical feminists in the United States or with preceding women's organizations that had not taken a clear stance in favor of socialism, the so-called "bourgeois feminists." In its very first program, *Grupp 8* defined socialism as a long-term goal, while short-term demands such as women's opportunities to work for pay, living wages, better childcare, and expanded social services were brought to the fore.[10] But this more reformist way of imagining the fight for socialism fell away almost immediately and was replaced by the notion that it should be possible to relate all *Grupp 8* campaigns and demands to the class struggle. This led to internal conflicts in relation to taking concrete action. One example is the successful—in the sense of well-attended and much-noted—meeting that *Grupp 8* arranged in 1971 to demand the right to pain relief during childbirth. The meeting was later criticized internally because it had no clear connection to the struggle for a socialist society.[11] Another example is the commotion surrounding the demonstration held by *Grupp 8* in the fall of 1974 requesting higher pay for women. When the demonstration, which combined slogans like "A single woman is only a slave, but a thousand sisters can make demands" with slogans like "Fight for women's liberation, Fight for human liberation, Fight for socialism," was about to begin, it turned out that a few members had, without the organizers' permission, removed a banner that urged all women to organize in their workplaces, since they thought it did not link the fight against women's subjugation clearly enough to the fight for socialism. The critics objected to the premise of the demonstration that all women were oppressed, as the saying went, regardless of class. The most scathing critics included a few leading members who cautioned that if *Grupp 8* continued along this line, the group was at risk of turning into a petty bourgeois reform movement.[12]

Another consequence of *Grupp 8*'s attempts to unite socialism and feminism and make the class struggle into a tool for fighting the subjugation of women was that any criticism of men of any kind was immediately seized upon and accused of fragmenting the class struggle. This type of criticism was voiced, for example, against a speech given by a *Grupp 8* member, in the name of the organization, at a solidarity meeting with a group of cleaning women on strike in 1975. The speech asserted that the cleaning women's strike was proof that men could no longer claim the sole right to decide what "class struggle" meant and that after the cleaning women's successful strike, the labor movement would have to also take the specific demands of women into account.[13] The speech triggered a heated debate within *Grupp 8* and one critic dismissed the address as "a really bad bourgeois feminist speech!"[14] The critics were particularly outraged over the statement that men would no longer be allowed to decide what was meant by the class struggle, which, they contended, suggested antagonism between men's and women's demands. They were also upset that the speech failed to mention that many working-class men had stood in solidarity with the women's strike.[15]

The demands that *Grupp 8* should design its actions against the subjugation of women in such a way that the class struggle was promoted and the world took a step closer to socialism culminated around the mid-1970s. When *Grupp 8* adopted a new program in the spring of 1976, "economic oppression"—capitalist exploitation of women both as cheap spare labor and as those responsible for the unpaid reproduction of labor through their work in the home—was put on par with "ideological oppression," the term *Grupp 8* used to designate the oppression to which women were subjected *as women.*[16] However, ideological oppression was transformed to become synonymous with the ideological capitalist offensive to instill in women a "false consciousness," that is, to make them blind to the oppression to which they were subjected.

Toward the end of the 1970s, *Grupp 8* abandoned its dogmatic socialist stance and allowed latitude to discuss various traditions of feminist thought. As one member wrote in the group's magazine, "The mood is so different now compared to the fraught leftist mania of the early days, when we were constantly worried, constantly asking ourselves: Is this Marxist enough? Is Big Brother going to approve this? They won't think we are feminists, will they? God forbid, they might think we are lesbians!"[17] The road to that point had been paved with conflict and attacks, not least from the various revolutionary leftist parties founded in the 1960s and 1970s—but the revolutionary socialist parties were not the only ones criticizing *Grupp 8.* In 1977 several former members and feminist activists voiced strong criticism of what they considered a dangerous ideological U-turn within *Grupp 8.* The criticism, which started out by comparing *Grupp 8*'s purported new ideology with fascism, was published in one of the biggest newspapers in Sweden. The critics seem to have been reacting to *Grupp 8* having begun to write more about sexual politics in its magazine, as well as to the favorable views of the magazine, and its editor, toward a book about radical feminism in the

United States.[18] The book expressed the opinion that men were responsible for the subjugation of women, that women should create their own societies, and that homosexuality could be a feminist strategy.[19] One of the more famous participants in the debate around *Grupp 8*'s attitude toward this book asserted that feminists in the United States had evolved into a lesbian sect that hated men, and that instead of discussing issues such as women's labor, they discussed the possibility of having children—but only girls—with no men involved. The lesbian feminists, she argued, were trying to "replace oppression of women with oppression of men," and she admonished *Grupp 8* that it would alienate itself from women's activists in schools, daycare centers, workplaces, and unions if it went the same route. The class struggle was still the best way to improve women's lot, in her opinion.[20] Another equally well-known intellectual, and also one of the founders of *Grupp 8,* cautioned the group against "a women's struggle whose goal is no longer equality but transfer of power. I see a glimpse of a master race ideology in which women are the new 'masters.'"[21] *Grupp 8*'s interest in issues such as lesbianism, prostitution, and women's sexuality in general were, in the eyes of this debater, a sign of an ideological turn in that direction, and *Grupp 8* was reprimanded for not having clearly repudiated American radical feminism.

It is paradoxical that the revolutionary left to which *Grupp 8* wanted to belong submitted the group to continuous criticism and attempted to influence its feminist politics several times, while the liberal feminists on their side were quite interested in discussing with *Grupp 8* but were most of the time pushed away.[22] The Social Democrats were also deemed too "bourgeois" to suit the socialist ambition of *Grupp 8*. When Prime Minister Olof Palme launched an ambitious gender equality program in 1972, *Grupp 8* was very critical and continued to be so during the following years.[23]

Did the strong socialist profile of *Grupp 8* affect the impact of the group's feminist claims? It is possible that *Grupp 8,* by choosing the revolutionary left instead of those who were about to launch Sweden's gender equality politics, alienated itself from direct influence on these politics. At the same time, stating over and over again its commitment to socialism seems to have been successful when it came to recruiting members to *Grupp 8*. The question was up for debate at an internal meeting in 1973, and the majority of the more than one hundred members present declared that they had joined *Grupp 8* because of the group's socialist and revolutionary profile. Not feeling sharp enough to join one of the revolutionary parties of that time, they said that they saw *Grupp 8* as an easier way to begin their socialist activism.[24] These recruitments helped the group to become better known and more visible. You can always argue that this visibility gave *Grupp 8* an indirect influence on gender politics, forcing the political parties that governed Sweden at that time to get into gender equality politics more quickly and more deeply than they would have done otherwise.

Ways of Organizing

The archives of *Grupp 8,* however, provide more than a basis for problematizing the dominating narratives about the 1970s feminist groups; they also provide avenues for fresh analysis that may lay the groundwork for various discussions about these groups. To illustrate this, I will analyze *Grupp 8*'s campaigning methods, its way of addressing its audience, and the new feminine *habitus* framed by *Grupp 8.*

Grupp 8's campaigns at the end of the 1960s and the beginning of the 1970s were often lighthearted and humorous. This is particularly apparent in the group's plans to tour over the highways and byways of the country a major exhibition that would reveal a number of "wizards"—politicians, capitalists, experts, as well as the socialist male activist—as symbols of how men and male society manipulated and dominated women.[25] In connection with the 1970 general election campaign, *Grupp 8* also displayed itself in the same good-humored way when the group pasted its slogan "The rights of children already born" over election posters proclaiming "The rights of unborn children" and traveled around heckling politicians of various parties at town square meetings. The leaflets the group distributed in connection with these actions read, "Dry Your Tears—Resist" and "Be Happy—Attack!"[26] These were ways of organizing inspired by the new feminists in the United States.

Starting in 1972, the slogans about being happy and going on the attack were replaced with rallying cries like "Fight for women's liberation—Fight for socialism." When *Grupp 8* arranged a demonstration in favor of women's right to work, the leaflet did indeed end with the slogans "Dry Your Tears," "Get Angry," and "Attack," but there was no longer any thought of being happy or resisting.[27] Women's situation was also increasingly being described in terms of victimhood. Ahead of the 1973 general election, *Grupp 8* and the Swedish section of Women's International Democratic Federation produced a joint leaflet. It was adorned with a picture of a woman constrained in an iron collar, manacles, and fetters, wearing a short dress and an apron, eyes wide open, arms and legs helplessly splayed like an inflatable sex doll. The shackles carried labels: "Capitalism" on the collar, "Patriarchy" on the manacles, "Gender Roles," and "Upbringing" on the fetters. Four iron balls weighted down the chains and were labeled "Women's Work," "Low Pay," "Inadequate Childcare," and "Unemployment."[28]

This change in campaign methods can be seen as a growing tendency to conform to leftist traditions for how demands related to the oppression of women should be articulated and how actions should be carried out. Why this change? The most obvious answer would be that it was a part of the dogmatization of *Grupp 8* that I have described above.

If we take this analysis a bit further we could ask to which extent *Grupp 8*'s dogmatic turn was linked to women's opportunities to act critically and independently in a society informed by the subjugation of women. The Swedish political scientist Maud Eduards has advocated that women organizing themselves are always seen as a threat by a male-dominated society.[29] By organizing without men, women put the finger on the existence of a hierarchy that many don't want to see. If we follow Eduards, the pressure from the left that was visible in both the precedent examples can be interpreted as a consequence of leftist activists' desire to stop *Grupp 8* as an independent women's organization.

Another noteworthy aspect of *Grupp 8*'s way of organizing is its mode of address. In this case, analyzing the mode of address provides an opportunity to discuss *Grupp 8*'s views on how change could be achieved, a matter that was not explicitly discussed. In the early years, *Grupp 8* employed a mode of address based on *talking with* the women they were addressing in their actions and encouraging them to start to act by themselves. When the group held a large opinion-shaping meeting in 1969 in protest of women's low wages and imposed part-time work in the retail sector, the group designed a leaflet with the following text:

> Can YOU live on your wages? Do you know that 45% of part-time workers are forced to work for financial reasons? 70% of workers at Tempo [a chain of department stores] are part-time.... Will YOU be allowed to keep your job? Do YOU have any job security as a part-time worker? ... It is the employer—not YOU—who profits from part-time work! Demand better conditions for part-time workers![30]

A few years on, the mode of address had changed and *Grupp 8* then spoke *on behalf of women*; that is, the group had made itself the representative of a larger women's collective—although there was some disagreement as to which collective. At the previously discussed demonstration urging higher pay for women held in the fall of 1974, the opening words of the leaflet were: "Everyone knows us women are oppressed. Women always do the cooking, do the laundry, scrub the toilet, become the sports widows, have poor self-esteem, etc."[31]

Some years later, yet another mode of address emerged. In some cases, *Grupp 8* began *talking to women* and offering them help; for example when the group arranged a meeting in 1978 in protest of women's unemployment and distributed a leaflet inviting women to the meeting, which among other things promised "information from unemployment counselors."[32] In another leaflet from the same period, we find under the heading "What every woman should know!" information about the benefits and training to which the unemployed were entitled.[33]

I interpret these variations in mode of address as evidence of *Grupp 8*'s belief in the early years that change could be achieved for women when the women affected joined together and decided to work for change. Thereafter, the mode of address indicates that *Grupp 8* increasingly saw itself as a vanguard for women and that change would occur when *Grupp 8* led women in actions that would tip the class struggle in favor of the working class. The mode of address in the late 1970s could reflect the fact that members of *Grupp 8* at this time were increasingly drawn to activities that provided an opportunity to do something concrete and immediate to improve women's lives, such as support systems for battered or raped women. The means of change then became helping and making contact with at-risk women in the hope that they would join the women's movement and thus make it stronger.

Did these changes in *Grupp 8*'s ways of campaigning and addressing itself to other women play a role for the impact on women's situation? You could in fact imagine that when the group adapted a more traditional left-wing way of organizing it lost some of its possibility to be a radical and independent voice in the discussion on gender equality politics that went on during the 1970s in Sweden. Talking like the radical left, marching like the radical left might have made it possible to neglect the group by identifying it with all the revolutionary parties at that time. The third turn of *Grupp 8*, toward a more helping activism, could also have had the same effect. Now it became possible to identify the group with what women's organization had done before: charity. But *Grupp 8* was not the sole group to step up for battered or sexually abused women, and the force of these groups together in getting these questions on the political agenda cannot be underestimated.

Starting in the archives we can also analyze how *Grupp 8* shaped a new way of being a woman. In the terminology of French sociologist Pierre Bourdieu, we might say that *Grupp 8* criticized the prevailing habitus for women by pointing out other strategies, another habitus, for women in the society of the time.

Bourdieu uses the term habitus to refer to a set of dispositions that vary among social groups and are learned through upbringing and observation.

These dispositions consist of tacit knowledge about the conditions of life and society as well as of rules for how those who belong to the group should live and act. Bourdieu argues that habitus is rooted in earlier successful strategies for survival and best possible outcome in a given situation.[34]

Grupp 8's behavior in connection with their actions, in contrast to other and earlier Swedish feminist groups, was characterized by marching, shouting, singing, and passing out leaflets on the streets and in public places in a way that was not designed to gain public sympathy but rather to demonstrate strength and rebelliousness. This behavior may be seen as a protest against the feminine ideal that *Grupp 8* contended was dominant in society. The habitus that *Grupp 8* called into question was, according to the group, based on the notion that women should concentrate on getting married (and therefore having to please men) in order to be supported by a man—a logical survival strategy for women in a society where women had limited opportunities. *Grupp 8* systematically criticized this habitus, which the group believed enslaved women. In its analyses, the group often emphasized a different survival strategy: to become financially independent through paid work and thus able to choose to live their lives in other ways.

Naturally, *Grupp 8* was not alone in this analysis at the time, but what set the group apart from others who promulgated the same thinking was that *Grupp 8*, in its behavior and mode of action, also performed loudness, disorder, and revolt as a survival strategy for women. By revolting, women could make themselves independent and break away from the habitus based on pleasing and waiting on men. In that way, *Grupp 8* framed a new norm.

Put in the context of the history of feminist activism I would argue that the habitus performed by *Grupp 8* and other new feminist groups in the 1970s has had the most long-lasting impact. Activists in these groups performed an independent and vindicatory woman, far from being uncritical about society and women's position in it, seeing women struggling together as a means to make change. It seems to me that this habitus has been present ever since.

Conclusion

In contemporary testimonies of early activists from the new Swedish feminist groups of the 1970s, the difficulties to marry socialism and feminism in concrete activism do not play any larger role. It rarely occupies a place in the narrative that corresponds to the importance it has in the archive material. This is probably not intentional; it is more reasonable to believe that the early activists, consciously or unconsciously, have chosen to emphasize the aspects that are relevant to them today, when it's not just a question of forgetfulness—they do not remember episodes that in hindsight seem insignificant. But for the historians it points to the fact that those testimonies are not reliable sources.

If testimonies of former activists are to be used as a starting point for studying the feminist groups of the 1970s, they must be examined from a source-critical perspective and compared to other source material. One of the source-critical questions that needs to be asked is how representative these testimonies are. Most feminist groups of the 1970s seem to have had flat organizations comprised of a number of small, independent groups, each of which might take a somewhat different approach and do somewhat different things. The activists' testimonies thus have bearing on only part of the organization, which presents a risk that other aspects of the organization will not emerge. More important however is the fact that often only the leading and long-standing activists have been afforded the opportunity to talk about 1970s feminism. The persons who were in more peripheral or obscure positions—in the 1970s or today—have rarely spoken or written publicly about their experiences.

In this chapter I have also tried to show that using archive material left behind by these groups gives very good grounds to make other analyses than those put forward by the activists. When it comes to the changing way of organizing as well as to the discussion about impact, the sort of analysis I have presented here is not to be found in the narratives of early activists. Such analysis and discussions need to stand on large historical accounts, built on relevant and reliable sources.

Elisabeth Elgán, is a professor of history at the Department of History at Stockholm University, Sweden. Her main field of research has been the relation between gender and politics as well as the history of feminism. She has recently published a book in Swedish about the new feminists of the 1970s (*Att ge sig själv makt: Grupp 8 och 1970-talets feminism,* 2015). Her publications in other languages comprise an analysis of the reason for the success of women politicians in the Nordic countries in the 1990s ("The Political Success of Scandinavian Women," in *Political and Historical Encyclopedia of Women,* ed. Christine Fauré, 2003: 473–80) and a relatively recent comparative analysis of the very different reception of gender equality politics in France and Sweden ("Regards croisés sur les politiques d'égalité femmes-hommes et leur réception en France et en Suède," in *Femmes-hommes: penser l'égalité,* ed. Sandrine Dauphin and Réjane Sénac, 2012: 191–98).

Notes

1. Gunilla Thorgren, *Grupp 8 & jag* (Stockholm: Norstedt, 2003); Ebba Witt-Brattström, *Å alla kära systrar!: Historien om mitt sjuttiotal* (Stockholm: Norstedt, 2010); Ingrid Sillén, ed., *Tusen systrar ställde krav: Minnen från 70-talets kvinnokamp* (Stockholm: Migra, 2010); Eva Schmitz, *Systerskap som politisk handling: Kvinnors organisering i Sverige, 1968 till 1982* (Lund: Lunds universitet, 2007); Emma Isaksson, *Kvinnokamp: Synen på underordning och motstånd i den nya kvinnorörelsen* (Stockholm: Atlas, 2007); Hanna Hallgren, *När lesbiska blev kvinnor: Lesbiskfeministiska kvinnors diskursproduktion rörande kön, sexualitet, kropp och identitet under 1970- och 1980-talen i Sverige* (Linköping: Linköpings universitet, 2008).
2. See for instance Inga-Lisa Sangregorio, "Kärlek vid första ögonkastet," and Solveig Roth Johansson, "Detta hade jag längtat efter," in Sillén, *Tusen systrar ställde krav,* 94, 117.
3. Hallgren, *När lesbiska blev kvinnor*; Schmitz, *Systerskap som politisk handling*; Isaksson, *Kvinnokamp.*
4. The lack of empirical studies giving an overview over the WLM does not seem to be only a Swedish problem. In her excellent PhD thesis *Pornografi er teori, voldtekt er praksis: Kvinnekamp mot voldtekt og pornografi i Frankrike og Norge ca 1970–1985* at Oslo University in 2014, the Norwegian historian Trine Rogg Korsvik struggles with getting a correct picture of the French and the Norwegian WLMs as a background to her analysis of feminist politics on pornography and prostitution.
5. An in-depth study of *Grupp 8,* by the author of this chapter, was published in Swedish in August 2015 under the title *Att ge sig själv makt: Grupp 8 och 1970-talets feminism* (Stockholm: Makadam förlag, 2015).
6. The curious name of the group is said to have come from its founding by eight women in 1968, and it seems that the intention was for the group to adopt a more explicit name later on but that this simply never happened.
7. All documents to which I refer are in Swedish. The citations should be understood as follows: ARBARK, Grupp 8, Volym 4, "Protokoll vid sammanträde med grupp 8 den 21 jan 1969," means that the source is found at the Labour Movement Archives and Library in Stockholm, where it is filed under the name *Grupp 8.* The following notation refers to the volume and the final notation is either the title of the document, if enclosed in quotation marks, or a description that makes it possible to find the document. RA, Föreningsarkiv, Grupp 8 i Stockholm, A1:1, Protokoll från Grupp 8:s årsmöte 1975, means that the source is found in the Swedish National Archives among the archives of voluntary associations and "Grupp 8" is the notation for the association archives used here. The following notation refers to the archive volume and the final notation is the title or a description of the document as such, as for documents at the Labour Movement Archives and Library in Stockholm. When multiple sources are cited, they are separated by semicolons. When I refer to *Grupp 8*'s magazine, *Kvinnobulletinen,* or to other periodicals, the names of the periodicals are italicized to distinguish them from other source material.
8. ARBARK, Grupp 8, Volym 4, Grönt skrivhäfte, "Protokoll från sammanträdet med Grupp 8 i Foajén på Hässelby Familjehotell den 7/1 1969."

9. Drude Dahlerup, *Rødstrømperne: Den danske Rødstrømpebevægelses udvikling, nytænkning og gennemslag 1970–1985. Vol. 2* (Copenhagen: Gyldendal, 1998), 93–107, 115–25.
10. RA, Föreningsarkiv, Grupp 8 i Stockholm, B3:1, Flygblad/Paroller 1970, "(Gamla) Grupp 8:s.första flygblad om sig själva, våren 1970"; "Grupp 8:s programförklaring," *Kvinnobulletinen,* no. 1 (1971).
11. ARBARK, Grupp 8, volym 1, "Diskussionsunderlag," undated/dated based on the text.
12. Photographs of the banners in *Kvinnobulletinen,* no. 4 (1974); RA, Föreningsarkiv, Grupp 8 i Stockholm, B3:1, Flygblad/Paroller 1974, untitled leaflets signed Grupp 8, dated by hand to 1974; RA, Föreningsarkiv, Grupp 8 i Stockholm, B3:1, Tal och resolutioner 1971–1974, "Kvinnor, kamrater!"; "Kvinnor, kamrater!" in *Kvinnobulletinen,* no. 4 (1974); "Resolution," *Kvinnobulletinen,* no. 4 (1974); RA, Föreningsarkiv, Grupp 8 i Stockholm, B3:1, Tal och resolutioner 1971–1974, "Resolution till demonstrationen den 16 november 1974"; RA, Föreningsarkiv, Grupp 8 i Stockholm, B1B:1, Interbulletin julen 1974, "Efter det deprimerande temamötet efter kampanjveckan"; RA, Föreningsarkiv, Grupp 8 i Stockholm, B1B:1, Internbulletin julen 1974, "Inlägg från massmediagruppen."
13. RA Föreningsarkiv, Grupp 8 i Stockholm, B1:1, volym 1, I-bullen maj 1975, "Tal hållet på Åsö gymnasium 2 februari 1975 av Anne Lidén."
14. RA Föreningsarkiv, Grupp 8 i Stockholm, B1:1, volym 1, I-bullen maj 1975, "Kritik angående talet på Åsö gymnasium 2/2 -75."
15. RA Föreningsarkiv, Grupp 8 i Stockholm, B1:1, volym 1, I-bullen maj 1975, "Kritik angående talet på Åsö gymnasium 2/2 -75."
16. RA, Föreningsarkiv, Grupp 8 i Stockholm, A1:1, Motioner Grupp 8:s årsmöte 25 april 1976, Motion nr 12.
17. Quoted by Inga-Lisa Sangregorio in "Kvinnor sitter fortfarande och väntar på att bli uppbjudna," *Kvinnobulletinen,* no. 3 (1977).
18. "Ibland känns det som om samhället är ett rivjärn och jag en grönsak," *Kvinnobulletinen,* no. 2 (1977); Witt-Brattström, *Å alla kära systrar!,* 144–46.
19. Britta Stövling, *Återtagandet: Feminismens andra våg ur kvinnorörelsen i USA* (Stockholm: Författarförlaget, 1977).
20. Margareta Garpe, "Har vi något att lära av kvinnorörelsen i Amerika?" *Aftonbladet* 12/7-1977; Margareta Garpe, "Y-kromosomen inte vår fiende," *Aftonbladet* 19/8-1977.
21. Barbro Werkmäster, "Splittring i kvinnornas kamp," *Aftonbladet* 13/7-1977.
22. RA, Gr. 8, B1B:1, internbulletin nr 1 1972, "Skildring från debattkväll med Göteborgs Fredrika Bremerförbund," RA, Gr. 8, B3:1, flygblad/paroller 1972, "Kvinnor, Kamrater."
23. ARBARK, Gr. 8, vol. 2, Grupp 8 stormöte den 10/10 1972 på Moderna museets filial, protokoll; "Sossarnas familjeprogram," *Kvinnobulletinen,* no. 2–3 (1972); RA, Gr. 8, B3:1, 1973, flygblad 1973, "Låt inte sossarna göra kvinnofrågan till ett valjippo"; "Ännu en femma i kapitalets tjänst," *Kvinnobulletinen,* no. 3 (1974); "Kvinnokamp på Palmes vis," *Kvinnobulletinen,* no. 2 (1975).
24. RA, Gr. 8, B1B:1, internbulletin fjärde kvartalet 1974, "Rapport från diskussionerna vid stormötesfesten hösten 1973."
25. ARBARK, Grupp 8, volym 4, "Trollkarlarnas hus."

26. RA, Föreningsarkiv, Grupp 8 i Stockholm, B3:1, Flygblad/Paroller 1970, handwritten title, "Flygblad valet1970."
27. RA, Föreningsarkiv, Grupp 8 i Stockholm, B3:1, Flygblad/Paroller 1972, "Vi är trötta på."
28. RA, Föreningsarkiv, Grupp 8 i Stockholm, B3:1, Flygblad/Paroller 1973, "Kvinnor! Vi måste höja våra röster. ..."
29. Maud Eduards, *Förbjuden handling: Om kvinnors organisering och feministisk teori* (Malmö: Liber, 2002).
30. ARBARK, Grupp 8, volym 4, "Protokoll från sammanträdet med Grupp 8 i Foajén på Hässelby Familjehotell den 7/1 1969."
31. RA, Föreningsarkiv, Grupp 8 i Stockholm, B3:1, Flygblad/Paroller 1974, untitled leaflet signed Grupp 8, dated by hand, 1974.
32. Föreningsarkiv, Grupp 8 i Stockholm, B3:1, flygblad/paroller 1978, "Öppet hus 5 mars om kvinnoarbetslösheten."
33. RA, Föreningsarkiv, Grupp 8 i Stockholm, B3:1, "Vad varje kvinna bör veta!" Undated leaflet. Dated by reference to other documents.
34. Pierre Bourdieu, *Questions de sociologie* (Paris: Éd. de Minuit, 1984), 134f. I was inspired to use Bourdieu's concept of habitus to analyze the WLM after reading Lynn Walter's article "The Embodiment of Ugliness and the Logic of Love: The Danish Redstocking Movement," *Feminist Review,* no. 36 (Autumn 1990): 103–26. In his book on the structures of men's domination and women's subordination, Pierre Bourdieu also uses the concept of habitus to signify gender and rules surrounding gender, even though it's not at the center of his reasoning; Pierre Bourdieu, *La domination masculine* (Paris: Seuil, 1998), 9, 45, 70.

Bibliography

Bourdieu, Pierre. *Questions de sociologie.* 2nd ed. Paris: Éd. de Minuit, 1984.

Dahlerup, Drude. *Rødstrømperne: den danske Rødstrømpebevægelses udvikling, nytænkning og gennemslag 1970–1985. 2 vols.* Copenhagen: Gyldendal, 1998.

Della Porta, Donatella, and Mario Diani. *Social Movements: An Introduction.* Oxford: Blackwell, 1999.

Isaksson, Emma. *Kvinnokamp: synen på underordning och motstånd i den nya kvinnorörelsen.* Stockholm: Atlas, 2007.

Schmitz, Eva. *Systerskap som politisk handling: kvinnors organisering i Sverige 1968 till 1982.* Lund: Lunds universitet, 2007.

Sillén, Ingrid, ed. *Tusen systrar ställde krav: minnen från 70-talets kvinnokamp.* Stockholm: Migra, 2010.

Stövling, Britta. *Återtagandet: feminismens andra våg ur kvinnorörelsen i USA.* Stockholm: Författarförlaget, 1977.

Thorgren, Gunilla. *Grupp 8 & jag.* Stockholm: Norstedt, 2003.

Walter, Lynn. "The Embodiment of Ugliness and the Logic of Love: The Danish Redstocking Movement." *Feminist Review,* no. 36 (Autumn 1990): 103–26.

Witt-Brattström, Ebba. *Å alla kära systrar!: historien om mitt sjuttiotal.* Stockholm: Norstedt, 2010.

Chapter 15

After the Protest

Biographical Consequences of Movement Activism in an Oral History of Women's Liberation in Britain

Margaretta Jolly

Sisterhood and After: The Women's Liberation Oral History Project (SAA) grew out of the determination of a group of older feminist activists and historians in Britain that the activism of their generation must not be forgotten.[1] Allying with a thirtysomething curator-researcher in the British Library's social science department and a fortysomething academic at the University of Sussex resulted in a grant from the Leverhulme Trust in 2010 for a three-year project involving the capture of sixty life history interviews with core activists across the UK, the making of ten related short films, as well as the interpretation of the interviews in an extensive schools-facing website.[2] Our primary aim was to create a permanent multimedia archive in a beautiful and powerful library where subsequent generations could discover the work of the movement pioneers of the 1960s–1980s. In this way, SAA attempts to speak to many publics at once, building on a strong tradition of feminist historiography. Feminists launched community activist archives as far back as the 1920s and have often favored oral history as a means to capture the women who do not write and the voices of all who speak out. But in many ways our oral history ironically restages the challenges that feminists themselves brought to the table in wanting to take the experiential and the personal into account and in terms of who can represent whom. Before turning to the results, let me say a few words on our methodological challenges for others interested in undertaking feminist oral history.

Oral Histories, Feminist Histories

There are two initial challenges that any oral historian must address: selection criteria and interview method. Unlike most social sciences, oral history is interested in the known individual, but also unlike journalism, it seeks to situate the individual in historical context. We dealt with this at the stage of selection by prioritizing the criteria of involvement in particular campaigns and political demands, with a spread across sector, region, ideology, and only secondarily by general "identities" including class, race, sexuality, disability. We also frankly identified those who had been political or intellectual catalysts—about a third of them—although we were mindful of the strong desire for "lesser-known" or "unsung" women to be represented, and these comprised the rest.[3] This raised an immediate methodological test, for an important aspect of our interviewees' self-perception is their almost unanimous rejection of claims to leadership. This reflects the horizontal nature of post-1960s social movements and the particularly fervent principles of equality and autonomy in the women's liberation movement (WLM), where, for example, anyone could speak to the media, no matter how inexperienced. Although feminists sometimes did work with political parties, particularly in Scotland, Wales, and Northern Ireland where the overlap between women's liberation and nationalist struggles necessitated it, there was always hostility to notions of hierarchy or even organized membership.[4]

The refusal of "leadership" has left us with the contradiction that our interviewees' self-description does not square with their position at the center of campaigns or ideas—a position for which, as we have seen, we selected them for interview. Juliet Mitchell, for example, explaining how she worked with others to organize the first national women's liberation conference, is adamant that she "wasn't the only person thinking [about women's liberation]. These things don't happen as one person: it's a misconception of history." And she goes on to warn, "If you look for people you find people, if you want to be the only heroine of the story, then you don't find [her]."[5] Much as this is true, we also have to acknowledge Mitchell's role as a formative intellectual, whose 1966 *Women: The Longest Revolution* was recognized even at the time as a breakthrough in understanding the structures of women's oppression. Mitchell was also, as her co-organization of the Ruskin conference itself suggests, an activist, effective media-woman, teacher, and feminist influence in and on the male New Left. Our view is therefore that in her own right she, and many others, can be described in Morris and Staggenborg's terms as "decision-makers who inspire and organise others to participate in social movements."[6]

Despite our sometimes contested interest in leadership, our archive offers a fair picture of the British movement. Campaigns represented include Women's Aid, Greenham Common Women's Peace Camp, Women in Manual Trades, the Organisation of Women of African and Asian Descent, Women Against Pit Closures; also represented are participants in magazines such as *Spare Rib* and *Shrew*.[7] Ideologically, most are at the socialist feminist end of the spectrum, but there is a sizeable minority of self-identified radical feminists and a small number of liberal feminists—and these categories include "Black feminist/womanist" activists who distinguished themselves by their commitment to simultaneously conceived race-gender liberation. We were less successful in capturing geographical diversity. Though we set aside a quota of five from Wales, Scotland, and Northern Ireland, respectively, to reflect the political importance of the four nations within the UK, within England we found it very difficult not to replicate a London-centric portrait. Thirty-one interviewees have lived most of their life in the capital with only fourteen living or working elsewhere, including Leeds, Halifax, Bradford, Hastings, Preston, and Bristol. Similarly, we did not succeed in representing working-class feminism as fully as we should have. Yet geographical and class categories are deceptive, for both conceal a mobility and fluidity that is crucial to the core experience of the WLM. We interviewed fifteen women of working-class origin, a few of whom still identified as working class, and at least another fifteen were from lower middle-class backgrounds, making up half of the interviewees. Many interviewees had traveled and settled away from childhood homes, and London was a seemingly irresistible draw for young activists. Stories of migration came from the three North Americans and one Australian who had settled in Britain, as well as from the ten Black or Asian-British and one British-Chinese woman, though most of the latter were themselves born in Britain. Seven Jewish women were also represented; ethnic minority interviewees therefore made up over a quarter of the whole. We did not select particularly for religious background, other than in Northern Ireland, but the results were interesting: fourteen were of Catholic origin (four from Northern Ireland); fifteen of Anglican origin, including from Scottish, Northern Irish, Chinese-Malay, and Kenyan backgrounds. In addition, five had experienced a Methodist upbringing, one Quaker, and one Hutterite Christian. Two had a Muslim family background, two a Hindu one, with the British-Chinese interviewee explaining her parents as Confucian. Interestingly, nine women describe themselves as still practicing, including three Anglicans, one who became an Anglican priest but has converted to Catholicism in her eighties; three others are still Catholics. Two declared themselves interested in a feminist spirituality; one has been interested in Buddism. Sexuality was also complex; we interviewed seventeen self-identified lesbian or bisexual women, but a much greater number had at some point had a sexual or romantic relationship with another woman. One interviewee self-identified as disabled/differently abled, and one had experienced institutional psychiatric care; many more, as we shall see, talked of challenges to mental or physical health.

This demography in some ways determines biographical consequence. By definition we have chosen those who self-identified as having belonged to the WLM (with a few notable exceptions), and for whom that epithet is still dear. It is not surprising that we therefore found that many of them are still activists in late life. That we recorded well-known movers and shakers, however, is a pricklier determinant. This is because movement leadership, even in the soft form we have described it, has been correlated with educational capital, which in turn correlates with a middle-class background. Feminist movements have indeed specifically followed a pattern of forming when women who are otherwise relatively privileged find their sexual or social status to be unfair. But even in workers' movements, such as the powerful British trade union movement of the late 1960s and 1970s, which for many working-class women was a far more important home than the WLM, those with more education are often more likely to lead.[8] One element we could anticipate, therefore, is that the later lives of many of our interviewees have also been affected by early advantages in education, status, or wealth, even if these were mixed with other disadvantages of gender, sexuality, race, religion, disability, or region. Cynthia Cockburn, a deeply conscientious labor and peace activist, made this point specifically in her interview, noting that she was one of many feminists who had been able to choose an insecure and principled working life because of a small inheritance that enabled her to buy her house back in the 1970s when she separated from her husband. Certainly the deregularization of the British housing market from the 1980s has been crucial to the life choices that our interviewees made, particularly if they lived in London, some getting lucky simply by having bought early on, others not.

In this light, we hope that our interview method has helped make these contexts visible. Modeled on the British Library oral history archive's "life story" approach, we also asked about relationships behind an interviewees' given name; about how their lives compared to their mothers'; about changing feelings about one's body; about pocket money, domestic arrangements, race, and national difference; and about how people felt about the method itself. Life story interviewing is well placed to reveal the emotional and physical relationships that are part of the formation as well as the consequence of ideas, actions, politics, and, indeed, the "passions" that can produce a lifetime commitment to activism.[9] It gives time to understanding the friendships and lovers in (and against) political networks, the way that work happens at home or in unpaid, informal spheres, the way that politics is defined with and without children, money, sexuality and sickness, depression, art, and parents. Thus, if it is inconveniently long to do, it is homologous to the way that material, sexual, relational, and reproductive life is long and various as well. The feminist principle of situated knowledge also influenced our method; we therefore archived short interviews *of* as well as *by* the team. Some of the inherent ethical challenges in undertaking such personal interviews were helped by the fact that the interview relationship could develop over the many hours we spent with each person.

Wrenching generalized meanings out of individual life stories is a painful act that Paul Thompson has identified as the "third and final choice" that an oral historian has to make.[10] However we hope that, even as we try to avoid *individualism* in interpretation, we may honor some of the *individuality* that our method has foregrounded, in turning now to consider the later lives of activists. Our interviewees' long and sometimes meandering narratives reveal expectations about work inside and outside the home, the relationships and children they were supposed to have, but also less obvious elements of where they expected to settle, the kinds of foods and fun they expected to consume, and even the sexual and emotional lives they expected to have. The interesting question is where this economic and social trajectory was thrown off course—or, conversely—enhanced, by their political participation, as we shall see.

The Biographical Consequences of Feminist Activism

> When I was young you were meant to meet people in your twenties, settle down, have children and … live in a kind of peaceful elderly middle age, and I've found my life's never gone according to that plan from early times. I initially rebelled against that pattern, but as I've got older I've been amazed that all the things that people expect to happen never seem to fit.[11]
>
> *Sheila Rowbotham, interviewed 2010*

Our oral history includes many for whom the movement was part of a personal transformation in which their lives became utterly different from those of their mothers. It thus powerfully testifies to the effects of political participation. Rowena Arshad, for example, described her Chinese-Malaysian Christian mother's life as hedged with shame and misplaced snobbery as an impoverished single mother and immigrant, hanging on to a fragile social status as a teacher who saw herself above other immigrants. In contrast, Rowena's discovery of a group of Black politicos and feminists at university took her into a new world where in middle age she became a pioneer of Black Trade Union activism and eventually Equal Opportunities Commissioner for Scotland. Now nearing retirement, she continues to define herself as a new kind of Scottish woman and mother, self-inventing, justice-seeking, but also filled with a fun and zest her mother could not allow herself. Similarly, Zoe Fairbairns describes her white middle-class mother as an unwaged domestic laborer, the wife of a man who did not love her, with no conception of divorce, three children, and no material help. Fairbairns describes the thrilling realization, around 1969, that she herself neither had to marry nor have children; she could stop assessing herself in terms of heterosexual attractiveness, give up disordered eating, and also be economically self-sufficient.

But not all our interviewees told such conversion narratives. For a good number, political socialization began in childhood. Notable examples include Valerie Wise, the chair of the Women's Committee in the Greater London Council in the 1980s, whose mother Audrey Wise had been a leading Member of Parliament in support of women's rights in the 1960s; and Amrit Wilson, whose mother was a human-rights activist in India. And the Communist mothers of Beatrix Campbell and Barbara Taylor became so interested in feminism that at times their radical daughters were irritated by their interference.[12] In fact, about half of our sixty interviewees were raised in left-wing or anti-imperialist families, seven of whose mothers were or became activists.

We can begin to measure the effects of activism more systematically by comparing our interviewees' stories with the life course of their peer generations, as well as longitudinally against their mother's destinies. Generational theory, which draws together kin relationships with social cohort identities,[13] allows us to identify three "generations" within our interviewees: a handful of so-called traditionalists/silent children born between 1925 and 1942; a large group of postwar "early baby-boomers" born between 1943 and 1955; and a second tranche of "late baby-boomers" born between 1956 and 1964.[14] Existing studies of these generations in Britain and the United States suggest that those born earlier in the century have been more likely to follow normative paths or, more concretely, to have clung to paid careers when they could get them and stayed in them once they had them. Women were expected principally to marry and mother, notwithstanding the experience of the Depression and Second World War in early life. In contrast, those born in the middle of the twentieth century have more often been willing to adopt an "alternative" lifestyle, aided by factors including postwar peace, secularization, and, importantly for women, contraception.[15] Life-course theorists have correlated this with the psychological effects of a widespread opening of opportunities and equalizing of incomes. This equality of opportunity has, since the 1970s, closed down again, creating newer, more conservative generations, sometimes termed the "Generation X" and now "Y," born roughly between 1968 and 1975 and the late 1970s onward.

Before proceeding further, we need to acknowledge that these generations are internally variable and also highly ideological categories in themselves. Gullette describes how the original use of the term "baby boomers" to describe a demographic "bulge" between 1946 and 1964 in the United States has become stretched and politicized.[16] According to the popular press, these are a vast demographic army of selfish, aging rock 'n' rollers sucking up their children's birthrights, still benefiting from the welfare state and the housing market boom, while their children strive to keep even miserable jobs and to patch the family up after their parents' misguided experiments with free love. This stereotype has its flipside; sixty- and seventy-year-olds looking ahead at ill and impoverished years as the life course extends, while their amoral yuppie kids fail to care. Gullette argues that this constructed generation war conveniently displaces the effects of free-market capitalism that has been transforming the life course over the second half of the twentieth century to create extreme economic insecurity at all ages. In this sense, there is truth in the "demographic time-bomb," in which even in developing countries the proportion of old people to potential younger carers of working age is increasing. Baby boomers' grandchildren are also undoubtedly coming of age in a world vastly more economically unequal than their own.[17] These contexts certainly shape the long lives of activists as they do everyone, and will be changing the "psychology" of each cohort as we speak.

Cohort generations are also internally differentiated by many factors—class, race, health, region, to name an obvious few. In Northern Ireland, for example, early baby boomer married Catholic women were twice as likely to work as Protestant women, despite the ideal of men as family breadwinners, because of employment discrimination against Catholic men, though both Protestant and Catholic professional women faced a marriage bar.[18] Afro-Caribbean migrants to England in the 1950s constitute a "generation" in themselves, as do East-African Asians who migrated in the late 1960s. Most of the Black women interviewed for SAA clearly situated their parents within a generational consciousness defined by migration and diasporic identity. Nadira Mirza, for example, speaks of the challenges of working with urbanized "second- and third-generation" British-Asians who were marrying peers from villages in Pakistan. Jewish women like Ursula Owen and Michelene Wandor also spoke vividly about their distinct sense of being "second generation," not only in relation to parental migrancy but also the Holocaust.[19] The evolution of Black and Jewish women's liberation needs to be understood in relation to the kinds of parenting they had, as well as to white racism and discrimination that their parents as well as they experienced. The pattern here too is that those who were active in the WLM of the 1970s and 1980s are more liberal than their parents.

The significance of this liberalization through the middle of the century is very debatable. Inglehart holds that economic and social growth allowed the baby-boomer generation to privilege self-expression and the quality of life.[20] But Easterlin has argued that as many responded to these opportunities by remaining normative, and it has rather been the more recent years of a stagnant economy that has prompted alternative lifestyles, in his rather punishing terms, "delaying entrance into adult roles."[21] McAdam's interpretation is more sympathetic to those who have seen their lives as a struggle for justice. For him, the easier climate of the postwar years allowed activists to reject normal life-course trajectories as a conscious choice.[22] Activists' lives in this way appear to be an extreme version of a generational shift.[23] Certainly we can see this in relation to paid employment, where there is a striking preponderance of public-sector, educational, and care work, often taken up in midlife, following years of activism while living on low-paid service-sector work, or as a student, or on government benefits. Although many SAA interviewees came of age at a time when the public sector in the UK was generally growing, they conform to the findings of studies of former New Left activists who are concentrated in teaching or other "helping" professions and have lower incomes than their age peers; they are also more likely than their age peers to have experienced an episodic or nontraditional work history.[24] About a third of our interviewees went on to become academics; just under a third are public sector, including teachers, equality consultants, or social workers; and most of the rest work in grassroots and voluntary organizations, such as Pragna Patel in Southall Black Sisters. A handful have become professional politicians, including Jane Hutt, who moved impressively from managing Welsh Women's Aid to becoming finance minister for the Welsh Assembly. A few manage to make a living in the arts, including the writer Michelene Wandor, artist Mary Kelly, and musician Alison Raynor, but many more write, make music, or knit for love. Only two are businesswomen, and neither one conventionally so. These are Ursula Owen, one-time director of the feminist Virago Press, and eco-builder Barbara Jones. Sue Lopez was exceptional as a professional soccer coach.

This work pattern makes our oldest interviewees, born between 1925 and 1939, more unusual in relation to their peers. Jalna Hanmer, Mary McIntosh, Cynthia Cockburn, Ellen Malos, Betty Cook, Una Kroll, Grace Lau, Mary Kennedy, and Sheila Kitzinger worked as academics, a nurse, a doctor, a photographer, an adult educator, and a birth activist respectively. Despite their very different class and ethnic backgrounds, they would have all been housewives had they followed their mothers' own paths, though some would also have been domestic servants, small businesswomen, and shopkeepers. Kroll's impoverished housekeeper mother had hoped her daughter would break through and become a brilliant surgeon. It is ironic that, instead, Kroll gave up medical school to become a nun, though she did later become a general practitioner and in old age, after women were finally allowed to be ordained in Britain in 1994, a lay priest. Poignantly, at that stage she was too old to gain a full-time post.

Giugni points out that such life-course effects belong to the category of unintended consequences of movement actions.[25] Jo Robinson's story furnishes another moving example. Born in 1942, in some ways a classic early baby boomer, Robinson grew up in a Blackpool suburb in which her father was a reasonably prosperous butcher, but her mother felt she had moved down a social class. Robinson's "hierarchically minded" parents expected their child to become a teacher and wife, but both died abruptly when she was still at college. Orphaned and traumatized, she took the bus to London with dreams of becoming a film director at age twenty-two. Her subsequent alternative life career of women's liberation and anarchism was mixed with hedonism, collective mothering, and uncertain mobility. Working first in a radical print collective, then as an art teacher, then midwife, she is now a gardener, a mid- to late-life job characteristic for a feminist of this generation. In her interview, she offers no regrets about this, but is equally clear that she imagined none of it on leaving home in 1964. "I thought that you got engaged at eighteen, married at twenty-one and had children at twenty-three, that's what I thought that you did. I was told and I believed that and then when I got to that age it wasn't like that at all…"[26]

The next generation down, Barbara Jones, a "late baby boomer" born in 1957, tells a similar story of serendipity and surprise. She describes growing up poor and Catholic in Barnsley, a good girl expected to go into a feminized profession such as social work, combined with having lots of children like her Catholic mother. Although she set off on this path, she encountered an inspiring feminist care-home manager who encouraged her to explore carpentry. This led to her taking a training course with Women in Manual Trades in the 1980s. She situates this decision as also deeply related to a profound, if at that time unconscious, sense of sexual difference. Jones now runs her own ecological building company in the lesbian-centered town of Todmorden. In some ways this took her back to her family's culture, looking at her six siblings who have almost all gone into small business. However it is obvious that her all-women eco-building business is as much a political project as an economic one, filled with ideals of self-sufficiency and women's relationship.[27]

Although examples like these suggest that activism may have involved some material self-sacrifice in later life, our archive also records upward mobility. I have suggested that this may be overdetermined by the fact that our oral history was focused upon those who were "inspirers" or leaders in some form, thus likely to have come into the movement with educational capital and possibly also financial resources, though the latter was not often inherited before midlife. Our rough sample confirms previous studies that suggest white lower/middle-class girls who finished grammar school form the nucleus of British activists.[28] Though many of our interviewees gave up a certain security, their movement years did not always prevent a midlife improvement in circumstance. Often, indeed, the former enabled the latter, through teaching women's studies or other professionalized feminist activities. Deirdre Beddoe, a working-class Welsh girl who at primary school was told she had to be a sailor's wife not a sailor, became a professor of history at the University of Glamorgan thanks in part to her brilliant uncovering of the history of Welsh working women.[29] We could also cite Betty Cook, Mary Kelly, Karen McMinn, Mukami McCrum, and many others who have in some way found that their politics has underwritten a profession that has enabled them to live at least as comfortably as their peers and certainly more than they had expected, Cook moving dramatically from life as a miner's wife to an educational advisor, and McCrum from a farming family in Kenya to a policy worker for the Scottish government.

Feminists are less comfortable talking about these gains, a discomfort that reflects the movement's much loftier ideals than mere equality of opportunity. Rosalind Delmar, whose father was a building laborer and mother a housewife in North Yorkshire, expresses the particular disappointment she felt in the 1980s when "friends of mine in the women's movement who had moved on to have careers related to the movement, like in women's studies or whatever, were not particularly interested in keeping up the connection when I had children. I thought that was very ironic as well, that, you know, the focus was on jobs and who was getting what job and, you know? … I was sad to see women in the women's movement behaving when they did get university jobs and so on, rather like male professors behaved."[30] This is perhaps the more striking given that Delmar was by then a psychotherapist and well known as a movement intellectual who had long previously moved into the world of university and adult education as well as literary translation.

If activists themselves have been so abashed about the modest career gains that they have made, popular opinion is even harsher in dismissing feminists as "middle class." This simplifies the mobile and precarious class status that our oral histories reveal is more often the truth. Yet the stereotype has certainly come back to haunt feminists in ironic ways. The free marketization of Western economies in the 1980s propelled a new generation of professional women who held few feminist allegiances but seemed to demonstrate that women were now "liberated." Was there a naiveté to the fact that many women were protesting at a time of general economic as well as political opportunity? And indeed, that feminism was itself generating small niches of employment in academia and equal opportunities training? Mitchell and Oakley's retrospection on "twenty years of feminism," published in 1986, considers the "unconscious function of the women's movement" to have been its complicity with a longer-term change in capitalism that set middle-class women's new employment against working-class women and men's redundancy.[31] Certainly in hindsight we can see that some of the well-known internal arguments over "difference" within the British movements reflected a generational lag in opportunity, as only in the 1980s, and then to a smaller extent, did Black, Asian, Catholic Northern Irish, and working-class late baby-boomer women gain the footing that white middle-class early baby-boomer women had begun to get in the 1960s. Stella Dadzie describes the poverty, educational exclusion, and policing that Black women faced in the 1970s as the reason she was far more quickly drawn to pan-African liberation movements than feminism at the time. Yet Dadzie's own story also shows the complexity of both class and identity, as she explains her own unlikely career as the daughter of a frail, poor white mother and feted Ghanian diplomat father. Like many Black women activists of her generation, she has become a freelance equal opportunities trainer and writer, having made her name with a groundbreaking book about resistance in 1985. Yet she also talks with brutal honestly about her financial naiveté at one point in choosing this over becoming a well-paid manager in a radical college.[32]

The mobility and flux of women's life courses is just as crucially defined by love, child bearing, and sexuality as by paid work. Transforming these aspects of life is of course at the heart of the WLM's aspirations. In the face of popular accusations that feminists were antimothering, antifamily, and also antiheterosexual, the WLM in the UK began with demands that included twenty-four-hour free childcare and evolved to ask for the right to define one's own sexuality. But what were the realities of activists' own lives? Most activists came into the movement unmarried and without children. This was partly because they were typically in their early twenties. The average age of becoming a mother in the UK in the 1970s was twenty-seven, and the mean age for women to marry in 1971, in England and Wales, was twenty-two.[33] Only a few of our older interviewees had done that. The minority who *were* mothers when they joined the movement, typically from our older cohort, became dramatic representatives of a new kind of life course. Ann Oakley, Catherine Hall, and Jenni Murray, for example, experimented with children's education, getting men to do the housework, giving birth at home, and combining mothering, activism, and paid work. Lynne Segal, like Jo

Robinson and Cynthia Cockburn, was a single mother who lived collectively as a means to create an alternative support system to the nuclear family. Since the key demand was for women to have reproductive choices, an alternative "consequence" was a new identity for women who did not have biological children and could more easily resist the sense of failure this brought. Many, like Beatrix Campbell, talk of the joy of parenting others' children, and lesbian women began to claim mothering as a life stage that they could own publicly.

Of course participation in the WLM did not magically solve the challenges of women's reproductive years. Forty-one of our sixty interviewees ended up being biological mothers, having one or two children, which was average for their peer group.[34] Many described how having them, typically in their thirties (and also generally in the 1980s) coincided with a period of retreat from activism, though sometimes a different set of political preoccupations emerged. They recounted ongoing divisions between biological and nonbiological mothers and child-free women, ambivalent feelings emerging around contraception and abortion, children who seemed to have been unhappy or rejected their mother's feminist values, the work and cost as well as the pleasures of childcare. The older interviewees were more directly faced with maternalist expectations, but all three generations testify to ongoing struggles to be "good enough" mothers. The young baby boomers seem little different from their peers in the way they now face new care responsibilities in relation to older relatives. At the same time the advent of The Pill, particularly after 1970 when it was available on the National Health Service to unmarried women, combined with the new expectations that women would compete with men professionally, created what Sylvia Ann Hewlitt has described provocatively as the "baby hunger" of professional baby-boomer women who delayed mothering until it was too late. Activists who have found themselves in this situation—admittedly only a couple—feel the irony particularly acutely, for obvious reasons. Zoe Fairbairns, one of the wittiest and most steadfast in her feminist refusal of maternity as destiny, expressed a realization that the absence of biological children has an impact in later life too:

> At my age, sixty-two, I look around and see my contemporaries …, I've chosen not to have kids and this is a joint choice with John, my partner, he never wanted to have kids either. And I look around and I see friends, contemporaries who have … now got these amazing grown-up kids who've all got wonderful jobs and they've got kids. And … the parents have got grandchildren and these people are going to be a consolation to them and look after them and look out for

> them in old age and suddenly I think, "Oh, you know, *that's* what it was all about. Maybe, you know, if I'd had kids, then now I'd have grandchildren and that would be nice." But, and then I think, "But you can't just have the good bits." And … if I run the video of my life—there's no point at which I think "Right, stop, that would be a point at which I could have kids and it would have worked out." I think that my decision not to have kids was the right decision for me, albeit perhaps made for the wrong reasons.

It is worth quoting this at some length because Fairbairns so clearly builds on the question of children to reflect on a broader sense of her life's shape as a feminist. She goes on to evoke the image of a scar, a fleshly trace that is startling in this context, and yet she is clearly proposing that what defines a feminist life course is autonomy. This means taking responsibility for youthful decisions in later life:

> So I'm not going to say that my not having kids is a scar that I bear from childhood because I don't think a decision is a scar. It's what you do. You know, you're responsible for your own decisions and if I had my time again I wouldn't make a different decision. But the reasons behind that decision, that is this perception that I had that really being a wife and a mother of young children was really horrible and a source of great misery and resentment for women, I think that perception was not entirely accurate. I think, you know, it can be a source of great joy and happiness for women and for men. Not for all, but it can be, but I didn't perceive that it could be. So that's a scar in a way, because I think I got it wrong.[35]

Feminists' feelings about childbearing are also entwined with sexuality, marriage and monogamy. McAdams reveals that former New Left activists are more likely than their age peers to have divorced, married later, or remained single, even in the context of decades in which life-long heterosexual marriage crumbled for the majority.[36] Again, are these chosen results, in a movement where patriarchal marriage and heterosexuality were themselves the objects of protest? It is somewhat a cliché now to talk of the baby-boomer activist looking back bemusedly on a youth of nonmonogamous experiment, but this does describe many of our interviews. Not one suggested explicitly that they still lived in an open relationship and forty-five have settled with a long-term partner, got married or civil-partnered. Yet it is obvious that the prism of sexual politics and rights has had enormous consequences in their unanimous insistence on sexual as well as economic equality in their later relationships. Many talk about how glad they are to have escaped the kinds of marital traps their parents endured before the English Divorce law of 1969, a law not passed in Northern Ireland until 1978, even if they have found their own relationships a struggle. Those who are single find comfort in their sense of independence and sometimes chosen celibacy. Several "live apart together," and all strive to divide housework fairly with their partner. Catherine and Stuart Hall's fifty-year marriage is an interesting as well as high-profile example of where a marriage preceded the movement and survived it. Catherine fascinatingly describes how an essential "emotional equality" underlay the stark disparity between his and her status—he an older star of the New Left who was typically masculinist in their early relationship, and she, a middle-class white woman who only in the 1980s learned deeply about the Caribbean culture of his ancestors.

A different kind of impact is evident in queer or lesbian relationships. A recent large-scale study of older lesbians in the UK reveals that the discovery of feminism allowed at least half them to come out.[37] Proportionally, this suggests a minimum of 250,000 queer women over seventy today owe their sense of sexuality in part to the WLM. Of the seventeen lesbian or bisexual women in our small study, four defined themselves as having entered the movement already identifying as lesbian; some, like Mary McIntosh, consciously attempted to link their original gay liberation work with feminism. However, thirteen attributed their sexuality as having begun in the movement, and many more talked of having had a period of "bisexuality" that was directly part of activist life even if it had not lasted. Here we see a political nurturing of a general fluidity and plasticity in women's sexualities that has also been important in extending "sex life" itself into older age. Lynne Segal's searing analysis of her male partner leaving her for a younger woman is interesting in that she is also testifying to making a new life in her sixties with a woman lover.

At the other end of the life course, activism has also had profound consequences for their experience of childhood, as interviewees realized belatedly the way they had been loved, dressed, punished, controlled as girls. This was most painful with the admission or remembering of sexual abuse in midlife. Beatrix Campbell's testimony is precisely sad because of this belatedness. She explained that though the subject was already thoroughly politicized and at the center of the 1970s WLM, it was only in the 1980s that she felt able to name and politicize her experience of being abused as a girl, or, as she put it, to "place children at the center of that narrative."[38] Here we should consider one final biographical consequence of activism: physical and mental health. Sheila Rowbotham's record of the ignominy of being treated for candida as if it were a shameful sexual disease in the mid-1960s is an ordinary but telling glimpse of the way that women's bodies were pathologized, and many interviewees mentioned the transformative effects of reading the feminist health handbook *Our Bodies, Ourselves,* of going to women's health workshops, and of seeing in other activists a new kind of physical beauty. Una Kroll's extraordinary description of giving the Eucharist while menstruating is a more unusual example, a protest against the church that was also an ecstatic reclaiming of her body from religious ideologies. Kirsten Hearn's interview, as a militant in Sisters Against Disablement, describes becoming feminist and lesbian as a blind woman, amusingly embracing "the dungaree with rapture" and experimenting with fat liberation.[39]

Although feminism has not been able to prevent disease or even necessarily help women manage weight issues when they want to, it has obviously transformed the terms in which women live in their bodies, or as Nadira Mirza put it, "recognising how much in control … you can be."[40] We can see too, in the contrast between Kroll and Hearn, the way that younger political generations pushed the bounds of normative femininity much further. This has helped in finding more positive ways to experience later life-course "turning points" of menopause and old age. But the relationship to mental health is more confusing. One of the most striking findings of our oral histories was the extent to which activists became preoccupied with their own or others' states of mind, in narratives where early political consciousness-raising often turned into prolonged therapeutic experiences in midlife. Out of the sixty we interviewed, thirty-two talk about having been depressed, with twenty-eight of those having sought therapy or counseling of some sort, though also, importantly, many also say their mothers had also been depressed; a "valium" generation of housewifery. Barbara Taylor, who has recently written a beautiful "memoir of madness" that followed a decade of excited activism at the center of London's feminist intelligentsia in the 1970s, subtly adds to this diagnosis in linking her breakdown in part to the effects of psychoanalytic treatment, though she also attributes her cure to it. Still, we must ask why so many feminists have seemed troubled and some of our most brilliant exponents even spectacularly mad.

Could we conclude that in some senses being a feminist *made* one oppressed or even ill? This is risky, in the face of ongoing popular stereotyping of feminists as dour and miserable. It is also tempting to attribute mental struggles to the challenges that come with refusing normative life courses and activist burnout. However, we need to contextualize our interviewees' stories in light of a large-scale study in 2001 that reported 15 percent of British adults had recently experienced an episode of anxiety or depression. This seems to hit mostly in middle age and is worse for women and those of Afro-Caribbean origin.[41] We might also admit that people are drawn to social movements because they are seeking meaning or remedy. Here we can see a correspondence between "biographical availability" for activism and its consequences.[42] A third explanation is that feminists' attention to private life constructed new emotional identities and even life courses, some of which have been enabling, some disabling. It would be foolish to simplify this, and again we need to situate it within a postmodern culture of confession that has also been stimulated by market forces and a therapeutic industry not at all feminist in origin or intent. Yet there is no doubt that feminists have often suffered, and personal breakdowns may be activism's unintended consequence in a peculiarly ironic form.

Conclusion

What can be said about individuals and impact? The portraits I have sketched show that feminist activists may not be heroic or even happy. But then, why should they be? Rather, they were, in Sara Ahmed's terms, trying to be alive, in the sense of putting the life course of a woman up for radical new definition.[43] In this respect, despite the obviously special nature of activists in the general population, the personal consequences of activism constitute an impact that is distinct from policy change. Movement veterans define an extended generation that is still more politically active than their peers. In this way they also carry "the political lessons and perspectives of the movement that shaped their enduring collective identity into other movements."[44] This is amply true of ours, even as they themselves learned from other movements.

Here we need to see generational life courses as entwined with the life cycle of movements too. The baby boomers came of age during the most fertile cycle of protest of the postwar period, in which there was an extraordinary diffusion of what social-movement theorists call tactical forms, identities, frames, within and across movements. Our project reveals their political education in civil rights, anticolonial movements, the New Left, and anti-Vietnam protests, often adapting ideas and tactics from constituencies unlike their own. We glimpse their influence in turn within the campaigns of the 1970s and 1980s, for example Amrit Wilson in Asian women's employment rights, Gail Chester in the International Feminist Book Fairs and libraries, Susie Orbach in women's mental health, or Lesley Abdela in campaigning for equal representation of women in the UK parliament. This historical fusing of movement life cycle with individual and generational life courses created a group of long-term activists and sustained networks. Wilson today chairs Imkaan, an organization challenging violence against Asian, Black, minority ethnic, and refugee women. Chester works with young feminist bloggers at the F-Word. Orbach has advised Dove's "Real Women" campaign. Abdela is a consultant for developing gender charters of postconflict governments like Tunisia. Now many are taking on new activisms around age.[45]

As "early adopters" of life courses that have become more common, activists also model a way of life that is part of the diffusion of feminist ideas into the general population. These include living apart together, extended or fluid family structures with no male breadwinner; shared housework; girl-centered education; ideals of personal and sexual autonomy; principles of care as well as social equality and opportunity. A new kind of bodily identity itself can be counted as a biographical consequence in these terms, from modeling Black dreadlocks or Jewish curls to enjoying fat and other non-normative bodies. This is the last of what McAdam defines as a three-stage process for these generations of activists, building on conscious rejection of normative life-course trajectories and their initial embedding of alternatives in local places and subcultures of opportunity such as campuses, low-rent neighborhoods, and upper middle-class suburbs to take them out to the culture at large.[46] A lovely instance of this is Michelene Wandor's reflection near the end of her interview that "I'm not, undervaluing the … power of … parenting and family, you know, genealogy, but I think … in cultural ways I have much, much more in common with my sons."[47]

Oral history interviewees also provide a valuable symbolic influence as the voices of a movement. Our interviewees are touchingly diffident when we ask them to assess their own contributions, but we think that the very particularity of their stories is what makes our project interesting to a public beyond the university or policymakers. In this they belong to a cultural arena of change particularly prized by women who have looked beyond and below the state or even the economy to know if we have won. Sisterhood and After's capture of some of the collective life of the UK WLM thus mimics women's movements themselves in attempting to create change through storytelling and through political education. Through the British Library's Learning Programme as well as the Sound Archive where our interviews will be kept, we hope to contribute to an alternative collective memory, one that acknowledges the differences between the four nations that make up the UK and the movement's richly varied communities. Della Porta and Diani argue that social-movement theorists have been too narrow in assessing what counts as a movement's "success" and that sustaining a campaign or cause in public consciousness should also be valued.[48] We take inspiration from the fact that the women we interviewed themselves looked back to the political generations that preceded them, whether in anticolonial, suffrage, workers', or other protests. In this way, the biographies of activists join an imagined women's community that stretches over time as well as nations.

Margaretta Jolly is Reader in Cultural Studies at the School of Media, Film and Music, University of Sussex, and directs the university's Centre for Life History and Life Writing Research. She is the editor of *The Encyclopedia of Life Writing* (2001) and the author of *In Love and Struggle: Letters in Contemporary Feminism* (2008), for which she won the Feminist and Women's Studies Association UK Book Prize. She is also principal investigator for Sisterhood and After: The Women's Liberation Oral History Project, partnered with the British Library at bl.uk/sisterhood, and oral history advisor to China Women's University in Beijing.

Notes

1. Sally Alexander, interviewed by Margaretta Jolly, Sisterhood and After: The Women's Liberation Oral History Project, 2010–13. British Library Sound & Moving Image Catalogue reference C1420/45, transcript 78–80/track 2. © The British Library and The University of Sussex.
2. For more information, see www.sussex.ac.uk/clhlwr/sisterhoodandafter and bl.uk/sisterhood.
3. Fifteen of them had already publicly archived their papers, and fourteen had already archived an oral history elsewhere, while a further six had done an unarchived oral history. We prioritized those who were frail or in ill health for obvious reasons.
4. Esther Breitenbach and Fiona Mackay, *Women and Contemporary Scottish Politics: An Anthology* (Edinburgh: Polygon at Edinburgh, 2001).
5. Juliet Mitchell, interviewed by Margaretta Jolly, Sisterhood and After: The Women's Liberation Oral History Project, 2010–13. British Library Sound & Moving Image Catalogue reference C1420/60, transcript 13/track 1. © The British Library and The University of Sussex.
6. Aldon D. Morris and Suzanne Staggenborg, "Leadership in Social Movements," in *The Blackwell Companion to Social Movements,* ed. David A. Snow, Sarah Anne Soule, and Hanspeter Kriesi (Oxford: Blackwell, 2004), 171.
7. Others include: Women's Aid; Greenham Common Women's Peace Camp; Women in Manual Trades; The Fawcett Society; Women Against Pit Closures; The 300 Group; The Movement for the Ordination of Women; The Organisation of Women of African and Asian Descent; Sisters Against Disablement; Southall Black Sisters; Gingerbread; Northern Ireland Women's Rights Movement; The Women's Research and Resources Centre; Working Women's Charter; National Abortion Campaign; The Women's Health Centre; The Gay Liberation Front.
8. Morris and Staggenborg, "Leadership in Social Movements."
9. Myra Marx Ferree and Carol McClurg Mueller, "Feminism and the Women's Movement: A Global Perspective," in *The Blackwell Companion to Social Movements,* ed. David A. Snow, Sarah Anne Soule, and Hanspeter Kriesi (Oxford: Blackwell, 2004), 596.
10. Paul Richard Thompson, *The Voice of the Past: Oral History,* 3rd ed. (Oxford: Oxford University Press, 2000), 269.

11. Sheila Rowbotham, interviewed by Rachel Cohen, Sisterhood and After: The Women's Liberation Oral History Project, 2010–13. British Library Sound & Moving Image Catalogue reference C1420/10, transcript 137/track 5. © The British Library and The University of Sussex.
12. Arshad, Catalogue reference C1420/21; Fairbairns, Catalogue reference C1420/45; Wise, Catalogue reference C1420/31; Wilson, Catalogue reference C1420/19; Taylor, Catalogue reference C1420/38; Campbell, Catalogue reference C1420/60, transcript 13/track 1. All from Sisterhood and After: The Women's Liberation Oral History Project, 2010–13. © The British Library and The University of Sussex.
13. Simon Biggs and Ariela Lowenstein, "Toward Generational Intelligence: Linking Cohorts, Families and Experience," in *Kinship and Cohort in an Aging Society: From Generation to Generation,* ed. Merril Silverstein and Roseann Giarrusso (Baltimore: Johns Hopkins University Press, 2013).
14. William Strauss and Neil Howe, *Generations: The History of America's Future, 1584 to 2069* (New York: Morrow, 1991).
15. Callum G. Brown, *Religion and the Demographic Revolution: Women and Secularisation in Canada, Ireland, UK and USA since the 1960s* (Woodbridge: Boydell, 2012).
16. Margaret Morganroth Gullette, *Aged by Culture* (Chicago: University of Chicago Press, 2004), 43–44.
17. Jan Baars, *Aging, Globalization, and Inequality: The New Critical Gerontology, Society and Aging Series* (Amityville, NY: Baywood Pub., 2006).
18. Rosemary Sales, *Women Divided: Gender, Religion and Politics in Northern Ireland* (London: Routledge, 1997), 32.
19. Mirza, Catalogue reference C1420/17, transcript 65/track 3; Owen, Catalogue reference C1420/36; Wandor, Catalogue reference C1420/09. All from Sisterhood and After: The Women's Liberation Oral History Project, 2010–13. © The British Library and The University of Sussex.
20. Ronald Inglehart, *Culture Shift in Advanced Industrial Society* (Princeton, NJ: Princeton University Press, 1990), 497.
21. Richard A. Easterlin, *Birth and Fortune: The Impact of Numbers on Personal Welfare,* 2nd ed. (Chicago: University of Chicago Press, 1987).
22. Doug McAdam, "The Biographical Impact of Activism," in *How Social Movements Matter,* ed. Marco Giugni, Doug McAdam, and Charles Tilly (Minneapolis: University of Minnesota Press, 1999), 135–36.
23. Jane Pilcher's study of white women in Southwest England across three generations showed that they were increasingly "progressive" and liberal on gender issues, though none called themselves feminist, with the generational cohort that matched that of the "second wave" being most consistently feminist in view. See Jane Pilcher, *Women of Their Time: Generation, Gender Issues and Femimism* (Aldershot: Ashgate, 1998).
24. Marco. G. Giugni, "Personal and Biographical Consequences," in *The Blackwell Companion to Social Movements,* ed. David A. Snow, Sarah Anne Soule, and Hanspeter Kriesi (Oxford: Blackwell, 2004), 494.
25. Giugni, "Personal and Biographical Consequences," 489.
26. Jo Robinson interviewed by Polly Russell, Sisterhood and After: The Women's Liberation Oral History Project, 2010–13. British Library Sound & Moving Image

Catalogue reference C1420/43, transcript 71/track 5. © The British Library and The University of Sussex.

27. Barbara Jones, interviewed by Margaretta Jolly, Sisterhood and After: The Women's Liberation Oral History Project, 2010–13. British Library Sound & Moving Image Catalogue reference C1420/53. © The British Library and The University of Sussex.
28. Martin Pugh, *Women and the Women's Movement in Britain, 1914–1999* (New York: St. Martin's Press, 2000).
29. Deirdre Beddoe, interviewed by Rachel Cohen, Sisterhood and After: The Women's Liberation Oral History Project, 2010–13. British Library Sound & Moving Image Catalogue reference C1420/23. © The British Library and The University of Sussex.
30. Rosalind Delmar, interviewed by Rachel Cohen, Sisterhood and After: The Women's Liberation Oral History Project, 2010–13. British Library Sound & Moving Image Catalogue reference C1420/03, transcript 150, track 5. © The British Library and The University of Sussex.
31. Juliet Mitchell and Ann Oakley, *What Is Feminism?* (Oxford: Basil Blackwell, 1986).
32. Stella Dadzie, interviewed by Rachel Cohen, Sisterhood and After: The Women's Liberation Oral History Project, 2010–13. British Library Sound & Moving Image Catalogue reference C1420/20, Interviewee-Edited transcript 93/track 5. © The British Library and The University of Sussex.
33. Birth Summary Tables, England and Wales 2013; Office of National Statistics; http://www.ons.gov.uk/ons/dcp171778_371129.pdf. See also Pat Thane, *Happy Families? History and Family Policy* (London: British Academy Policy Centre, 2010), 24.
34. Birth Summary Tables, England and Wales 2013; Office of National Statistics; http://www.ons.gov.uk/ons/dcp171778_371129.pdf.
35. Zoe Fairbairns, interviewed by Margaretta Jolly, Sisterhood and After: The Women's Liberation Oral History Project, 2010–13. British Library Sound & Moving Image Catalogue reference C1420/60, Interviewee-Edited transcript 27/track 1. © The British Library and The University of Sussex.
36. McAdam, "The Biographical Impact of Activism."
37. Jane Traies, *Lives of Older Lesbians: Sexuality, Identity & the Life Course* (London: Palgrave Macmillan, 2016).
38. Campbell Catalogue reference C1420/60, transcript 2/track 1. Sisterhood and After: The Women's Liberation Oral History Project, 2010–13. © The British Library and The University of Sussex.
39. Kirsten Hearn, interviewed by Rachel Cohen, Sisterhood and After: The Women's Liberation Oral History Project, 2010–13. British Library Sound & Moving Image Catalogue reference C1420/44, Interviewee-Edited transcript 75–77/track 3. © The British Library and The University of Sussex.
40. Nadira Mirza, interviewed by Rachel Cohen, Sisterhood and After: The Women's Liberation Oral History Project, 2010–13. British Library Sound & Moving Image Catalogue reference C1420/17, Interviewee-Edited transcript 111/track 4. © The British Library and The University of Sussex. Interestingly our interviewees seem to conform to an average pattern of physical health, with a handful getting cancer and other serious conditions and one Black woman experiencing sickle cell anemia.

41. See Ed Halliwell, Liz Main, and Celia Richardson, *The Fundamental Facts: The Latest Facts and Figures on Mental Health* (London: Mental Health Foundation, 2007), 9.
42. Catherine Corrigall-Brown, *Patterns of Protest: Trajectories of Participation in Social Movements* (Stanford, CA: Stanford University Press, 2012).
43. Sara Ahmed, *The Promise of Happiness* (Durham, NC: Duke University Press, 2010).
44. Giugni, "Personal and Biographical Consequences," 541.
45. Lynne Segal, *Out of Time: The Pleasures and Perils of Ageing* (London: Verso, 2013).
46. McAdam, "The Biographical Impact of Activism."
47. Michelene Wandor, interviewed by Rachel Cohen, Sisterhood and After: The Women's Liberation Oral History Project, 2010–13. British Library Sound & Moving Image Catalogue reference C1420/09, Interviewee-Edited transcript 151/track 5. © The British Library and The University of Sussex.
48. Donatella Della Porta and Mario Diani, *Social Movements: An Introduction,* 2nd ed. (Malden, MA: Blackwell, 2006).

Bibliography

Ahmed, Sara. *The Promise of Happiness.* Durham, NC: Duke University Press, 2010.

Baars, Jan. *Aging, Globalization, and Inequality: The New Critical Gerontology.* Society and Aging Series. Amityville, NY: Baywood Pub., 2006.

Biggs, Simon, and Ariela Lowenstein. "Toward Generational Intelligence: Linking Cohorts, Families and Experience." In *Kinship and Cohort in an Aging Society: From Generation to Generation,* edited by Merril Silverstein and Roseann Giarrusso, 159–75. Baltimore: Johns Hopkins University Press, 2013.

Breitenbach, Esther, and Fiona Mackay. *Women and Contemporary Scottish Politics: An Anthology.* Edinburgh: Polygon at Edinburgh, 2001.

Brown, Callum G. *Religion and the Demographic Revolution: Women and Secularisation in Canada, Ireland, UK and USA since the 1960s.* Woodbridge: Boydell, 2012.

Corrigall-Brown, Catherine. *Patterns of Protest: Trajectories of Participation in Social Movements.* Stanford, CA: Stanford University Press, 2012.

Della Porta, Donatella, and Mario Diani. *Social Movements: An Introduction.* 2nd ed. Malden, MA: Blackwell, 2006.

Easterlin, Richard A. *Birth and Fortune: The Impact of Numbers on Personal Welfare.* 2nd ed. Chicago: University of Chicago Press, 1987.

Ferree, Myra Marx, and Carol McClurg Mueller. "Feminism and the Women's Movement: A Global Perspective." In *The Blackwell Companion to Social Movements,* edited by David A. Snow, Sarah Anne Soule, and Hanspeter Kriesi, 576–607. Oxford: Blackwell, 2004.

Giugni, Marco. G. "Personal and Biographical Consequences." In *The Blackwell Companion to Social Movements,* edited by David A. Snow, Sarah Anne Soule, and Hanspeter Kriesi, 489–507. Oxford: Blackwell, 2004.

Gullette, Margaret Morganroth. *Aged by Culture.* Chicago: University of Chicago Press, 2004.

Halliwell, Ed, Liz Main, and Celia Richardson. *The Fundamental Facts: The Latest Facts and Figures on Mental Health.* London: Mental Health Foundation, 2007.

Hewlett, Sylvia Ann. *Baby Hunger: The New Battle for Motherhood.* London: Atlantic, 2002.

Inglehart, Ronald. *Culture Shift in Advanced Industrial Society.* Princeton, NJ: Princeton University Press, 1990.

McAdam, Doug. "The Biographical Impact of Activism." In *How Social Movements Matter,* edited by Marco Giugni, Doug McAdam, and Charles Tilly, 119–48. Minneapolis: University of Minnesota Press, 1999.

Mitchell, Juliet, and Ann Oakley. *What Is Feminism?* Oxford: Basil Blackwell, 1986.

Morris, Aldon D., and Suzanne Staggenborg. "Leadership in Social Movements." In *The Blackwell Companion to Social Movements,* edited by David A. Snow, Sarah Anne Soule, and Hanspeter Kriesi, 171–96. Oxford: Blackwell, 2004.

Pilcher, Jane. *Women of Their Time: Generation, Gender Issues and Femimism.* Aldershot: Ashgate, 1998.

Pugh, Martin. *Women and the Women's Movement in Britain, 1914–1999.* New York: St. Martin's Press, 2000.

Sales, Rosemary. *Women Divided: Gender, Religion and Politics in Northern Ireland.* London: Routledge, 1997.

Segal, Lynne. *Out of Time: The Pleasures and Perils of Ageing.* London: Verso, 2013.

Strauss, William, and Neil Howe. *Generations: The History of America's Future, 1584 to 2069.* New York: Morrow, 1991.

Thane, Pat. *Happy Families? History and Family Policy.* London: British Academy Policy Centre, 2010.

Thompson, Paul Richard. *The Voice of the Past: Oral History.* 3rd ed. Oxford: Oxford University Press, 2000.

Traies, Jane. *Lives of Older Lesbians : Sexuality, Identity & the Life Course* (London: Palgrave Macmillan, 2016)

Chapter 16

Writing the History of Feminisms (Old and New)

Impacts and Impatience

Karen Offen

My work on the comparative history of European feminisms takes a long as well as a wide-angle view. From a vantage point that spans several centuries, as well as multiple countries, it is easier to ascertain the dimensions of the dramatic challenges posed by feminist demands to the fabric of most societies. Similarly, it is easier to see the equally momentous changes that feminist demands have brought about to date, particularly (though not only) in the developing nation-states of the Western world.

The specific demands made by feminists in Europe in the four centuries before 1950 have addressed the subjects of educational opportunity, changes in laws governing marriage, control of property and one's own person, valuation of women's unpaid labor, opportunities for economic self-reliance, and ending the maligning of women in print. Their demands also call for admission to the more prestigious professions; adjustment of inequitable sexual mores (including a single standard of morality); ending government-licensed prostitution and sexual exploitation; control over women's health, birthing, and childrearing practices; state financial aid to mothers; as well as representation—and decision-making power—in political and religious organizations. Feminists have addressed issues of economic injustice, criticized male sexual practices, and promoted peace and arbitration instead of war. To be sure, these claims included the vote—as the key to enabling other changes—but the vote was never the only goal. It was a means, not an end in itself.

Today, girls and women in Europe and the rest of the West do have access to educational and economic opportunities that they did not have even a century ago; the struggle for more equitable laws of marriage has, by and large, succeeded, at least in societies in which secular law prevails; women have access to formal citizenship—in most democratic societies (though in the earliest democracies, Switzerland and France, it took over a century).

Even the demand for equal pay for equal work, sought after for many decades, is now taken seriously, and some nation-states and supranational bodies such as the European Union have taken action to implement it. The United Nations proclaims "women's rights are human rights"; it promotes gender equality and continues to monitor progress through its Commission on the Status of Women and the CEDAW Committee that monitors implementation of the Convention on the Elimination of All Forms of Discrimination Against Women. In some countries, pressure from feminists has even begun to dent the androcentric grammatical conventions of their respective languages. These are enormously important developments.

Yet in other parts of the world, still today, even basic literacy cannot be assumed, much less clean water, safe childbirth, and other basic necessities of life for women and men alike. Joni Seager's *Penguin Atlas of Women in the World* graphically documents the fact that progress for women has been uneven.[1] Women's health issues dominate today's international aid programs. Yet even girls who have access to a solid education are not taught in school about the history of feminism. Why is that? Why is it that we, as historians of women and feminisms, do not insist that learning about women's history and, in particular, the history of feminism is essential for women's mental health, an essential aspect of women's empowerment?

Has "feminism changed our lives"?[2] Absolutely. "Zooming in" on our own profession provides an example that Seager does not document: in academia, specifically in the historical profession. Certainly the situation varies from one country to another. In the United States, we do have good news to report over the last forty years. Women's numbers among PhD's rose from 12 or 13 percent in 1971 to somewhere around 40 percent today; the presence of women on history faculties has greatly increased; they get promoted and even serve as department chairs. History students can now study one aspect or another of women's history at a number of leading universities; aspiring researchers can now undertake doctoral dissertations on such topics without inciting the ridicule of male advisors. In fact, we have gained critical support from a number of sympathetic male colleagues. What is more, we have challenged the masculine "gender" of earlier historical writing—by "outing" the gender assumptions and assertions of its earlier male authors and by initiating and insisting upon a gendered analysis of the past, one in which women's voices are heard and women's contributions are taken as seriously as those of men.[3] We have fought "the knowledge wars" and we are winning, even though we have not been able to impose a gendered perspective on some of our colleagues or on certain book editors and publishing houses. On the practical side, feminist historians in the United States have succeeded in forcing open advertising for positions; professional rules for recruitment interviews that forbid interviewees to be seated on the bed in a hotel room; faculty bathrooms that are not exclusively for male professors; and institutional procedures to combat sexual harassment. We have opportunities to teach women's history and also the history of feminisms, and to focus our research on women and gender. Women scholars are eligible for and even win research grants from the major foundations, which was practically impossible forty years ago. Women's historians have been elected as presidents of all the major associations of historians, including the American Historical Association, and have directly influenced their policies in the direction of gender equity. As the Virginia Slims cigarette advertisements once put it, "You've come a long way, baby." And yet … we ask, is history still being written—and taught—without women? Despite all our progress and all our assertiveness, the answer—unfortunately—is yes.

In the short term, it can be more difficult to recognize progress or change, especially as many of the initial problems addressed by feminists before the 1970s were easier to resolve than those we have faced since, or than those we still face today. In most other professions besides our own the "glass ceiling" still exists, not only in government decision-making positions but especially in those professions involved with making large sums of money. And, for women who are employed and also want or already have a family, work/life balance issues, especially shared parenting, remain extremely difficult to resolve in the absence of adequate daycare arrangements, whether private or community- or state-supported. Thus, as we embark on writing the histories of what some call the "second wave," the women's liberation efforts that began in the late 1960s, we have run up against issues—anti-woman attitudes, habits, and practices—that are etched very deeply into the sociopolitical and cultural fabric. These issues include continuing violence (both physical and symbolic) against women; resistance to women's quest for control of their own bodies, which includes their reproductive freedom; controversy around expressions of sexual identity; demeaning, destructive, and even insulting imagery of women in the media. The list is long. And we might be tempted to think we have arrived at "success without impact," as Kurt Tucholsky put it. As we achieve some successes, the list of problems only seems to grow. Are we underestimating success? Or our impact? Or are we underestimating the complexity of the problems we are trying to solve?

How, indeed, do we gauge success? What constitutes success, what are the markers? And how do we measure impact over the course of a "mere" forty years? We might, for example, look at women's arrival in positions of political authority—as prime ministers, as representatives in elected assemblies, or as candidates for president, or the fact that women are now a majority of students in universities, or that some women have access to reliable contraception that gives them control over their reproductive powers. And, with regard to effects, how long is "long-term"? Decades? Centuries? Millenia? The so-called "second wave" has only been rolling in for four decades—this is very short relative to the long "first wave" of over 150 years, not to mention the centuries of feminist protest that preceded it. We live in an age of enhanced worldwide communications, an age that demands instant results, but in matters of restructuring relations between the sexes, instant results may not be possible. We need to be hopeful, but we also need to be realistic. We also need to be well organized, and we need to remain vigilant. We need to work both on the macro and micro levels. We need to change practices and policies, but most importantly we need to change minds.

Why? Because the threat of backlash is always present. Feminists must be constantly watchful to see that their achievements, however partial, are not rolled back, even as we struggle to advance. For, as history teaches us, the tide can turn. And sometimes it does so aggressively—as it did in Afghanistan. As it did in Iran. And as it did in that small Shi'ite valley in Pakistan. It can and does turn whenever certain men in situations of authority feel threatened in their masculine privileges, when they express a need to reclaim patriarchal control under what they call "tradition" or "religion," invoking "cultural heritage" to rein in women; in such instances every aspect of women's freedom and equality can be at risk. Even in the United States we are currently witnessing such efforts by those who call themselves "conservatives" to turn back the clock on the subject of women's hard-won reproductive rights—the right to choose whether or not to bear a child. We are subjected to a media and popular culture onslaught, especially through television programming and advertising but also in the cinema, in the fashion industry, and via internet pornography that is nothing less than scandalous: what one recent filmmaker calls "MissRepresentation" and a feminist author has labeled "the rise of enlightened sexism," the reobjectification of women's bodies for men's amusement and sexual gratification.[4] Under the sanction of "freedom of speech," this sort of pornography is on the rise, and it threatens the future of our youth, especially our girls but also our boys, by promoting and implicitly endorsing retrograde and fundamentally unhealthy images of relations between the sexes that objectify women and that promote and celebrate male domination. As one feminist author wrote in the *New York Times Book Review* concerning a new book about the controversial author Henry Miller, "The question is not art versus pornography or sexuality versus censorship or any question about achievement. The question is: why do men revel in the degradation of women?"[5] Not all men, to be sure, but all too many.

As historians we recognize all too well that the advances of women (and other subordinate groups) are indeed historical constructions. What has been gained by and for women during the last several centuries, not to mention in the second half of the twentieth century, can all too easily be taken away. In particular, the dreadful lack of historical memory of women's struggles for equality worldwide, both among our peers and among the young, works to the advantage of antifeminists. Until equality, or at least equity, for women becomes an unquestioned cultural norm, it is not secured. There is no gain that cannot be rolled back. Although Hélène Cixous, writing in 1975, insisted that the past must no longer condition the present and that we should not consolidate it by repeating it, the past and its patterns nevertheless carry enormous cultural weight.[6] It depends, of course, on whose version of the past we are talking about. Cixous was not referring to the new women's history or the history of feminism.

In our impatience, we might pause a moment to take counsel from our predecessors. In the first decade of the twentieth century, one of my favorite French feminists, the Swiss-born Madame Avril de Sainte-Croix, then secretary-general of the Conseil National des Femmes Françaises (National Council of French Women), had felt "rather disheartened by the complexity of the problems and the slow progress of our work." She reported that her older colleague in the International Abolitionist Federation, the English reformer Josephine Butler, wrote her as follows: "I feel you are a little discouraged. Do not lose confidence … progress is not like a great flood that submerges everything; it is more like a rising tide which reaches its goal in the end, though sometimes it may seem to be ebbing away."[7]

Indeed, the rising tide did rise and retreat repeatedly during that long period we once referred to as "the first wave."[8] And its intermittent ebbs also obliterated the remaining traces of the struggle from our collective memory. Which is precisely why the French historian Michelle Perrot insists on the continuing importance of our writing history, "the sole way to stabilize the shifting sands of an uncertain memory."[9]

Contemporaries of Madame Avril were extremely impressed with the magnitude of the challenge posed by the quest for women's emancipation. Here I share some quotations from the first decades of the twentieth century—over a hundred years ago. Consider this 1904 assertion by the Swedish writer and mother's advocate Ellen Key: "The struggle that woman is now carrying on is far more far-reaching than any other; and if no diversion occurs, it will finally surpass in fanaticism any war of religion or race."[10] In 1912 the German socialist-feminist Lily Braun wrote in her introduction to Adele Schreiber's *Die Mutterschaft* (Motherhood) that "the women's movement … turns out to be revolutionary in the profoundest sense of the word." As its initial demands—economic, legal, and political—are resolved, the real challenge appears. "On its solution will depend not only the future of women but the future of the human race."[11] In 1913 the British suffragist Millicent Garrett Fawcett remarked that "the women's movement is one of the biggest things that has ever taken place in the history of the world."

> Other movements towards freedom have aimed at raising the status of a comparatively small group or class. But the women's movement aims at nothing less than raising the status of an entire sex—half the human race—to lift it up to the freedom and value of womanhood. It affects more people than any former reform movement, for it spreads over the whole world. It is more deep seated, for it enters into the home and modifies the personal character.[12]

Half a century later the British feminist Juliet Mitchell entitled her influential tract "Women: The Longest Revolution."[13] Think for a moment about the extraordinary implications of this long-term revolution we are still experiencing. One hundred years later, Fawcett's words still ring true, as do those of Mitchell some fifty years after Fawcett. The emancipation of women is not just one cause among others or one that must give precedence to the issue of class, as the socialists long claimed.[14] It challenges the very core of sociopolitical organization in the human species, which, in virtually every known society, centers on the relations between women and men.

Are we still too focused on the trees themselves to see the forest as a whole? Can we actually tell whether the tide is ebbing away, or preparing another wave? Are the eruptions of feminist activism diminishing or gathering momentum for yet another, hopefully devastating, attack on what remains of male privilege? Or, are today's mounting antifeminist campaigns going to triumph? Whatever outcome we hope for, whatever metaphor we choose, it seems clear that at this moment we have arrived at a generational turning point—a moment of recollection, reassessment, and regrouping that must encompass the next generation. In evaluating what has happened since 1970, can we afford to take only the short view?

One significant aspect of the women's liberation movement (WLM) since 1968, which is not as well known as it should be, is that feminist historians have recaptured so many facets of women's history and, more especially, the histories of feminisms past. There is no doubt that in the last forty years our investigations have been fruitful beyond our wildest dreams. We have learned so much about women's thoughts and action in both the recent and distant past, and about the campaigns they waged—singly or in groups, and frequently with male-feminist allies—to challenge masculine domination. After carefully situating these campaigns in their social, economic, political, and cultural context, some of us can say with certainty that feminism deserves recognition as a major historical movement. As I have claimed for many years, and as the team of European editors of *Le Siècle des féminismes* (the century of feminisms) insisted in 2004, "feminism is a major event of the 20th century ..." that should be considered as "a true social, political and cultural movement" and "an incontestable actor in twentieth-century history."[15] My recent claim that "the history of feminism IS political history" is valid not only for the twentieth century; it can be extended backward in time into the eighteenth and nineteenth centuries as well. I have demonstrated this in my book *European Feminisms, 1700-1950: A Political History,* as have many other authors, both those featured in my edited volume, *Globalizing Feminisms, 1789-1945,* and those referenced in its extensive bibliography.[16] This is a particularly important message to deliver to colleagues who are unfamiliar with this field of history, to our students, and to the general public. Yes, I repeat: "the history of feminism IS political history." We need to get this message out, and to show what a difference it makes to our understanding of the past and what significance it has for our approach to the future.

When Simone de Beauvoir published *Le Deuxième Sexe* (*The Second Sex*) in 1949, she did not have access to the historical data that we now have at our fingertips; consequently, her account of earlier developments left a great deal to be desired. "Why do women not contest male sovereignty?" asks Beauvoir in her introduction: she could only affirm, on the following page, that women "have no past, no history, no religion of their own" because she had only superficial knowledge of the facts. What she knew of the history of feminisms was entirely second- or third-hand. Instead, we now know that women (and their male-feminist allies) had been contesting male sovereignty for centuries, and especially in France.[17]

Beauvoir's account, including her inadequate history, influenced an entire generation—or even two generations—of feminist activists before women's historians set about uncovering the full story. And what a story it is. My own investigation of the history of feminisms in France, and ultimately in Europe, began as an effort to recover and reclaim the historical evidence that Beauvoir omitted—or wrote badly, lacking the appropriate sources and the time and interest to ferret them out. It seemed important to set the story straight. Obviously, many other women's historians felt the same way, and the results of their efforts underlie the comparative synthesis that I was able to achieve. But while it took Beauvoir a bit over two years to write her entire book, it has taken another two generations to provide a more complete, more contextualized story—as the work of pioneers like Christine Bard and Sylvie Chaperon in France, Eliane Gubin in Belgium, and Beatrix Mesmer and others in Switzerland attests.

Should historians of feminisms focus on the struggles or only on the outcomes? Like other reputable historians, we historians of feminisms are "objective," but this does not mean that we lack a point of view. In fact, we have something of a mission—to convey the truth about the history of feminism and to underscore its enormous significance. We are, of course, interested in the social movement aspects—in the necessary acts of organizing, mobilization, etc., but that is only one part of it. We are interested in conveying the ideas and analyses that women—and male sympathizers—bring to the table, in reporting on women's challenges to and outcomes of women's struggles against masculine domination. To be sure, we take pleasure in telling success stories, in highlighting progressive outcomes. But we are also interested in documenting and analyzing failures and understanding their meaning. We can be as fascinated by the process of struggle as in the outcomes; we care about highlighting the political debates, feminist efforts to convince, to persuade others of the importance of feminist objectives—the strategies and tactics deployed to achieve results *without resorting to force.* Until quite recently, feminist networks and struggles were local; then they became regional and national; but it was only from the late nineteenth century on, with the founding of international women's organizations that met on a regular basis, that they become truly international or transnational. Today they have become global to a certain degree but sometimes do not take local conditions and cultures sufficiently into account.

In some national cultures, earlier feminists have made extraordinary contributions to documenting their own campaigns, such as the six-volume *History of Woman Suffrage* compiled by Elizabeth Cady Stanton and Susan B. Anthony and their colleagues (1881–1922). A related initiative was Theodore Stanton's groundbreaking compilation *The Woman Question in Europe* (1884). These early projects established a precedent. They provided the kind of priceless documentation we all need to be thinking about gathering—for who will document our campaigns if we don't?[18]

Let's look around to see what's been happening in several countries that share borders or languages with Switzerland. In France, our colleague Christine Bard has created the *Archives du Féminisme* (Archives of Feminism) to supplement the holdings of the remarkable *Bibliothèque Marguerite Durand* [Marguerite Durand Library]) as well as the website *Musea* to showcase feminist history for the general public. She has organized two historical conferences (2010 in Angers, 2011 in Paris) devoted to history of the "first" and "second" waves of French feminism, and has published the proceedings of both. She and her colleagues have just published *Dictionnaire des féministes: France XVIIIe–XXIe siècle* (Dictionary of Feminists: 18th to 21st

Century France; 2017), a *lieu de mémoire* comparable to the "*Maitron*" for the workers' movement. Bard is also writing for the general public.[19] In the 1990s a team assembled around Françoise Thébaud launched a very important journal: *Clio—Histoire, Femmes, Sociétés (Clio*—history, women, societies), which has completed over twenty years of publication. Our French colleagues have also launched a variety of projects designed to get women's history into the schools—the most recent being a *manual scolaire* (textbook), *La place des femmes dans l'histoire: une histoire mixte* (the place of women in history: a co-ed history; Paris: Belin, 2010), designed specifically to address and reshape the history programs in France's secondary schools.[20]

In Belgium (which is a linguistic neighbor, although it does not share borders with Switzerland), Eliane Gubin and her team produce the excellent Francophone review *Sextant*. The CARHIF (*Centre d'Archives pour l'histoire des femmes*; Archive Centre for Women's History) in Brussels has provided an institutional resting place for the archives of the International Council of Women, which has stimulated scholarly investigation of this significant international women's organization, the very first of its kind in the world. Other archives in Brussels and the *Mundaneum* in Mons hold the papers of leading feminists. Our Belgian colleagues have also produced a *Dictionnaire des femmes belges* (Dictionary of Belgian Women; 2006) in which many feminists appear. In 2010 Julie Carlier defended a dissertation at the University of Ghent, that sets bilingual Belgian feminism in comparative context with France and the Netherlands.

In Germany several major feminist archives exist, including the Helene Lange archives in Berlin and the Archive of the German Women's Movement in Kassel, which publishes *Ariadne*. The scholarly German-language publication *L'Homme: Zeitschrift fur feministische Geschichte* (L'Homme: Review for feminist history) is a joint project of Austrian, German, and some Swiss historians. Our Austrian colleagues have also launched a rather elaborate web presence for women's and gender history, Salon 21, at *www.univie.ac.at/Geschichte/salon21/*. Other transnational projects are in development at Atria (formerly Aletta) and the Institute for Social History in Amsterdam, as well as the Women and Social Movements International (WASMI) web-based project of Kathryn Kish Sklar and Thomas Dublin in cooperation with Alexander Street Press.

I particularly want to single out one collaborative transnational effort by non-neighbors, focused on the "forgotten" feminists of Europe—Central, Eastern, and Southeastern. This effort has already produced several important publications, including a biographical dictionary of women's movements and feminisms covering the countries of that region and an annual journal, Aspasia, the first volume of which addressed the history of feminisms in the region.[21] Despite these successful ventures, efforts to establish women's history archives in Eastern and Southern Europe have not yet materialized. The only exception is in Turkey.

Other comparative historical assessments are in progress. A few years ago the English historian of feminism, Krista Cowman, launched a cross-national and comparative project to explore the question of "Feminism and Historical Memory in Europe." The project's objective (as explained on the website) is to investigate the ways in which "different feminist movements in both the 19th and the 20th centuries devised and utilized their own history as a means of creating a strong political identity." Becoming self-conscious about preserving and transmitting the historical record is essential. If we don't do it, who will?

In 1995 Susan Stanford Friedman complained that "the loss of collective memories, of myriad stories about the past, has contributed greatly to the ongoing subordination of women. The unending, cumulative building of broadly-defined histories of women, including histories of feminism, is a critical component of resistance and change."[22] This is still true today. Even those who may have once believed that 1970 was the *Année Zéro* for feminism now acknowledge that feminisms in Europe have a history going back some six centuries—or more. Retrieving those sources has been extremely time consuming, not least for lack of adequate archiving and biased classification systems. Many sources were destroyed because they were deemed "unimportant."

Efforts are now underway throughout the world to document the most recent collective surge of feminist activity. Networks have formed internationally to promote research and publication in women's and gender history; the newsletters of the International Federation for Research in Women's History attest to a thriving interest in advancing the field (not only for the most recent period).[23] Efforts to popularize the history of feminist thought include the recent two-volume, globe-spanning documentary source collection, *Feminist Writings from Ancient Times to the Modern World: A Global Sourcebook and History*, ed. Tiffany K. Wayne (Greenwood/ABC-CLIO, 2011). Along with biographical entries on each author, the volumes include a significant text, followed by analysis and additional bibliography. Recent publications of this sort in France include *La Mémoire des femmes*, ed. Pauline Bascou-Bance (Cestis: Elytis Edition, 2002) and Nicole Pellegrin's collection, *Écrits féministes de Christine de Pizan à Simone de Beauvoir* (Feminist Writings from Christine de Pizan to Simone de Beauvoir; Paris: Flammarion, 2011).

We need more carefully designed—and more extensive—source anthologies. We also need more in-depth biographical studies. It would certainly be worthwhile, for example, to compile (or put online) an all-Swiss volume to complement the superb illustrated volume *Les Femmes dans l'Histoire de Genève* (2005), which includes a range of significant Swiss feminists.

I am not here to raise critical questions about the artificiality of the "archive" and the "fictions" it may contain but rather to suggest that without archived sources, writing the history of the women's movement since 1970 will be extremely difficult. We want curators to collect the kinds of sources that we need to document the histories of feminisms. Fortunately there is still time to gather those sources and preserve them in secure circumstances for future use.[24] But this task also requires resources—time, money, and, above all, human energy.

We need our feminist publications scanned and available on the internet so that we don't have to contend with crumbling newsprint. I was delighted to learn that the principal French-language Swiss feminist publication, *Le Mouvement Féministe* (subsequently *Femmes Suisses* and now *Emilie*), has been scanned and is consultable online at www.lemilie.ch. We need more oral interviews and, preferably, videography; we need to encourage "second-wave" activists to deposit their own papers, and we need to archive our own. It is not possible to do sound historical work without documentary sources and without developing rich context to situate them. Our histories must be based on a broad investigation of sources; cherry-picking the past to prove a preconceived theoretical point—as some political theorists like doing—is not good scholarship. We need to test our hypotheses against a mass of concrete evidence, and let the theories emerge from the sources.

And what about the critics who fret about the artificiality of the category "women"? Despite some contemporary feminist theorists' debates over whether "sex" constructs "gender" or "gender" constructs "sex," we know that there has long been a "class" historically constituted as "women" by laws, institutions, customs, and practices of all sorts. We know that women are differently embodied than men, that they come in all different shapes, sizes, and colors. Bodies and their functions do matter: we recognize that menstruation, pregnancy, parturition, nursing, child-raising, etc., continue to provide most women with common physical experiences that transcend these other differences, as well as distinguishing them from men. Moreover, we know that feminism represents a political effort to ensure the equality of opportunity and possibilities of women with men, and to assure women's autonomy as *embodied* individuals. The history of feminism IS political history, and it encompasses intellectual, social, economic, and cultural history too; the debates on the so-called "woman question" continue to this day.[25] It may still be too soon to tell whether the last generation's women's movement has had a lasting effect. What is clear, though, is that, in the short term, it has had a substantial effect on the lives of individual women, though clearly more in some countries than in others.

Conclusion: Three Wishes for the Future of the History of Feminism

The English novelist and essayist Virginia Woolf poured out nearly two hundred pages of reflections on how she might invest *Three Guineas* in the interest of preventing war. I will devote only three paragraphs to offering three wishes that concern the preservation and transmission of the histories of feminisms, in the interest of assuring women's future equality and healthy relations between the sexes, of implanting the notion that there must be a balance of power between women and men.

1) My first wish is that we stand up for and reaffirm publicly the importance of historical knowledge in general for informing present and future action, and especially feminist action. We need to build a knowledge bridge that spans the generations, a bridge that will make it unnecessary to reinvent the wheel every quarter-century. As the Australian historian of feminism Barbara Caine wrote in 1995, "The historiography of feminism is hampered by ... lack of a functioning feminist tradition ... transmitted from one generation to the next.... Few of those who have protested about women's oppression in any given generation have known about predecessors—and even those who did rarely acknowledged them."[26] We know that once people encounter the history of feminisms, they become very upset with their earlier education: "Why didn't we learn about that in school?" they say.

2) My second wish is that, in considering what history is important and what we will research and write about, we continue to broaden our focus, both personally and professionally so that we can see beyond our own personal, regional, and national borders. Comparative history is especially illuminating; it helps us see what is specific about any given national culture by throwing it into relief through comparison with another. The Portuguese-based historian Anne Cova has argued in the historiographical introduction to her volume *Comparative Women's History: New Approaches* (2006) that "cautious comparative research can contribute towards a reassessment and rewriting of history from a broader perspective."[27] This includes the rewriting of any given "national" history. In *European Feminisms* I wrote: "We still have a great deal to learn about the history of feminisms not only in European countries but throughout the world."

> We are seeing recurrent patterns that we are only beginning to understand. We are learning more about the intricacies of constructing—and reconstructing—patriarchal institutions, about the particular conditions that force fissures to open, the molten lava of feminist protest to erupt, and about the advances and retreats in women's situation that allow it to flow and ebb—or the resistances that force it to recede—over time. But of one thing we can be certain: the history of this path-breaking, multifaceted, centuries-long feminist tradition in European societies can teach us all a great deal. Knowledge and historical memory can be used to address problems as they arise and to avoid mistakes in the future. They can be powerful tools for assuring that efforts to subordinate women are met with sustained resistance. In short, they can provide a springboard.

I still believe this to be true.

3) My third wish concerns teaching and transmission of our hard-won comparative and local knowledge. We need to figure out ways to broadcast the histories of feminisms not only to each other and to our own students but also and especially to the public that lies outside the universities. We need to reach our friends and neighbors, to be sure, but we also need to reach our counterparts in other parts of the world. By engaging with the internet and harnessing the new global media for our purposes, we can open up unprecedented possibilities for spreading the word about the history of feminisms.[28] How many of you—or your students—have posted notices about historical feminists on Wikipedia? How many of you have set up websites where you can post documents, illustrations, and the like to illuminate the histories of feminisms that lie closest to your hearts? How many of you have considered writing a women's history "blog"?[29] Or an op-ed article relating some aspect of the history to current issues?

In *European Feminisms,* I asserted that "the long, rich history of European feminisms from 1700 to 1950 is a heritage that belongs to all of us, women and men alike, wherever in the world we live, whatever the color of our skin or our ethnicity, whatever our religion or our national origin." And I added:

> What is at stake here is not merely a more systematic knowledge of the complex history of the European past, of events that took place in particular cultural configurations that may never be repeated. What is at stake is access to knowledge that can help us, women and men, Europeans, neo-Europeans, Asians, Africans, Indians (subcontinent), people of all backgrounds and persuasions who have been

> touched by the "woman question" in some aspect of our lives (as indeed, we all have been), to learn to live more amicably with one another—to build futures in which partnership and mutual respect, not institutionalized dominance and subordination, nor physical, psychological, or symbolic violence become the norm. Women and men need to stand side by side as partners, not face to face as antagonists. Men need to learn that telling women who they are and what they need to be, using force to ensure their submission, will no longer be tolerated… The challenge, then, is to inform ourselves about what has been "already in place," the victories, the mistakes, the arguments, and to use this knowledge as a springboard to future feminist thought and action. We have far more important things to do than continually to reinvent the wheel.

I still believe this. And, as I have said for the last decade and will reiterate here, "amnesia, not lack of history, is feminism's worst enemy today." Let us, then, gather the documentation we need to recount the history of the last forty years of feminism, in a spirit of gratitude for the ways in which this movement, which now involves hundreds and thousands (perhaps even millions) of women—and men—worldwide, has enormously changed our own lives—for the better—but also impacts the lives of our daughters and sons, and our grandchildren.

Let's get going! We've got work to do!

Karen Offen (PhD, Stanford University) is a historian and independent scholar, affiliated as a Senior Scholar with the Clayman Institute for Gender Research, Stanford University. She publishes on the history of modern Europe, especially France and its global influence. Author of *European Feminisms, 1700–1950: A Political History* (2000; French translation, 2012; Spanish translation, 2015; Serbian translation, 2016); editor of *Globalizing Feminisms, 1789–1945* (2010); and co-editor (with Susan Groag Bell) of the acclaimed documentary, *Women, the Family, and Freedom: The Debate in Documents,* 2 vols. (1983), she has also published many articles on feminism and women's/gender history in various languages. A cofounder of the International Federation for Research in Women's History in 1987, she also coedited IFRWH's first publication, *Writing Women's History: International Perspectives* (1991). With Chen Yan, she co-edited a special issue of *Women's History Review,* entitled "Women's History at the Cutting Edge," forthcoming in 2017, and currently available online. Her two-volume study of "the woman question" debates in France is forthcoming from Cambridge University Press.

Notes

1. Joni Seager, ed., *The Penguin Atlas of Women in the World,* 3rd ed. (New York: Penguin Group, 2003).
2. See Delphine Gardey, *Le féminisme change-t-il nos vies?* (Paris: Textuel, 2011).
3. See Bonnie G. Smith, *The Gender of History: Men, Women, and Historical Practice* (Cambridge, MA: Harvard University Press, 1998), and Bonnie G. Smith, ed., *The Oxford Encyclopedia of Women in World History,* 4 vols. (New York: Oxford University Press, 2010).
4. *MissRepresentation* (2011), a documentary film produced and directed by Jennifer Siebel Newsom. See also Susan J. Douglas, *The Rise of Enlightened Sexism: How Pop Culture Took Us from Girl Power to Girls Gone Wild* (New York: St. Martin's Griffin, 2010).
5. Jeanette Winterson, "The Male Mystique of Henry Miller," *New York Times Book Review,* January 29, 2012, 1.
6. See Hélène Cixous, *Le Rire de la Méduse* (1975; Paris: Galilée, 2010), 37.
7. Josephine Butler, letter, quoted by Ghénia Avril de Sainte-Croix, "The Work of the Traffic in Women and Children Committee," *Bulletin, International Council of Women* (June 1936): 82. Consulted at the *Centre d'Archives pour l'Histoire des Femmes* (CARHIF) in Brussels. I have yet to discover the whereabouts of Butler's original letter, which has not so far turned up in the papers of Mme Avril at the *Bibliothèque Marguerite Durand* in Paris.
8. To the metaphor of "waves," I prefer the geologic metaphor of "eruptions." Another approach is Nancy Hewitt's proposal of "radio waves": see her article in the spring 2013 issue of *Feminist Studies.*
9. Michelle Perrot, "Préface," *Le Siècle des féminismes,* ed. Eliane Gubin, Catherine Jacques, Florence Rochefort, Brigitte Studer, Françoise Thébaud, and Michelle Zancarini-Fournel (Paris: Éditions de l'Atelier, 2004), 10.
10. Ellen Key, *Love and Marriage,* trans. Arthur G. Chater (New York: G. P. Putnam's Sons, 1911), 214; originally published in Swedish as *Lifslinjer af Ellen Key* (1904).
11. Lily Braun, "'Introduction' to Motherhood," in Lily Braun, *Selected Writing on Feminism and Socialism,* trans. and ed. by Alfred G. Meyer (Bloomington: Indiana University Press, 1987), 113. Originally published as "Einleitung," in *Die Mutterschaft: ein Sammelwerk fur die Probleme der Frau als Mutter,* ed. Adele Schreiber (Munich: A Langen, 1911).
12. Millicent Garrett Fawcett, "Introduction," in *The Future of the Women's Movement,* ed. Helena M. Swanwick (London: G. Bell, 1913), xii.
13. Juliet Mitchell, "Women: The Longest Revolution," *New Left Review,* no. 40 (November–December 1966): 11–37. Reprinted as a pamphlet and widely circulated.
14. Marilyn J. Boxer, "Rethinking the Socialist Construction and International Career of the Concept 'Bourgeois Feminism'," *American Historical Review* 112, no. 1 (February 2007): 131–58. Reprinted in Karen Offen, ed., *Globalizing Feminisms 1789–1950* (London: Routledge, 2010).
15. *Le Siècle des féminismes,* cited above.
16. See Karen Offen, "The History of Feminism IS Political History," *AHA Perspectives on History* 49, no. 5 (May 2011): 22–24.
17. See Simone de Beauvoir, *The Second Sex: A New Translation by Constance Borde and*

Sheila Malovany-Chevalier (London: Jonathan Cape, 2009), "Introduction," 7, 8. I have written about Beauvoir's "problem" with history in "History, Memory, and Simone de Beauvoir's *Second Sex,*" lecture, Vassar College, 2009. Unpublished.

18. For a good example of the kind of documentary collections I am suggesting, see the sourcebook compiled by Ilse Lenz, *Die Neue Frauenbewegung in Deutschland* (Wiesbaden: VS Verlag, 2008).
19. See Christine Bard's newest book, *Le Féminisme au-delà des idées reçues* (Paris: Le Cavalier Bleu, 2012).
20. For additional information on developments in France, see Françoise Thèbaud (2016) "The History of Women and Gender: French perspectives on the last twenty years," *Women's History Review,* DOI:10.1080/09612025.2016.1250529 . Posted 01 December 2016 on the journal's website; forthcoming in hard copy, 2017. Online at: http://dx.doi.org/10.1080/09612025.2016.1250529.
21. See *A Biographical Dictionary of Women's Movements and Feminisms: Central, Eastern, and South Eastern Europe, 19th and 20th Centuries,* ed. Francisca de Haan, Krassimira Daskalova, and Anna Loutfi (Budapest: Central European University Press, 2006), and the scholarly review *Aspasia: International Yearbook of Central, Eastern, and Southeastern European Women's and Gender History.*
22. Susan Stanford Friedman, "Making History: Reflections on Feminism, Narrative, and Desire," in *Feminism beside Itself,* ed. Diane Elam and Robyn Wiegman (New York: Routledge, 1995), 29.
23. IFRWH; see the International Federation's website, http://www.ifrwh.com.
24. See the recent publications by Liz Stanley, Carolyn Steedman, and Antoinette Burton on the "problem" of the archive. See also Nupur Chaudhuri, Sherry J. Katz, and Mary Elizabeth Perry, eds., *Contesting Archives: Finding Women in the Sources* (Urbana: University of Illinois Press, 2010).
25. Offen, "History of Feminism IS Political History."
26. Barbara Caine, in "Women's Studies, Feminist Traditions and the Problem of History," in *Transitions: New Australian Feminisms,* ed. Barbara Caine and Rosemary Pringle (New York: St. Martin's, 1995), 3.
27. Anne Cova, "Introduction: The Promise of Comparative Women's History," in *Comparative Women's History: New Approaches,* ed. Anne Cova (Boulder, CO: Social Science Monographs, 2000), 37. This book has since appeared in French, Spanish, and Portuguese translations.
28. Cf. Karen Offen, "The Potential for Research in Women's and Gender History in the Age of the Global Internet," paper given in Helsinki, May 2011. Unpublished.
29. From 2008 to 2015 I published a women's history blog called "Clio Talks Back" for the International Museum of Women's "Her Blueprint" at http://imowblog.blogspot.com. These blogs are now archived, but the need continues. Historians of feminism in other countries, with other languages, should consider launching blogs.

Bibliography

Bard, Christine. *Le Féminisme au-delà des idées reçues.* Paris: Le Cavalier Bleu, 2012.

Beauvoir, Simone de. *The Second Sex: A New Translation by Constance Borde and Sheila Malovany-Chevalier.* London: Jonathan Cape, 2009.

Boxer, Marilyn J. "Rethinking the Socialist Construction and International Career of the Concept 'Bourgeois Feminism'." *American Historical Review* 112, no. 1 (February 2007): 131–158. Reprinted in *Globalizing Feminisms 1789–1950,* edited by Karen Offen. London: Routledge, 2010.

Braun, Lily. "'Introduction' to Motherhood." In Lily Braun, *Selected Writing on Feminism and Socialism,* translated and edited by Alfred G. Meyer. Bloomington: Indiana University Press, 1987. (Orig. publ. as "Einleitung." In *Die Mutterschaft: ein Sammelwerk fur die Probleme der Frau als Mutter,* edited by Adele Schreiber. Munich: A Langen, 1911).

Caine, Barbara. "Women's Studies, Feminist Traditions and the Problem of History." In *Transitions: New Australian Feminisms,* edited by Barbara Caine and Rosemary Pringle. New York: St. Martin's, 1995.

Chaudhuri, Nupur, Sherry J. Katz, and Mary Elizabeth Perry, eds. *Contesting Archives: Finding Women in the Sources.* Urbana: University of Illinois Press, 2010.

Cixous, Hélène. *Le Rire de la Méduse.* Paris: L'Arc, 1975; Galilée, 2010.

Cova, Anne. "Introduction: The Promise of Comparative Women's History." In *Comparative Women's History: New Approaches,* edited by Anne Cova. Boulder, CO: Social Science Monographs, 2000.

Douglas, Susan J. *The Rise of Enlightened Sexism: How Pop Culture Took Us from Girl Power to Girls Gone Wild.* New York: St. Martin's Griffin, 2010.

Fawcett, Millicent Garrett. "Introduction." In *The Future of the Women's Movement,* edited by Helena M. Swanwick. London: G. Bell, 1913.

Friedman, Susan Stanford. "Making History: Reflections on Feminism, Narrative, and Desire." In *Feminism beside Itself,* edited by Diane Elam and Robyn Wiegman, 11–53. New York & London: Routledge, 1995.

Gardey, Delphine. *Le féminisme change-t-il nos vies?* Paris: Textuel, 2011.

Key, Ellen. *Love and Marriage,* translated by Arthur G. Chater. New York: G. P. Putnam's Sons, 1911.

Lenz, Ilse. *Die Neue Frauenbewegung in Deutschland.* Wiesbaden: VS Verlag, 2008.

Mitchell, Juliet. "Women: The Longest Revolution." *New Left Review,* no. 40 (November–December 1966): 11–37.

Offen, Karen. *European Feminisms, 1700-1950: A Political History.* Stanford, CA: Stanford University Press, 2000. (Editions also in French, Spanish, and Serbian).

Offen, Karen. "The History of Feminism IS Political History." *AHA Perspectives on History* 49, no. 5 (May 2011).

Perrot, Michelle. "Preface." In *Le Siècle des féminismes,* edited by Eliane Gubin, Catherine Jacques, Florence Rochefort, Brigitte Studer, Françoise Thébaud, and Michelle Zancarini-Fournel, 9–13. Paris: Éditions de l'Atelier, 2004.

Seager, Joni. *The Penguin Atlas of Women in the World.* 3rd edition. New York: Penguin Group, 2003.

Smith, Bonnie G. *The Gender of History: Men, Women, and Historical Practice.* Cambridge, MA: Harvard University Press, 1998.

———, ed. *The Oxford Encyclopedia of Women in World History.* 4 vols. New York: Oxford University Press, 2010.

Winterson, Jeanette. "The Male Mystique of Henry Miller." *New York Times Book Review,* 29 January 2012, 1.

Postscript

Kristina Schulz

The last decades of the twentieth century saw significant change in the way women, claiming equality and freedom—"liberation" in their own words—appeared on the public stage. Our collected essays have critically analyzed the depth of change achieved. Clearly, the women's liberation movements experienced moments of great success in terms of mobilization; their long-term consequences are less clear cut. Based on case studies from the perspective of history and cultural studies, the present volume offers some elements of an answer to the complex question of impact.

The first element points to the need for a differentiated look at the specific logics of functioning in the different social and political settings where challenge can take effect. Several chapters of this book deal with the political and the institutional realm from a state-centered perspective. They show that the WLMs had an influence on the political agenda and its institutional implementation. By focusing on realms beyond institutionalized politics, other chapters make clear that the WLMs also had an impact on public opinion, on print culture, and on the patterns of women's life courses. As all of the contributions suggest, the movements have "radically transformed many of the laws and policies, and the public and personal practices of everyday life."[1] Those shifts, some of which emerged plainly in the context of the 1970s, others slower or more discretely, took place within and beyond the fluid boundaries of the WLMs.

Different paths have been explored in this volume in order to assess the movements' impact, on scales that range from micro to macro, and spanning the local to the (trans)national. Several chapters have analyzed the WLMs' relation to public institutions, such as the organization and curricula of higher education, the construction of equality in the professional area, and the link to international organizations. The chapters here demonstrate clearly that no generalization can be made about the strategies that WLMs applied in order to induce change. These strategies not only differed from country to country according to political opportunity structure—hence the "formal institutional structure" of the political system, its "informal procedures and prevailing strategies with regard to challengers," and the "configuration of power"[2] in the very moment of agenda setting; they were also debated and controversial within the movements themselves. The Swiss pro-choice activists, for example, did pursue a strategy of extraparliamentary mobilization, but at the same time, some of them were campaigning in the run-up of the popular initiatives, thereby using the political channels intended for legislative reform in Switzerland. By tracing back the intertwined ways of institutional reform in some selected areas, the contribution of women's liberation becomes more visible than the anti-institutional impetus of the movement might suggest.

Far from being extensive or representative for the developments in Europe as a whole, the examinations of the women's movements' relationship to political and public institutions presented in the first section of the volume point to a hypothesis that William Gamson put forward in his path-breaking study on "The Strategy of Social Protest" (1975). He asserted that "challenging groups should enjoy relatively greater success in times of general crisis than in quiet times."[3] While Gamson himself was not able to discover full evidence for his assertion from his sample (fifty-three challenging groups in the early nineteenth century, during World War I, and during the Great depression), his thesis invites closer attention to the specific historical contexts in which the WLMs acted. If historians consider the 1970s as a period of civil disturbance in many European countries—as the French term *les années 68* emphasizes—in what respect did this affect the chances of the WLM realizing its concrete political demands? The chapters gathered here suggest that institutional change occurred where feminist claims were adjusted to the means, and even the language, of the institutions being addressed. Success was also more likely to be achieved by groups with clearly defined structures—even if they did not represent the full women's movement in a given national, regional, or local setting. Successful groups were sharply contoured and, in the eyes of power holders, were considered as a "valid spokesman [*sic*] for a legitimate set of interests."[4] Such contouring did not occur as a matter of course but was the result of multiple negotiations within and outside the movement. Such negotiations, at any moment, ran the risk of failing. This might be one reason—underlying many others—why the policy outcomes of women's liberation movements have taken so long to be perceptible.

Gamson's view of social protest—even if criticized—has significantly influenced research on the political outcomes of social movements.[5] However, the different cases explored in the second section of this volume suggest that this theory may be inadequate to assess cultural consequences of social movements. Feminist cultural interventions are reviewed by Sylvie Chaperon, Ana Martins, Christa Binswanger, and Kathy Davis, who have assessed and historicized the WLMs' influence on print culture, as has my own chapter on feminist reading culture and bookshops in Switzerland. These chapters suggest shifting the focus of research from groups and claims to collective practices. This shift in perspective constitutes a second contribution to the overall question of how to investigate the consequences of the WLMs. Most of the authors suggest a critical reading produced by, on the one hand, thoroughly analyzing and recognizing the sense that feminist activists gave to their literary activities and, on the other hand, showing the ongoing (and most of the time unconscious) processes of (d)evaluation, selection and in/exclusion at work within and between the movements in different local, regional, national, and international settings. To be able to build a collective identity is essential for social movements.[6] Hence, the history of the WLMs in Europe shows that, against their claim of "sisterhood" being "powerful,"[7] they were not free from reproducing the social and racial exclusion prevailing in the societies they sought to change.

Another lesson can be drawn from the section on "Sharing Words": The cultural consequences of the WLMs were not limited to internal dynamics in the movement sector. By producing, translating, printing, selling, and talking about women's literature (including the question what this expression exactly meant), the movement reached a broad range of audiences (of different genders), rendering thereby the boundaries of "the" movement more fluid. The advantage of an approach that focuses on practices rather than groups or claims is that it allows historical enquiry to go beyond the narrow understanding of "movement impact" as "policy impact." It also goes beyond the "individual-level consequences of participation in social movements and activism."[8] To read and to write does not necessarily imply any kind of activist stance. But women's liberation activists gave new meaning to female cultural practices that, from the age of the Enlightenment on, have been seen as a sign of consent to a new bourgeois gender order based on individual pursuit of *Bildung* (education). Above all, this was a gender order that located women's agency in the domestic realm. Against it, the literary practices investigated in this volume aimed at reappropriating words and symbols. They also prioritized "going public," be it a general public or a delineated feminist or women's public in search of a collective identity. How exactly reading and writing practices shaped women's lives beyond the movement is nevertheless a methodologically challenging question that invites further research and archival exploration.[9]

The third element offered by this collection concerns the heuristic surplus value added by an expanded perspective, one that embraces parallel and subsequent movements as well as other forms of "contentious politics."[10] The WLMs emerged in a configuration, which social scientists have termed "movement society" (*Bewegungsgesellschaft*).[11] It provided conditions favoring the formation and stabilization of social movements, each with specific focal points concerning aims, mobilizing strategies, and social groups represented. Nonetheless, the chapters of the third section, "Identities at Stake: Gender, Race, Class," point to the fact that social movements were not just coexisting but relating to each other, be it in mutual support, conflict, or rivalry. Moreover, the lines between "movements" were not clearly drawn. Was the French lesbian movement a different movement or a challenge from within? How was the feminist struggle interwoven with other struggles, especially in the areas of class and ethnic belonging? The authors explore the interaction of multiple identifications and distinctions in the 1970s and 1980s. The categories of class, race, and sexual orientation challenged the idea of a social movement based on the affirmation of a common gender identity as the connecting bond. The WLM therefore definitely had a legacy for feminist debates of the 1990s and 2000s, revolving around key notions such as "diversity" and "intersectionality."

The fourth section, "Beyond National Boundaries," adds a transnational perspective, revealing that impact can transgress borders in very complex and not always linear ways. As American feminist, writer, and journalist Robin Morgan's mid-1980s anthology *Sisterhood Is Global* demonstrated, the aspirations of the WLMs were global.[12] However, this did not prevent the reproduction of power structures between regions considered more central (Western Europe and the Northern Atlantics) and those considered to be at the margins (Southern and Eastern Europe and the Global South). New information technologies allowed for a multiplication of international contacts, nourishing the utopia of a global feminist network. At the same time, technologies introduced new boundaries, such as that between those women who had access to the internet and those who, by social, geographical, or generational reasons, did not.

While historians have given detailed accounts of the numerous encounters between feminist activism and organisations in different countries during the nineteenth century and the beginning of the twentieth,[13] research on such connections is fragmentary for the last decades of the twentieth century. Interestingly enough, in recent years, "global feminism" has gathered more attention than European feminism. A transnational history of the WLM in Europe still remains to be written.[14] By putting national case studies in dialogue, the authors in this volume hope to encourage a cross-national conversation between WLM scholars. In bringing together different methodological approaches, empirically based studies of nationally anchored grassroots dynamics, and divers research foci, the volume reflects theoretical and methodological problems regarding the analysis of the impacts of social movements. The chapters shed light on the impact that women's movement's campaigning had upon different aspects of society. In addition, several chapters, such as Stefanie Ehmsen's, Kirsten Harting's, Ana Martin's, or Karen Offen's, place findings from national case studies in a broader international and comparative perspective. They take into account the transfer of ideas and mobilization practices between different movements and countries. Further work needs to be done.[15] To apply a differentiated view on the multiple areas of concern movements address, to shift the focus from studying groups and claims to investigating collective practices, and to adopt an expanded perspective in terms of time and space are approaches that might usefully be explored.

I would like to close this book with a personal note: I have been trained in German and French contemporary history. To discover the place of feminism in this historical landscape was not a simple task, as women's activism was hardly ever mentioned in history books. This was particularly true for the women's movement after 1968, a mere object of feuilleton. The archives and oral testimonies, on the contrary, showed that the WLM was one of the most important new social movements in both societies. After researching the WLM in France and the Federal Republic for several years, I was given the opportunity to study the fascinating history of the WLM in Switzerland; not just its specificities but also the striking parallels with developments in other European contexts and, of course, its connections and relations to a transnational feminist community. During all this time I was convinced that the German-speaking historiography was the last one to have discovered women's liberation as a topic of historical research. It was not until trying to get a greater view on the European scenery that I became aware that European (so-called) second-wave feminism is still underresearched, or, at least, that research is still not available outside the linguistic community in which it has been produced. Little of the dense work about the French case has been translated to other languages, and texts about Germany available in English, aside from Myra Marx Ferree's groundbreaking works,[16] still only cover the beginning of the women's liberation movement and its relation to the upheavals of 1968.[17] Research about Switzerland's WLM is virtually nonexistent outside Switzerland, whereas, recently, Great Britain and Norway, as well as Southern European contemporary women's movements, have been studied from a comparative perspective within the international project "FEMCIT: Gendered Citizenship in Multicultural Europe: The Impact of Women's Movements."[18] Moreover, since Bonnie Smith's collection *Global Feminisms since 1945*,[19] it has become easier to examine and juxtapose Egyptian, Kenyan, or Vietnamese feminist movements, and this has been a productive and welcome expansion of the historical field. Karen Offen's encompassing research on European feminism from the 1700s to the aftermath of World War II has also been inspirational.[20] Both collections have encouraged a fresh look at "Western" feminism and feminist activism in the second half of the twentieth century, assessing opportunities to produce social change and trying to find out what impact feminists had.

To be able to work on women's liberation, especially for early career scholars engaged in unsecure careers, still cannot be taken for granted. I recently met a young scholar who was working on the manuscript of her excellent PhD thesis, about one facet of WLM activism, to get it ready for publishing. She explained to me that she was about to rewrite some chapters of the manuscript in order to make her book more interesting for "general" historians. Whereas the history of feminism(s) in the United States may have become a widely accepted topic, equal to, for example, works on the Cold War or the peace movement, in the European context, this is far from accepted. Early career researchers of feminism still feel obliged to demonstrate the scientific base and empirical contribution of their research in ways that apply to "general historians." In addition, they have to be very careful to remain in contact with what are perceived as "general" historical debates, because a strong contribution in feminism's history does not always provide many career opportunities. However, as to judge from the many events—conferences, book launches, internet activities, and so on—that have taken place in the last few years also in European settings, hopefully feminism's past has a future in the European academy as well.

Kristina Schulz, PhD, is Senior Lecturer for Contemporary History and Migration History at the University of Berne. She is a specialist of Western feminist history in comparative perspective and is the author of a book on the French and German WLM: *"Der lange Atem der Provokation": Die Frauenbewegung in der Bundesrepublik und in Frankreich (1968–1976)*. Together with Leena Schmitter and Sarah Kiani she published a source and archive guide about the Swiss Women's Liberation Movement in 2014. With Magda Kaspar she is currently preparing an audio archive and interactive website about the feminist movement in Switzerland from the 1970s to the present (*Frauenbewegun 2.0*).

Notes

1. Sasha Roseneil, Beatrice Halsaa, and Sevil Sümer, "Remaking Citizenship on Multicultural Europe: Women's Movements, Gender and Diversity," in *Remaking Citizenship in Multicultural Europe: Women's Movements, Gender and Diversity*, ed. Beatrice Halsaa, Sasha Roseneil, and Sevil Sümer (Basingstoke: Palgrave Macmillan, 2012), 1.
2. Cf. Hanspeter Kriesi, "The Political Opportunity Structure of New Social Movements: Its Impact on Their Mobilization," in *The Politics of Social Protest: Com-*

parative Perspectives on States and Social Movements, ed. J. Craig Jenkins and Bert Klandermans (Minneapolis: University of Minnesota Press, 1995), 167–198, 186.

3. William Gamson, *The Strategy of Social Protest* (2nd edition, Belmont: Wadsworth Publishing Company, 1990), 112.
4. Ibid., 28
5. Marco Giugni, "Was It Worth the Effort? The Outcomes and Consequences of Social Movements," *Annual Review of Sociology* (1998): 383.
6. For an overview of new approaches and questions, cf. Stephen Wulff, Mary Bernstein, and Verta Taylor, "New Theoretical Directions from the Study of Gender and Sexuality Movements: Collective Identity, Multi-Institutional Politics, and Emotions," in *The Oxford Handbook of Social Movements,* ed. Donatella della Porta and Mario Diani (Oxford: Oxford University Press, 2016), 108–30.
7. Robin Morgan, *Sisterhood Is Powerful: An Anthology of Writings from the Women's Liberation Movement* (New York: Vintage, 1970).
8. Giugni, "Was It Worth the Effort?" 386.
9. For example: Kristina Schulz, "'Wort um wort, begriff um begriff' Weibliches Schreiben als Praxis der Veränderung: Überlegungen zu den kulturellen Wirkungen der neuen Frauenbewegung," *Internationales Archiv für Sozialgeschichte der deutschen Literatur* 37 (2012): 307–22.
10. Cf. Charles Tilly and Sidney Tarrow, *Contentious Politics* (Oxford: University Press, 2015).
11. Dieter Rucht and Friedhelm Neidhardt, "'Auf dem Weg in eine Bewegungsgesellschaft'? Über die Stabilisierbarkeit sozialer Bewegungen," *Soziale Welt* 44, no. 3 (1993): 305–26.
12. Robin Morgan, ed., *Sisterhood Is Global: The International Women's Movement Anthology* (New York: Doubleday, 1984).
13. Among others: Sylvia Paletschek, ed., *Women's Emancipation Movements in the Nineteenth Century: A European Perspective* (Stanford, CA: Stanford University Press, 2004); Lucy Delap, *The Feminist Avant-Garde: Transnational Encounters of the Early Twentieth Century* (Cambridge: Cambridge University Press, 2007); Alison Fell and Ingrid Sharp, *The Women's Movement in Wartime: International Perspectives, 1914–1919* (New York: Palgrave Macmillan, 2007); Leila Rupp, *Worlds of Women: The Making of an International Women's Movement* (Princeton, NJ: Princeton University Press, 1997); Annika Wilmers, *Pazifismus in der internationalen Frauenbewegung (1914–1920): Handlungsspielräume, politische Konzeptionen und gesellschaftliche Auseinandersetzungen* (Essen: Klartext-Verlag, 2008); Karen Offen, ed., *Globalizing Feminisms, 1789–1945* (London: Routledge 2010).
14. Without a special focus on the women's liberation movement: Bonnie S. Anderson and Judith P. Zinsser, *A History of Their Own; Women in Europe from Prehistory to the Present,* 2 vols. (New York: Oxford University Press, 2000).
15. As, for instance, the project *Translating Feminism: Transfers, Transgression, Transformation (1945–1991),* funded by the Leverhulme International Network Grant and directed by Maud Bracke (2016–18, University of Glasgow).
16. Myra Marx Ferree, *Varieties of Feminism: German Gender Politics in Global Perspective* (Stanford, CA: Stanford University Press, 2012).

17. For a comparative view, see Kristina Schulz, "Echoes of Provocation: 1968 and the Women's Movements in France and Germany," in *Transnational Moments of Change: Europe 1945, 1968, 1989,* ed. Gerd-Rainer Horn and Padraic Kenney (Lanham, MD: Rowman & Littlefield, 2004), 137–54, and Kristina Schulz, "Feminist Echoes of 1968: Women's Movements in Europe and the United States," in *"Wreckage of Modernity" or "Revolution of Perception"? 1968: Consequences and Echoes,* ed. Ingrid Gilcher Holtey (New York: Berghahn Books, 2014), 124–47.
18. To mention two major publications out of many related to FEMCIT, a project founded by the European Commission (2007–11): Line Nyhagen Predelli and Beatrice Halsaa, *Majority-Minority Relations in Contemporary Women's Movements* (London: Palgrave Macmillan 2012); Ana Cristina Santos, *Social Movements and Sexual Citizenship in Southern Europe* (London: Palgrave Macmillan, 2013). For Italy cf. Maud Bracke, *Women and the Reinvention of the Political: Feminism in Italy, 1968-1983* (New York: Routledge 2014). For Britain recently Natalie Thomlinson, *Race, Ethnicity, and the Women's Movement in England, 1968-1993* (New York: Palgrave, 2016).
19. Bonnie G. Smith, *Global Feminisms since 1945* (New York: Routledge, 2000).
20. Karen Offen, *European Feminism, 1700–1950: A Political History* (Stanford, CA: Stanford University Press, 2000).

Bibliography

Anderson, Bonnie S., and Judith P. Zinsser. *A History of Their Own: Women in Europe from Prehistory to the Present.* 2 vols. New York: Oxford University Press, 2000.

Bracke, Maude. *Women and the Re-Invention of the Political: Feminism in Italy (1968–1983).* New York: Routledge, 2014.

Delap, Lucy. *The Feminist Avant-Garde: Transnational Encounters of the Early Twentieth Century.* Cambridge: Cambridge University Press, 2007.

Fell, Alison, and Ingrid Sharp. *The Women's Movement in Wartime: International Perspectives, 1914–1919.* New York: Palgrave Macmillan, 2007.

Ferree, Myra Marx. *Varieties of Feminism: German Gender Politics in Global Perspective.* Stanford, CA: Stanford University Press, 2012.

Gamson, William. *The Strategy of Social Protest.* Belmont: Wadsworth Publishing Company, 1990.

Giugni, Marco. "Was It Worth the Effort? The Outcomes and Consequences of Social Movements." *Annual Review of Sociology* (1998): 371–93.

Morgan, Robin. *Sisterhood Is Powerful: An Anthology of Writings from the Women's Liberation Movement.* New York: Vintage, 1970.

———, ed. *Sisterhood Is global. The International Women's Movement Anthology.* New York: Doubleday, 1984.

Offen, Karen. *European Feminism, 1700–1950: A Political History.* Stanford, CA: Stanford University Press, 2000.

———. *Globalizing Feminisms, 1789–1945.* London: Palgrave Macmillan, 2010.

Paletschek, Sylvia, ed. *Women's Emancipation Movements in the Nineteenth Century: A European Perspective.* Stanford, CA: Stanford University Press, 2006.

Predelli, Line Nyhagen, and Beatrice Halsaa. *Majority-Minority Relations in Contemporary Women's Movements.* London: Palgrave Macmillan, 2012.

Roseneil, Sasha, Beatrice Halsaa, and Sevil Sümer. "Remaking Citizenship on Multicultural Europe: Women's Movements, Gender and Diversity." In *Remaking Citizenship in Multicultural Europe: Women's Movements, Gender and Diversity,* ed. Beatrice Halsaa, Sasha Roseneil, and Sevil Sümer, 1–20. Basingstoke: Palgrave Macmillan, 2012.

Rucht, Dieter, and Friedhelm Neidhardt. "Auf dem Weg in eine 'Bewegungsgesellschaft'? Über die Stabilisierbarkeit sozialer Bewegungen." *Soziale Welt* 44, no. 3 (1993): 305–26.

Rupp, Leila. *Worlds of Women: The Making of an International Women's Movement.* Princeton, NJ: University Press, 1997.

Santos, Ana Cristina. *Social Movements and Sexual Citizenship in Southern Europe.* London: Palgrave Macmillan, 2013.

Schulz, Kristina. "'Wort um wort, begriff um begriff' Weibliches Schreiben als Praxis der Veränderung: Überlegungen zu den kulturellen Wirkungen der neuen Frauenbewegung." *Internationales Archiv für Sozialgeschichte der deutschen Literatur* 37 (2012): 307–22.

———. "Echoes of Provocation: 1968 and the Women's Movements in France and Germany." In *Transnational Moments of Change: Europe 1945, 1968, 1989,* ed. Gerd-Rainer Horn and Padraic Kenney, 137–54. Lanham, MD: Rowman & Littlefield, 2004.

———. "Feminist Echoes of 1968: Women's Movements in Europe and the United States." In *"Wreckage of Modernity" or "Revolution of Perception"? 1968: Consequences and Echoes,* edited by Ingrid Gilcher Holtey, 124–47. New York: Berghahn Books 2014.

Smith, Bonnie G. *Global Feminisms since 1945.* New York: Routledge, 2000.

Tilly, Charles, and Sidney Tarrow. *Contentious Politics.* Oxford: Oxford University Press, 2015.

Natalie Thomlinson, *Race, Ethnicity, and the Women's Movement in England, 1968-1993.* New York: Palgrave, 2016.

Wilmers, Annika. *Pazifismus in der internationalen Frauenbewegung (1914–1920): Handlungsspielräume, politische Konzeptionen und gesellschaftliche Auseinandersetzungen.* Essen: Klartext-Verlag, 2008.

Wulff, Stephen, Mary Bernstein, and Verta Taylor. "New Theoretical Directions from the Study of Gender and Sexuality Movements: Collective Identity, Multi-Institutional Politics, and Emotions." In *The Oxford Handbook of Social Movements,* edited by Donatella della Porta und Mario Diani, 108–30. Oxford: Oxford University Press, 2016.

Index

D

M

T

Protest, Culture and Society

Protest movements have been recognized as significant contributors to processes of political participation and transformations of culture and value systems, as well as to the development of both a national and transnational civil society.

This series brings together the various innovative approaches to phenomena of social change, protest and dissent which have emerged in recent years, from an interdisciplinary perspective. It contextualizes social protest and cultures of dissent in larger political processes and socio-cultural transformations by examining the influence of historical trajectories and the response of various segments of society, political and legal institutions on a national and international level. In doing so, the series offers a more comprehensive and multi-dimensional view of historical and cultural change in the twentieth and twenty-first centuries.

Volume 1
Voices of the Valley, Voices of the Straits: How Protest Creates Communities
Donatella della Porta and Gianni Piazza

Volume 2
Transformations and Crises: The Left and the Nation in Denmark and Sweden, 1956–1980
Thomas Ekman Jørgensen

Volume 3
Changing the World, Changing Oneself: Political Protest and Collective Identities in West Germany and the U.S. in the 1960s and 1970s
Edited by Belinda Davis, Wilfried Mausbach, Martin Klimke, and Carla MacDougall

Volume 4
The Transnational Condition: Protest Dynamics in an Entangled Europe
Edited by Simon Teune

Volume 5
Protest Beyond Borders: Contentious Politics in Europe since 1945
Edited by Hara Kouki and Eduardo Romanos

Volume 6
Between the Avant-Garde and the Everyday: Subversive Politics in Europe from 1957 to the Present
Edited by Timothy Brown and Lorena Anton

Volume 7
Between Prague Spring and French May: Opposition and Revolt in Europe, 1960–1980
Edited by Martin Klimke, Jacco Pekelder, and Joachim Scharloth

Volume 8
The Third World in the Global 1960s
Edited by Samantha Christiansen and Zachary A. Scarlett

Volume 9
The German Student Movement and the Literary Imagination: Transnational Memories of Protest and Dissent
Susanne Rinner

Volume 10
Children of the Dictatorship: Student Resistance, Cultural Politics, and the 'Long 1960s' in Greece
Kostis Kornetis

Volume 11
Media and Revolt: Strategies and Performances from the 1960s to the Present
Edited by Kathrin Fahlenbrach, Erling Sivertsen, and Rolf Werenskjold

Volume 12
Europeanizing Contention: The Protest Against 'Fortress Europe' in France and Germany
Pierre Monforte

Volume 13
Militant Around the Clock? Left-Wing Youth Politics, Leisure, and Sexuality in Post-Dictatorship Greece, 1974–1981
Nikolaos Papadogiannis

Volume 14
Protest in Hitler's 'National Community': Popular Unrest and the Nazi Response
Edited by Nathan Stoltzfus and Birgit Maier-Katkin

Volume 15
Comrades of Color: East Germany in the Cold War World
Edited by Quinn Slobodian

Volume 16
Social Movement Studies in Europe: The State of the Art
Edited by Olivier Fillieule and Guya Accornero

Volume 17
Protest Cultures: A Companion
Edited by Kathrin Fahlenbrach, Martin Klimke, and Joachim Scharloth

Volume 18
The Revolution before the Revolution: Late Authoritarianism and Student Protest in Portugal
By Guya Accornero

Volume 19
The Nuclear Crisis: The Arms Race, Cold War Anxiety, and the German Peace Movement of the 1980s
Edited by Christoph Becker-Schaum, Philipp Gassert, Wilfried Mausbach, Martin Klimke, and Marianne Zepp

Volume 20
A Fragmented Landscape: Abortion Governance and Protest Logics in Europe
Edited by Silvia De Zordo, Joanna Mishtal, and Lorena Anton

Volume 21
Hairy Hippies and Bloody Butchers: The Greenpeace Anti-Whaling Campaign in Norway
Juliane Riese

Volume 22
The Women's Liberation Movement: Impacts and Outcomes
Edited by Kristina Schulz